ASTOUNDING

ASTOUNDING

JOHN W. CAMPBELL, ISAAC ASIMOV, ROBERT A. HEINLEIN, L. RON HUBBARD, AND THE GOLDEN AGE OF SCIENCE FICTION

Alec Nevala-Lee

DEY ST.

An Imprint of WILLIAM MORROW

DEY ST.

Excerpts of letters by John W. Campbell, Jr., are reprinted with permission of AC Projects, Inc., 7111 Sweetgum Road, Fairview, TN, 37062.

HarperCollins books may be purchased for educational, business, or sales promotional use. For information, please e-mail the Special Markets Department at SPsales@harpercollins.com.

FIRST EDITION

Designed by Renata De Oliveira

Library of Congress Cataloging-in-Publication Data has been applied for.

ISBN 978-0-06-257194-6

18 19 20 21 22 DIX/LSC 10 9 8 7 6 5 4 3 2 1

To Beatrix

I thought it was for your sake that I came alone, so obviously alone, so vulnerable, that I could in myself pose no threat, change no balance: not an invasion, but a mere messenger boy. But there's more to it than that. Alone, I cannot change your world. But I can be changed by it. Alone, I must listen, as well as speak. . . . So was I sent alone, for your sake? Or for my own?

—URSULA K. LE GUIN, *THE LEFT HAND OF DARKNESS*

We are what we pretend to be, so we must be careful about what we pretend to be.

—KURT VONNEGUT, JR., *MOTHER NIGHT*

CONTENTS

Prologue
ASIMOV'S SWORD

My feeling is that as far as creativity is concerned, isolation is required. . . . Nevertheless, a meeting of such people may be desirable for reasons other than the act of creation itself. . . . If a single individual present . . . has a distinctly more commanding personality, he may well take over the conference and reduce the rest to little more than passive obedience. . . . The optimum number of the group would probably not be very high. I should guess that no more than five would be wanted.

—ISAAC ASIMOV, "ON CREATIVITY"

On June 13, 1963, New York University welcomed a hundred scientists to the Conference on Education for Creativity in the Sciences. The gathering, which lasted for three days, was the brainchild of the science advisor to President John F. Kennedy, who had pledged two years earlier to send a man to the moon. America was looking with mingled anxiety and anticipation toward the future, which seemed inseparable from its destiny as a nation. As the event's organizer said in his introductory remarks, the challenge of tomorrow was clear: "That world will be more complex than it is today [and] will be changing more rapidly than now."

One of the attendees was Isaac Asimov, an associate professor of biochemistry at Boston University. At the age of forty-three, Asimov was not quite the celebrity he later became—he had yet to grow his trademark sideburns—but he was already the most famous science fiction author alive. He was revered within the genre for the Foundation trilogy and the stories collected under the title *I, Robot,* but he was better known to general readers for his works of nonfiction. After the launch of Sputnik in 1957, Asimov had been awakened to the importance of educating the next generation of scientists, and over the course of thirty books and counting, he had reinvented himself as the world's best explainer.

The day before the conference, Asimov had taken a bus from Boston to New York. It was a trip of over four hours, but he was afraid of flying, and he welcomed the chance to get out of the house—he was going through a difficult period in his marriage. On the morning of his departure, the papers carried photographs of the death of the Vietnamese monk Thích Quảng Đức, who had set himself on fire in Saigon, and coverage of George Wallace, who had blocked a doorway at the University of Alabama to protest the registration of two black students. Just after midnight on June 12, the civil rights activist Medgar Evers had been shot in Mississippi, although his murder would not be widely reported until later that afternoon.

Asimov followed the news closely, but on his arrival in New York, he was more concerned by the loss of a bankroll of two hundred dollars that he was carrying as emergency cash—"I just dropped it somewhere." It left him distracted throughout the conference, and afterward, he remembered almost nothing about it. What he recalled most clearly was a discussion of the basic problem facing the scientists who had gathered there, which was how to identify children who had the potential to affect the future. If you could spot such promising students, you could give them the attention they needed while they were still young—but you had to find them first.

It was a question of obvious significance, and it had particular resonance for Asimov. He had always thought of himself as a child prodigy—he had mixed feelings about entering middle age, noting that "there is no possibility of pretending to youth at forty"—and his life had been radically transformed by a mentor who had found him at just the right time. At the conference, he proposed what he felt was a practical test for recognizing creative youngsters, but no one else took it seriously.

Two days after returning home to West Newton, Massachusetts, Asimov was asked to write an article for the *Bulletin of the Atomic Scientists,* the journal best known for its Doomsday Clock, a visual representation of the risk of nuclear war that currently stood at seven minutes to midnight. Asimov, who was deeply concerned by the bomb, decided to return to the idea that he had raised in New York. He went to work, typing away in his attic office, which had become a refuge from his unhappy personal life— his wife was talking openly about divorce, and he was worried about their son David, who seemed to have nothing in common with his famous father.

Asimov began his essay, "The Sword of Achilles," with an episode from the Trojan War. The Greeks desperately wanted to recruit the warrior Achilles, but his mother, Thetis, feared that he would die at Troy. To protect her son, she sent him to the island of Scyros, where he dressed as a woman and concealed himself among the ladies of the court. The clever Odysseus arrived in the guise of a merchant, laying out clothing and jewelry for the maidens to admire. Among the other goods, he hid a sword. Achilles seized and brandished it, giving himself away, and after being identified, he was persuaded to go to war.

"Wars are different these days," Asimov continued. "Both in

wars against human enemies and in wars against the forces of nature, the crucial warriors now are our creative scientists." It was a technological vision of American supremacy that Asimov had carried over from World War II, and it was about to be tested in Vietnam. For now, however, he only noted that while it was necessary to provide gifted students with ways to develop their creativity, it was too impractical and expensive to lavish the same resources on everyone.

"What we need is a simple test, something as simple as the sword of Achilles," Asimov wrote. "We want a measure that will serve, quickly and without ambiguity, to select the potentially creative from the general rank and file." He then outlined what he saw as a useful method for finding the innovators of tomorrow. It was elegant and straightforward, and in the events of his own remarkable life, Asimov had witnessed its power firsthand: "I would like to suggest such a sword of Achilles. It is simply this: an interest in good science fiction."

HALF A CENTURY LATER, SCIENCE FICTION HAS CONQUERED THE WORLD. ON THE SAME DAY THAT Asimov rode the bus down to New York, a huge crowd gathered at the Rivoli Theatre on Broadway for the premiere of *Cleopatra*, the Elizabeth Taylor epic that became the highest-grossing film of 1963. Today, the view from Hollywood has changed. For the last two decades, the most successful movie in any given year has nearly always featured elements of science fiction or fantasy, often refracted through the related medium of comic books, in what amounts to a universal language that can captivate or divert audiences worldwide.

The same holds true for literature and television. By the early sixties, Asimov had sold hundreds of thousands of copies of his books, but he had never reached the bestseller lists. Nowadays, science fiction and fantasy fill the front tables of chain bookstores, and they make up much of the reading of the young adults of whom Asimov wrote in "The Sword of Achilles." When his essay appeared, the first episode of *Star Trek* was three years away. The franchise created by Gene Roddenberry—who later became Asimov's friend—is still thriving, and its successors on the networks, cable, and streaming services dominate the cultural conversation.

In recent years, such movies as *Interstellar* and *The Martian* have made a conscious return to the values of what Asimov described as "good science fiction," but their success would have been unimaginable when he wrote these words. Using the sales of his own books as a proxy, he estimated that just one out of every four hundred and fifty Americans was interested in science fiction. Today, it would be harder to find someone who wasn't bombarded by it. The genre has been absorbed so completely into the mainstream that it can be easy to take its presence there for granted—or to forget that its most recognizable incarnation arose at a specific turning point in the thirties, when it seized hold of its readers and never let go.

Despite its darker and dystopian streak, science fiction offers a vision of the world into which many fans still long to escape. It reached maturity at a time of economic depression and war, in which there was no guarantee that the future would be bright, and it was uniquely positioned to provide America with the new mythology—or religion—that it needed. This book is an attempt to figure out how this happened and what it means for us today, through the lives of a handful of extraordinary men and women who had an outsized influence on the outcome.

By some definitions, science fiction is as old as Achilles himself. Even if we restrict it, as Asimov did, to "that branch of literature which deals with the reaction of human beings to changes in science and technology," it goes back as far as Mary Shelley's *Frankenstein,* with signal contributions from such authors as Edgar Allan Poe, Jules Verne, Arthur Conan Doyle, Rudyard Kipling, and

H. G. Wells. Its emergence as a viable genre was thanks largely to an immigrant from Luxembourg named Hugo Gernsback, who first published science fiction in the cheap magazines known as the pulps, culminating in the debut of *Amazing Stories* in 1926.

These early stories were crude, but they fired up the imaginations of readers, and a vibrant fan culture was born, with dynamics strikingly like those of modern online communities. Toward the end of the thirties, fans who had grown up with science fiction became old enough to write for themselves, and unlike the mercenary authors of the earlier phase, they didn't do it for the money, but out of love. Gradually, they built on the discoveries of their predecessors, and they pushed the field by trial and error into directions that no one could have foreseen.

This advance would have occurred in one form or another, but it came to focus on the magazine *Astounding Science Fiction*, and in particular on its editor, who was nothing less than Asimov's intellectual father. By the sixties, Asimov had grown apart from the mentor and friend whom he later called "the most powerful force in science fiction ever," but he never forgot his debt to the man who had first thrust the sword of Achilles into his hands. His name was John W. Campbell, Jr.

CAMPBELL NEVER BECAME AS FAMOUS AS MANY OF THE WRITERS HE PUBLISHED, BUT HE INFLU-enced the dreamlife of millions. For more than three decades, an unparalleled series of visions of the future passed through his tiny office in New York, where he inaugurated the main sequence of science fiction that runs through works from *2001* to *Westworld*. Despite his flaws, he deserves to be seen as one of the key cultural figures of the twentieth century, and his singular career—which has never been the subject of a full biography until now—is one of its great untold stories.

He was born in Newark in 1910. As an undergraduate at the Massachusetts Institute of Technology, he became one of the most popular authors of superscience, or space opera, cranking out futuristic pulp adventures that spanned the entire galaxy. His more mature stories—which he wrote under the pen name Don A. Stuart, in a tribute to his first wife, Doña—heralded the beginning of the genre's modern age, and his most famous work, the novella "Who Goes There?," would have been enough to ensure his immortality, if only through its multiple filmed adaptations as *The Thing*.

By the time it appeared, Campbell had already moved away from writing. At twenty-seven, he landed the job as the editor of *Astounding*, stumbling into it almost by accident. He took control of the magazine just as fans were emerging as a formidable force in their own right, and he assumed the role of a gatekeeper who controlled access to the top of the genre, in which the pulps were the only game in town. Science fiction, which was still defining itself, was changed forever by his whims, prejudices, and private life. For more than thirty years, Campbell relentlessly worked a virtual staff of hundreds of writers, and they rewarded him with stories ranging from Asimov's "Nightfall" to Frank Herbert's *Dune*.

Their peak became known as the golden age of science fiction, which ran roughly from 1939 to 1950—and Campbell was the most brilliant of them all. Asimov called him "the brain of the superorganism," while the writer Harlan Ellison, one of his harshest critics, conceded that he was "the single most important formative force" in modern science fiction. He was synonymous with the genre, and his influence lasted long after his death in 1971. As a teenager in the seventies, Neil Gaiman paid more than he could afford for a box of old *Astoundings*, and decades later, when asked if *Game of Thrones* had been inspired by the mythologist Joseph Campbell, George R. R. Martin responded, "The Campbell that influenced me was John W., not Joseph."

If Campbell loomed large in the imaginations of his readers, he was even more daunting in person. He stood an inch over six feet tall and weighed over two hundred pounds, with sharp blue eyes and a black cigarette holder with a Chesterfield perpetually clutched in one hand. As a young man, he wore his light brown hair slicked back, emphasizing his aquiline profile, which bore a striking resemblance, he liked to say, to both Hermann Göring and the Shadow. In middle age, he switched to browline glasses and a crew cut, and he always struck others as huge. For much of his career, he was hated as much as he was loved, and he was inescapable even for writers he neglected, such as Ray Bradbury, who tried and failed repeatedly to break into the magazine.

Science fiction might have evolved into a viable art form with or without Campbell, but his presence meant that it happened at a crucial time, and his true legacy lies in the specific shape that it took under his watch. Campbell had wanted to be an inventor or scientist, and when he found himself working as an editor instead, he redefined the pulps as a laboratory for ideas—improving the writing, developing talent, and handing out entire plots for stories. America's future, by definition, was unknown, with a rate of change that would only increase. To prepare for this coming acceleration, he turned science fiction from a literature of escapism into a machine for generating analogies, which was why, in the sixties, he renamed the magazine *Analog*.

He also expanded the range of the genre's concerns. Before his editorship, most stories had centered on physics and engineering, but the rise of the Nazis led him to wonder if the study of civilization itself could be refined into a science. Working with Asimov, he developed the fictional field of psychohistory, which could predict events for thousands of years in the future, and he openly dreamed of a similar revolution in psychology.

After Hiroshima, history seemed on the verge of overtaking science fiction. With his audience looking to him for answers, Campbell felt that the next step was clear. His ultimate goal was to turn his writers and readers into a new kind of human being, exemplified by "the competent man," who would lead in turn to the superman. As the atomic age dawned, nothing less than humanity's survival seemed at stake, and Campbell teamed up with one of his own authors—L. Ron Hubbard—to achieve this transformation in the real world. But none of it went according to plan.

CAMPBELL AND HIS THREE MOST IMPORTANT COLLABORATORS MET WHEN THEY WERE ALL YOUNG men. One was Hubbard, who seemed at first like an unlikely partner. In 1938, Hubbard was a successful pulp writer without any interest in science fiction, and he and the editor were paired up almost against their wills. They became friends, and a decade later, Hubbard approached Campbell with a new mental therapy that he claimed would turn psychology into an exact science. It was the expression of a longing inherent to the genre—many fans had always hoped that it would produce a major scientific discovery—and Campbell became the enthusiastic promoter and editor of the bestselling book *Dianetics: The Modern Science of Mental Health*.

Their partnership collapsed after just one year, but they continued to affect each other from a distance. Campbell spent hours every night exploring the mysteries of the mind that dianetics had been unable to explain, while Hubbard inherited his original circle of followers from *Astounding*. He wasn't a science fiction fan, but his disciples were, and in shaping his theories for his available audience, he emerged with the Church of Scientology, the doctrines of which rivaled the wildest excesses of space opera. Campbell despised it, but he grudgingly envied the cult that Hubbard had managed to create, with tens of thousands of members who still honor its founder as the most important human being of all time.

For all his efforts, Campbell was unable to replicate Hubbard's success in building a lasting social movement. He had to content himself with the influence that he held over his readers, a legion of fans epitomized by Isaac Asimov, who wandered into the editor's office as a teenager to submit the first story that he ever wrote. The bright child that Asimov evoked in "The Sword of Achilles" was a portrait of the artist himself—he was an awkward prodigy who escaped into science fiction—and Campbell took him on as an experiment to develop a writer from scratch, feeding him the premise for his landmark story "Nightfall," the psychohistory of the Foundation series, and the revolutionary Three Laws of Robotics.

In time, Asimov outgrew him, and their friendship was strained by Campbell's fixation on psychic powers. Asimov was too cautious and rational to follow the editor's example, but he was unable to tear himself away. Instead, he diverted his energies into nonfiction, which rewarded him with a level of recognition unmatched by any other science fiction writer. With more than four hundred books to his credit, he became, incredibly, the most prolific author in American history, although he never forgot what he owed to Campbell: "In the essential characteristics that made him my literary father, I am but a pygmy to him."

But Campbell's most intriguing partnership was with the man who became the leading science fiction writer of his generation, with an unsurpassed body of work that often left both Hubbard and Asimov in its shadow. A prominent critic once called Robert A. Heinlein "the hand of John Campbell's mind," but he was already a major talent when he mailed in his first submission, and Campbell's primary contribution was to recognize it. With his skills as a storyteller and his dazzling range of interests, he was everything that Campbell had ever wanted in a writer, and Heinlein seized the chance to express his ideas in a form that could reach a vast readership.

The two men lived on opposite sides of the country, but they fed off each other's obsessions, and their friendship grew astonishingly intense, even if, as Heinlein's wife later recalled, "[it] carried in it the seeds of its own destruction." Its peak lasted for less than four years, but more than any body of work, it defined the golden age. After he and Campbell fell out in the early fifties, Heinlein went on to write such classic novels as *Starship Troopers, Stranger in a Strange Land,* and *The Moon Is a Harsh Mistress,* turning him into an intellectual hero to wildly different audiences. He was far from the first science fiction writer to advise his readers on how to live, but he did it more effectively than anyone else ever would.

Campbell never reached the same heights of fame as Hubbard, Asimov, or Heinlein, but he marked each of them in turn. They drew energy from their rivalries, learning from one another's triumphs and mistakes, and they had profound similarities. All were gifted children who endured professional or academic setbacks in their early twenties. Each remarried at a hinge point in his career, leaving the wife who had supported him at his most vulnerable for another as soon as he was ready to enter a new phase. All were generalists who saw science fiction as an educational tool—although to radically different ends. And they all embodied Campbell's conviction, which he never abandoned, that science fiction could change lives.

AND THEY CHANGED THE LIVES OF THOUSANDS OF READERS. AS ASIMOV NOTED IN "THE SWORD OF Achilles," most fans discover the genre at a young age for many of the same reasons that it speaks to a huge popular audience. It offers fantasies of escape and control; it can be enjoyed by children or teenagers who might be intellectually precocious but emotionally inexperienced; and it tends to catch them at a moment when they are uniquely receptive to new ideas. As one fan famously observed, "The real golden age of science fiction is twelve."

This impact has both its light and its dark sides. In 1963, Asimov estimated that half of all creative scientists were interested in science fiction, and he acknowledged that this was probably an understatement. Campbell's magazine counted Albert Einstein and the scientists of Bell Labs among its subscribers, and it made an indelible impression on such fans as the young Carl Sagan, who stumbled across it in a candy store: "A glance at the cover and a quick riffle through the interior showed me it was what I had been looking for. . . . I was hooked. Each month I eagerly awaited the arrival of *Astounding*." Public figures of all political persuasions—from Paul Krugman to Elon Musk to Newt Gingrich—have confessed to being influenced by its stories.

Campbell and his writers were creating nothing less than a shared vision of the future, which inevitably informs how we approach the present. Science fiction's track record for prediction is decidedly mixed, but at its finest, it was a proving ground for entire fields—such as artificial intelligence, which frequently invokes the Three Laws of Robotics—that wouldn't exist for decades. Yet it also encourages us to see all problems as provinces of engineering, and science as the solution to the dilemmas that it creates. When we propose technological fixes for climate change, or place our hopes in the good intentions of a few visionary billionaires, we unconsciously endorse a view of the world straight out of the pages of *Astounding*.

These values were expressed through the figure of "the competent man," whose very name points to the way in which science fiction encourages certain assumptions. Editors like Campbell tended to favor writers who looked like them, and from the start, fandom was overwhelmingly male. Women were often regarded with suspicion, and even when they were welcomed, they could still be treated poorly—Asimov, who described himself as a feminist, casually groped female fans for years. Such women as Doña Campbell, Leslyn Heinlein, and Campbell's assistant editor Kay Tarrant have fallen out of the history of the genre, while Hubbard's first two wives have been erased from his official biography. This is their story as well.

Many of the same factors apply to race. Campbell's writers and their characters were almost exclusively white, and he bears part of the blame for limiting the genre's diversity. At best, this was a huge missed opportunity. *Astounding*, which questioned so many other orthodoxies and systems of power, rarely looked at racial inequality, and its lack of historically underrepresented voices severely constrained the stories that it could tell. At his worst, Campbell expressed views that were unforgivably racist, and even today, the most reactionary movements in modern fandom—with their deep distrust of women and minorities—have openly stated, "We have called for a Campbellian revolution in science fiction."

This book is not a comprehensive history of the genre, and its focus on Campbell's circle means that many other writers receive less attention than they deserve. It was inspired by the realization that the nature of Asimov's sword has changed. In 1963, Asimov argued that science fiction appealed to an existing type of curious reader, but today, it seems more likely to subtly alter the way in which we all think and feel. This is closer to Campbell's original intentions, and the implications can only be understood by considering why the genre evolved along the lines that it did. Science fiction can seem inevitable, but it arose from luck, specific decisions, and the experiences of its creators at a particular moment in time. Their subculture has become our global culture, and its pattern is strangely like that of their lives.

These stories are fascinating in themselves, and they shed light on issues of inclusion and representation that still matter today. Science fiction is far too large now to be directed or defined by any one person, but this book concentrates on a period in which one man was thought to oversee it—until many of his readers broke free. Campbell liked to say that the genre's true protagonist was all of mankind, but he saw it in terms of heroic figures, starting with himself. If his audience ultimately refused to fall in line, it led, paradoxically, to the outcome that he wanted. Science fiction became an ongoing collaboration between writers and fans, and the most convincing proof of Campbell's success is the fact that he lost control of it.

Campbell can seem like a tragic figure, and the last act of his life vividly illustrates the risks of trying to put the ideals of science fiction into practice. He wanted to turn psychology and history into exact sciences, but the lunatic trajectory of his career proves how little any man can foresee of his own fate. In pursuing his dream of a great discovery that would emerge from the magazine, he was all too ready to sacrifice everything else—his friendships, his family, even science itself. Yet he was right that the future demands new ways of thinking, even if their ends remain unknown. If the Three Laws of Robotics and the Church of Scientology came from the same place, it only means that the sword of Achilles cuts both ways.

Asimov himself may have sensed this. As a boy growing up in Brooklyn, he knew that the life of a warrior—or superman—could end in tragedy, but he never ceased to believe that he could imagine his hero into a more glorious future: "I even told myself stories designed to continue the *Iliad* after Homer had left off. I was Achilles, and although Homer clearly indicated that Achilles was slated for an early death, he never died in my daydreams."

I.

WHO GOES THERE?

1907–1937

You may have had troubles heaped on you for being a Jew; I had troubles heaped on me for being John W. Campbell, individual. You felt set apart and excluded from the great group; my friend, they had me set apart from the whole damn human race!

—JOHN W. CAMPBELL: IN A LETTER TO ISAAC ASIMOV

1.
THE BOY FROM ANOTHER WORLD

1910–1931

*Do not take on a Junior for your first case if you can avoid it.
If father was named George and the patient is called George,
beware of trouble.*

—L. RON HUBBARD, *DIANETICS*

For most of his life, John W. Campbell, Jr., the editor of *Astounding Science Fiction,* had trouble remembering his childhood. He had filled his stories with extravagant images, but he had no visual memory, to the point that he was unable to picture the faces of his own wife and children. When L. Ron Hubbard, one of his most prolific writers, approached him with the promise of a new science of the mind, he was understandably intrigued. And he was especially attracted by the possibility that it would allow him to recall events that he had forgotten or repressed.

In the summer of 1949, Campbell was thirty-nine years old. At his invitation, Hubbard, who was a year younger, had moved with his wife to Elizabeth, New Jersey, just up the road from the offices of *Astounding.* Hubbard could hardly have found a more receptive subject—Campbell had been openly searching for a scientific psychology that could save mankind from nuclear war and provide insights into his own faltering marriage. Yet it soon became clear that Hubbard's therapy wasn't working on the one man in the world whom he most desperately needed to persuade.

The treatment, which became known as dianetics, was designed to relieve the psychological pressure caused by repressed memories. Hubbard later wrote, "The prize case in difficulty in dianetics is a patient who is a Junior named after either father or mother." If the subject shared a parent's name, he said, it led to subconscious trauma before birth, as the mother spoke badly of the father and the fetus absorbed her words as a negative description of itself.

Campbell, of course, had been named for his father, and he turned out to be a difficult patient in other ways. In its earliest incarnation, dianetics amounted to a form of hypnotism—Hubbard was an accomplished hypnotist who liked to show off at parties—but the editor was stubbornly resistant to suggestion. It was a defense mechanism, he said, that he had used to deal with his mother, leaving him with "a permanent—but useful!—scar." But it also left him unable to recover any of the memories that had to be accessed for Hubbard's treatment to proceed.

They decided to try drugs. Campbell, who didn't even like to drink at home, agreed to take phenobarbital, a sedative, followed by scopolamine, a notorious truth serum. He hated one course of the latter so much that he refused to try it again—it left him dehydrated, confused, and listless—but he was willing to consider other approaches. Hubbard, in turn, knew that the editor was his best hope of bringing his ideas to a wider audience, and he was equally determined to continue.

By all indications, they had reached a dead end, but Hubbard had one last idea, which he claimed to have based on an apparatus described by the neurologist Jean-Martin Charcot, who had taught hypnosis to Sigmund Freud. Four mirrors were arranged in a truncated pyramid on a record player, with a lit candle placed nearby. When the turntable revolved at its highest speed, the result was a flicker of light that flashed at more than three hundred times per minute.

Campbell sat across from the phonograph. They turned it on. Almost immediately, he found himself overwhelmed by a feeling of pure horror, followed by a wave of memories that he had locked away. The editor confessed, "I'd been scared before in my life, but never that scared. I had to have Ron hold my hand—literally—while I spilled some of the fear. He's a fairly big guy, and fairly rugged, but twice I damned near crushed his hand when some of the really hot ones hit."

In the end, Campbell spoke like a frightened child for six hours, and his terror was contagious—Hubbard was allegedly so shaken by the technique that they never used it again. The mirrors, Campbell came to believe, had accidentally coincided with his brain's alpha rhythms, and he compared its effects to electroshock therapy or the use of drugs to induce seizures in psychiatric patients.

It would be months before he remembered what he had said. Hubbard supposedly erased the experiences themselves, leaving only the memory of the session behind—but it was enough. Later that summer, after additional treatment, Campbell wrote to Robert A. Heinlein, who was also friends with Hubbard, "Do I know things about my family I never knew I knew! . . . Come visit us, sometime, Bob, and I'll show you how to get data to blackmail the hell out of parents—blackmail the hell out of them so they back down and behave like human beings instead of the high and mighty and perfect."

Many of the episodes that he recovered did, in fact, revolve around his family, including a traumatic memory of his birth. According to Campbell, the doctor at the delivery had barked at his mother in a German accent, "The cord is caught around his neck and it is strangling him. You must stop fighting—you are killing him. Relax! You are killing him with your fighting! You must think your way out of this!" The forceps had slashed open the baby's cheek, and afterward, a nurse had put drops in his eyes and remarked, "He's just not interested in people!"

Campbell concluded that these words had shaped his personality, leading to much of his subsequent unhappiness. Other memories were equally disturbing. When he was six weeks old, he claimed, his mother—who had wanted to go to a party—had given him salt water to make him sick, which provided her with an excuse to leave him with his grandmother. He had almost drowned at age three, and a few months later, he had swallowed morphine pills and nearly overdosed.

Or so he thought. In reality, most of these incidents were probably imaginary, either knowingly implanted by Hubbard, or, more plausibly, drawn out of what Campbell honestly believed about himself. But they undoubtedly reflected his feelings about his family—and, in particular, about the women in his life.

Everyone agreed that his grandmother, Laura Harrison, had once been "a shrew." Her first husband had been Harry Strahorn, Campbell's maternal grandfather, to whom she bore identical twin girls, Dorothy and Josephine, in 1888. When he beat her, she left him for Joseph Kerr, whom she divorced after he ran out of money. Her third husband took a different approach, taming her into submission by playing on her feelings of guilt. It became a family legend, and Campbell heard it from all sides—because her last husband, William W. Campbell, was his paternal grandfather.

Campbell liked to describe his family history, with characteristic understatement, as "somewhat involved." William W. Campbell's first wife had been a woman named Florence van Campen, who gave birth to Campbell's father, John. After they divorced, William wed Laura Harrison Strahorn—and, years later, John married Dorothy Strahorn, his stepmother's daughter by her first marriage. It meant that Campbell, in practice, had only one grandmother, and it also had the effect of combining the two lines of his ancestry into a single imposing tree.

His ancestors ran back through the *Mayflower,* the American Revolution, and both sides of the Salem witch trials, with traces of Irish, Dutch, Hungarian, English, and other nationalities—although Campbell always thought of himself as Scottish. His grandfather William had been raised in Rochester, Vermont. After obtaining a law degree and serving one term as a Republican congressman in Washington, William became a master in chancery and a judge in Napoleon, Ohio, where his son John Wood Campbell was born in 1884.

John studied electrical engineering at the University of Michigan, returning home to marry Dorothy Strahorn. Instead of remaining in Napoleon, where their combined families ran the town, they moved to Newark. John Wood Campbell, Jr., their first child, was born in a frame house at 16 Treacy Avenue, a block away from the cemetery, on June 8, 1910. Decades later, he wrote to Heinlein, "Every individual starts out in life with a basic purpose. . . . Mine was 'to understand and explain.' " And the first mystery he had to confront was that of his own parents.

CAMPBELL'S FATHER WAS SEVERELY RATIONAL, WHICH SERVED HIM WELL IN HIS PROFESSIONAL life. After ten years with Bell Telephone in Newark, he was promoted to the company's New York headquarters, where he worked as an expert in business methods, rising to the position of chief engineer for plant practices at American Telephone and Telegraph. In private, he was exacting and unemotional—he was a religious conservative who refused to allow his children to see movies on Sundays—and he never laughed at home, although he could be charming in public.

He argued constantly with his wife, usually over money, and instead of "taming" her, as his father had done with her mother, he fought her to a draw. Their son felt ground between them—

"Mentally speaking, I was brought up in hellfire, high water, and earthquake country"—and he looked elsewhere for affection. Campbell's only friends as a boy were two women in the neighborhood, one French, one German, to whom he listened carefully, searching for points of view that were easier to grasp than the ones that he received from his parents.

When he was six, they moved from Newark to nearby Maplewood, where his sister, Laura, was born on September 2, 1917. His life became incrementally less miserable—his father learned to leave the house during his mother's tantrums, and they went from constant quarreling to an icy politeness—and the siblings got along well. They spent most of their summers with his grandparents in Ohio, where Campbell's grandfather, a legendary arguer in the courtroom, taught him that the law was a game that rewarded those who could be truthful and biased at the same time.

His parents presented him with different challenges. Campbell saw his father as an arrogant man who believed himself to be admirably humble and tolerant. He rarely showed affection toward his children. Instead of using the first person, he issued his commands as impersonal statements: "It is necessary." "One must." "One should." He laid down endless rules, adding more without any warning, and approvingly recited the poem that began "The boy stood on the burning deck," about a son who would rather die than disobey his father's orders.

Occasionally, Campbell remembered his father more fondly, particularly as he began to resemble him as he aged. He once described him as "a good and sincere guy" who introduced him at the age of three to science, which was the only way that they could be close. When Campbell was six, his father hung a crowbar from a thread, inviting him to marvel at how magnetic forces swung it around to the north, and he later said in all seriousness, "I feel there must be a wise creator who organized this universe—it can't be just an accident that the coefficient of thermal expansion for steel and concrete come out so nearly the same."

After he started school, his father reviewed his homework, asking him to revise the answers if he didn't approve—which taught him the useful skill of rewriting in the space that he had available. He also encouraged his son to solve math problems in two different ways. An analog approximation, he pointed out, was usually right to the first few places, while a digital calculation could make a mistake in the units as easily as in the millionths, with each one serving as a check on the other. At times, he criticized his son for being "a good beginner" who was unable to finish what he started, and Campbell often had reason to recall his father's favorite saying: "Well, it was a good idea, John. But it didn't work. Now clean it up."

His mother, by contrast, made so many inconsistent statements that he didn't know what to believe. Campbell later dismissed her as "a would-be aesthete" and paranoid sadist whose Episcopalian upbringing taught her that her role in life was to give orders—to men, to servants, and to her own family. She would contradict herself in the same breath or apologize tearfully after flying into a rage, in a cycle that Campbell compared to brainwashing, and her children found their own ways of dealing with it. Laura learned to independently verify everything that their mother said, while Campbell, who identified as agnostic from an early age, came to doubt all pronouncements made by any adult whatsoever.

Many of these recollections come from letters written years after the fact, and there were times when Campbell thought more kindly of his mother: "She was a very brilliant woman, who had an extremely wide range of information, high intelligence, great personal charm. . . . She was very pretty as a girl and young woman, and gave an appearance of being generous and thoughtful." He once described his father as "a failure" who "almost destroyed my ability to enjoy life," adding without explanation, "My mother helped to preserve that for me."

Campbell was also marked by his mother's twin. Dorothy and Josephine were impossible to tell apart, and they had been in constant competition since girlhood. Like their mother, who had attended Wellesley College, they were strikingly intelligent, and they despised each other: "They clawed each other viciously, with the most fiendishly expert belittling imaginable, for some fifty-five years. Sugar, with strychnine sauce. They wouldn't have used cyanide; it produces too easy a death." Campbell thought that his aunt "cordially detested" him, and she handled him roughly on her visits until he figured out that she was afraid of reptiles. After he started keeping a garter snake or toad in his pocket, she learned to stay away.

His mother and her twin also stand at the center of the single most famous anecdote from his childhood. As a boy, Campbell recounted, he would rush home from school to see the woman who he thought was his mother, only to be greeted by a distant figure—his aunt—who treated him like a stranger. In some versions of the story, which are hard to believe, the sisters dressed to fool him deliberately. But he always concluded by saying that he could never be sure whether the person with his mother's face would turn out to be his friend or his enemy.

Much later, he claimed that this memory inspired the most famous story that he, or perhaps any other science fiction author, would ever write—about an alien that could assume the form of any living thing, until it was impossible to know whether you were facing an ally or a murderous impostor. But this was only half true. Campbell's real enemy, as he repeatedly indicated, wasn't his aunt, but his mother, and his ambivalence toward her cast a shadow across the rest of his life.

If he owed his mother anything, it was the fact that she introduced him to science fiction and fantasy. Campbell turned to books for escape, and he devoured works of popular science, Greek and Norse myths, and the *Arabian Nights*. Mythology and science were both potential sources of answers, and he read them indiscriminately, along with such pioneers of speculative fiction as Jules Verne, Rudyard Kipling, and Edgar Rice Burroughs.

He had no choice but to take comfort in reading, because he didn't have any friends. Campbell's kindergarten teacher was convinced that he would grow up to be either a genius or a criminal, and he was insufferable in elementary school: "[I was] the damn fool who, while in first grade, lectured the third grade class on the annual and diurnal motions of the earth. Boy, was I smart!" Writing years later to Heinlein, he spoke from bitter experience of the price of precocity:

> *Kids who don't get angry, get teased. Adolescents who think freely in terms of nuclear physics, spaceships and wonder fascinatedly about the origin of the solar system lose friends at a remarkable rate. They get kidded, and rejected by the group until they learn the lesson of not thinking. If they persist in thinking, they get completely rejected. Until they succeed in finding a group of* [Homo superior] *and gradually learn what the trouble is.*

"I was unpopular with local kids, because I solved games," Campbell wrote elsewhere, explaining that he had figured out a way to win hide-and-seek: "Once I taught the kids the formula"—based on a standard naval search pattern, with a spiral moving out from the center—"that ended hide-and-seek in the neighborhood." His size didn't stop the bullies, and although he went after them, "heart set on dismemberment," it was easier to seek protection from friendly adults on the walk home. Genius, he decided, was the worst handicap of all—which later made him less than sympathetic to those who felt like outcasts for other reasons.

He was happiest in a workshop. In grade school, he built a catapult in his yard, using an iron pipe as a lever arm, and conked himself soundly on the head. He loved his Meccano set, constructing a crane that won a contest sponsored by a department store. At thirteen, he assembled a radio receiver with lead ore and a steel phonograph needle, and he put together his first car using two batteries and a Studebaker starting motor. He blew up his basement chemistry lab, fixed bikes and appliances, and constructed an eavesdropper that could hear a conversation from a block away.

Gradually, he also figured out how to deal with his parents. He took pleasure in bending the rules by following their instructions to the letter, and he loved science because it allowed him to counter his father with facts: "The old son of a bitch couldn't cram in a new rule anymore." With his mother, he perfected a "mental beating technique" that worked because his attention span was longer than hers: "My childhood battles with her did a great deal to build, in me, the ability to put a given set of facts together in sixteen dozen new and unsuspected ways in the space between two sentences. She's good at that; I had to be better at it."

Campbell was twelve when his parents separated. His mother moved to Lemon Grove Avenue in Hollywood, California, with the children, and their divorce was finalized a year later. By then, Campbell was a tall, lanky kid, and in his father's absence, his mother began to feel physically threatened by him. None of her old tactics were working, and her son finally "had her so thoroughly scared that she didn't want me in the same house with her."

When they returned to the East Coast after the divorce, his mother sent him away for the summer to Kittatinny Campground in Barryville, New York, and then to Blair Academy, an exclusive boarding school for boys in Blairstown, New Jersey. Campbell tried to approach the situation with a positive outlook. Instead of his mother's assumption that everyone was against her, he experimented with the opposite point of view: "Everybody is trying to be nice to me."

It didn't quite work. At Blair, he made a few friends, but in general, he did an admirable job of failing to get along with anybody. His intelligence was scored at 145—"I'd have gotten a higher score if I hadn't known so damn much"—but he earned mediocre grades, excelling at physics but nearly flunking English. Campbell applied himself to subjects that he found interesting, ignored the rest, and never passed up the opportunity to correct his teachers in class. He joined no teams or societies, and he listed one of his weekly activities as "hiking," perhaps because it allowed him to think for extended periods on his own.

On the social side, he was as unbearable as before. His size gave him an advantage at sports like football, but he tended to spoil the game. In tennis, he taught himself a few dirty tricks with a steel racket, spinning the ball so that it dropped dead on the court or striking the top of the net so that it barely toppled over to the other side. When he played chess against the school's best player, he traded pieces savagely until they were each down to four, proceeding to win the simplified game three times in a row. Campbell only wanted the contests to end, as if he were conserving his energy for the greater challenges to come.

He never received his diploma. A student could graduate only if he had enough credits for the college of his choice, and he lacked French and trigonometry. Yet an attractive prospect beckoned. His father had proposed that he apply to the Massachusetts Institute of Technology, promising that he would cover the full cost of his tuition. Campbell plowed through two years of French in a single summer and got a high score on the trig exam after skimming the book the night before—and, like that, he was headed for Cambridge.

As far as he was concerned, it was just in time. Years later, he wrote, "I've felt a vast need for love and affection—and a complete lack of ability to go outward seeking to establish those human contacts necessary to fulfill my needs." College, he felt, was the one place where he could find the emotional connection that he craved, using nothing but his brain. In Orange, New Jersey, he said goodbye to his mother and her second husband, an unassuming appliance salesman named James A. Middleton. Then he left without looking back, hoping to finally escape the trap of his childhood.

But he had been changed by it in ways that he would never overcome. As he told his father decades afterward, "You and Mother between you gave me immunity to many things that neither one of you could have; either of you would have crippled me. . . . At the time, of course, I felt a vast injustice; I do not forgive you, because that's a useless and arrogant thing."

John W. Campbell, circa 1928.
Courtesy of Leslyn Randazzo

WHEN CAMPBELL ENTERED COLLEGE IN THE FALL OF 1928, HE SENSED THE DIFFERENCE AT ONCE. HE described Cambridge as "a little, dingy town," but his nostalgia for it remained a constant throughout his career, particularly toward his professors. In high school, the teachers had seemed certain of everything, while at MIT, he wrote, "I found a bunch of rather bewildered men." They acknowledged that they didn't have all the answers, and for Campbell, who would make questioning others his life's work, it felt like a place that he could call home.

In his freshman year, he was associated with the department of physics, where he read through his textbook at the beginning of the semester, plowing through it like a novel in three days. Sometimes, as he had at Blair Academy, he failed to make a good impression. During a course in analytical chemistry, he was asked to identify a sample of an unknown substance. Instead of going by the book, he looked at the reddish crystals, guessed that they were ferric nitrate, and performed two tests to confirm his hunch, which only annoyed his instructor. On another occasion, he brought an entire experimental apparatus to the classroom just to prove a professor wrong.

His most significant influence was Norbert Wiener, an associate professor of mathematics who later achieved worldwide fame as the founder of cybernetics. Like Campbell, Wiener had been a child prodigy with a complicated relationship to his father, whom he called his "dearest antagonist." Campbell later described him as the worst teacher he had ever seen—he would write a complicated expression on the blackboard, state that the result was clear, and move on without elaboration.

Yet Wiener's genius was undeniable, and his example left a lasting impression. Decades later, Campbell fondly remembered college as the place where dirty limericks were born, where students spread chemicals on locker room benches in order to play practical jokes, and where handwritten signs in dorm rooms proclaimed Finagle's Law: "Anything that can go wrong, will—at the worst possible moment." He rowed crew, played tennis, and began smoking two packs of cigarettes a day, a habit that he would retain for the next forty years.

Almost by accident, he also became a science fiction writer. He had been a fan of the pulps since high school, buying *Argosy, Weird Tales,* and the first issue of Hugo Gernsback's *Amazing Stories,* which might have been conceived with him in mind—it emerged from a close community of electronics hobbyists, with stories in which intelligence was rewarded not with ostracism but with infinite power. In 1928, in particular, Gernsback had published a novel that opened up the genre overnight to a vaster sense of scale than it had ever known before, with an atomic spacecraft that one character casually estimates as capable of "a velocity of something like seven billion four hundred thirteen million miles per second."

Campbell was fascinated by *The Skylark of Space.* The serial by E. E. "Doc" Smith and Lee Hawkins Garby—with a dashing villain who steals the hero's ship and leads him on a chase six quadrillion miles from home—inaugurated the field of superscience, or space opera. It inspired endless imitations, and it even influenced Campbell's decision to major in physics—atomic energy, he felt, was the big scoop of his lifetime, a conviction shared by few of his professors. Yet it didn't occur to him to write until he was a freshman, and when it did, it was for a reason that the captain of the *Skylark* might have approved. He wanted a new car.

A Model A Ford cost five hundred dollars, and his father informed him, "I owe you a good education; luxuries you get for yourself." *Amazing* paid half a cent per word, so Campbell cranked out "Invaders from the Infinite," writing it as fast as he could because he needed the money. He showed the result to his father, who liked it enough to send it to editor T. O'Conor Sloane. Incredibly, it was accepted, along with his next effort, "When the Atoms Failed."

As the months passed, however, neither story appeared, and the magazine only paid on publication. The summer after his freshman year, Campbell decided to visit the editor in person. Going to the publisher's offices on Fourth Avenue in New York, he was ushered inside to meet Sloane, who was notorious both for his stodginess—he didn't believe that humans would ever enter space—and for his tendency to hold on to submissions until the pages crumbled. He was also eighty years old.

Campbell was only nineteen. To his eyes, Sloane, with his flowing white beard, must have seemed ancient, and neither man suspected that the encounter was a passing of the torch. Sloane treated him kindly, and he confessed that "Invaders from the Infinite" had been lost. Campbell didn't have a carbon, so the story was gone forever. All that he later remembered of it was that it turned on the problem of heating a ship in space, with its hero harnessing "material energy," which was a thousand times greater than the power of the atom.

Yet it isn't hard to guess how it read. His second story, "When the Atoms Failed," ran on the cover of *Amazing* in January 1930, and it felt like E. E. Smith with the excitement, love interest, and villain removed. Its protagonist uses an integraph—a machine for doing calculus—to develop atomic power and fend off an invasion from Mars, but its author was less interested in action than in describing the spaceship, with its "six-inch iridio-tungsten alloy shell," and in delivering endless technical lectures that might have been transcribed straight from his textbooks.

It must have pleased his father, but it also struck a chord with fans. Campbell was one of the only writers at the time with any knowledge of theoretical physics at the college level, and his use of scientific jargon made readers feel as if they could almost understand what was happening, with enough realism to offer the illusion of more. The integraph, for example, was an actual instrument that was used to solve differential equations at MIT, and by incorporating it into his story, Campbell provided one of the first descriptions of a computer in science fiction.

He was off and running, and between sessions of summer school, he churned out stories, falling back repeatedly on the same formulas. Once he figured out how to recombine the pieces, it became just another game to solve, and none of his early stories is worth reading today. *The Skylark of Space,* which was written with real passion, can still put a silly grin on a reader's face, while "When the Atoms Failed" showed barely any competence as a writer and minimal affection for the genre. Its sequel, "The Metal Horde," featured a machine that could build more copies of itself, resulting in a story with millions of spaceships and no recognizable human beings.

His next effort, "Piracy Preferred," marked the debut of Arcot, Morey, and Wade, a trio of adventurers who deliver huge blocks of exposition while puffing on pipes. None of them had anything resembling an inner life, including Arcot, who otherwise might have seemed like a wishful portrait of the author—he was six feet tall and the son of a famous scientist. Yet there were hints of developments to come. One character says in an aside, "You've grown up in a world where the psychomedical techniques really work. When I was growing up, psychomedical techniques were strictly rule of thumb—and the doctors were all thumbs."

Campbell pressed on with "The Voice of the Void," which he wrote in a single afternoon, and the Arcot stories "Islands of Space," "The Black Star Passes," and "Solarite," which expanded outward from the solar system to encompass the entire galaxy. His aliens were often more interesting than his men. An extraterrestrial could be flawed, while his human protagonists were all generic heroes—invariably tall and strong—who represented the kind of genius inventor he wanted to be. The results read, accurately, like the work of a bright, lonely kid who knew everything about chemistry and nothing about people. And there were no women in sight.

Before long, Campbell became second in popularity only to "Doc" Smith, whom he challenged directly in the letters column of *Amazing*, pointing out errors in his rival's stories while daring all comers to do the same to him: "I'm waiting anxiously for all comments, from anyone, and in particular Dr. Smith." Yet it never seems to have occurred to him to submit to the magazine *Astounding Stories of Super-Science*, which had appeared on newsstands at the end of 1929.

His professors were skeptical. One told him that he was prostituting his talents, while his freshman English teacher, William Chace Greene, Jr., disliked science fiction, giving him a poor grade for a story that stated that light had mass. Campbell responded with a signed note from the physics department, but Greene flunked him anyway. The only professor who ever helped him was Norbert Wiener, who advised him on "Islands of Space." As for his father, he had merely remarked, after hearing of his first acceptance by *Amazing*, "It isn't *The Saturday Evening Post*."

But Campbell had bought his car. It was a Model A Ford Coupe that he rebuilt from the ground up, like one of his heroes constructing a spaceship. Driving from his mother's house in Orange to Cambridge, he spent eight hours on twisty roads, taking pride in going as fast as he could without killing himself. He had passed every test that he had been given, and he seemed on the verge of achieving the ideals of his fiction in real life—until, inexplicably, he failed.

His grades had been good but unexceptional, with high marks in physics and chemistry and fair ones in calculus, although he was "constitutionally opposed to math." He was also required to learn German, the language of international research, which he failed to pass after three tries. Campbell evidently blamed this later on the repressed memory of the doctor at his birth, who had shouted in a German accent, but at the time, he only found it hard to care about something so trivial as declining nouns: "If *das Haus* means 'the house,' why isn't that good enough for anybody?"

None of it mattered. After spending the first half of his junior year as an unclassified student at MIT, he was asked to leave. His last day was February 7, 1931. At the age of twenty, Campbell had seemingly proven his father's accusation that he was unable to see anything through to the end, and his dreams of finding a place where he belonged lay in ruins. Worst of all, he had been let down by his mind. It was the one game that he had been unable to solve, and as he slunk back to his mother's house in New Jersey, he had no real idea of what his future might hold.

2.
THREE AGAINST THE GODS

1907—1935

The adventurer is an outlaw. Adventure must start with running away from home.

—WILLIAM BOLITHO, *TWELVE AGAINST THE GODS*

In 1931, shortly after his demoralizing departure from MIT, Campbell boarded a ship to Europe, where he traveled alone for two months. It was an act that was deliberately out of character. Campbell's fiction ranged across the universe, but he was not a natural wanderer. His father's relative affluence granted him physical, if not emotional, security, and for most of his life, he was rarely more than a day's drive from where he had been born and raised.

His three most important collaborators, by contrast, all ended up far from home. From an early age, they had invented identities for themselves, out of choice or necessity, and they were profoundly marked by their travels. One wandered as a pragmatic solution to his problems; another, in pursuit of his dreams; and the last, an immigrant who went the farthest, left when he was only a child.

ONE DAY IN 1912, ROBERT A. HEINLEIN LIKED TO RECALL, A YOUNG COUPLE WAS WALKING THROUGH Swope Park in Kansas City, Missouri. They were crossing the railroad tracks when the wife caught her heel in a switch—the pair of tapering rails that guided the cars—as a train's whistle sounded its approach. A passerby, identified in press accounts as a tramp, stopped to help, but the men were unable to free her before the engine struck them all. The woman and the stranger were killed at once.

Heinlein, who was only five at the time, remembered being in the park that day with his family. The incident became one of his earliest memories, and he never got over it. What obsessed him the most was the second man, who could have saved himself at the last moment but died instead. It informed Heinlein's ongoing effort to find meaning in a world defined by death, as embodied by the message of the tramp on the tracks: "This is how a man lives. And this is how a *man* dies."

Or so he claimed. In reality, the incident didn't occur when he was five, but twelve, and it took place over four hundred miles away, in Winnetka, Illinois. On September 1, 1919, William Tanner was killed while trying to save his wife from an oncoming train, while a flagman—not a tramp—named John Miller lost a leg in the rescue attempt but survived. Heinlein had listened intently as his father read the coverage aloud from the *Kansas City Star*, and the fact that he quietly assimilated it into his own biography was revealing in itself.

Robert Anson Heinlein was born on July 7, 1907, in Butler, Missouri, eighty miles southeast of Kansas City. His parents, Rex Ivar Heinlein and Bam Lyle, had been sweethearts in high school, and Rex, a veteran of the Spanish-American War, worked for his family's agricultural tools company and as a cashier for International Harvester. Heinlein was the third of seven children. He stammered, but he was an excellent student, and as a child, he had mystical experiences, including memories of past lives. At school, he found himself looking at another boy—a bully—and feeling overwhelmed by the certainty that they were different aspects of the same person.

He never shared these convictions with his parents, who had more pressing worries. They were always poor—there were simply too many kids—and they once survived on potato soup for three months. In their crowded house, Heinlein slept on a mattress on the floor, and on summer nights, he snuck out to the park to play naked as Tarzan. He earned pocket money by selling *The Saturday Evening Post*, reading his homework on the streetcar, while such writers as Edward Bellamy, H. G. Wells, and Will Durant turned him into a budding socialist.

At night, under the bedcovers, he studied pages by candlelight—Kipling, Burroughs, the Tom Swift series, Horatio Alger, and the Gernsback science fiction magazines. They filled him with a resolve to conquer his limitations, and he took forensics to overcome his stammer. During a high school debate on shipping regulations, he quoted the annual reports of the British Colonial Shipping Board to support his argument. A week later, the students on the opposing team realized that the organization didn't exist—but Heinlein had already won. At night, he studied the stars from the top of a billboard, and he contemplated a career as an astronomer.

His family was more focused on this world. The Heinleins had a strong military tradition—their ancestors had supposedly fought in every American war—and his father had used a patronage job to secure a place for Heinlein's older brother at the U.S. Naval Academy at Annapolis, Maryland. When Heinlein was old enough to follow suit, his father didn't offer to do the same. Heinlein took matters into his own hands, writing dozens of letters until he landed an appointment, and he prepared himself by strengthening his eyes, which had always been weak, using the Bates Method, a system of exercises intended to improve his vision.

On June 16, 1925, he was sworn in as a midshipman at Annapolis. During his plebe year, he was hazed by upperclassmen, who forced him to answer questions in the mess hall. Heinlein, who was six feet tall and painfully skinny, lost ten pounds, and he had nightmares about the beatings for decades. He was drawn to aviation, thinking that he might become a pilot, and he took up fencing and dancing, seeing them as ways in which the mind and body could be harmonized. The academy's structure seemed to offer a corrective to personality flaws—his impulsiveness, his temper, his impatience with others—that he would always struggle to overcome.

In May 1926, his favorite sister, Rose Elizabeth, died at the age of seven, after falling out of the family car. His father, who had been driving, never forgave himself. Heinlein was heartbroken, but he had to return to the academy, where he hoped to join the aviation squad. Even after his eye exercises, however, his stereoscopic vision was terrible, and he failed the qualifying exam. He turned to engineering instead, and although he remained fascinated by planes, he would never fly.

The following year, he sailed on a practice cruise to the Panama Canal on the USS *Oklahoma*. Heinlein was a dreamer, but he knew that the details were what counted, and he crawled over the battleship with his sketchbook, taking pleasure in memorizing its systems. Yet life continued to present him with devastating surprises. While on leave, he had dated Alice McBee, one of his high school classmates, and he had been planning to ask her to marry him. In 1928, he learned that she had died from appendicitis, and after hearing the news, he felt suicidal.

Heinlein was commissioned as an ensign on June 6, 1929, but he skipped his graduation. On the train home, he met and slept with a woman named Mary Briggs, who was on her way to see her fiancé in St. Louis. When he climbed into her berth, he wasn't entirely inexperienced—he had lost his virginity to "a grandmother"

Robert A. Heinlein at the Naval Academy in Annapolis, 1929.
Courtesy of Geo Rule

five years earlier—but it was his first fulfilling sexual encounter, and it led to an awareness of sex as another interface between the body and the mind. Decades later, he wrote to Briggs, "Had you not been engaged when I met you, I suspect that we would have married within weeks or even days."

Like Campbell, he had been impressed by the story *The Skylark of Space*, but his interests ran equally toward the spiritual side. A classmate named Cal Laning had taught him hypnosis, and they joined a third friend in a project called the Quest—if one of them died, he promised to contact the others from beyond the grave, and they conducted experiments in telepathy, following the instructions in a book by the socialist writer Upton Sinclair. Heinlein was searching for approaches to mysticism, and he even considered joining the Freemasons.

Instead, the revelation of the girl on the train led him to take an uncharacteristic risk. In Kansas City, he reunited with another high school friend, Elinor Curry, whom he married without telling his parents. Elinor was "sexually adventurous," and the impulsive act was driven by a desire to further explore sex—but he was disturbed when she slept with another man on their honeymoon. Heinlein had done much the same with Mary Briggs, who was engaged to someone else, but was evidently unprepared when it didn't occur on his terms.

The marriage also required a sacrifice. Earlier that year, Heinlein had asked to be considered for a Rhodes Scholarship. It was a long shot—his grades were only fair—but it seemed like a plausible path to astronomy. Rhodes Scholars had to be single, however, so he withdrew his application, giving it up in exchange for a sex life. Within a year, their marriage was over, and Elinor, whom he called "poisonous, like mistletoe," filed for divorce in 1930.

Heinlein was serving on the USS *Lexington,* an aircraft carrier based in San Pedro, California. In 1932, he reconnected with Cal Laning, who had become infatuated with a woman named Leslyn MacDonald. Leslyn, who was born in Boston on August 29, 1904, had been raised in the Los Angeles area by a mother devoted to Theosophy—an occult philosophy that Heinlein also studied—and worked in the music department at Columbia Pictures after graduating from the University of California, Los Angeles. She was three years older than Heinlein, just over five feet tall, and undeniably striking.

Although he knew that Laning was in love with Leslyn, Heinlein, who had felt so betrayed by Elinor under similar circumstances, slept with her on the night that they met. The following morning, he startled all three of them by proposing. It was the second time that Heinlein, who was otherwise so disciplined, had rushed headlong toward marriage—but Leslyn was a far more promising partner. She was more than his match intellectually,

Leslyn MacDonald in 1926.
Special Collections, UCLA Library

shared his interest in mysticism, and hinted that she would be receptive to an open relationship.

On March 28, 1932, Heinlein, wearing his dress uniform and carrying his saber, married Leslyn, who wore a borrowed gown. The groom was slim and handsome, with an air of studied sophistication. Laning, who had turned out to be a remarkably good sport, attended the ceremony. A few months later, Heinlein was promoted to lieutenant, junior grade. His life seemed to be coming together, and he had no way of knowing that it was about to fall apart.

That summer, he was transferred to the USS *Roper,* a destroyer on which he was slated to serve as a gunnery officer. It was smaller than the other ships to which he had been assigned, and its motion made him desperately seasick. After losing weight and suffering stomach pains, he checked into the naval hospital in San Diego. For years, he had endured minor ailments—his eyes, his wrist, attacks of urethritis that would disrupt his sexual relations with Leslyn—and now he was at open war with his body. The diagnosis was tuberculosis.

At first, he recovered quickly, but after his transfer to a hospital in Denver, where the quality of care was far worse, Heinlein developed bedsores—inspiring him to work up an early design for a waterbed—and an infection that went misdiagnosed. He was facing an involuntary retirement, and with his lungs damaged, he would never serve at sea again. Looking for a new career, he put up the exploration money for a silver mine in Colorado, only to lose everything when his backer turned out to be a gangster who was shot to death before the deal closed.

On August 1, 1934, he was found "totally and permanently disabled." At the age of twenty-seven, his career was over. Heinlein had hoped to honor his family's tradition in the Navy, but although he had done everything right, he had failed. His body, which he had spent most of his life trying to control, had betrayed him, and now he had to find answers somewhere else.

WHEN HE WAS JUST A BOY, L. RON HUBBARD OFTEN SAID, HE MET A MEDICINE MAN NAMED OLD Tom Madfeathers. Old Tom lived with a small group of Blackfoot Indians in a camp on the outskirts of Helena, Montana, not far from where Hubbard's grandfather owned a gigantic cattle ranch, and could jump fifteen feet from the ground while seated to the top of his tent—a lesson, it seemed, in how reality could be far stranger than anything one might imagine.

According to Hubbard's account, the Blackfeet saw him as a kindred spirit. As a toddler, he had charmed them by forcing his way into their tribal dance, during which the braves threatened his father with tomahawks when he tried to take him away. Hubbard boasted that he learned to ride before he could walk, that he was breaking horses at three and a half, and that the Blackfeet made him a blood brother—a custom that is otherwise unattested— when he was six years old.

All these stories are almost certainly false. Hubbard's grandfather didn't own a ranch, but a farm of a few hundred acres where horses were raised for parades, and it was miles from the nearest reservation. If Hubbard ever encountered the Blackfeet, he would have seen himself in them, and not the other way around. For most of his life, he idealized the freedom that they seemed to represent, and the dream of being a blood brother was a variation on an idea to which he repeatedly returned—an initiation in which an ordinary man could become something more.

Hubbard's embellishments were often based on a grain of truth, but in the long run, their only effect was to trivialize what had been an indisputably colorful boyhood. His mother, Leodora May Waterbury, was born in 1885 in Tilden, Nebraska. She was an intelligent woman who studied to become a teacher in Omaha, marrying a naval recruiter, Harry Ross Hubbard, who was one year her junior. After she became pregnant, May returned with her husband to her hometown, where their son Lafayette Ronald Hubbard was born on March 13, 1911.

The boy had orange hair, gray eyes, and immense charm. He loved to tell stories and invent games, and after moving to Helena, he was so spoiled by his relatives that he came to expect the same treatment from everyone. Hubbard attended grade school within sight of the Cathedral of Saint Helena, walking nearly every day past its Gothic spires. During World War I, his father returned to the Navy, where he served as an assistant paymaster, and he was ultimately posted to the USS *Oklahoma*, on which Heinlein later took a practice cruise.

When his father was reassigned to Washington, D.C., Hubbard and his mother joined him by ship. On the voyage, Hubbard met Joseph C. "Snake" Thompson, an eccentric herpetologist, psychoanalyst, and former spy. Hubbard credited Thompson with introducing him to the principles of psychology, and he was undoubtedly fascinated by him. After arriving in Washington, Hubbard, at thirteen, allegedly became the youngest Eagle Scout in the country. In reality, no such age records were kept, but he had clearly advanced very quickly.

His father was promoted to full lieutenant, bringing his wife and son to Puget Sound, where he served as a disbursing officer. In 1927, he was put in charge of the commissary at the U.S. naval station in Guam. Hubbard assumed that he was coming, too, but his parents were wary of the native girls, and they decided that he would live with his grandparents in Helena. It felt like an abandonment, and Hubbard was only slightly mollified by a visit that took him through Japan, China, and the Philippines. He remained in Guam for six weeks, teaching English to local kids, who were more intrigued by his red hair: "Whenever I sat down outside of a doorway, the children would gather around with a very dumb and astonished look upon their faces."

After leaving Guam in July 1927, he enrolled in high school in Helena, lying about his age to enlist in the National Guard. The following May, after the annual Vigilante Day Parade, in which Hubbard and his friends dressed as buccaneers—he would always be drawn to images of piracy—he vanished. He caught a train to Seattle, and after a nasty spill left him bleeding on a hiking trail, he decided to return to Guam. Like many young men, he was looking for answers that his ordinary life couldn't provide, and he was neither the first nor the last to invent his way out.

When he arrived in Guam, his parents, although upset by his departure from school, decided that he could stay, with his mother tutoring him for the entrance exam to Annapolis. Hubbard also had time for another visit to China, writing of the locals in his journal, "They smell of all the baths they didn't take. The trouble with China is, there are too many chinks here." All the while, he was filling notebooks with ideas for short stories, interspersed with algebra homework, that revolved around the exploits of white heroes in the Far East.

Yet a writer's life wasn't sufficiently exciting, and he wanted real adventure. Unfortunately, he lacked the necessary practical skills, and he failed the math section of the Annapolis exam. When he tried again, he was disqualified by his poor vision, which he later said he used "to escape the Naval Academy." In contrast to Heinlein, who diligently did his eye exercises, Hubbard welcomed it as a convenient excuse—he didn't have any patience for details, and it was easier to daydream.

In the fall of 1930, at the urging of his father, he enrolled at George Washington University: "[He said] I should study engineering and mathematics and so I found myself obediently studying." Hubbard liked to refer to himself as a nuclear physicist who had taken "the first American class on atomic and molecular phenomena," but in fact, he had failed it. He was more interested in the gliding club, and he claimed to have found a spiritual protector in the air—a "smiling woman" who appeared on his wing in moments of danger. Years later, he called her Flavia Julia—another name for Saint Helena, whose cathedral had loomed over his town in Montana.

When Hubbard wasn't flying, he was writing, with a short piece about his barnstorming adventures for *Sportsman Pilot* followed by a few stories for the college literary review—but the sea was still calling. In the spring of 1932, after hearing that a schooner was available for charter in Baltimore, he conceived of what he grandly called the Caribbean Motion Picture Expedition. He convinced fifty other students to sign up, saying that they would film "strongholds and bivouacs of the Spanish Main," gather specimens, and stage pirate movies for the camera.

The ship set sail on June 23, although a lack of wind meant that it had to be towed out of Chesapeake Bay. After encountering stormy weather, it made an unscheduled stop in Bermuda to procure water for its leaking tanks. Eleven members of the voyage promptly left, followed by more after their fresh stock of water dribbled away. They were stuck in the Sargasso Sea for days, with Hubbard hung in effigy by his passengers, and their captain was ordered to return. "Despite these difficulties, we had a wonderful summer," Hubbard glibly wrote, and he never gave up on his fantasy of sailing from one port of call to another.

In his second year of college, his grades remained low, and he dropped out. His father made one last effort on his behalf, arranging for Hubbard to volunteer for the Red Cross in Puerto Rico. Instead, he prospected for gold, which was more in line with his sensibilities, and briefly worked for a mining company. Deep down, he was aware that he had disappointed his family. He later dismissed his mother as a "whore" whom he claimed to have caught in bed with another woman, and his reduction of his life to a series of invented episodes amounted to a small act of revenge against the parents who had genuinely loved him.

By February 1933, he was back in Washington, D.C., and for once he had a tangible goal in mind. One year earlier, before his departure for San Juan, he had encountered a woman named Margaret Louise Grubb, who was known to her friends as Polly. They had met on a gliding field—Polly, who hoped to get a pilot's license, had cut her blond hair in a bob just like Amelia Earhart's. But she was even more charmed by Hubbard, who was attracted to her as well.

At first her parents disapproved—Hubbard was six years younger, with no obvious prospects—but they were married on April 13. Hubbard seemed as aimless as always. He boasted that he had found gold on his new wife's family farm, but when his glider pilot's license expired, he was unable to afford the flight time required to renew it. Over the course of the previous year, working as a freelance writer, he had earned less than a hundred dollars.

Only then did he realize that the answer had been in front of him all along. His one undisputable gift had always been storytelling, and toward the end of 1933, he went to a newsstand and used some of his remaining cash to buy copies of all the fiction magazines on sale. He had never taken any interest in the pulps before, but now he saw them as a possible vehicle for his talents, reading them closely to see what the editors were buying. Polly was pregnant, and he sensed that this was his best shot at earning enough to survive on his own terms.

It isn't clear whether *Astounding Stories*—which had recently been acquired by the publishing firm Street & Smith, after the bankruptcy of its previous owner—was among the titles that he purchased, but it wouldn't have mattered. At twenty-two, Hubbard was about to embark on a remarkable career, but he had no interest whatsoever in science fiction.

THERE WAS NO DOCTOR IN THE VILLAGE IN RUSSIA, SO THE MOTHER HAD TO DELIVER HER BABY with only a midwife. She was twenty-five and diminutive, with blue eyes and light hair. For three days and two nights, she labored, walking back and forth as she leaned on her husband for support. Finally, she gave birth to a boy. He would never know his exact birthday, but he ultimately settled on January 2, 1920.

She named him Isaac Asimov, after his maternal grandfather. Petrovichi, his birthplace, was located in Great Russia, or the Russian Soviet Federated Socialist Republic, and it was too tiny to appear on most maps. Decades later, during World War II, Asimov was marking troop movements with pins on a map of Europe. Looking closely, he was astonished to see Petrovichi for the first time. He stuck a special pin there, and for the duration, he found it easier than usual to explain where he had been born: "A few miles south of Smolensk."

Judah, his father, was born there in 1896. His wife, Anna Berman, was a year older, and she married Judah, their son speculated, "as the only way of getting rid of him." They were inseparable, but never publicly affectionate, and Judah rarely cracked a smile, while Anna laughed loudly at jokes. She was fiercely protective of her son and his younger sister, Manya, who would later be known as Marcia. When he was two, Asimov nearly died of pneumonia—according to his mother, sixteen local children came down with it, and he was the only one who survived.

His father was content to run a food cooperative in their village, and they might have stayed there forever if it hadn't been for an unexpected opportunity. Anna's half brother had emigrated to Brooklyn, and when the news came of the Russian Revolution, he wrote to say that he would vouch for them if they immigrated to the United States. They decided to accept, reasoning that one could become rich in America—which didn't make it any less of a risk. After securing the necessary bribes for passports, the family left on Christmas Eve of 1922. Asimov was just three, and in Moscow, it was so bitterly cold that his mother buttoned him up in her coat.

After a stormy crossing, they arrived at Ellis Island on February 3, 1923. It was the last year of relatively unobstructed immigration, and if they had waited any longer, they might not have been allowed to enter. They settled in East New York, a Jewish and Italian neighborhood in Brooklyn, in an apartment that used a woodstove for heat. His parents knew only Russian and Yiddish, the latter of which the family spoke at home, but they worked themselves hard, and they were too proud to ask for help from their relatives.

Asimov had trouble adjusting—he had to be told not to urinate into the gutter—but he was already showing flashes of something special. He learned the alphabet from a jump-rope rhyme, and by five, he could read. When he was ready for kindergarten, his mother said that he had been born on September 7, 1919, allowing him to enter the first grade. His teacher skipped him ahead again, which only increased his sense of isolation. Unlike Campbell, Heinlein, or Hubbard, he didn't have to invent forms of exile for himself, and he learned to value stability.

He never had close friends, and he was about to be set even further apart. In 1926, his father bought a candy store with a soda counter and a phone for the use of the neighborhood. Asimov had to be available to pitch in and run errands, but in practice, the store effectively orphaned him. It was open seven days a week, except for Jewish holidays, and he rarely had dinner with his father again—his mother and the children would eat first, finishing quickly so that Judah could have his meal alone, which left Asimov with a lifelong habit of wolfing down his food.

His solitude led him to take an interest in reading, and there was one obvious source of material. Along with candy and cigarettes, the store sold such pulps as *Nick Carter*, but when he tried to read them, his father replied, "Junk! It is not fit to read. The only people who read magazines like that are *bums*."

Asimov responded with the obvious objection. "You sell them to other boys."

"I have to make a living. If their fathers don't stop them, I can't stop them."

It was clearly hopeless, but he gave it one last shot. "*You* read them, Pappa."

His father ended the discussion. "I have to learn English. You learn it in school, but I don't go to school. I have to learn it from these books."

In the end, his father gave him a library card. Soon he was reading everywhere, and once he learned something, he never forgot it. He made no attempt to conceal his intelligence—to avoid being bullied, he helped a big kid with his homework in exchange for protection—and his identification as a prodigy became a preemptive form of defense. In third grade, he made a point of insisting that his real birthday was January 2, 1920, and the records were dutifully revised, in a seemingly trivial change that had significant consequences much later on.

Like Campbell, Asimov read through his textbooks at the beginning of the year. The only bad marks that he ever received were for talking in class, which led to spankings—his father never hit the children, but his mother kept a clothesline for whippings, during which she scolded him, calling him a *paskudnyak,* or nasty boy. They didn't maintain a kosher house, and Asimov received minimal religious education, despite the fact that the synagogue was an obvious place for his talents. He never had a bar mitzvah, and early on, he began to identify as an atheist.

After they moved into the apartment upstairs from a new candy store on Essex Street, Asimov had to devote all of his spare time to it. When he wasn't in school, he was working, and it seemed his fate to be set apart by some combination of Jewishness, youth, intelligence, and the family business. In 1928, his mother accidentally conceived again, and he had to work even longer hours.

The magazines still beckoned, and after the rare treat of a school trip to the Statue of Liberty on July 2, 1929, he was filled with a renewed determination. Showing his father a copy of Gernsback's *Science Wonder Stories,* with its pictures of futuristic machinery, he argued that it was educational. Science, after all, was right there in the title. His father was skeptical. "Science fiction? Like Jules Verne?"

He pronounced the author's name in the proper French style, and Asimov, who was nine, didn't recognize it. His father became annoyed. "He wrote about going to the moon and to the center of the earth and, oh yes, about a man going around the world in eighty days."

As he listened to these words, Asimov's face lit up. "Oh! You mean Jooles Voine!"

At last, his father agreed. In all likelihood, he was in no mood to argue—his second son, Stanley, would be born just three weeks later—and he said that Asimov could read the magazines, with the exception of *The Shadow.* Asimov promptly took to peeking at it while his father took his nap, only to be caught in the act one afternoon. His father looked at him wearily. "Well, Isaac, rather than have you steal and learn to be a gangster, you can read the magazines."

Asimov counted the hours until his favorite titles came out each month, and he handled them carefully, since they had to be sold or returned—if it hadn't been for the store, he couldn't have read them at all. As he neared his teens, however, his thoughts turned to more urgent concerns. His parents wanted him to become a doctor, but to stand out from other Jewish applicants—a quota system was still in place—he had to graduate from a good school. Boys High of Brooklyn was the best available choice, but after Asimov enrolled, he felt more alone than ever. There were no girls, of course, and he had to hurry back to the store every day.

There were small consolations. He was allowed to check out three books from the library, reading as he walked, with one volume in front of his face and two tucked under his arms. After successfully persuading his father to spend ten dollars on a used typewriter, he made his first stab at science fiction, which was his ideal medium: "It was just enough of a slipping of bonds to give freedom, and not enough to seem folly and anarchy." When he read an introspective story in *Astounding,* "Twilight" by Don A. Stuart, he didn't like it, and he later wrote to the editor:

> Astounding Stories *as a whole is the best magazine on the market, and people who claim otherwise show lack of taste. . . . I find that your stories tend to harp rather too much on hackneyed themes such as earth-demolishing wars. . . . Interplanetary stories are getting painfully rare, and I do wish that some would appear in the very near future.*

He wouldn't publish another fan letter for years, and he had other things on his mind. It was time to go to college, and it had to be in New York—even if he had been inclined to live elsewhere, which he wasn't, he had to stay near the store. City College, the most practical choice, wasn't prestigious enough for the medical schools, so he decided to apply to Columbia.

His interview was scheduled for April 10, 1935. At fifteen, Asimov had never been to Manhattan on his own, so his father accompanied him, waiting outside until he was done. As usual, he was awkward and overeager, and he made a bad impression. Taking pity on him, his interviewer proposed that he apply to Seth Low Junior College in Brooklyn, which would allow him to attend classes at Columbia as an upperclassman. It was also predominantly Jewish, which was no coincidence.

Asimov went out to tell his father, who agreed that Seth Low was just as good as Columbia, although neither of them really believed it. Later that day, they went to a museum, where they saw Albert Einstein being trailed by a crowd of admirers. If it was a sign, it failed to comfort Asimov. He was a child prodigy, but it hadn't been enough, and without a scholarship, he couldn't even afford to attend Seth Low—it had to be City College after all.

No matter where he ended up, he had to leave the circle of security that he had created for himself. Asimov was fond of enclosed, windowless spaces, like the kitchen at the rear of the store, and he fantasized about running a newsstand in the subway. He also loved being alone, going on long walks in the cemetery with the latest issue of *Astounding*. One day, the caretaker had to ask him not to disturb visitors who might be there to mourn. Asimov had been whistling.

Now he faced an uncertain future. He had been three when his family left Russia, and the memory of that passage, along with the concerns of his parents, caused him to stay as close to home as possible, even as his imagination took him throughout the galaxy. For most of his life, he had lived just a short train ride away from Coney Island, but after his first crossing, he had never even seen the ocean.

3.
TWO LOST SOULS
1931–1937

No one should be a freelance writer who isn't naturally irresponsible. . . . To support your wife and children on a regular and predictable food supply, in a predictable housing, with predictable supply of clothes—if you feel such regularities are important . . . then you aren't cut out to be a freelance writer.

—JOHN W. CAMPBELL, IN A LETTER TO BEN BOVA

In 1933, while living in Durham, North Carolina, John W. Campbell had his first close encounter with the unknown. He was seated on the porch of his house, looking across the road at a thunderstorm that was lashing the field on the other side. With a clap of thunder, a bolt of lightning struck the damp ground directly in front of him, and when his eyes recovered, he found himself staring at a small glowing sphere that was drifting across the grass.

The sphere was the size of a bowling ball, roughly ten inches across, with the greenish color and apparent temperature of a mercury vapor arc lamp. It bounced three times along the tops of the stalks, moving at about ten miles per hour for a distance of fifty feet. After rebounding off the side of an old barn, it abruptly changed course, floating toward an oak tree at the edge of the road. Striking the trunk three feet above the base, it exploded.

With a crack, the tree shattered and came crashing down. Afterward, when Campbell went to examine the remains, he found that the wood seemed strangely frayed—like the ends of a length of rope—but not scorched or burned, as if the water inside had expanded suddenly into steam. The entire incident, which had lasted for just ten seconds, was witnessed by four other people at the house, two of whom later cut up the fallen tree for firewood.

Campbell, who had seen a similar phenomenon at the age of eleven at his grandmother's house in Ohio, reported the incident to a physics professor at MIT. To his chagrin, his old teacher said that what he was describing was impossible, and that the sphere had been nothing but the afterimage of the initial flash on his retinas. No competent observer, he was informed, had ever witnessed ball lightning, the existence of which would not be widely acknowledged for decades.

The response infuriated him—he didn't see how an afterimage could splinter a tree into toothpicks—and it only confirmed a growing suspicion. In college, he had been impressed by how little his instructors took for granted, but in practice, scientists could be as resistant to new ideas as anyone. When it came to challenging orthodoxy, he concluded, he would be on his own.

His departure from MIT had inserted a pause into his life. After returning briefly to his mother's house, he had left on a trip for Europe. For two months, he explored Spain, France, Switzerland, and Germany, returning to Paris by way of Holland before flying across the channel to London. He told Heinlein years later that he had been searching for social patterns: "My one advantage is that, at twenty, with remarkably sound physical constitution and an immense interest in anything and everything, plus a constitutional objection to wasting time sleeping, I was able to absorb at least two years' worth of data. . . . I still haven't sorted out all the stuff I soaked up then!"

In reality, his observations were about as perceptive as those of the average American male in his twenties. He found the Spanish childlike and "stupid," though friendly, while in Paris, which he described as "the city where every pimp spoke at least six different languages," he was relieved of his camera, watch, and fountain pen on three successive days. In an echo of what Hubbard had written about China, he concluded, "Paris itself is fine; too bad there are so many French in it."

He was looking for alternatives to the traditions that he had spent most of his life trying to escape, but he also benefited from his family's position, which gave him more options than most college dropouts. On his return, he was accepted by Duke University, stating that his intended occupation was "physics research." As before, his father would cover the entire cost of his education.

After a short stay in Wilson, North Carolina, Campbell enrolled at Duke, where he was listed as a student in 1932, although he didn't move to Durham until the following spring. His performance in his first semester, which consisted mostly of math and physics classes, was undistinguished—a B, two Cs, a D. But after an intensive summer course, he finally passed German, freeing him to pursue his interests without a language requirement hanging over his head.

He was searching for direction, and he was naturally drawn to Joseph B. Rhine, who was the most insistent questioner in sight. Rhine, who had established a lab for parapsychology at Duke, was best known for his statistical studies of telepathy, which he tested using the cards designed by the psychologist Karl Zener, with a circle, a cross, a set of wavy lines, a square, or a star. At the time of Campbell's arrival, Rhine had allegedly obtained exceptional results from two students, but his findings were never convincingly replicated.

Campbell underwent runs with the Zener cards, but failed to demonstrate any psychic abilities—although he did become convinced of the existence of "the evil eye." He never became close to Rhine, as he had with Norbert Wiener, but both left their mark on his work. Rhine would be frequently invoked in Campbell's stories, as well as in those that he published by others, and the entire genre was subtly shaped by his undergraduate encounters with the paranormal.

Otherwise, he was rudderless, and he had mixed feelings about North Carolina, which wasn't the sort of place where he could feel at home. Still, he explored it as thoroughly as he had in Europe, visiting family farms—"You can generally smell them before you see them"—and small towns. He also kept an eye on race relations, which were more visible here than they had been in New Jersey or Massachusetts, and his opinions on the subject began to grow silently inside of him.

Campbell was drifting away from physics. He later presented himself as an aspiring physicist who had been unable to find work in the Great Depression, but his transcript told a different story. In his last year at Duke, he took no science classes at all, with electives in English, philosophy, and religion. Apart from two As in philosophy, his grades were average, and it looked for all the world like the schedule of a student who was questioning his priorities.

A different writer might have worked out these issues in his fiction, and Campbell eventually did, but not in ways that were immediately visible. He had continued to write during his gap year between MIT and Duke, which saw the appearance of "The Derelicts of Ganymede," "Invaders from the Infinite"—which reused the title of the story that Sloane had lost—and "The Electronic Siege." None moved beyond the easy formulas that he had established, and he seemed interested mostly in keeping his name in print, as well as in the money.

Campbell's only memorable effort from this period was "The Last Evolution," which described the creation of a vast army of intelligent robots to turn back an invasion by extraterrestrials. It fails—mankind is annihilated—but the machines survive to defeat the aliens, and with their masters gone, they spread across the universe as the heirs of humanity. The story, which ran in *Amazing,* was the strongest work that he ever published under his own name, and it looked ahead to themes that would later become central to science fiction.

At Duke, he remained as mercenary an author as always, cranking out "Beyond the End of Space," "The Battery of Hate," and a chapter of *Cosmos,* a collaborative novel for a fanzine by seventeen different writers. "Space Rays," which appeared in *Wonder Stories,* was so far-fetched that it inspired a rebuke in print from the editor Hugo Gernsback, and Campbell never forgot the slight. Yet most of these stories were undeniably poor. His heart wasn't in it, any more than it was in his studies, and when he earned a bachelor of arts degree in physics, with a minor in math, he didn't even attend his graduation ceremony.

When he left college in 1934, he entered one of the worst economies imaginable for recent graduates. Franklin D. Roosevelt had begun his first term as president the year before, and Campbell had been impressed by his policies. During a visit home, however, he had made the mistake of mentioning his views to his father, who demolished his notions in three minutes. It marked the last time that he held political beliefs that were even remotely progressive, and he came to despise Roosevelt, despite the black cigarette holder that they both affected.

Campbell's future seemed just as uncertain as ever, but there was one important difference. He was no longer alone. Two years earlier, in the summer after his flight from MIT, he had married a young woman who would turn out to be his most important ally.

She would play a pivotal role in his career and, by extension, in the history of science fiction as a whole, and in many ways, she remains the most intriguing figure in his life story.

DOÑA LOUISE STEWART STEBBINS WAS BORN IN OHIO IN 1913. HER PARENTS, GEORGE AND MOLLY Stebbins, divorced shortly thereafter, and she moved with her mother to the Boston area. Doña's mother, a Canadian citizen, was her closest friend and confidante for most of her childhood, which appears to have been a lonely one. Her father wasn't a part of her life, and she was set apart from her peers from an early age by her obvious wit, irony, and intelligence.

She was attractive but not conventionally pretty, with a long nose and dark complexion, although her background, like Campbell's, was primarily Scottish and English. Doña first encountered her future husband while attending a Latin high school in Waltham, but not even their children ever knew how they met.

Doña Stebbins in her late teens.
Courtesy of Leslyn Randazzo

She was evidently the first woman with whom he was ever romantically involved, and years later, she only said to her daughter, "We were two lost souls looking for love." They married after she graduated in 1931, and while she never legally changed her name, from the beginning, Campbell introduced her to everyone as Doña Stuart.

Decades afterward, with the benefit of hindsight, Campbell wrote, "I quit MIT at twenty-one and got married—to the wrong gal for me, too. Doña's a very nice, basically sweet girl—there's nothing wrong with her, any more than there's anything wrong with a well-made left shoe on your right foot." He also said that she disapproved of his writing and wanted him to enter respectable research. But he was speaking at a time when he was inclined to minimize her impact on his career, and he overlooked the remarkable patience that she demonstrated during their marriage, in which they endured countless hardships—many of his own creation—as a team.

They depended on each other enormously. By any standard, Doña was the first wholly positive female influence in Campbell's life, apart from his sister, and despite their differences, they fulfilled each other. Campbell was drawn to her artistic and theatrical side, and he gave her the intellectual partner she had always wanted. She was smart, creative, and widely read, and he stimulated her as no one else ever would, as a friend remembered: "When his wife Doña was new, she would sit on a hassock at his feet in adoring puppy dog style, while he discoursed on the problems of the universe."

In most respects, however, she was his equal, and she served as his ambassador to the world. Doña was as outgoing as Campbell was introverted, with a good singing voice and a sense of humor that came through in her letters. She was a talented homemaker who attended the Boston School of Cooking, as well as a cheerful hostess at parties, which her husband grudgingly tolerated. Doña also enjoyed a glass of beer in the evening, while Campbell claimed to rarely drink, saying that alcohol made him feel as if his brain "were walking in about two feet of water."

They had their disagreements. Doña, Campbell said, had trouble dealing with conflict directly, and because she wouldn't hold still for long enough to have a real conversation, they were unable to address any underlying issues: "She considered the proper thing to do with problems was to shove them out of sight in a closet somewhere and pretend they didn't exist." But he defended her faithfully, even against his family. When his mother tried to dominate Doña, as she did with most other people, Campbell put her savagely in her place.

Above all else, Doña—who wrote at least one unpublished story, "Beyond the Door," when she was twenty—changed his writing, although it took years for the full implications to emerge. Campbell was a lousy speller and typist, and Doña took it on herself to retype his stories, silently correcting his spelling and grammar. She became his first reader, taking his father's place, and he submitted ideas and openings for her approval. According to a friend who later knew them both well, Doña was a "sounding board" who reminded Campbell "that science was for *people*." The man who said this was L. Ron Hubbard.

In 1932, while they were living in Wilson, North Carolina, Campbell—still smarting over Gernsback's dismissal of "Space Rays"—began a new project. He had recently read the adventure novel *The Red Gods Call*, by C. E. Scoggins, which had awakened him to a new appreciation of tone. Campbell conceived of a story that started in a similar fashion, with its narrator picking up a hitchhiker who has returned from seven million years in the future, in an era when humanity has been robbed of all initiative by machines that fulfill its every need.

The result, with its evocation of "the lingering, dying glow of man's twilight," was haunting, atmospheric, and like nothing else that Campbell had ever written. There had been hints of it in the opening of "The Black Star Passes," which elegiacally described a waning alien culture—but here, crucially, it was the human race. On some level, it was only revisiting themes that H. G. Wells had already explored, but by reintroducing a sense of melancholy to the pulps, it single-handedly ushered in the modern age of science fiction.

At first, however, it didn't seem that the story he called "Twilight" would have any impact at all. Campbell worked on it for longer than usual, but it was turned down everywhere, even by *Amazing*. He set it aside, focusing in the meantime on an unsuccessful effort to unload a backlog of his unsold manuscripts on *Wonder Stories,* and nothing might ever have come of it without the encouragement of an editor named F. Orlin Tremaine.

In 1933, Tremaine had assumed the helm of *Astounding Stories,* after it was acquired from the bankrupt publisher William Clayton by the pulp powerhouse Street & Smith. He had no particular interest in science fiction, but he was a seasoned professional who knew how to build an audience, and he began by systematically courting the field's top writers. Tremaine went aggressively after E. E. Smith, and the next name on his list was Campbell's.

When Tremaine reached out to him, Campbell had a story ready to go. A serial called *The Mightiest Machine* had been out for consideration with *Amazing* for a full year without being accepted. He pulled it and sent it to Tremaine, who took it at once—and Campbell was pleased to find that the editor paid on acceptance, rather than publication. It was slated to run in five installments, starting in the December 1934 issue, and its appearance was treated as a major event, with an announcement in the magazine proclaiming, "And Now Campbell!"

For better or worse, it was the epitome of the superscience genre. Its hero, Aarn Munro, was born on Jupiter, granting him superhuman strength to go with his enormous intelligence. When he and his friends stumble across a war between two alien cultures, they pick sides based solely on one race's devilish appearance—a notion that Arthur C. Clarke would later borrow for *Childhood's End*—and deploy an entire moon as a weapon. It was comparatively brisk, but only slightly more readable than usual, and cheerfully accepting of genocide on a planetary scale.

Tremaine liked "Twilight" as well, but he was concerned that its publication alongside *The Mightiest Machine* would confuse readers, since it was so different from the author's previous work. He asked Campbell to use a pseudonym, which he did, choosing a pen name that would double as a private tribute to the most important person in his life. When it appeared in the November issue, it was credited to Don A. Stuart. A second story under that name, "Atomic Power," came out the following month, and before long, Tremaine could write in the magazine that Stuart had emerged as a reader favorite "almost overnight."

In the years that followed, Campbell, who otherwise would have been happy to recycle his stock plots forever, grew considerably as a writer. It was a transformation that he owed to two people. One was Doña, who was unlikely to have found his superscience stories particularly interesting. When she replaced his father as his reader of choice, she nudged him toward fiction that was more conscious of style and theme. Their collaboration, if not literal, was very meaningful, and they often worked together, smoking, on two typewriters set side by side.

His other major influence was Tremaine, who forced Campbell to evolve by closing off certain avenues while encouraging others. He personally preferred works of the Stuart type, and by rejecting all of Campbell's superscience stories, including the sequels to *The Mightiest Machine,* he offered a model of an editor's guiding hand. Campbell seethed at this, but he never forgot it. Occasionally, he would make a splash with a gimmick story—"The Irrelevant," which he published under the name Karl van Campen, led to a scientific debate in the letters column that ran for months—but he found his greatest success with stories that focused on mood and atmosphere.

It led to a profound change in his published work. His superscience stories, which he had written for his father, had often shared the same basic plot. A lone genius develops atomic power and uses it to build a spacecraft, drawing on the limitless resources of a wealthy benefactor. After a loving description of the ship, he encounters a war between two alien races, takes sides without hesitation, and triumphs through his superior weaponry. Technology was portrayed as an unalloyed good, while the heroic scientist or engineer—the avatar of the technocratic movement of the early thirties—was elevated to the status of a god.

In the Don A. Stuart stories, Campbell interrogated his previous assumptions with an intensity that recalled the boy who had been forced to question every statement that his mother made. He described them as "a dirty, underhanded crack at the pretensions of science fiction—dressed in the most accepted terms of science fiction," and they were aware of the limits of technology, which could deprive mankind of its most precious qualities—its curiosity and initiative. The shift in tone has often been interpreted as a response to the Great Depression, but in fact, he engaged in both modes simultaneously, and it was Tremaine who favored one over the other.

Readers responded strongly to the ambivalence of the Stuart stories, which resonated with issues of personal and cultural insecurity, even as the author was about to enter the most frustrating chapter of his life. In one of his defenses of "The Irrelevant"—which appeared on the same page of the magazine as the first letter from a fan named Isaac Asimov—he mentioned offhandedly, "I'm doing some work now in connection with automobiles." This was true, but not entirely forthcoming. Campbell, who had studied physics at MIT, was working as a car salesman at MacKenzie Motors in Brighton, Massachusetts.

AFTER CAMPBELL GRADUATED FROM DUKE IN 1934, HE AND DOÑA HAD MOVED TO THE BOSTON area, where they became friends with a prominent science fiction fan named Robert Swisher and his wife, Frances. Their apartment in Cambridge was just a short walk from MIT, but the gap between Campbell's aspirations as an undergraduate and his current situation could hardly have seemed more stark. He wanted to move into research work, but no jobs were available, so he ended up selling the Ford V8 when he couldn't afford a new car of his own.

Yet he was a natural salesman—he would be peddling one idea or another for most of his life—and he approached it as another game to solve. After leaving the dealership, he worked for an air-conditioning company in Boston. He convinced a restaurant to buy fans and leave its windows open to create a pleasant flow of air, advertising the result with his most profitable piece of writing from that year: "Always a Breeze." In another sales position, he sold so many gas heaters that it left the company with more orders than it could fill, which put him out of a job.

His father gave them some money, but Campbell still had to write to make ends meet. In "The Machine," "The Invaders," and "Rebellion," he returned to his favorite theme—the death of initiative—and he produced three unusually bleak stories, "Blindness," "The Escape," and "Night," all of which were credited to Don A. Stuart. He also clung to his earlier mode in "Conquest of the Planets" and the unpublished "All," which imagined an invasion of the United States by Asia. His most ambitious effort was *The Moon Is Hell,* a genuine hard science fiction novel about an expedition stranded on the far side of the moon, and although it went unsold, it remained at the back of his mind, informing his private sense of what the genre might be.

In the end, he never sold another story under his own name to Tremaine, who asked him instead to write a series of articles on the solar system. It was an influential piece of popular science that impressed Asimov and Heinlein, among others, and it kept his byline alive, while providing some badly needed income. He and Doña had left for New Jersey in February 1936, with their car threatening to break down for the entire drive. After staying briefly with his mother in Orange, they made their way to Hoboken and settled at last in New Brunswick.

Doña called it "a factory town" and "a terrible hole." Their apartment was tiny, with hideous mahogany furniture, and their finances were equally dismal. Street & Smith was culling its titles, and Tremaine, who had to keep costs down to avoid attracting attention, wasn't sending any checks. Campbell had tried unsuccessfully to get a job at *Wonder Stories,* and he was casting about for technical writing positions when he landed an offer from International Motors, better known as Mack Truck. His title, he proudly announced, was "Experimental Engineer."

In reality, Campbell was a secretary, drafting memos for a supervisor for whom he worked for two days on a single letter, prompting Doña to observe, "Poor John, who has spent seven years or so making two words do where one is sufficient." He hoped to turn it into a research role—he still dreamed of becoming an inventor—but no such opportunity presented itself, and his work left him too exhausted at night to do any writing of his own.

Money was a constant concern. After complaining once too often to their landlord in New Brunswick about the lack of heat, the couple was evicted. They were down to their last five dollars, and they spent all day looking for a new place, with Doña's spirits growing steadily lower. When they slunk back home, they found, miraculously, that Tremaine had sent a check for "Frictional Losses," an alien conquest story most notable for its anticipation of kamikaze attacks by the Japanese.

The reprieve was brief. Mack Truck was reducing overhead, and in late April, Campbell was laid off. During this dark period, he wrote two of his best stories, "Elimination," about a machine that allows the user to preview the decision points of his own future, and "Forgetfulness," in which mankind abandons its technology in favor of a life of the mind. Campbell later wrote that the latter story came directly out of his "rejection of an up-till-then idea that I wanted to be the Great Inventor." It was a fantasy that seemed increasingly out of reach.

Swallowing his pride, Campbell decided to leverage his family connections, reaching out to his father and to his uncle, Samuel B. Pettengill, an Indiana congressman who was married to his mother's twin sister. In the meantime, they survived on as little as possible. It was a hot summer, and they spent evenings at a beer garden in New York, where Doña ordered one drink, Campbell stuck with water, and they asked the singer to perform "Die Lorelei." Tremaine was bouncing all his stories "with a nasty little sneer," but Doña maintained her sense of humor: "I'm beginning to get restless. We haven't moved in over a month!"

In June, thanks to his uncle's efforts, Campbell found work at the Pioneer Instrument Company, a manufacturer of electronic equipment for ships. They moved back to Hoboken, where he started punching a time clock. Technically, he was in research, but in practice, the job meant walking seventy blocks to fetch machinery or dipping pressure gauges into kerosene that was kept below freezing with dry ice. It was painful, tedious work, and it couldn't have been further from the ideal of engineering that he had described so often in his stories.

His employers were unimpressed by his low "tweezer dexterity," and Campbell quit after two months. Remarkably, he found a new job right away at the chemical firm Carleton Ellis, where he rewrote stacks of abstracts for the second volume of *The Chemistry of Petroleum Derivatives*. The job allowed them to move to a nicer place in Orange, but Campbell grew bored. After failing to find any teaching positions, he left anyway in February 1937. He was still writing, selling the unremarkable story "Uncertainty," but his financial difficulties contributed to his belief, which he would later share with his authors, that fiction was no way to make a living.

Yet he was growing as an artist. After a conversation with a chemist, he came up with the idea of a creature that could change itself into any living being. The result was "Imitation," his first attempt at a humorous story, in which two fugitives named Penton and Blake wrangle with a species of shape-shifting alien. It was bought by Mort Weisinger of *Thrilling Wonder Stories*, who retitled it "Brain Stealers of Mars," and Campbell followed it with three sequels—"The Double Minds," "The Immortality Seekers," and "The Tenth World"—that amounted to the most likable work that ever appeared under his real name.

"The Double Minds" also looked ahead by describing a science of psychology that allowed both halves of the brain to work together. In an earlier story, Campbell had written that "no man in all history ever used even half of the thinking part of his brain," and he expanded on this "pet idea" in an author's note: "The total capacity of the mind, even at present, is to all intents and purposes, infinite. Could the full equipment be hooked into a functioning unit, the resulting intelligence should be able to conquer a world without much difficulty."

He found time for an excellent novella, "Out of Night," which depicted the conquest of mankind by an alien matriarchy—but a different sort of extraterrestrial formed the basis of the work that would ensure his lasting fame, to the point that it threatened to overshadow all of his later accomplishments. It occurred to him that "Brain Stealers of Mars" could be rewritten as a horror story set on Earth, playing up the idea, which was left implicit in the original, that no one could be trusted. Once he situated it in Antarctica and wrote the first scene, he said, the rest was easy.

In fact, he worked hard on the story that he called "Frozen Hell," generating five false starts and cutting an opening section of more than forty pages. He based the setting on a book by the explorer Richard Byrd, but he may also have been inspired by H. P. Lovecraft's "At the Mountains of Madness," which had been serialized in *Astounding*. Campbell was no fan of Lovecraft's— particularly of his trick of hinting at terrors "too frightful to mention"—but he was drawn to the challenge of depicting horrors that others left undescribed, and it gave him more pleasure than anything else he had ever written: "Doña says I clicked."

And he had. It would ultimately appear in *Astounding* as "Who Goes There?," and it remains the greatest science fiction suspense story of all time, with iconic scenes—as the characters confront the alien killer in their midst—that have lost none of their power. The premise was so good that Campbell was unable to resist it, although he was pointedly uninterested in exploring its philosophical implications, perhaps because it reminded him of his childhood. Years later, he quoted the line: "We've got monsters, madmen, and murderers. Any more 'M's' you can think of?" Campbell added sardonically, "M, my friend, stands for 'mother!' She belonged."

But this all lay in the future. Campbell was still revising the story when he was felled by an attack of appendicitis in July 1937. The operation lasted for hours, and when the anesthetic wore off prematurely, he heard the doctors talking over his helpless body— an unpleasant experience that would later contribute to his interest in dianetics. For now, it left him depressed, unable to climb stairs more than once a day, and even deeper in debt than before.

He was distracted by rumors at Street & Smith. The firm's president had died in 1933, leading to a series of estate disputes. In September, ten titles were dropped, and the following month, Tremaine was promoted to managing editor, with oversight of multiple magazines—which pointed to another possible development. As Campbell wrote to his friend Robert Swisher on October 4, "But Tremaine, while able to keep a watchful, fatherly eye over

Astounding, his pet, will not be in direct charge of it. Who will be, I don't know yet."

At that point, Campbell had no apparent interest in a magazine job. He was on good terms with Tremaine—he had finished a long story, "Dead Knowledge," in six days to fill a gap in inventory—and he planned to submit "Frozen Hell" soon. But he was still focused on finding a technical writing position, and if it ever occurred to him to hope for anything more, he kept it to himself.

What happened next was something that no one could have foreseen, with Tremaine playing the role of one of the improbable benefactors in his stories. On October 5, Campbell wrote to Swisher on the letterhead of *Astounding.* The letter just said, "Hiya, Bob!" And it was signed "John W. Campbell, Editor."

Campbell had stumbled, unbelievably, into the job that he had been born to have—and his talent, which was undeniable, was less important than the fact that he was available. He was always hanging around the office; he was a dependable writer with a loyal following; and he was in a position to start right away. His background in technical writing and editing may have played a role, but above all else, it was a stroke of luck—and far from the last—without which the history of science fiction might have unfolded along utterly different lines.

At twenty-seven, Campbell couldn't have known any of this, but he knew what he had in *Astounding.* It was the perfect outlet for all of his frustrated ambitions, and he was bursting with ideas. For now, some would remain unfulfilled—Tremaine retained editorial control, and a backlog of stories still had to be published. But one change became visible almost at once. A few months later, when the March 1938 issue arrived at the candy store in Brooklyn, Isaac Asimov saw with approval that its title was no longer *Astounding Stories.* Now it was *Astounding Science Fiction.*

II.

GOLDEN AGE

1937—1941

I am not solitary whilst I read and write, though nobody is with me. But if a man would be alone, let him look at the stars. . . . Seen in the streets of cities, how great they are! If the stars should appear one night in a thousand years, how would men believe and adore; and preserve for many generations the remembrance of the city of God which had been shown!

—RALPH WALDO EMERSON, "NATURE"

4.
BRASS TACKS

1937–1939

There are times of evolutionary stress that have immensely hastened developments. Now I claim that this is, and will continue to be, such a time.

—ARTHUR MCCANN, IN A LETTER TO *ASTOUNDING*, APRIL 1938

For readers of *Astounding Science Fiction* in the late thirties, the name of Arthur McCann would have been a familiar one. McCann was described as a Harvard-educated endocrinologist, originally from the Midwest, "a tall, rather thin, good-natured, easy-going guy." He contributed nonfiction articles and filler pieces to the magazine, and he became a regular presence in Brass Tacks, the letters column, often to respond to a point that the new editor had made.

In fact, he never existed. McCann was an alter ego for Campbell, named after an ancestor on his mother's side, that he assumed whenever he wanted to write an unofficial editorial or nudge the conversation in a particular direction. In April 1938, he used it for a letter that amounted to a declaration of principles that he would follow for decades: "The conditions [man] tries to adjust to are going to change, and change so darned fast that he never will actually adjust to a given set of conditions. He'll have to adjust in a different way: he'll adjust to an environment of *change*."

What was left unstated was the important point that the subjects of this transformation would be the readers of *Astounding* itself. It was an impossibly ambitious agenda, and it was built on a foundation that Campbell never could have made on his own. He had stumbled into the editorship after the magazine had reached a position of unprecedented strength, and much of what followed might have occurred without him, if not nearly in the same form. The groundwork had been laid by others—and when he took over, it was as if he had been entrusted with a spacecraft at the precise instant that it was ready to make its next leap into the unknown.

TO MOST OUTSIDERS, CAMPBELL'S NEW JOB WOULD HAVE SEEMED ANYTHING BUT GLAMOROUS. THE offices of Street & Smith were housed in a decaying hulk of a building—actually several older structures that had been joined together—on Seventh Avenue and West Seventeenth Street, not far from a women's prison. Campbell took the train and ferry from Orange, New Jersey, and when he arrived, he went through a side entrance, where he had to punch a time clock. As the floor vibrated underfoot from the printing press, he headed for an ancient elevator, which he operated by yanking a rope, and rode it up to a storage level filled with massive rolls of paper.

At the rear, next to the office occupied by John Nanovic, the editor of *Doc Savage,* was a tiny room with two desks and a spare chair for visitors. This was where Campbell would be stationed for years. Because of all the paper, smoking was officially forbidden, and he learned to hide the copper ashtray in his rolltop desk whenever the fire inspector paid a visit. He also suffered from a chronic sinus condition, giving him "a continuous very mild sniffle," and he began to keep a vaporizer on hand, using it to periodically spray his nostrils.

Campbell was feeling his way into a magazine that had spent most of its existence in a state of transition. Its founder, William Clayton, was a publisher whose company had put out thirteen titles in the genres of love, adventure, western, and detective fiction. The pulps, named after their cheap, rough paper, were a hugely successful form of mass entertainment—the most popular sold a million copies each month, and a prolific writer could make a living by cranking out stories—and Clayton's offerings, including *Air Adventures* and *Danger Trail*, all had the garish painted covers that had become synonymous with the field.

For reasons of economy, the covers for all thirteen magazines were printed each month on the same enormous sheet of paper, which had four rows and four columns, leaving it with three blank spaces. In 1929, as Clayton looked at the proofs in his office, he realized that the empty areas, which were going to waste, could be used to print three more covers—the most expensive part—at minimal cost. He mentioned this to the editor Harry Bates, who pitched the title *Astounding Stories of Super-Science*. A year after its launch, in 1931, it became *Astounding Stories*.

The market was already there. In 1908, Hugo Gernsback, who had recently emigrated from Luxembourg, started *Modern Electrics* to educate prospective customers of his radio supply business, with fiction—he came to call it "scientifiction"—that described the inventions of the future. Eighteen years later, he launched *Amazing Stories*, which was the first pure science fiction magazine. Its main attraction was the cover art by Frank R. Paul, who defined the look of the entire genre, and its contents were mostly unremarkable. As Theodore Sturgeon said decades afterward, "Ninety percent of science fiction is crud. But then ninety percent of everything is crud."

This was certainly true of *Amazing*, but there were a few note-worthy efforts, including *The Skylark of Space* and the Buck Rogers series. Its circulation eventually rose to over 100,000, but it remained on financially shaky ground, and Gernsback was eventually forced out of his own company, rebounding with a family of titles known collectively as *Wonder Stories*. Its unquestioned peak was "A Martian Odyssey" by Stanley Weinbaum, whose untimely death in 1935 prompted Asimov to write later, "If Weinbaum had lived . . . there would have been no Campbell revolution. All that Campbell could have done would have been to reinforce what would undoubtedly have come to be called 'the Weinbaum revolution.' "

In the meantime, *Astounding* had appeared, with a debut issue dated January 1930. It cost twenty cents, a nickel cheaper than *Amazing* or *Wonder Stories,* and unlike its competitors, which had the large format of the "slicks," it was the same small size as the titles with which it shared its proof sheet, as well as its literary qualities. Harry Bates wasn't a science fiction fan, but a professional editor going after an existing audience, and despite its obligatory nods to Gernsback's educational goals, *Astounding* was pure pulp—its writers simply transferred their stock western or war stories to space, and its first cover showed a hero in a flight suit punching out a gigantic bug.

Forty years later, when Asimov recalled this period, he couldn't think of a single story worth remembering. In time, Bates might have been able to turn it into something special—the magazine paid promptly and well, which naturally drew the best authors—but it was hitched to the sinking ship of Clayton, whose company suffered from financial problems that had nothing to do with any one title's performance. Sensing that the clock was ticking, Bates tried a series of frantic innovations. He wrote editorials on science, published nonfiction, included a ballot for story grades, and promised to focus more on ideas and less on action, in response to reader demand.

None of it mattered, and the magazine ceased publication in March 1933. For half a year, there was silence—and then, to the relief of fans, it was revived by the pulp publisher Street & Smith, which had bought it at an auction of Clayton's assets. Its new owners were primarily interested in such titles as *Clues* and *Cowboy Stories,* and *Astounding,* which reappeared in October, was just part of the package. Fortunately, it was placed in the capable hands of F. Orlin Tremaine and his assistant editor, Desmond Hall, and within six months, they had totally transformed it.

Tremaine wasn't particularly fond of science fiction—he relied mostly on Hall's advice—but he entered on a program of purposeful change. He introduced the "thought variant" story, which would develop some strikingly original idea, and sought out star writers like E. E. Smith and Campbell. He also made fascinating experiments, including serializing *Lo!* by Charles Fort, a collection of such unexplained phenomena as rains of frogs and poltergeists. His greatest finds were *At the Mountains of Madness* and *The Shadow Out of Time* by H. P. Lovecraft, which are the only works from that era that a casual fan is likely to have read today.

By 1935, *Astounding* had a circulation of fifty thousand, or more than twice that of its nearest rivals. In general, however, its stories weren't appreciably higher in quality than those of its competitors, and if it ultimately developed a reputation as the best in its field, this was due in part to the structure of the market. By the late thirties, each title had evolved to fill a niche—*Amazing* for juveniles, *Wonder Stories* for teens, *Astounding* for adults. The first two served as essential bridges to the third, and all three had legitimate readerships.

When Campbell arrived, the magazine was serializing E. E. Smith's *Galactic Patrol,* the first novel in the Lensman series, which Asimov would remember as the climax of his infatuation with the genre. It was as close as any story can get to pure action, jumping from one thrilling high point to the next, and it represented the summit of what was possible under the traditional model. Campbell would carry it to the next level, but he had to move slowly. Tremaine, as managing editor, still had final discretion over stories, and although Campbell effectively took control of the contents by March 1938, apart from the title change to *Astounding Science Fiction*, most readers probably never even noticed the transition.

From the beginning, Campbell's workload was physically exhausting. He later said that he had read more lousy science fiction than anyone else alive, and he was spending up to twelve hours a day on manuscripts alone. The fact that he managed to survive—while still keeping his overall objectives in mind—was thanks largely to two women. One was Doña, who became his unofficial first reader, showing him the best submissions and offering notes for writers. After one session, she wrote, "At present my eyes feel as though they are resting uncomfortably on my jowls, from all the reading I've been doing at home, the most frightful stuff."

His second key partner was Catherine Tarrant, known as Kay, or, more often, as Miss Tarrant. Half a year after Campbell was hired, Tarrant, an outwardly nondescript woman in her early thirties, took the desk next to his, where she would remain for the next three decades. A devout Roman Catholic from Hoboken, Tarrant never married, and she would inevitably become known as a spinster. Campbell kept their relationship strictly professional—he always addressed her by her last name, and he never took her to lunch—and he continued to refer to her as his secretary for years. In fact, she handled the entire practical and administrative end of the magazine, assuming her role shortly after R. W. Happel, the previous assistant editor, had left the firm.

The division of labor soon became clear. Campbell selected the fiction and the art, while Tarrant oversaw proofreading, copyediting, and production. In person, she had a salty sense of humor, but she occasionally took it on herself to remove bad language from stories—and her prudish reputation also provided Campbell with a convenient excuse whenever a writer objected to any changes. Throughout their partnership, she saw "Campbell," as she always called him, as an oversize boy who would never get the magazine out on his own, and in all the anecdotes from those years, she was the unacknowledged presence in the room, seated a few feet away from the editor and the authors whom he was transforming into his kind of writer.

Word of his appointment had spread rapidly through fandom, with the agent Julius Schwartz warning his clients to be more careful about their science: "Campbell's editing *Astounding*." He began by dividing submissions into two piles. Bad ones got a printed rejection slip, while those that showed promise received a note explaining how they could be revised to the new standards. Campbell also wrote to writers directly, telling them that the magazine was targeting mature readers, in an extension of Tremaine's policy from "about fourteen months ago."

His task was complicated by the fact that he was about to lose the services of Don A. Stuart. He was working on the revision of "Who Goes There?" and on "Cloak of Aesir," a sequel to "Out of Night," while a few older sales—"The Brain Pirates" and "Planet of Eternal Night"—trickled into *Thrilling Wonder Stories*. Yet while there were no real obstacles to selling to himself, he no longer had the time to write anything new, as he hinted to a reader who innocently asked where Stuart had gone: "Stuart, I'm afraid, has had to retire due to pressure of outside work."

But this was less a retirement than a change of title. Campbell later said that it was Don A. Stuart who was really editing *Astounding*, and he became an inexhaustible source of plots for others, writing to Robert Swisher, "I'm thinking up ideas at a furious rate nowadays, and passing 'em out." As an editor, he wanted good writing, accurate science, believable characters, and stories that logically accounted for multiple variables: "The future doesn't happen one at a time." It was a tricky needle to thread, and he learned to give the same premise to multiple writers, trusting that each one would come up with a different story entirely.

As Campbell searched for new talent, his first regular visitor was a seventeen-year-old fan and aspiring writer from Brooklyn. Frederik Pohl, who was born in 1919, had submitted his stories in person to Tremaine, since it was cheaper to take the subway than to buy postage. After Campbell was hired, he paid a visit to the new editor, unsure of how he would be received.

When Pohl arrived, Campbell sat back in his chair, inserted a cigarette into its holder, and said without preamble, "Television will never replace radio in the home. I'll bet you don't know why."

"Gee, no, Mr. Campbell," Pohl replied hesitantly. "I never thought of that."

"Right, Pohl, and no one else did, either. But what is the audience for radio? The *primary* audience is bored housewives. They turn the radio on to keep them company while they do the dishes."

Pohl made an effort to squeeze a word in. "Yeah, I guess that's right—"

"And the point is, you can't ignore television," Campbell finished triumphantly. "You have to *look* at it."

Pohl concluded that Campbell was workshopping his editorials by trying out a new outrageous statement on everyone he saw, but it would be just as accurate to say that his editorials were an extension of his conversation. Campbell, who was naturally shy, was most comfortable in small spaces that he could fill with his presence—a big man in a tiny office. And he loved arguing with a worthy opponent like Pohl, with whom he often debated the merits of communism—the editor had a natural respect for business, while Pohl was a member of the Young Communist League.

Tarrant didn't care for Pohl, writing later to Campbell, "I've never liked him. If you'll think back for a moment, you'll recall that I never chatted with him when he came in. A sixth sense always seemed to say 'Watch your step with this one.' " Campbell, in turn, seemed wary of the younger man's energy, and there were occasional signs of animosity—when the editor learned that Pohl obtained free magazines from a friend in the circulation department, he told her to stop. Yet he also took him seriously. The ranks of fans who had come of age with the pulps were old enough to be authors themselves, and Pohl was their first emissary to *Astounding*.

Pohl dreamed of becoming an editor one day, and Campbell shared what little he knew, even as he was figuring the job out for himself. He had been lucky to join the firm when it was undergoing a reorganization, leaving it with less inertia than usual, and he sought advice from Mort Weisinger at *Thrilling Wonder Stories*. To attract more sophisticated readers, he worked to improve the art—he would later ask authors to write stories around paintings that he had commissioned—and he hoped to change the title to the more refined *Science Fiction*. He was frustrated by the debut of a pulp of that name the following year, and he learned to live with *Astounding*.

There were a few telling editorial changes. Campbell introduced a readers' poll and a separate section called "In Times to Come" to discuss the upcoming issue, which freed up the editor's page to become his primary creative outlet. Advances in science made this platform seem all the more important, and nuclear physics was his favorite topic, beginning with a proclamation in 1938: "The discoverer of the secret of atomic power is alive on Earth today." He later said that he had been speaking, without knowing it, of Enrico Fermi.

On the fiction side, Campbell had already made one major discovery. Jack Williamson, who was born in 1908, was a writer from New Mexico who had been a popular pulp author for years. He submitted a pitch that revolved around two possible futures, one utopian, the other apocalyptic, the emergence of which depended on the outcome of a single event in the present. To complicate matters, the hero was in love with women from both timelines—and while his heart may have belonged to the virtuous Lethonee, he was also drawn to the sinister Sorainya.

"The Legion of Time," which began its run in the May 1938 issue, was the first great story that Campbell acquired. When its parallel worlds—and heroines—fuse together in the end, the effect was unbelievably satisfying, and the serial itself read like a superimposition of possible futures for the genre, with a newfound respect for ideas and characterization mingling with all the primal pleasures of the pulps. Campbell told readers that it pointed to a new direction for the entire field, and—in a revealing choice of words that he used to describe covers or whole issues—he referred to it as the first "mutant" story of his editorship.

He was also farming out ideas for stories. One early effort involved Arthur J. Burks, whose prolific output had led *The New Yorker* to call him "an ace of the pulps." Campbell wasn't a fan, but when he gave Burks a premise about a replication machine, the author wrote up a serial in three days. It was far from a classic, but Campbell needed writers like this. After joining the firm, he had asked Frank Blackwell, the editor in chief, what would happen if he couldn't find enough stories to fill an issue. Blackwell had replied, "An *editor* does."

By the beginning of 1938, however, he was faced with an alarmingly lean inventory. He blamed it on writers submitting to the revived *Amazing,* which had been acquired by a new publisher, but his own higher standards were also to blame. Campbell was buying just one out of every fifteen submissions, and while he got a few good stories, he didn't have as many as he needed.

This was the situation that he faced when he was called out of his office for a meeting with Tremaine and Blackwell in the spring of 1938. When Campbell arrived, he discovered that two writers were already there, and as he listened, disbelieving, he was ordered to buy everything that they wrote. One was Burks. The other was a tall, imposing man of twenty-seven with red hair and skin so pale that it was almost transparent. It was L. Ron Hubbard.

HUBBARD'S FIRST PROFESSIONAL SALE, "THE GREEN GOD," HAD APPEARED IN THE FEBRUARY 1934 issue of *Thrilling Adventure*. Like all his earliest efforts, it had been written at a feverish pace—in the beginning, he wrote a story every day for six weeks. He would leaf through a magazine before going to bed, come up with the plot in his sleep, and write it the next morning, mailing it out without bothering to read it again. The approach bore fruit almost immediately. His first two acceptance checks came to three hundred dollars, which was more money than he had ever seen at any one time.

Much later, he wrote, "A story jammed and packed with blow-by-blow accounts of what the hero did to the villain and the villain did to the hero, with fists, knives, guns, bombs, machine guns, belaying pins, bayonets, poison gas, strychnine, teeth, knees, and calks, is about as interesting to read as the *Congressional Record* and about twice as dull." He might have been describing his own debut, a bloodbath set in Tientsin with the same casual disregard for accuracy that led him to refer to China, in another story, as "a country almost as large as the United States."

To celebrate the sale, he took his pregnant wife, Polly, on a vacation to Encinitas, California, where she went into premature labor. L. Ron Hubbard, Jr., was born on May 7, 1934, weighing just over two pounds. As soon as their son, whom they called Nibs, was healthy enough, Hubbard left on a trip to New York. He had no particular interest in being a father, and he had new worlds to conquer.

For the first time in his life, he did a creditable job of it. In Manhattan, he checked into a run-down hotel with a reputation as a haven for writers. The only other author in sight was a man named Frank Gruber, who was hardly an advertisement for success—he told Hubbard how to get a free lunch of tomato soup by filling a bowl with hot water, ketchup, and crackers at the Automat.

In exchange for a meal, Gruber brought him to a meeting of the American Fiction Guild, an association of pulp authors. Its president was Arthur J. Burks, who took a shine to the newcomer, and Hubbard soon broke through. A note in *Thrilling Adventure* stated, "I guess L. Ron Hubbard needs no introduction. From the letters you send in, his yarns are about the most popular we have published. Several of you have wondered, too, how he gets the splendid color which always characterizes his stories of the faraway places. The answer is, he's been there, brothers. He's been, and seen, and done, and plenty of all three of them!"

Hubbard knew that his energy was more profitably spent on developing himself as a personality than on refining his craft. In 1935, he was elected president of the chapter, lining up speakers for their weekly lunches, including the New York coroner, who told him, "The morgue is open to you anytime, Hubbard." He also became notorious for his rate of production, analyzing the percentage of stories that sold to each magazine and focusing on those with the highest return. Hubbard boasted that he wrote only first drafts, but he was occasionally capable of more, and the closer a story was to the sea, which he loved, the better it became.

For the most part, however, it was just a job. Hubbard invested in an electric typewriter—a rarity in itself—and was rumored to work on a continuous scroll of butcher paper. He claimed to write a hundred thousand words a month, which was a gross exaggeration. As always, he turned himself into whatever he thought would impress everyone else in the room, whether they were pilots, explorers, or authors, and since he couldn't be the best writer, he would settle for being the most prolific in a field defined by its monstrous productivity.

Hubbard's second child, Catherine, was born on January 15, 1936. After they moved to South Colby, Washington, Polly began to think that he was cheating on her, and when she found a pair of letters that he had written to two different girlfriends, she took her revenge by switching the envelopes. Hubbard later wrote, "Because of her coldness physically, the falsity of her pretensions, I believed myself a near eunuch. . . . When I found I was attractive to other women, I had many affairs."

If his home life didn't meet his expectations, he was making progress elsewhere. He met H. P. Lovecraft, who called him "a remarkable young man," and Columbia Pictures bought the rights to an unpublished novella that he adapted into the serial *The Secret of Treasure Island,* which featured an erupting volcano and a scientist forced to build "death bombs." In 1937, he spent ten weeks doing uncredited rewrites in Hollywood, and he later said, without any evidence, that he had worked on *Stagecoach, Dive Bomber,* and *The Plainsman.*

In fact, Hubbard had finished a different sort of western, which was acquired by the publisher Macaulay for an advance of $2,500. Hubbard spent all the money on a boat, but the deal for *Buckskin Brigades* was noteworthy in itself—few pulp authors of the time ever made it into hardcover. Remarkably enough, it turned out to be a real novel. Its hero, Yellow Hair, was a stock white savior figure, but the plot vigorously took the side of the Native Americans, and it drew energy from Hubbard's identification with his protagonist, who was the earliest version of a character type to which he would often return—the last honorable man in a world of ignorance.

Despite favorable notices, *Buckskin Brigades* failed to sell out its first printing. Shortly afterward, Hubbard was invited to his fateful meeting at Street & Smith, where he had written for such titles as *Top-Notch* and *Western Story.* By his own account, he and Burks were met by Tremaine and "an executive named Black"—probably Frank Blackwell—who asked them to write for *Astounding.* They were unhappy, he recalled, with the magazine's performance, as well as the fact that it "was mainly publishing stories about machines and machinery."

After airing their concerns, Hubbard remembered, the executives called in Campbell, who was told to buy everything that the two writers submitted: "He was going to get *people* into his stories and get something going besides *machines*." The only source for this story is Hubbard himself, which is reason enough to be skeptical of it—but the timing is basically right, and it seems plausible that a meeting more or less like what he described did take place.

In all likelihood, the ultimatum was inspired less by poor numbers—*Astounding* was still the leading title in its field—than by a desire to fill out the magazine's inventory. Hubbard and Burks were known for generating copy on demand, and they had both been officers of the American Fiction Guild, which gave them useful connections to other writers. In an editor's note that appeared a few months later, Campbell confirmed that Hubbard's debut was part of "the effort to get the best stories of the science fiction type by the best authors available."

Initially, however, the partnership seemed like a step backward. In a letter dated April 5, 1938, Campbell accused his new writer, whom he addressed as "Hubbard Snubbard," of deliberately avoiding him, and Hubbard had misgivings of his own. He wasn't a science fiction fan—he later wrote that he was "quite ignorant of the field and regarded it, in fact, a bit diffidently"—and his only work of speculative fiction, aside from *The Secret of Treasure Island*, had been "The Death Flyer," a throwaway about a ghost train. But he was happy to take work wherever he could find it, and within a few weeks, he had sent in his first submission.

At first, Campbell wasn't sure how he felt about "The Dangerous Dimension," a work of borderline fantasy about a scientist who discovers an equation that teleports him wherever he thinks, willingly or otherwise. It was amusing, but little else, and it made the editor uncomfortable—he repeatedly asked his friends and family what they thought of it, and in his note on the upcoming issue, he mentioned every writer except Hubbard. Yet the response was positive. It introduced a welcome note of humor, and in the monthly readers' poll, the Analytical Laboratory, it placed first in fiction, above the final installment of "The Legion of Time."

This reaction, more than anything else, reconciled Campbell to Hubbard, whose name appeared on the cover two months later with "The Tramp." Like "The Dangerous Dimension," it featured a weak, milquetoast lead who couldn't have been further from the heroes of Hubbard's adventure fiction—which hinted, perhaps, at his secret opinion of his audience. But the relationship between the two men had thawed just in time. After a corporate reorganization, Blackwell and Tremaine were fired in May, leaving Campbell with complete control of the magazine. If he had still wanted to drop Hubbard, he could have—but he didn't.

It helped that Campbell had discovered a better venue for Hubbard's talents. The idea of a companion fantasy magazine had been kicked around by Tremaine, who spoke of starting "a weird or occult mag," and in 1938, Campbell took the first serious steps toward launching it. He wrote to authors asking for fantasy, but he didn't mention the new title. Instead, he spread a rumor that he was following up on the success of stories like "The Dangerous Dimension," which led Hubbard to believe that the magazine, *Unknown*, had been founded expressly for him.

In reality, the true catalyst was an extraordinary novel titled *Forbidden Acres,* by Eric Frank Russell, a writer based in Liverpool. It was a wild fantasy, inspired by the writings of Charles Fort, that proposed that countless unexplained events were the work of a race called the Vitons, who took the form of ball lightning and fed on human fear. After receiving a requested rewrite, Campbell thought that it was the best story that he had read in a decade—it still deserves to be ranked as one of the greatest science fiction novels ever written—and it was published as *Sinister Bar-*

rier in the inaugural issue of *Unknown,* which was dated March 1939.

The following month, the lead novel was Hubbard's *The Ultimate Adventure,* which introduced a formula that its author would frequently exploit—an ordinary man magically plunged into a story straight out of *The Arabian Nights.* Using a protagonist from the real world made it easier to deliver exposition, but it also reflected a fascination with personal transformation that Hubbard shared with Campbell. Much of his work parodied the visions of change that were on the verge of becoming central to science fiction, but he also wouldn't have taken so naturally to *Unknown* if he hadn't had so much in common with its editor.

Hubbard was cultivating Campbell, as he did with other useful contacts, and he began to pay visits to the editor's home, filling his ears with stories about running a cruise ship in the Caribbean and serving with the U.S. Marines in China. "Ron can do almost anything extraordinarily well," Campbell wrote to Swisher, and a mutual respect was growing on both sides—when Hubbard visited a university science department, he found that everyone there wanted to ask him about Campbell.

Yet there was one aspect of his life that he kept secret. On New Year's Day, 1938, while undergoing a dental operation under anesthesia, Hubbard had felt himself leaving his body. Rising as a spirit from his chair, he drifted toward a gate behind which lay the answers to all of mankind's questions, but before he could reach the final revelation, he was pulled back. Opening his eyes, he asked, "I was dead, wasn't I?" And he was allegedly told that his heart had indeed stopped beating.

The vision faded, and he spent several days trying in vain to recover it. At last, early one morning, he awoke with the memory of what he had seen. Working like a madman, he produced a draft of over two hundred pages. It took the form of a fable about a sage from the time of *The Arabian Nights* who tried to distill all of human wisdom into one book, cutting it down to a tenth of its length, then to one line, and finally to a single word: *SURVIVE*.

When Hubbard finished the manuscript, which he titled *Excalibur* or *The One Command*, he cabled publishers, telling them to meet him in Penn Station to bid for the rights. Hubbard later claimed to have withdrawn the book after the first six people who read it went insane, while another jumped from the window of an office tower, and he wrote of his ambitions to Polly:

> *Foolishly perhaps, but determined none the less, I have high hopes of smashing my name into history so violently that it will take a legendary form even if all books are destroyed. . . . I do know that I could form a political platform, for instance, which would encompass the support of the unemployed, the industrialist and the clerk and day laborer all at one and the same time.*

He showed it to Arthur J. Burks, who recalled, "It was the strangest book I ever read. Reading it seemed to open queer windows in the bodies of everyone one thereafter met. It was a *squirmy,* self-revealing book." Yet Hubbard didn't mention it to Campbell, perhaps because he suspected that the editor would try to take control of the project—a hunch that later turned out to be more than justified.

Years afterward, Hubbard implied that such stories as "The Dangerous Dimension" reflected his interest in philosophy: "I didn't tell John that the idea was actually as old as Buddha." In fact, his published fiction showed minimal regard for ideas, and he was content to work within the pulps, where he became popular among fans. One raved in a letter to *Unknown*, "Give me the L. Ron Hubbard fairy tale any time and I'm happy." In the following issue, he added: "With Hubbard . . . I consider anything below perfect a letdown." The reader who wrote these words was Isaac Asimov.

IN THE FALL OF 1935, ON HIS FIRST DAY AT CITY COLLEGE, ASIMOV TOOK TWO EXAMS. THE FIRST was a physical. With his bad complexion and scrawny build, Asimov was classified as "poorly developed"—the only student in his group to earn that designation. The second was an intelligence test. His score was off the charts, and the college wrote an astonished letter asking him to report back for further testing. By then, Asimov was already gone. He had been there for a total of three days.

Asimov had assumed that he wouldn't be able to afford Seth Low Junior College, the Columbia University affiliate in Brooklyn, but he landed a scholarship and a job with the National Youth Administration. A year after he enrolled, Seth Low closed, and he was transferred to the main campus of Columbia, in Morningside Heights. He still had to come back in the afternoon to work at the candy store, however, and he failed to make any friends.

In December 1936, his father bought a new store in Park Slope. The family moved into a railroad apartment across the street, with their rooms laid out in a line: Asimov, his sister, Marcia—whom he constantly annoyed with his wisecracks—and the bedroom that his mother shared with his brother, Stanley. The store was doing well, so he didn't have to worry about a summer job, and the uninterrupted stretch of time got him thinking about fiction again. He began a time travel story, "Cosmic Corkscrew," but abandoned it halfway through.

Asimov was also writing every month to Brass Tacks, stating in one letter, "When we want science fiction, we don't want swooning dames." His nervousness around girls—he had never been on a date—could express itself as hostility, as it did throughout the fan community, and in a later issue, he added, "Let me point out that women never affected the world directly. They always grabbed hold of some poor, innocent man, worked their insidious wiles on him . . . and then affected history through him." Asimov concluded that he should stop before he created a "vendetta" of all the female fans in the country: "There must be at least twenty of them!"

Astounding arrived at the store on the third Tuesday of each month, and Asimov was always ready to slice open the bundle as soon as it came. On May 10, 1938, it didn't appear. Fearing that it had been canceled, he called Street & Smith. Whoever answered the phone informed him that it was still being published, but he spent the next week staring at the magazine rack with dread—and on the following Tuesday, sure enough, there was no sign of it.

He made a fateful decision. After obtaining permission from his mother to take two hours off, he boarded the train to Manhattan. He was eighteen years old, but it was one of the first times that he had ventured into the city by himself, except for school—and if he had lived even as far away as Staten Island, it might never have occurred to him to go at all. When he arrived, he confirmed that the publication date was now the third Friday of each month, and he immediately went home again.

The episode seemed like a minor one, but it made the magazine feel closer in his imagination, and he realized that he wasn't content with just being a fan—he wanted to be a writer. By now, his junior year was over, and he had the summer off. Pulling out "Cosmic Corkscrew," he noticed that part of it was reminiscent of "Dead Knowledge," by Don A. Stuart, but he decided that it wasn't worth worrying about the similarities, and he finished it.

Like Pohl, he wondered if it might not be better to hand it over in person. As it happened, the current issue was late again, which gave him an excuse to pay another visit. He consulted his father, who advised him to put the manuscript directly into Campbell's hands, as well as to shave and put on a good suit. Asimov decided to compromise—he shaved, but he didn't change clothes—and then he headed for the train. It was June 21, 1938.

At Street & Smith, he was told that the magazine was now slated to come out on the fourth Friday of the month. From there, he went to find the editor, and he was astonished when the receptionist said, "Mr. Campbell will see you."

Following her directions, Asimov made his way through a storage room filled with stacks of magazines and rolls of paper. He finally arrived at the rear office, where he saw Campbell—and probably Tarrant—for the first time.

Campbell was friendly. He liked having an audience, and he recognized the skinny, pimpled fan's name from Brass Tacks. Asimov had letters in the July and August issues, and when he eagerly pointed them out in the advance copies on the editor's desk, Campbell only smiled. "I know."

They talked for more than an hour. Campbell revealed that he was Don A. Stuart, whose stories Asimov hadn't liked, and promised to read "Cosmic Corkscrew." Two days later, Asimov received a polite rejection that cited its slow beginning and poor dialogue. But he was overjoyed, and he began another submission, mostly for the excuse to visit Campbell again.

Asimov went back on July 18 with "Stowaway," a story about alien worms that killed using magnetic fields. When he asked hesitantly if it was all right to keep bringing his work in person, Campbell told him that it was fine, as long as he didn't come when they were laying out an issue. He refused to say when this was, however, and Asimov suspected that the editor just wanted to have an excuse whenever he didn't feel like seeing him. His second effort was bounced as well, but Asimov wrote in his diary, "It was the nicest possible rejection you could imagine."

At the end of July, Asimov finished "Marooned Off Vesta." It was a scientific problem story—about astronauts coping with their damaged ship—of the kind that later came to dominate the magazine, and Asimov, whose rational personality drew him to mysteries and puzzles, latched on to it instinctively. Reasoning that one submission each month was plenty, he waited until August to deliver it. At the office, Campbell, who had been on vacation, indicated a stack of manuscripts. "I've got to skim over these and put aside the hopeless ones for rejection."

Asimov wondered if there might be a hidden message there. "Is that personal?"

Campbell regarded the younger man kindly. "No. I don't consider you hopeless."

But the story was soon back in Asimov's hands. Campbell later wrote that he thought it was "a sound, and pretty fair piece of work, just lacking humanity," but the curt rejection gave Asimov a crisis of confidence. He sent it to *Amazing*, even though he considered the magazine "trash," and felt that his visits with Campbell were all that was keeping him going.

On October 22, Asimov returned home from school to find his mother and sister smiling. Going upstairs, he learned that he had received a letter—which his father had blithely gone ahead and opened—from Raymond Palmer of *Amazing*. He was buying "Marooned Off Vesta."

It was Asimov's first sale. The money came to sixty-four dollars, or enough to pay for a full month's tuition. Asimov wrote about it proudly to the author Clifford Simak, with whom he was corresponding. Simak congratulated him, but he also disclosed that he had just sold a serial to Campbell for more than five hundred dollars. *Astounding*, Asimov saw, remained the top of the market.

And he was still unable to break in. When Campbell told him that one of his stories was "hackneyed," Asimov wrote back to apologize. Elsewhere, Campbell noted that his work was "definitely improving, especially where you are not straining for effect," but he also said that it lacked an indefinable "umph." Asimov continued his monthly visits—he was speaking to Campbell by now at greater length than he did to his own father—but he was feeling discouraged.

For his job with the National Youth Administration, he had been assigned to the sociologist Bernhard J. Stern, who asked him to type up excerpts from books that described opposition to technological change. It occurred to Asimov that the same reaction might apply to spaceflight, and he submitted the resulting story, "Ad Astra," before Christmas. A week later, he received an invitation to discuss it after the holidays. He worked himself into a state of frenzied anticipation, and he went to see Campbell on the first possible day, which was January 5, 1939.

Campbell didn't want to buy the story outright, but he was intrigued by the notion of resistance to space travel, and he asked Asimov to revise it with that theme in mind. Asimov was nervous, but he was encouraged by the appearance of "Marooned Off Vesta" in *Amazing,* in which he described himself in an author's note: "I am of medium height, dark, and my mother thinks I'm handsome. . . . I hope and hope again that this first story does not prove to be a flash in the pan."

The revision of "Ad Astra" took him three weeks, interrupted by the distraction of his first fistfight, with a local kid who left him "properly banged up." It had the same flat dialogue and characters as all of his early work, but the idea of a reaction against science— and the implication that it followed a historical cycle—was exactly the kind of concept that Campbell loved to explore. Asimov also allowed one character to express his anxieties about the mounting tensions in Europe: "It was a time of political chaos and international anarchy; a suicidal, brainless, insane period—and it culminated in the Second World War."

And it was enough. One week after Asimov brought Campbell the rewrite, his father called from downstairs, "Isaac, a check!"

There was no letter. When Campbell bought a story, he sent the payment alone, and "Ad Astra," his ninth submission, had sold for sixty-nine dollars. He was nineteen years old.

Much later, Asimov asked Campbell why he had encouraged him, saying that it must have seemed impossible. Campbell agreed: "Yes, it was impossible. On the other hand, I saw something in *you*. You were eager and listened and I knew you wouldn't quit no matter how many rejections I handed you." And his eagerness was visible to everyone, including Tarrant, who remembered how the young Asimov "sat in adoring admiration of Campbell, drinking in every word he said."

Campbell had also encouraged Asimov as much for what he represented as for what he was in himself. The editor had successfully given ideas to established writers, but he wondered whether it might be possible to build an author from the ground up, and Asimov came along at just the right time to serve as an experimental subject. In a letter, Campbell referred to him as "the fan who's been trying to be a writer," which was precisely how he saw him—as a representative, located conveniently nearby, of a rising generation of fans who had grown up with the magazine.

It didn't occur to him to lavish the same attention on Pohl, who never sold Campbell a story that he wrote on his own. Pohl was just as available and arguably more promising, but he was also pushy, aggressive, and manifestly eager to take the editor's place. Asimov was more deferential, recalling of Campbell, "I could endure him. . . . I was fortunate in the sense that he was in some ways a lot like my father." He would submit to an apprenticeship that no professional would tolerate, and the editor began to think of other ways to put him to use.

In the meantime, Campbell rejected "Robbie," Asimov's first attempt at a robot story, and there was also the slight problem of his name. Asimov had heard that the fan Milton A. Rothman, who had sold two stories to Campbell, had been asked to use the

pseudonym Lee Gregor, which he was advised would be more acceptable to readers. Asimov never felt the slightest hint of personal
anti-Semitism in their interactions, but it was evident that Campbell generally regarded gentile names—and their bearers—as preferable to the alternative.

Eventually, Campbell brought up the possibility of a pen name.
"On this point," Asimov recalled, "I clearly expressed intransi-
gence. My name was my name and it would go on my stories."
Campbell never pressed it, in all likelihood because it wasn't important to his overall plans.

Later that month, exactly one year after his first visit, Asimov
dropped off a new story. As he was leaving, he passed a stack of the
July 1939 issue. He knew that it included "Ad Astra," so he helped
himself to a copy. In the previous issue, Campbell had written,
"Next month, *Astounding* introduces a new author, and one of unusual promise." It wasn't Asimov—who wasn't even mentioned—
but A. E. van Vogt, whose debut, "Black Destroyer," was featured
on the cover.

Leafing through the issue, Asimov saw that "Ad Astra" had
been retitled "Trends," which struck him as an improvement.
There were stories by van Vogt, Nat Schachner, Nelson S. Bond,
Ross Rocklynne, Amelia Reynolds Long, and Catherine L. Moore;
an article titled "Tools for Brains"; and an editorial on uranium fission in which Campbell said, "A university equipped with the necessary cyclotron has already arranged for the purchase of a cubic
foot of uranium oxide."

Asimov didn't know it, but the university was Columbia,
where Campbell would later visit the cyclotron in person—and the
editorial was as significant, in its way, as any of the stories in the
issue. With atomic energy on the threshold of becoming a reality,
predicting the future was no longer merely an educational strategy,
as it had been for Gernsback, or a pretext for stock adventures,

as it had been for the other magazines. Now it was something far more urgent.

A month earlier, Asimov had earned his bachelor of science degree, but he wasn't in the mood to celebrate—he had been rejected by the medical schools to which he had applied. As he took home his copy of *Astounding*, he had no reason to suspect that it would come to be seen as the first issue of the golden age of science fiction, due in no small part to his presence there. But there had been signs. Asimov had once ventured to ask, "Mr. Campbell, how can you bear not to write?"

"I discovered something better, Asimov," Campbell replied. "I'm an editor. When I was a writer, I could only write one story at a time. Now I can write fifty stories at a time. There are fifty writers out there writing stories they've talked with me about." On another occasion, he clarified, "When I give an idea to a writer and it comes back to me exactly the way I gave it to him, I don't give that writer any more ideas. I don't want it my way; I can do that myself. I want my idea *his* way."

Asimov remembered, "That was the way he saw us all. We were extensions of himself; we were his literary clones; each of us doing, in his or her own way, things Campbell felt needed doing; things that he could do but not quite the way we could; things that got done in fifty different varieties of ways."

And the team was about to expand. In the September 1939 issue, Campbell predicted, "*Astounding* will find and develop not less than four now-unknown *top-rank* new authors during the next year." Van Vogt was one obvious discovery. Others were waiting in the wings. And before the summer was over, the golden age would find its embodiment in a writer whose life would entwine with Campbell's—and Asimov's—in ways that none of them could have foreseen.

5.
THE ANALYTICAL LABORATORY
1938–1940

[Science fiction] writers, confronted with desperate problems, may mope, but are much more likely to break out by some dazzling improvisation; they have what Arthur Koestler calls "the coward's courage."

—DAMON KNIGHT, *THE FUTURIANS*

While Asimov was paying his monthly visits to Campbell, he was engaged in another life that seemed for a time to be equally significant. It began with a postcard on August 2, 1938, from Jack Rubinson, a high school classmate who had recognized Asimov's name from his letters to *Astounding*. When he wrote to strike up a correspondence, Asimov responded eagerly, and a month later, Rubinson sent him a package so big that it cost an extra penny to mail.

Inside were three issues of a fan magazine, which Asimov found "fairly interesting." He was more intrigued by the postcard that came the following week, in which Rubinson mentioned that he was a member of the Greater New York Science Fiction League in Queens. As soon as he heard about it, Asimov badly wanted to join—even if getting there would mean "double carfare"—and he asked Rubinson to let him know when the next meeting would take place.

Three days later, he got a postcard from Frederik Pohl, who didn't mention the Greater New York Science Fiction League at all. Instead, he invited him to the first meeting of the Futurian Science Literary Society in Brooklyn. Asimov wasn't clear about the reasons for the change, but he was glad that it was closer to home. He wrote back to ask if it was a house or an apartment—in fact, it was a hall used by the Young Communist League—and concluded, "That's all right, I'll get to the right place somehow and I'll bring the card you sent me as identification."

He was innocently wandering into a drama that had been unfolding around him for years. Science fiction fandom had sprung into existence almost by accident, after Hugo Gernsback printed letters from readers in *Amazing*, along with their addresses, allowing them to correspond in private with like-minded fans. In cities with a critical mass of enthusiasts, like New York, Philadelphia, or Los Angeles, they gathered in small groups and printed mimeographed fanzines full of inside jokes—a meeting ground for such creative teenagers as Jerry Siegel and Joe Shuster of Cleveland, who went on to create the character of Superman.

The first officially sanctioned club, the Science Fiction League, was established in 1934 by Gernsback and Charles Hornig of *Wonder Stories*. It received free coverage in the magazine, but it also became seen as a tool of the publishers, drawing attacks from fandom's radical wing. The key figure among the extremists was Donald A. Wollheim, who later became a major figure in science fiction in his own right—although in his late teens, he was closer to what today would be called a troll, boasting that he could single-handedly drive "any fan from the field."

It was a small world—by one estimate, there were fewer than

fifty active fans—that magnified certain personality traits. The most devoted members were usually young, obsessive, and confrontational. Disputes between clubs were driven by personal grudges, and a lone player like Wollheim could exert a disproportionate influence. The dynamics were much like those of modern online communities, except considerably slower, and a pattern was established in which a club would be founded, persist for a while, and then implode, either because of internal tensions or because Wollheim came in and dissolved it.

Before long, fandom in New York had broken into two rough divisions. One was led by Sam Moskowitz, an athletic kid of eighteen who was less interested in political disputes than in running conventions and meeting professionals. The other group gathered around Wollheim and his friend John Michel, whose views were expressed in a leftist manifesto, "Mutation or Death," that argued that fans should strive for the kind of social change that they saw in their favorite stories.

In May 1938, Moskowitz and the fan William Sykora, who had formed an alliance against Wollheim, organized the First National Science Fiction Convention in Newark. When Campbell showed up with the writers John Clark and L. Sprague de Camp, there were fifteen people in attendance. Looking out at the gathering, the editor remarked dryly, "Better than I expected."

By the time Campbell rose to speak, the crowd had grown to over a hundred fans. The editor held forth on the importance of fandom, which he described as the inner circle of his readership, and expressed his support for a World Science Fiction Convention, or Worldcon, to be held next summer. Wollheim had asked to speak as well, but permission was denied out of fear that Campbell would be offended by his prepared remarks, which questioned why anyone with a college degree in science would want to edit a pulp magazine.

Fandom quickly split into factions over who would run the

Worldcon. In July, Campbell and Leo Margulies of *Thrilling Wonder Stories* had lunch with Sykora and Wollheim to settle the issue. Margulies did most of the talking—Campbell was uncharacteristically quiet—and ruled that Wollheim would be in charge. Moskowitz responded by founding a rival organization, New Fandom, to wrest back control. The situation became so rancorous that Margulies was forced to dissolve the Greater New York Science Fiction League, and Wollheim and Michel responded by starting the group that became known as the Futurians.

When Asimov arrived at the inaugural meeting on September 18, he was aware of none of this. The other attendees included Wollheim, Michel, Pohl, Rubinson, Dick Wilson, Robert Lowndes, and Cyril Kornbluth. Many were Jewish, and most were fervent communists, more out of the excitement of being part of a movement than from any deep ideological conviction. Asimov was especially interested in their fanzine, of which he wrote in his diary, "I intend to write for [the magazine], but hesitate to put my name to violently radical and probably atheistical articles, so I am wondering if they will allow me to write under a pseudonym."

Afterward, they went out for banana splits and sandwiches, although Asimov, who was smarting from the expense of joining—the initiation fee was a quarter—ate nothing. He was powerfully drawn to the combative Wollheim, and the others seemed like fellow outsiders. Wollheim had suffered from polio, while Michel—whose stammer made it impossible for him to speak in public—had been paralyzed by diphtheria as a child. Pohl had missed a year of school because of scarlet fever, Lowndes had a clubfoot, Kornbluth's teeth were green, and they were all poor.

Asimov saw them as kindred spirits. The Great Depression had led to a contraction of possibilities for fans who were already on the edge, and science fiction told them that there was a point to it all—although most of the factors that kept them apart could

The Futurians, circa 1939. (*Front row:*) Harry Dockweiler, John Michel, Isaac Asimov, Donald Wollheim, Herbert Levantman. (*Middle row:*) Chester Cohen, Walter Kubilis, Frederik Pohl, Richard Wilson. (*Back row:*) Cyril Kornbluth, Jack Gillespie, Jack Rubinson.
Courtesy of the Richard Wilson estate and the Damon Knight papers,
Special Collections Research Center, Syracuse University Libraries

be overcome with time or effort, with little to keep them from becoming productive members of society once they had emerged from their larval stages. Science fiction had less to offer those who felt excluded for reasons that couldn't be outgrown, and with few exceptions, most fans were white males.

None of these points would have occurred to Asimov, who was happy to have found a world where he belonged—although he might have been equally pleased to have stumbled into the ranks of their rivals. In any case, he was caught up by their fervor. On September 28, he went to see Campbell at the office, where he expounded on his new Futurian ideals. He was shocked to learn that the editor was a conservative, and he worried that he might have offended him.

By the third meeting, Wollheim and Michel, typically, were growing bored, and they moved that the club be recognized along new lines—a motion that Asimov opposed "like hell." On October 30, the Mercury Theatre broadcast its adaptation of *The War of the Worlds*, narrated by Orson Welles. Campbell seemed to resent Welles's intrusion on his turf, but the Futurians loved it, and at their next gathering, they held a debate on the prospect of an alien invasion, with Wollheim speaking for the Martians. Asimov took the side of mankind and lost, but he made up for it by picking out "The Internationale" on the piano.

He was enjoying the atmosphere of mild rebelliousness—at the next meeting, he actually smoked two cigarettes—but the other members were mixed on his presence. On one occasion, he was ejected for talking too loudly, and after failing to receive invitations for two meetings, he wrote to Pohl, "Have I been blackballed out?" He once brought his sister, Marcia, along, only to have the others yank her inside and lock the door as a joke: "I got very panicky. I had some vague notion that they might do something to her, and I'd never be able to explain it to my parents."

At times, Asimov felt out of place—his friends were all ambitious, but he was the only one who had sold a story to Campbell—and he even attended a meeting of the rival Queens Science Fiction League, at which he rose to introduce himself: "Now you see the world's worst science fiction writer!" Of the Futurians, he was the closest to Pohl, who tried to become his agent, offering to rewrite his unsold stories "in accordance with certain suggestions previously given me by Campbell, Weisinger, and Tremaine," in exchange for the majority of his earnings. Asimov declined: "Campbell is a good friend of mine."

Campbell was a constant presence in their letters, as if they were rival siblings competing for a father's love. Pohl wrote, "Campbell once remarked to me that he could pick out a specific flaw in a story and identify [it] so that the author could correct it with ease; but that he could do nothing when a story simply did not click." In another letter, he added, "Through your acquaintance with Campbell, you're in a better position than most beginning or even fairly well established authors."

Asimov would later deny knowing anything about Marx, but in his late teens, he characterized his politics rather differently, as Pohl revealed in the same letter: "You call yourself a communist; well, if you'll allow me to handle some of your manuscripts and will contribute any profits therefrom to the [Communist Party], I'll waive commission—and I do need the money. . . . If you don't need money yourself, they certainly do." Asimov replied that he might not need the money, but he welcomed it. Finally, he agreed to take on Pohl as his agent for three months.

In the meantime, the dispute over the World Science Fiction Convention—which was scheduled for the Fourth of July weekend, to coincide with the World's Fair—grew more acrimonious. New Fandom won back the sponsorship, due in part to the widespread assumption that Campbell was on its side. The editor became a regular guest of the Queens Science Fiction League, an affiliate of New Fandom, and even Doña was dragged along, "much against her will," to one meeting.

Campbell had little reason to be sympathetic to the Futurians. Their politics couldn't have been more different; he was ambivalent toward Pohl; and he had tangled with Wollheim before. A year earlier, Wollheim had circulated an open letter criticizing him for publishing "Three Thousand Years," by Thomas McClary. Wollheim had blasted the serial—of which Pohl had also written to complain—as "fascistic" and "an outrage," and Campbell forwarded his comments to Robert Swisher with a wry note: "Maybe he didn't like the story?"

As a rule, however, the editor was content to let fandom take its course. He took a practical interest in its existence, and he occasionally tossed a coin with the fan H. C. Koenig to see who would host visitors from out of town, but he had never been active in such circles, and he was a decade older than its most vocal members. Campbell hoped to utilize its growth, but he was also aware of how quickly it could turn against him, and he mostly kept his distance.

On July 2, 1939, the doors opened at last for the first World Science Fiction Convention. At ten in the morning, a crowd began to gather on the fourth floor of the Caravan Hall on East Fifty-Ninth Street, which had been decorated with cover art from the pulps. The fans Forrest J Ackerman and Ray Bradbury had come all the way out from Los Angeles, and the professional attendees included Jack Williamson, L. Sprague de Camp, and Campbell himself.

When Asimov arrived, freshly shaved and wearing a new suit, he was nervous. There were rumors that all the Futurians would be excluded, and he wasn't sure whether Moskowitz, who knew that he was a published author, would extend the ban to him or not. He found his friends lurking across the street in the Automat, and they all headed upstairs together.

On the fourth floor, they were met by James Taurasi, one of Moskowitz's cronies. New Fandom had decided that the Futurians would be allowed inside if they swore to behave themselves, but Moskowitz and Sykora hadn't arrived, and without their approval, Taurasi didn't want to admit them.

When Moskowitz showed up, Taurasi was still arguing with the Futurians by the elevators. Wollheim asked if they could enter, but before Moskowitz could respond, a fan named Louis Kuslan passed him a leaflet that he had been handed outside. It referred to New Fandom as "ruthless scoundrels," and its headline was *BEWARE OF THE DICTATORSHIP.*

Moskowitz showed it to Wollheim. Both he and Taurasi were big guys—they each weighed close to two hundred pounds, and Moskowitz was an amateur boxer—who outsized most of the Futurians. "I thought you just stated that you would do nothing to hurt the convention."

"I didn't print them," Wollheim replied. In fact, they were the work of a fan named David Kyle, a Futurian who had printed them on the presses of a newspaper owned by his brother in upstate New York.

"But his group was passing them out," Kuslan piped up. In response, Moskowitz went downstairs to look for Sykora. Instead, he saw the police—Taurasi, anticipating trouble, had called the cops. He also found piles of leftist tracts, which he assumed the Futurians were planning to distribute.

Moskowitz told the police to come back in an hour. Then he went up to see Wollheim again. "If we let you in, will you promise on your word of honor that you will do nothing in any way to disturb the progress of the convention?"

"If we do anything to disturb the convention," Wollheim said, "you can kick us out."

"We don't want to kick you out," Moskowitz replied. "We simply want your honored promise not to harm the convention."

When Wollheim refused, Moskowitz asked the others in turn, including Asimov and Jack Rubinson, who promised not to make trouble. He later recalled, "But the core of the group . . . chose to remain without."

Asimov remembered it differently: "No one tried to stop me. I just walked in." Once he was inside, he regretted it, and he wondered whether he should leave in a show of solidarity. Looking around the room, however, he saw Campbell, the artist Frank R. Paul, de Camp, and Williamson, whom he had met earlier that summer, and he guiltily decided to stay.

As the morning wore on, the Futurians kept trying to enter in pairs, but they were repeatedly turned back. Williamson came out to see them, and Campbell tried to persuade Sykora to let them in, but was refused. At lunch, Asimov crept out to buy coffee and a chicken sandwich. Instead of branding him as a traitor, as he had feared, the others saw him as an undercover operative. They badgered him for details, and Leslie Perri, Pohl's girlfriend, joined him as he went back inside.

At two in the afternoon, Moskowitz called the convention to order. After a screening of the film *Metropolis,* which Asimov hated, Campbell delivered a talk on the evolution of science fiction, pointing to the movie as an example of what the genre could accomplish. He stated that their goal should be one of constant advancement, and he proclaimed that his magazine was prepared to lead the charge.

Around seven in the evening, Sykora rose to introduce various notables in the audience. The writer John Clark yelled, "How about Asimov?" As the crowd shouted its approval, Asimov stood up, delighted and bewildered, to make his way toward the front. As he passed Campbell, the editor grinned and gave him a friendly shove forward, nearly toppling him over.

Asimov climbed onto the stage. He saw that Perri was gesticulating furiously, but he wasn't sure what she wanted. After a brief speech in which he referred to himself as "the worst science fiction writer unlynched," he sat down again, relieved. Later, he learned that Perri had wanted him to deliver a statement in support of the exiled Futurians, which had never even crossed his mind.

Afterward, it was generally agreed that the first Worldcon had been a resounding success, heralding a closer relationship between fans and professionals and setting a precedent for conventions to follow. The fact that it had taken place just as the July 1939 issue of *Astounding* ushered in the golden age was no coincidence—fandom and the magazine had reached a new level of maturity together.

In the short term, the Great Exclusion Act, as it became known, had the effect of stabilizing the community. New Fandom and its successors would run conventions, while the Futurians—who were less a real club than a cult of personality around Wollheim and Michel—withdrew into themselves to produce writers and editors. What they shared was a sense of identity that science fiction afforded. Many were young men about to be swallowed up by the war, and the genre, which taught that outsiders were the ones who made the future, told them that their lives had value.

Ironically, most of the Futurians would never break through with the editor who was more responsible than anyone else for awakening them to the field's possibilities. Campbell regarded them with suspicion, to the extent that he thought of them at all, and they didn't go out of their way to endear themselves. At one meeting, Pohl brought along Cyril Kornbluth, who was openly disrespectful toward Campbell. Afterward, Kornbluth explained, "I wanted to make sure he remembered me."

In time, the Futurians formed what amounted to a counterculture to the establishment that Campbell represented, with Asimov caught somewhere in the middle. Campbell was less interested in fans who were willing to suffer for science fiction than in technically minded professionals who wrote on the side—which made them more receptive to his notes—or in reliable writers for hire. Hubbard, to his eyes, was one of the latter. And he was about to make his greatest discovery of all, a former Navy man and political activist who fulfilled his wildest hopes almost overnight.

FOR ALL THEIR AVOWED RADICALISM, THE FUTURIANS APPROACHED POLITICS AS SOMETHING TO BE debated over table tennis and banana splits. Robert A. Heinlein, who later called it the only game fit for adults, got to know it on the ground. He had entered the political arena out of admiration for Upton Sinclair, the author of *The Jungle,* who was drafted to run for governor of California in 1933. Sinclair, a progressive socialist, based his platform on a program called End Poverty in California, or EPIC, that called on the state to provide jobs for more than a million unemployed workers.

Heinlein had settled with his wife, Leslyn, in Southern California, where he was living off his naval pension. He was attracted by Sinclair's politics, which reflected his conviction that economic freedom was the basis of liberty, and he volunteered at EPIC, where he was given oversight of seven precincts. After a decisive loss, Heinlein remained at the group's newspaper, and he became friends with Cleve Cartmill, a journalist and aspiring science fiction writer.

During the municipal elections of April 1935, Heinlein served as a district chairman, and he began to see the danger of being associated with radical movements. In May, he was admonished by the secretary of the Navy for writing a letter to the *Hollywood Citizen-News*—to which he had signed his rank—condemning the police response to a student riot. He took responsibility, but he grew wary of being labeled an extremist. Unlike the Futurians, many of whom held a rosy view of Moscow, he saw the Soviet Union as "a grisly horror."

Later that summer, he and Leslyn bought a house on Lookout Mountain Avenue in Laurel Canyon. With another election on the way, he spent hours campaigning in person and held weekly breakfasts for his district workers, with Leslyn baking the cookies. They were so in tune that they finished each other's sentences, but both were feeling the stress of politics, as well as a lack of money—Heinlein had made an unsuccessful stab at real estate, and he fell short in his attempt to run for a seat in the California State Assembly in 1938.

Heinlein also became interested in General Semantics, a discipline developed by the Polish philosopher Alfred Korzybski. In his monumental book *Science and Sanity*, Korzybski warned against the fallacy of confusing words with their underlying objects, as expressed in the aphorism for which he would be best remembered: "The map is not the territory." General Semantics was a mental engineering program that trained its users to avoid such mistakes, and Heinlein was particularly drawn to the concept of "time binding," which stated that man was the one animal that could build on the abstractions created by previous generations—but only if it knew how.

In any event, he had to find a real job, and he was weighing his options when his eye was caught by a call for submissions in the October 1938 issue of *Thrilling Wonder Stories*. It occurred to him to try his hand at writing, and while Leslyn was hospitalized for an appendectomy, he began work on a novel that he conceived as an extension of his politics. Many of his favorite writers, such as Edward Bellamy and H. G. Wells, had used fiction to advance their ideas, and just as Campbell had used the genre to indulge in his fantasy of being a great inventor, Heinlein saw it as a vehicle for the political convictions that he had been unable to put into practice.

Heinlein decided to structure *For Us, the Living* around his interest in a proposal for a universal basic income, and he worked on it diligently until Christmas. After Leslyn returned from the hospital, he asked for her advice, searching "for plot twists and climaxes" as they sat together in the kitchen. In the end, it wasn't very good. Heinlein saw it less as a human story than as an excuse for long discussions of monetary theory, and it showed—but there were also scattered signs of promise, along with elements of a future history that he would continue to mine for decades.

The novel failed to get any traction with publishers, but the appearance of *Unknown* inspired him to turn to short fiction. After pitching ideas to Leslyn, he settled on a story about a machine that can predict when a person will die—a premise inspired by the death of Alice McBee, the woman he had once hoped to marry. Its centerpiece was a vivid description of the shape of an individual life: "Imagine this space-time event . . . as a long pink worm, continuous through the years. . . . The cross section we see appears as a single, discrete body. But that is illusion."

Heinlein finished it in four days in April 1939. He wasn't sure if "Life-Line" was science fiction or fantasy, so he sent it to the one editor with titles in both genres, along with postage for its return: "I hope you won't need it." Two weeks later he received a short letter from Campbell offering to buy the story for seventy dollars, which prompted him to demand, "How long has this racket been going on? And why didn't anybody tell me about it sooner?"

It wasn't hard to see how he broke in so quickly. Unlike Asimov, who submitted all his first efforts, Heinlein, at thirty-one, had already written a whole novel, and the didactic ambitions that sank *For Us, the Living* had also allowed him to practice for thousands of words in private. Without the example of Wells or Bellamy, it never would have occurred to him to write at length, since there was no viable market for science fiction in book form. And "Life-Line" wouldn't have been nearly as good if Heinlein hadn't gotten so many bad habits out of his system.

If Campbell had treated him as ruthlessly as Asimov, Heinlein might well have given up on writing altogether. Unlike Asimov, who was obsessed with science fiction, Heinlein saw it as just another potential career, and without outside encouragement, he might have dropped it. Thankfully, Campbell liked the story, and Heinlein responded with just the kind of résumé that the editor would find enticing: "I am a retired naval officer. When I was in the fleet, my specialty was ballistics, with emphasis on the electro-mechanical integrators used in fire control."

Campbell was interested, but this didn't mean that he took everything, and Heinlein's second effort was sent back. The editor told him that it suffered from a contrived villain: "I think if you would amputate you'd have a much better yarn." Heinlein took him literally, cutting out the character and splicing the ends together, and Campbell bought the revision, which was published as "Misfit." His next two submissions were rejected, but the editor remained encouraging: "Your work is good. Even this is good, despite the fact it's bouncing."

Taking a page from Sinclair Lewis, who had prepared a timeline of events while writing the novel *Babbitt*, Heinlein hung up an old navigational chart and began to map out a future history. He depended enormously on Leslyn: "I work very slowly, three to six pages a day at the beginning, and spend much more time discussing the story with Mrs. Heinlein than in actual composition. My stories are actually collaborations with her, although I do all the actual writing. We talk it out, until we are both satisfied with each notion, then I set it down in its final form."

Heinlein labored over a novella, eventually titled "If This Goes On—," that he finished in August. The account of a revolution against a false prophet in a dystopian America was his first great story, with an unconventional structure that he would often employ in his subsequent work—a riveting opening followed by a second half that picked apart its assumptions. It displayed his matchless ability to follow a story down unexpected byways without losing the reader's attention, and Campbell praised its logic as magnificent, especially "the mass of small details that made it real," which he identified decades later as the author's primary contribution to the genre:

> *Cultural patterns change; one of the things Heinlein*
> *"invented" was the use of that fact. . . . Like the highly*
> *skilled acrobat, he makes his feats seem the natural,*
> *easy, simple way—but after you've finished and enjoyed*
> *one of his stories . . . notice how much of the cultural-*
> *technological pattern he has put over, without impressing*
> *you, at any point, with a two-minute lecture on the*
> *pattern of the time.*

The editor called it "one of the strongest novels I have seen in science fiction," and he would publish it as a "Nova" story, a designation reserved for exceptional work. He particularly liked its awareness that societies could evolve, as well as the implication that psychology could be turned into a science. As one character noted darkly, "The American people have been conditioned from the cradle by the cleverest and most thorough psychotechnicians to believe in and trust the dictatorship which rules them.... If you free them without adequate psychological preparation, like horses led from a burning barn, they will return to their accustomed place."

Campbell was slightly worried by the religious angle, which was "a definitely warmish subject to handle," and when he proposed a few changes to clarify that the cult was fake, Heinlein said that he would be more careful. They were feeling each other out, with subtle moves on both sides. The editor thought that the story "Requiem," which Heinlein called "my pet," was saccharine, but he bought it as an experiment to see if readers would accept it, and he was interested to hear that Heinlein was contemplating a series set in a shared future history.

Heinlein rapidly became a fan favorite. Asimov praised "Life-Line" in a letter to the magazine, and he also wrote Heinlein directly. Pohl, who had talked his way into editing the pulps *Astonishing* and *Super Science Stories* at the age of nineteen, bought "Let There Be Light," a gadget story that Heinlein published as Lyle Monroe. He was saving his real name for Campbell, to whom he sent the ambitious "Lost Legacy," which was inspired by an item that the editor had written in *Unknown* about the apparently unused structures of the brain.

Campbell rejected it: "It's good. It should be great." He saw it as a superman story, which he was starting to think was impossible to tell, and advised Heinlein to avoid forcing the narrative: "L. Ron Hubbard, who is my idea of a man who is both professional and artist in his writing, refuses to write any story that is hard work. That's not laziness; that's because, if it's hard for a writer to work out his story, somewhere there's a motivating principle missing."

It was a generous rejection, but Heinlein felt that Campbell had missed the point—the story wasn't about supermen, but the capacities inherent in everyone. He was also irritated by the final version of "Requiem," to which the editor had added an ending that ruined the tone. Yet he knew that *Astounding* was the best possible platform for his ideas, and as long as he retained enough freedom to express himself, he intended to provide more or less what Campbell wanted.

He decided to focus on straight science fiction, which was all that he had sold so far. Campbell took "The Roads Must Roll," and he gave Heinlein a premise, based on his visit to the Columbia cyclotron, about atomic engineers: "They'll nearly all go mad one way or another after about ten years of work." It was one of his first explicit connections between psychology and nuclear power, and Heinlein wrote it up as "Blowups Happen," with a cover letter that reflected their growing closeness: "I hope that both Don A. Stuart and Doña Stuart will enjoy it."

In the meantime, Heinlein was getting to know other writers in Los Angeles, with the breakfasts that he had held for his precinct workers evolving into a writer's group called the Mañana Literary Society. It allowed him to assume a leadership role, which suited his personality—although Leslyn was equally prominent—and he passed ideas from Campbell to its members, who included an eager, unpublished nineteen-year-old named Ray Bradbury. Years later, Bradbury gratefully remembered his mentorship: "Heinlein taught me human beings."

But Heinlein was its unquestioned star. After the check from "Blowups Happen" allowed him to pay off his mortgage, he contemplated cutting back on his output, prompting Campbell to lament to Pohl, "The trouble with Bob Heinlein is that he doesn't need to write." When the author mentioned the possibility of a visit to New York, Campbell said that he would reschedule his vacation so that they could meet. Heinlein and Leslyn drove across the country, financing their trip with the sale of his novella "Magic, Inc.," and arrived in the city on May 18, 1940.

Campbell wasn't there. Doña's mother had been sick, and they were in Boston when she died on Sunday, May 19. They spent the following week settling up the estate, returning on Friday to New York, where they attended a war game hosted by the writer Fletcher Pratt. The weekly battles—in which wooden ships were moved across the floor according to an elaborate set of rules—were a regular meeting place for science fiction authors, and it was there that the Campbells met the Heinleins. Campbell told Swisher, "Heinlein puts on a bit of Annapolis manners, and Mrs. H is naturally reserved—but they loosened up quickly, and they both are darned interesting."

The four of them stayed out until two in the morning—Doña didn't want to go home alone—and from the beginning, they had a remarkably intense connection. Doña had just lost her mother, to whom she had been close, and she was pregnant with their first child, which made her more receptive than usual to new friends. Campbell, in turn, was fascinated by Heinlein's naval stories, and he later invited them over for dinner in New Jersey, where they discussed a story that never came to fruition:

> The gag was that our mad scientist of two or three or more generations back had spilled some sort of a catalyst in the oceans which caused the formation of an as-yet-unnumbered type of ice, heavier than water and stable at ordinary temperatures. The oceans "freeze" solid, many persons die, the remaining few build up a culture in which fresh water is semi-precious.

It was based on an idea, current in science fiction circles, that was originally developed by the chemist Irving Langmuir. Decades later, Kurt Vonnegut would use it as the premise for the novel *Cat's Cradle.*

On another night, the Campbells attended a party at the apartment of Heinlein's friend John Arwine, where the visiting couple was staying. Leslyn served a tamale pie, while Doña asked Heinlein to define his political beliefs. The conversation moved on before he could answer, but he took the question seriously, and he stayed up until three in the morning to type up his response. He had taken the time to write it, he informed Doña, because "you and John are of the small group whose approval and understanding I need to be happy."

Hubbard was also there. Heinlein had been impressed by a serial that the younger author had written, telling Campbell, "If you write to L. Ron Hubbard, please tell him for me that I consider his *Final Blackout* one of the most nearly perfect examples of literary art it has been my privilege to read. His comprehension and ability to portray the character of the commissioned professional military man is startling. I find myself wondering intently as to whether he himself has been such a man, or whether he is an incredibly astute observer and artist."

At their first meeting, Hubbard struck Heinlein as "a red-headed boy" with whom he shared many opinions: "He is our kind of people in every possible way." During the party, Hubbard and Campbell hashed out a plot together, with the editor concluding, "No, I know you. Once you've talked out a story you're through with it. You won't bother with it." Hubbard decided to prove him wrong. After leaving the apartment that night, he went to the train at Penn Station. He wrote the entire story—probably "One Was Stubborn"—on the way home to Washington, mailing the first half from Chicago and the second from Seattle.

On June 2, Heinlein attended a meeting of the Queens Science Fiction League and hosted the Futurians, although Asimov—who was moping over the departure of a college crush—was absent. A week later, Campbell proposed that Heinlein rewrite "All," the editor's unpublished story about the conquest of America by an Asian empire. Since it wouldn't fit into his future history, Campbell advised him to use a pseudonym—Anson MacDonald—based in part on Leslyn's maiden name, much as the editor had once written as Don A. Stuart.

Heinlein agreed, and he gave Campbell a copy of *For Us, the Living*. He and Leslyn left on June 14. In just a few weeks, they had developed a powerful bond with the Campbells, and the feeling that something significant had passed between them was shared on both sides. As Doña wrote to them much later, "Our personal contact was of such short duration—why or rather how did we come to feel so strongly about you, individually and as a couple?"

ON THE MORNING OF AUGUST 23, 1940, DOÑA'S WATER BROKE WHILE SHE WAS ALONE AT HOME. She was seven months pregnant. They had recently moved to Maple Hill Farms, a housing development in Scotch Plains, New Jersey. It was their first house, with an enclosed porch, two bedrooms half a flight up, and a basement that soon became cluttered with equipment from Campbell's electronics hobby—he was working on an improved kind of fuel battery.

For several months, they had been gardening, refinishing furniture, and preparing for the family that they had postponed, although they failed to make many friends. Campbell wrote to Heinlein, "My personality is too cold. . . . Friendship with me seems to require a sort of mutual, friendly respect, something I can build up only in certain limited types of people. . . . Doña doesn't belong to the Ladies Bridge Club; it would bore her silly. . . . As far as I can make out, normal people . . . are unhappy, uncomfortable, in the presence of genuine intensity of any sort."

Campbell may have been projecting onto Doña, who was considerably more social than he was—but when she felt her water break, "scaring the living daylights out of her," she didn't know any of their neighbors well enough to ask for help. Fortunately, Campbell had a cousin nearby who drove her to Orange Memorial Hospital. Before the pregnancy, Doña had suffered from health issues—a year earlier, after an operation for a uterine cyst, she had been hospitalized for weeks. Now she was experiencing false labor, and both she and her husband were terrified for the baby.

After she didn't give birth after her fourth day at the hospital, she was sent home on Tuesday. On Wednesday, around midnight, she felt persistent pains. Campbell took her back to the hospital, driving so carefully that they didn't arrive for forty minutes, and active labor began an hour later. The doctor gave Doña phenobarbital as an anesthetic, but she had an unusual reaction to it—her pelvic muscles relaxed completely, and the baby just slipped out.

Philinda Duane Campbell, or Peedee, was born early in the morning of August 29. She seemed likely to survive, but her organs were incompletely developed, and she had to remain in an incubator until she reached five pounds. Doña was given a breast pump for the daily milk delivery, and they had to don gloves whenever they wanted to see their daughter at the hospital.

In his letter of congratulations, Heinlein noted that Philinda had the same birthday as Leslyn: "That ought to make her a patroness, or a godmother, or something." Campbell responded that Leslyn could be a fairy godmother, and that he hoped that she could wish away the curse of the baby's nose, which she had inherited from her father. At the end of October, Philinda finally came home, and Campbell told Heinlein that Doña was still intrigued by their offer to be godparents: "D'ja mean it?"

When Heinlein confirmed that they were serious, Campbell replied, "Among friends of our own generation, you *two* rate tops. . . . We are now trying to line things up in a practical and legal way as well as we can." In the end, Campbell's father—who had married a woman named Helen Putnam—asked to be the godfather, but Heinlein and Leslyn would be next in line, and everyone thought of Philinda as their goddaughter. Campbell wrote, "You and Leslyn were the type of people we'd want to have as guardians for any children we might have."

The exchange spoke to the intensity of their relationship, although they had only met a handful of times. Heinlein had finished his new version of "All," retitled *Sixth Column*, in which he clarified why the resistance against the Asian invaders took the form of a fake religion—"This will just look like any one of half a dozen cockeyed cults of the sort that spring up overnight in Southern California"—and attempted to tone down the racism. He wasn't entirely successful, in part because he was a stronger writer, and he was unable to keep from investing his characters with rhetorical vigor as they spoke of "our slant-eyed lords."

They were soon discussing other possible stories. Heinlein sent the editor a list of potential plots, including one about a house that collapses into a tesseract and another about extreme longevity, which respectively became "—And He Built a Crooked House—" and *Methuselah's Children*. Campbell, in turn, proposed an idea about a generation starship—a spacecraft designed to travel for centuries—that forgets its original mission, which Heinlein turned into the classic "Universe."

Kay Tarrant was skeptical—she thought that Heinlein's writing was "bad clear through"—but he had become the writer closest to Campbell's heart. Despite their political differences, they had more in common with each other than either one ever would with anyone else. They both loved a good argument; Leslyn and Doña had played similar roles in their careers; and Heinlein, who appreciated how Campbell treated him as an equal, was everything that the editor had wanted in a writer. They saw each other as men in a genre dominated by overgrown boys, and both were convinced that science fiction could change lives.

But Heinlein wasn't alone. *Astounding* was publishing such

landmarks as "Farewell to the Master" by Harry Bates, which would later be adapted as *The Day the Earth Stood Still,* and *Unknown* was flourishing creatively. Campbell had rewritten an unreadable submission by Arthur J. Burks, "The Elder Gods," into a minor masterpiece, and his two magazines gave him room to indulge all sides of his personality. It purified science fiction and fantasy at a crucial time, and both genres might have evolved along different lines if they had continued to mingle in adjacent pages.

Campbell was building his research team, and there was always room for more. Because of Street & Smith's strong finances, he could afford to pay the highest rates on acceptance, which came to a penny and a half per word for a popular author like Hubbard. Combined with his relatively mature readership, it made him the editor of choice for the most talented and innovative writers. The pulps may have been a literary ghetto, but those same conditions—a closed world with rapid feedback from fans—enabled him to deploy and test new ideas with a minimum of interference.

The editor wanted writers who embraced the challenge, and many became his friends. One was L. Sprague de Camp, a Caltech graduate who was born in 1907. Campbell liked de Camp's background—he was an expert on inventions and patent law—and they had many interests in common. In February 1938, they saw Orson Welles's famous modern-dress staging of *Julius Caesar,* which led Campbell to remark, "It represented, in a way, what I'm trying to do in the magazine. Those humans of two thousand years ago thought and acted as we do—even if they did dress differently."

Another aspect of the performance stuck in his head. A few months later, he asked de Camp, John Clark, and Willy Ley—a rocket scientist and science writer who had recently fled the Nazis—what they would do if they found themselves in ancient Rome. He initially planned to write up their responses as an editorial, but de

Camp turned the premise into *Lest Darkness Fall*, a time travel novel for *Unknown* that read like a wishful hymn to the hero's sheer competence—he distills brandy, constructs the first printing press, and single-handedly saves Europe from the Dark Ages.

A second key protégé was the short, bespectacled Lester del Rey, whom Campbell greeted at their first meeting: "You're not at all what I pictured." Del Rey had started out as a prominent fan, but unlike Asimov, he sold his first submission, which he wrote on a dare from his girlfriend when he was twenty-two. Campbell wanted more, and del Rey responded with the robot romance "Helen O'Loy" and "The Day Is Done," which was based on the editor's idea that the Neanderthals had died of heartbreak. When a lack of money left him unable to write, Campbell, an avid photographer, paid him to print enlargements.

Del Rey's masterpiece was "Nerves," a thriller about a nuclear accident that the editor pitched "not merely as an idea, but as to the viewpoint and the technique that made it possible." Like *Lest Darkness Fall*, it reflected Campbell's desire to develop a new kind of protagonist—a hero with the sensibilities of an engineer, confronting challenges that only science could solve. This figure became known as "the competent man," as memorably evoked decades later by Heinlein:

> *A human being should be able to change a diaper, plan an*
> *invasion, butcher a hog, conn a ship, design a building,*
> *write a sonnet, balance accounts, build a wall, set a bone,*
> *comfort the dying, take orders, give orders, cooperate,*
> *act alone, solve equations, analyze a new problem, pitch*
> *manure, program a computer, cook a tasty meal, fight*
> *efficiently, die gallantly. Specialization is for insects.*

The next step was the superman—a being of superior intellect who would emerge, perhaps by mutation, from within the human race—and Campbell began to make efforts "to get some superman stories of a new type written."

His answer came from an unlikely direction. If Heinlein was the writer whom Campbell had always hoped to find, A. E. van Vogt, a Canadian born in 1912, gave him what he never knew he wanted. Van Vogt had been galvanized by the publication of "Who Goes There?," half of which he read standing up at a newsstand, and he based many of his hallucinatory plots on his dreams. Most of the stories from those years could have been credibly attributed to Heinlein, whose versatility seemingly knew no bounds—but there was nobody else like van Vogt.

It culminated in the sensational *Slan*, the first installment of which appeared in September 1940. Campbell had concluded that a superman was only believable if you kept him offstage or showed him before the onset of his powers, and van Vogt took the latter approach, inventing a young mutant with psychic abilities, or a slan, whose race is being hunted down in a genocide meant to re-call the situation of the Jews. It was embraced by readers who saw themselves as persecuted geniuses, leading to a widespread rally-ing cry: "Fans are slans."

More authors soon followed. In late 1939, Campbell bought two submissions in one week from Leigh Brackett, who recalled of her first acceptance at the age of twenty-four, "No matter what may come after, the unforgettable day in any writer's life is the day when he sold his first story. The day upon which he could stop saying 'I hope to be' and say 'I am.' John Campbell gave me that day. I shall always be grateful." Brackett later expressed surprise at her early success—"They weren't very good stories"—but Camp-bell clearly saw her as a major find, and he took obvious pleasure in correcting a reader: "The 'Leigh' in 'Leigh Brackett' is feminine."

Brackett, who lived in Venice, California, joined the Mañana Literary Society, where she attended gatherings hosted by the Heinleins and became close friends with the teenage Ray Bradbury, whose drafts she read as they lay together on the beach. She displayed a rare ability to translate the conventions of other genres—the western, the war story—into science fiction, but she was insecure about her lack of a scientific background, and after Campbell rejected one of her efforts "rather viciously," she moved on to other markets, commencing a successful career as a novelist and screenwriter that culminated decades later with *The Empire Strikes Back*.

Campbell steered writers to *Astounding* or *Unknown* based on their strengths, and one who was comfortable in both worlds was Theodore Sturgeon. Sturgeon, who was born in 1918, was fascinated by the challenges that the editor presented to his authors, including "Write me a story about a creature that thinks *as well* as a man, but not *like* a man." He later called Campbell "my best friend and my worst enemy" for labeling him as a science fiction writer in the eyes of critics, but he maintained to the end, "I owe him more than I owe any other single human being in the world."

Sturgeon's finest work—and perhaps the single most spellbinding story ever to appear under Campbell's editorship—was "Microcosmic God," which was published in April 1941. Its hero, a biochemist named Kidder, might have been a thinly disguised version of Campbell himself:

> He was always asking questions, and didn't mind very much when they were embarrassing. . . . If he was talking to someone who had knowledge, he went in there and got it, leaving his victim breathless. If he was talking to someone whose knowledge was already in his possession, he only asked repeatedly, "How do you know?"

Frustrated by the slow progress of scientific research, Kidder develops an artificial civilization in his laboratory, populated by tiny creatures who live and think at a rate hundreds of times faster than humans. When he poses problems to them in the guise of their god, it takes them just two hundred days to replicate all known science, followed by unprecedented discoveries.

It was nothing less than an allegory for *Astounding,* which Campbell saw as a kind of time binding—an evolutionary collaboration between authors and fans to develop ideas at blinding speed. Campbell encouraged his writers to compete, to the point of handing out manuscripts to read at parties, and his ultimate goal was to create a new kind of person in both the magazine and its audience—a competent man who might pave the way for the superman to come. Even as he enthralled his readers, he was training them to think about the future.

The stakes would soon seem enormous. Campbell's thoughts were never far from the war in Europe—his sister Laura, who had attended Swarthmore College, had been in Paris when it fell, working with her husband at the U.S. embassy. The situation also affected the pulps, many of which had sold their remainders in England, where they were brought over as ballast on cargo ships. This source of revenue was gone, and publishers were unable to collect on their existing debts. Sales suffered, and the circulation of *Astounding* declined to around fifty thousand.

But Campbell was looking ahead to the next phase, in which he felt that science fiction would play a crucial role. He wrote that the Nazis had to be "science fiction addicts," judging from the part in the conflict that mechanization had assumed: "The battle of robots is on." And in his first editorial after the invasion of Poland, Campbell had written, "May we hope that attempts to release the unimaginable energy locked in uranium atoms, on a useful scale, remain complete and unmitigated failures until such time as the family fight in Europe is concluded?"

6.
IN TIMES TO COME
1939–1941

In 1939 and 1940 I deliberately took the war news about a month later, via Time *magazine, in order to dilute the emotional impact. Otherwise I would not have been able to concentrate on fiction writing at all. Emotional detachment is rather hard for me to achieve, so I cultivate it by various dodges whenever the situation is one over which I have no control.*

—ROBERT A. HEINLEIN, IN A LETTER TO JOHN W. CAMPBELL

Early in 1940, Hubbard decided to go to Alaska. He was one of the most highly paid authors in the pulps—his novel *Slaves of Sleep* had sold to *Unknown* for the largest check in that magazine's short history—and he was contributing regularly to Campbell, both in his own name and under such pseudonyms as René Lafayette, Kurt von Rachen, and Frederick Engelhardt. Campbell was a reliable market, and Hubbard was more than happy to use the editor's ideas. Yet he also had expectations for himself that a writing life was unable to satisfy.

Hubbard was dividing his time between South Colby, Washington, where he spent his summers, and New York, where he rented a winter apartment on Riverside Drive, setting up a typing nook with a curtain and a blue bulb that reduced the shine on the paper. He still didn't care much for science fiction, but he enjoyed fantasy. Despite his considerable following, he had minimal contact with fans, with whom he had little in common and who failed to strike him as immediately useful.

He was more interested in expanding his professional circle. At Campbell's invitation, he became a fixture at the war games at Fletcher Pratt's apartment, of which the editor wrote to him, "If you have the interest therein that you might well have, you would probably be welcomed with open arms." At these weekly gatherings, Hubbard met John Clark and de Camp, with whom he played poker, and he impressed everyone with his improvised voodoo drumming, beating out the rhythm so furiously that his hands were left bruised.

His work for *Astounding* had settled into a pattern, alternating between humorous fantasy, war or adventure yarns with superficially futuristic settings, and stories that looked like space opera but hinged on predictable twists. All were undermined by a palpable lack of interest in science. Hubbard, who had spun a colorful persona for himself out of thin air, saw through Campbell's pretensions about the competent man—many of his heroes were pointedly incompetent, and even when he offered up a more conventional lead, it was with a trace of contempt.

His stories for *Unknown* were much more diverting. *The Ultimate Adventure* had established the basic formula, which was driven by his fascination with the British explorer, spy, and scholar Sir Richard Francis Burton, who came closer than anyone else in history to his vision of himself, and whom he often mentioned by name. Campbell encouraged his strengths: "I'm convinced that you do like fantasy, enjoy it, and have a greater gift for fantasy than for almost any other type. . . . I'm reserving *The Arabian Nights* to you entirely."

There were occasional hints of things to come. Hubbard's alter ego, René Lafayette, appeared in a pair of stories in the role of a psychiatrist. "One Was Stubborn" described a cult leader who plans to rule the world by convincing his followers that it exists only in the brain, vaguely anticipating its author's later career, and in *The Indigestible Triton,* he echoed a growing interest of Campbell's: "The fact that psychiatry has succeeded in healing but a small percentage of the known ills of mind rather indicates that the subject is not, as yet, ready for its place among the sciences."

At times Hubbard grew tired of Campbell. In an essay titled "How to Drive a Writer Crazy," he listed the ways in which an editor could infuriate his authors: "When he starts to outline a story, immediately give him several stories just like it to read and tell him three other plots. . . . By showing his vast knowledge of a field, an editor can almost always frighten a writer into mental paralysis, especially on subjects where nothing is known anyway." But they remained close. In 1939, the Campbells invited Hubbard to Thanksgiving, and he was fond of Doña, who "kept things smooth" at the house and could make him bray with laughter.

Hubbard's stories appealed to such fans as Asimov and Ray Bradbury, but most were forgettable. The exceptions were *Death's Deputy,* perhaps his best story, which came out of conversations with Campbell about "a man who officiates, all unwillingly, for the god of destruction"; *Final Blackout,* the postnuclear war novel that had impressed Heinlein; and *Fear,* a work of straight horror that had been conceived over grilled steaks at the editor's house. Bradbury called this last story a "landmark novel in my life," and he was so taken by it that he privately recorded it as a play.

These three novels, which came out within six months of one another, benefited from a slight degree of extra attention. Hubbard's output was slowing, in part because he was seeking new outlets for his talents. Unlike Heinlein, he didn't see the pulps as an educational tool—Campbell was still in charge, and the stories weren't being read by the audience that he wanted to reach. Hubbard had a larger stage in mind, writing to the War Department on the day that hostilities broke out in Europe, "I wish to offer my services to the government in whatever capacity they might be of the greatest use." The proposal went unacknowledged.

He was longing to break out of his confines, and his attention turned to the Explorers Club, a society on East Seventieth Street founded to advance the cause of exploration. Hubbard, who wanted to be recognized as an explorer, was proposed for membership in December 1939, on the strength of his unremarkable excursions to the Caribbean and Puerto Rico. The following February he was accepted, and it remained a source of pride for the rest of his life.

In 1940, he began preparing for an expedition on which he would fly the club's flag for the first time, sailing the *Magician,* which he had bought with the advance from *Buckskin Brigades,* from Washington to Alaska. The voyage was supposedly intended to update navigational guides and test out new models of radio and camera gear, and Hubbard used it as an excuse to outfit his boat for free, writing letters to manufacturers on a special letterhead.

It may also have been one last attempt to save his relationship with Polly. Around this time, Hubbard's son, who was known as Nibs, was awakened one night by screaming. He was six years old. Peeking into his parents' room, he saw his father seated on his mother in their bed with a twisted coat hanger in his hands. Nibs went back to sleep, and the next day, he found a bloodstained sheet in the trash. Hubbard later said that Polly had undergone "five abortions" during their marriage.

In July, after submitting a few stories to Campbell and leaving their children with his aunt, Hubbard sailed out of Yukon Harbor with Polly, who was described in subsequent accounts of the voyage as "a deckhand." On the second day their engine failed in a heavy fog, and it conked out again off the coast of British Columbia. At last, on August 30, they made it to Ketchikan, a fishing community on the Alaska Panhandle. Their crankshaft was broken. Hubbard wrote in his log, "I anchored and lashed up. The town, despite rain, was awake. Ketchikan we have won. We arrived in Alaska. And maybe tomorrow we will even go ashore."

They were stranded there for months. Hubbard didn't have the money to fix the *Magician*, so he wrote letters instead to his friends, including Campbell, and mailed film and navigational notes to the Hydrographic Office in Washington, D.C. He befriended the owner of the local radio station, where he became a regular presence on the air, sharing tall tales of his adventures. One was an encounter with a swimming brown bear that he had allegedly lassoed at sea—it clawed its way on board, forcing Hubbard to flee into the cabin, and after the boat beached itself, it devoured the salmon in the hold and lumbered off.

As soon as the boat was repaired, they left Ketchikan, returning home shortly before Christmas. Hubbard, characteristically, spun it into the sort of colorful story that made him seem larger than life. Campbell ran an update on his travels in *Unknown*, stating that the author had suffered "a slight case of shipwreck," and he wrote to Swisher, "Ron, I think, is in for some kidding when he comes east again." On his return to New York, he got a phone call that began, "Cap'n, do you *like* to wrassle with bears?" And at the next war game, Clark, Pratt, and de Camp sang a satirical song in his honor—but it was the kind of affectionate ribbing that he enjoyed.

Hubbard went back to work. A few stories had appeared in his absence, notably the metafictional *Typewriter in the Sky*, and he connected with writers, including Pohl, whom he struck as a flamboyant character who seized the attention of everyone within earshot. Other distractions were less welcome. His most serious affair in New York had been with a woman named Helen, who cheated on him as well. When he found out about it, shortly after his return from Alaska, he almost took violent action: "I waited on the stairway with a gun, just for a moment. Then I said they are flies. I realized who and what I was and left."

In any case, his mind was elsewhere. Hubbard was convinced that the Japanese would attack sooner or later, and he still hoped to get into the Navy, soliciting recommendations from anyone he could find. When a state representative gave him a blank page of stationery and told him to write it himself, he obliged with a letter that began, "This will introduce one of the most brilliant men I have ever known." Campbell wrote on his behalf to Commander Lucius C. Dunn, noting that Hubbard produced good stories on deadline and concluding, "In personal relationships, I have the highest opinion of him as a thoroughly American gentleman."

When Hubbard took the medical exam for the Naval Reserve, however, he failed it—his eyes, which had kept him out of Annapolis, were just as bad as before. Shortly thereafter, President Roosevelt declared a state of national emergency in response to the rise of the Nazis, and the results of the vision test were waived. Hubbard was commissioned as a lieutenant, junior grade, in July 1941. On a visit to Campbell's office, he ran into Doña, who described him as delighted by his blue-and-gold uniform: "He was very beautiful and pleased with L. Ron."

Hubbard joined a public relations division in New York, where he worked on recruiting and pitched ideas for magazine articles, none of which was published. After a short trip to the Hydrographic Office in Washington, D.C., to annotate his pictures from Alaska, he returned to the city, where he began training at the headquarters of the Third Naval District. From there, he expected to head to the Philippines, where he would be ready for the war that he knew was coming.

BY THE TIME HUBBARD RETURNED FROM ALASKA, THERE WAS NO DOUBT THAT HE RANKED AMONG the most valued authors in Campbell's circle. The editor wrote to Heinlein, "There are about five consistent, adult-material science fiction writers in the business: de Camp, Heinlein, Hubbard, van Vogt, and, if he'll only work at it a little, del Rey." Asimov's name was notably absent, and Campbell's attitude toward his most junior writer was summed up in the faint praise he offered in the magazine: "Asimov is one of those authors who has to work long and hard to get his story, but is apt to have something worthwhile when he comes up for air."

Asimov bore only a passing resemblance to many of the authors developed by Campbell, who felt that most writers didn't "work their way up," and he didn't see himself as a competent man. He just wanted to be in the magazine—but even that often seemed out of reach. After "Trends," the editor bounced his next two stories, holding on to the second, "Pilgrimage," for a whole month. Asimov later learned that Campbell had been waiting on Heinlein's "If This Goes On—," because he didn't want to publish two works with religious themes too closely together, and when one turned out to be a masterpiece, he sent the other back.

After another round of rejections, Asimov wrote nothing for three months, depressed by the war and by troubles at school. In July 1939, Columbia had turned down his application for graduate study, which lacked a required course in physical chemistry. When he tried to sign up anyway, the department head, the Nobel laureate Harold Urey, almost threw him out of the building. Asimov finally found a loophole that allowed him to register, and he quietly applied to medical schools on the side, although he had doubts about whether he even wanted to become a doctor.

He remained close to the Futurians, but their lives were diverging. Most of his friends were unemployed and trying unsuccessfully to break into the magazines, and several had moved into an apartment on Bedford Avenue that became known as the Ivory

Tower. The Futurians also began hanging around the candy store, and his mother grew fond of Pohl, who encouraged Asimov by buying some of the stories that Campbell had rejected.

In December, Asimov came up with a premise in which Earth, after developing spaceflight, is approached for membership in the Galactic Federation but refuses. Unexpectedly, Campbell loved it. His casual assumption that Europeans had an advantage over other races led to stories in which humans were shown to be superior to aliens, and Asimov's idea fit perfectly into that theme.

On January 4, 1940, Asimov delivered "Homo Sol." At the office, he met three writers for the first time—Sturgeon, Willy Ley, and Hubbard. He was surprised by Hubbard's impressive appearance. Most of Hubbard's fiction was about small, weak men, and Asimov blurted out, "You don't look at all like your stories."

Hubbard seemed amused by the younger author. "Why? How are my stories?"

"Oh, they're *great*," Asimov said. Everybody laughed as he awkwardly clarified that he didn't mean that Hubbard wasn't great, too, and he left feeling embarrassed by the encounter.

Campbell eventually took "Homo Sol," but Asimov had trouble following up. A sequel lacked the theme of human excellence, and the editor didn't buy it. In a letter to the magazine, Asimov wrote, "I can detect that fiendish look that comes over editor Campbell's face when about to give me his opinion of the tripe *I* cook and call—*heh, heh*—stories." Yet it clearly bothered him. When Campbell spoke highly of another writer's work, Asimov's face fell, prompting the editor to say gently, "Do you think, Asimov, that because I like his stories, I like yours any less?"

Asimov was also displeased by the version of "Homo Sol" that appeared in the magazine. Campbell had inserted a new speech and an ending that he didn't like, and Asimov had reluctantly added a section that contrasted the differing reactions of Africans, Asians, and Europeans, in a sign of the editor's interest in mass psychology. It was a theme that was figuring prominently in *Astounding*. In his note for "If This Goes On—," Campbell had written:

> *Robert Heinlein . . . presents a civilization in which mob psychology and propaganda have become sciences. They aren't, yet. . . . Psychology isn't a science, so long as a trained psychologist does—and must—say "there's no telling how an individual man will react to a given stimulus." Properly developed, psychology could determine that.*

Campbell—who consulted a psychologist about his recurrent panic attacks—was eager to explore the subject. Developments in atomic energy had made it impossible to write about the invention of nuclear power ever again, and a new kind of discovery story was needed. Pulling back from galactic expanses, he focused on the mind and on society, and readers noticed. Toward the end of 1940, a fan named Lynn Bridges wrote in a prescient letter:

> *The* Astounding Science Fiction *of the past year has brought forth a new type of story, best described, perhaps, as "sociological" science fiction. . . . Both Asimov [in "Homo Sol"] and Heinlein treat psychology as an exact science, usable in formulas, certain in results. I feel called upon to protest. Its very nature prevents psychology from achieving the exactness of mathematics.*

Bridges went on to express concern that a true science of psychology would mark an end to human progress, to which Campbell replied, "Psychology could improve a lot, though, without becoming dangerously oppressive!"

"Homo Sol" was an early example of Campbell's fondness for incorporating gratuitous psychological elements into stories, and Asimov smarted under it. Campbell had also added a few lines on Earth's ability to make war, giving it a militaristic tone that Asimov thought was poorly timed. The whole experience left a bad taste in his mouth, and he decided to avoid aliens entirely—a choice that would have important consequences for his career.

Later that summer, Asimov went to the beach for the first time, and he was about to reach a milestone as a writer as well. "Robbie," which Pohl had bought for *Super Science Stories*, was his personal favorite of all his works, and he realized that writing about robots would neatly sidestep the problem of humans and aliens. Recalling Campbell's interest in religious themes, he pitched a story about a robot who refused to believe that he had been created by human beings. Campbell was enthusiastic, and as Asimov left, the editor said, "Remember, I want to see that story."

Asimov felt the pressure, and it took him four tries to find the right opening. When he confessed his problems, Campbell offered some useful advice: "Asimov, when you have trouble with the beginning of the story, that is because you are starting in the wrong place, and almost certainly too soon. Pick out a later point in the story and begin again." It was a rule that the editor had learned firsthand—Campbell had ruthlessly cut the original openings from many of his own stories—and it did the trick. When Asimov submitted "Reason," with a pair of characters inspired by Campbell's Penton and Blake, he received an acceptance check within a week.

Another turning point was just around the corner. On December 23, Asimov proposed a sequel about a robot that could read minds. Campbell liked it, and after they had tossed the idea back and forth, the editor said, "Look, Asimov, in working this out, you have to realize that there are three rules that robots have to follow. In the first place, they can't do any harm to human beings; in the second place, they have to obey orders without doing harm;

in the third, they have to protect themselves, without doing harm or proving disobedient."

The result, after some refinement, would become known as Three Laws of Robotics, and their impact would be felt endlessly in Asimov's fiction, in stories by other writers, and in the fields of robotics—a word that Asimov coined without realizing it—and artificial intelligence. When Asimov later tried to give credit to Campbell, the editor replied, "No, Asimov, I picked them out of your stories and your discussions. You didn't state them explicitly, but they were there." Asimov thought that he was just being polite, and in fact, only a rudimentary version of the First Law was visible in any of the earlier stories.

They also reflected Campbell's fascination with the mind. The editor later wrote that the laws were "the basic desires of a small child," and they foreshadowed his subsequent efforts to define the rules of human behavior. Asimov—who compared them to the principles of "a good many of the world's ethical systems"—was interested in this problem as well. In his story "The Imaginary," he evoked the equations of a "mathematical psychology," and he expressed hope in a letter to the magazine that it might result in fewer Hitlers and more Einsteins. Campbell responded, "Psychology isn't an exact science—but it can be."

Asimov's robot stories "Reason" and "Liar!"—the latter of which featured the debut of the robopsychologist Dr. Susan Calvin—appeared in successive issues, establishing the series in the eyes of readers. Campbell cautioned him against becoming tied down to a formula, however, and when Asimov came to visit on March 17, 1941, the editor wanted to discuss an idea of his own. Campbell read him a line from an essay by Ralph Waldo Emerson: "If the stars should appear one night in a thousand years, how would men believe and adore; and preserve for many generations the remembrance of the city of God which had been shown!"

He set the book aside. "What do you think would happen,

Asimov, if men were to see the stars for the first time in a thousand years?"

Asimov—who never read the essay himself and tried unsuccessfully to find it later—replied lamely, "I don't know."

"I think they would go mad," Campbell said. "I want you to write a story about that."

It was the second plot that the editor had pitched on the theme of men going mad, after "Blowups Happen," and it emerged directly from his interest in psychology. Campbell had never entrusted him with an idea before—Asimov wasn't sure if the editor had been saving it for him in particular, or if he just happened to be the first author who came into the office that day—and it felt like a test. For now, they brainstormed reasons why the stars might not be visible at other times, and the editor closed by saying, "Go home and write the story."

They agreed to call it "Nightfall," and it came quickly. Asimov wrote in his diary, "I never had anything write itself so easily." When he submitted it, Campbell asked for a few revisions, taking the opportunity to snap some pictures of Asimov, who had "a lean and hungry, somewhat pimply, mustached look." A new draft came in shortly afterward. Willy Ley was staying overnight in Scotch Plains, and after reading it, he said, "From what you told me about the story, I knew it would be good, but I didn't know it would be *this* good."

When Asimov got the check, he called Campbell to say that he had been overpaid—which was how he found out that he had been awarded a bonus. "Nightfall" would later be voted the greatest science fiction story of all time, although its themes—the cyclical fall of civilizations, the warnings of disaster that go unheeded, the foundation of scientists who preserve knowledge for the coming dark age—would be more fully developed elsewhere. And in stating that humanity would be unprepared to confront its insignificance in the universe, it looked faintly ahead to the possibility of a solution, despite the bleakness of its last line: "The long night had come again."

On August 1, Asimov was riding the train to his monthly visit when he decided to try coming up with another story idea. Opening the book that he was carrying—a collection of Gilbert and Sullivan lyrics—to a random page, he saw an illustration of a scene from the comic opera *Iolanthe*. His eyes skipped past the Fairy Queen, who may have seemed too feminine, to the unassuming figure of Private Willis. It made him think of soldiers and empires, and when he got to the office, he told Campbell that he wanted to write a future history, like Heinlein's, that chronicled the collapse of the Galactic Empire, inspired by Gibbon's *Decline and Fall*.

Campbell grew excited. Working together, they came up with the premise of a foundation of psychohistorians who had turned the study of human behavior into a science that could accurately forecast the fate of a civilization far into the future. It also drew on another of Campbell's interests: "He felt in our discussion that symbolic logic, further developed, would so clear up the mysteries of the human mind as to leave human actions predictable."

The editor had already been thinking along these lines. He had published an article by de Camp on theories of history from Spengler to Toynbee, which had gained a new resonance in light of the crisis in Europe, and, even more significantly, on April 16, 1941—more than three months before his meeting with Asimov— Jack Williamson had written to him, "I'm interested in theories of the growth and decay of cultures. . . . It would be interesting, I think, to show the logical culmination of that process in an interstellar civilization."

When Asimov made his pitch, Williamson's "Backlash" had been on newsstands for nearly two weeks. It featured "a scientific Shangri-La, to be a lamp of culture through the dark ages ahead," while a later story, "Breakdown," spoke of "politicotechnic theories" that could "reduce the laws of the rise and fall of human cultures to [an] exact science." If Campbell decided to pursue the same concept more aggressively with another writer, it was largely because Asimov was younger, compliant, and closer at hand. He made his choice. "That's too large a theme for a short story."

For once in his life, Asimov was ready with a reply. "I was thinking of a novelette."

"Or a novelette," Campbell said. "It will have to be an open-ended series of stories."

Asimov hadn't been expecting this. He found himself at a loss for words. "What?"

"Short stories, novelettes, serials, all fitting into a particular future history, involving the fall of the First Galactic Empire, the period of feudalism that follows, and the rise of the Second Galactic Empire." The editor advised him to establish another, secret foundation on the other side of the galaxy—"You may need the second one later on"—and ended with an order: "I want you to write an outline of the future history. Go home and write the outline."

Asimov tried to do as he had been told. When he started the timeline, however, he felt stuck. Tearing it up, he got to work on the first story, "Foundation," which would take place in a galaxy inhabited entirely by humans, avoiding the issue of aliens altogether. Campbell took it, but without a bonus—it was less striking as a story than for the concept of psychohistory, which it treated only in passing. It ended with the words "The solution to this first crisis was obvious. Obvious as all hell!" But Asimov didn't know the answer himself, and he had to deliver a sequel soon.

At their meeting on October 27, Campbell's first words were "I want that Foundation story." It was enough to bring Asimov's work, which had been going well, to a halt. Feeling desperate, Asimov went for a stroll across the Brooklyn Bridge with Pohl, who made a few suggestions that allowed the series to continue. He was deeply grateful, although he later learned that they had gone for a walk mostly because Pohl's girlfriend, Leslie Perri, disliked him intensely.

Asimov was drifting away from the Futurians. He had tired of all the drama, and he didn't fit in with the others—he didn't drink, smoke, or have sex. Instead, he grew closer to his fellow writers, and he even attended one of Pratt's war games, where his three destroyers were sunk by a cruiser. Asimov sat out the rest, eating peanuts and drinking two beers. Hubbard was there as well, but he never made any effort to befriend Asimov, who clearly wasn't worth his time.

The younger author's mind was on other matters. Earlier that year, Campbell had told him that there was a cubic foot of uranium in Pupin Hall at Columbia. It was the first time that Asimov had ever heard of nuclear fission, and when he expressed concern, Campbell replied, "Why? Do you think you would be any safer in Brooklyn if that uranium exploded?"

In fact, there was no danger of an explosion, but the knowledge weighed on Asimov, who had just obtained his master's degree. He later attended a lecture on thermodynamics delivered by his old nemesis, Professor Harold Urey, who lamented that he was the only one in his department who didn't have interesting war work. Asimov piped up, "But Professor Urey, what are you talking about? What about the cubic foot of uranium in Pupin? Isn't that your field?"

Urey turned crimson. Finally, he managed to say, "Some people talk too much."

Asimov knew exactly what was going on, and a few months later, he registered for the draft. Because he was still in school, he was given a deferred classification, but events in the wider world were moving inexorably forward.

On June 22, 1941, the Nazis had invaded Russia. When the news broke, Campbell argued about it with Lester del Rey for four hours, insisting that Russia wouldn't last six weeks. The two men then took the train to New Jersey, where the author watched with amazement as Campbell told another passenger that the Nazis didn't stand a chance—and added a few new points of his own. Not only had he changed his mind, but he had even improved on the argument.

Asimov had a rather different reaction to the invasion. When the word came that the Nazis had taken the Smolensk district, he knew exactly what would happen to the villagers who had remained in Petrovichi. Deep down, he wanted to believe that psychohistory meant that Hitler's defeat was inevitable, but at the rate that the war was going, he feared that he could expect nothing but an early death. When de Camp asked him why, Asimov simply replied, "Because I'm a Jew."

BY 1941, HEINLEIN WAS ON THE VERGE OF BECOMING THE MOST RESPECTED WRITER IN SCIENCE fiction. The high point was the May issue of *Astounding,* which included the complete timeline of his Future History. It was an unprecedented act of generosity toward an individual writer, as well as the first hint of a hidden theme in his stories—in his future, the earth fell apart after the most competent people went into space. In an editor's note, Campbell wrote to readers:

> *It might be of very real interest to you to trace in on this suggestion of the future your own life line. My own, I imagine, should extend up to about 1980—a bit beyond the time of "Roads Must Roll" and "Blowups Happen." My children may see the days of "The Logic of Empire."*

The issue also featured Heinlein's "Universe," which was based on Campbell's premise about a lost generation starship. Heinlein hadn't been sure that he was right for it—"Van Vogt probably could do a better job"—but it became one of his most acclaimed works, with a plot that turned, like "Nightfall," on the psychological impact of a first glimpse of the stars.

Its most interesting story, however, was one that Heinlein published as Anson MacDonald. Years before the Cold War, Campbell pitched the idea of a superweapon, based on radioactive dust, that led to a destructive arms race. He proposed a twist ending that revealed that the narrator was a member of a new, superior species created by mutation, but Heinlein didn't like it: "Too reminiscent of *Slan* and too much like a rabbit out of a hat." But he failed to come up with anything better, and the finished story ended with the creation of a global police force that has monopoly power over the weapon, effectively holding the rest of the world hostage.

When Campbell read it, he replied, "The story is weak, because the solution is so palpably synthetic and unsatisfactory—and that very fact can be made, by proper blurbing, the greatest strength of the story." It was a masterstroke of editing, and "Solution Unsatisfactory" closed with a note to the reader: "Can any solution not invoking the aid of the Arisian super-beings"—the aliens in E. E. Smith's Lensman stories—"protect mankind against the irresistible weapon?" And the editor's answer, which arose years later in dianetics, turned out to depend on a certain kind of superman after all.

Campbell and Heinlein moved on to an ambitious story about extreme longevity, with a colorful protagonist, Lazarus Long, who was over two hundred years old. Heinlein sent in the first section for notes before proceeding further, and they corresponded about it at length. *Methuselah's Children* turned out to be an exuberant, if superficial, masterpiece, and it testified to the extent to which the editor had replaced Leslyn as Heinlein's reader of choice. It was followed by "By His Bootstraps," a fully realized attempt to exploit the paradoxes of time travel. Heinlein thought it was "cotton candy," but Campbell loved it.

John W. Campbell, circa 1942.
Courtesy of Leslyn Randazzo

All the while, the question lurked of what would happen if Campbell rejected a submission. Heinlein said that he valued their friendship too highly to risk it over work: "If you someday find it necessary to start rejecting my stuff, I expect to take a crack at some other forms." For now, the prospect seemed remote, and Heinlein was touched when the editor casually numbered him among his best authors: "To be classed as one among the sort of writers you have attracted to *Astounding* is one of the most completely satisfying things that has ever happened to me."

Campbell's praise was more than justified—the genre was still confined to the pulps, but within that closed world, Heinlein had inspired greater devotion than any writer since E. E. Smith. As the guest of honor at the third World Science Fiction Convention in Denver, he was pestered by a group of Futurians and told the crowd in his speech, "Mrs. Heinlein and I are in almost complete collaboration on everything. She never signs any of the stories, but I do better if she's there." On his return, he submitted "Creation Took Eight Days," a story inspired by the work of the paranormal researcher Charles Fort, and he had no reason to expect anything but the usual reception.

On August 21, Campbell rejected it. The letter that he sent was weirdly impersonal, addressed to "Mr. Heinlein" rather than the familiar "Bob," and signed with the editor's full name. Instead of the customary detailed critique, it was brief to the point of opacity: "The basic trouble is that it lacks point; nothing of particularly convincing importance occurs in the story. I'm afraid it simply has no punch." He didn't elaborate further, although he may also have been concerned by its parallels to Eric Frank Russell's *Sinister Barrier*.

When Heinlein received the rejection, he felt a twinge of regret, but he was secretly relieved that he no longer had to write. A few days later he wrote to propose that the editor send a weekly letter to the Mañana Literary Society, for which Heinlein would serve as an "unofficial scout." He had generous words for "Nightfall" and its author: "We were delighted to see Asimov in the cover position. . . . As a young prodigy yourself, I think you will admit that Isaac's present stuff is more subtle, sensitive, and mature than yours of ten years back."

Campbell replied a week later. His tone was friendly again, and he said that he hoped Heinlein would send more fiction soon, adding, "Asimov is one of my personal finds; he had ideas, word-sense, but couldn't write up an obituary when he first submitted." There was no discussion of retirement, and in his response, Heinlein made the situation more explicit:

> *You are apparently under the impression that I am still writing. To be sure, I did not drop you a card saying,*

*"I retired today." I could not—under the circumstances
it would have seemed like a childish piece of petulance.
Nevertheless I knew that I would retire and exactly when
and why, and I sent a letter to you a number of months
back in which I set forth my intention and my reasons.
Surely you recall it?*

The letter exuded a sense of wounded pride that must have troubled him even as he was typing it, and he ended by softening the threat, offering to write as a hobby whenever an idea occurred to him: "It seems funny that I should be retiring on page two and suggesting a serial on page five."

In his reply, Campbell apologized, saying that he had been sick with the flu when he wrote the rejection. He added that it was the product of "pressure and uncertainty" at the office, and he hinted that perhaps the story could be saved. When Heinlein replied that he would try to write occasionally, the editor was relieved: "If you retire abruptly at this particular moment, *Astounding* is going to feel it in much the way one's tongue feels a missing tooth just after it's been yanked."

Heinlein revised the submission according to the editor's instructions, and it was published as "Goldfish Bowl." It was a seemingly inconclusive episode, but it marked a fundamental shift. At worst, Heinlein had been cutting back, not retiring, but he framed it as an ultimatum. If Campbell blinked first, it was for much the same reason that he hadn't pushed Asimov to use a pen name—in the long run, it was less important than everything he had in mind.

It effectively put them on equal footing, and within weeks they were trading ideas as avidly as ever. Heinlein pitched a serial about a society that used selective breeding to create a superman, but he wasn't sure how to write it. Campbell proposed that instead of a straight utopia, he frame it as a conflict between two opposing philosophies, and in the same letter he included a striking tribute:

What you contributed to science fiction was a direct expression of what I'd been vaguely groping for—personalized, emotionalized science fiction instead of intellectualized stuff. Your prime strengths are two—reality of personalities who have reasonable emotional reactions, and a reality of technical-political-social culture against which they can react.

It was an acknowledgment of what both of them knew, but had never said aloud. Campbell was looking for stories that felt like they could appear in a "slick" magazine a century in the future, and Heinlein was the realization of everything that he had wanted, but had been unable to bring off on his own.

The hint got Heinlein unstuck, and he set the story in an aggressive dueling culture, for which he coined the problematic aphorism "An armed society is a polite society." Campbell proposed that he come out to work on it in New Jersey, but Heinlein feared that it was too late—he had been asked to volunteer to route merchant traffic in San Pedro, which was a transparent excuse to ensure his availability in case of war. In a phone call to Campbell in the last week of November, he said, "If the Japanese start a war with us, as it looks as if they intend to, then they will do so this coming weekend and probably on Sunday."

As it turned out, he was off by a few days. He finished *Beyond This Horizon* in a burst of activity and mailed it on December 1. It included the earliest definition in his fiction of the "encyclopedic synthesist," a figure capable of consolidating information from a wide range of disciplines, but when Doña wrote that Heinlein seemed like one himself, he demurred, "I would like to have been a synthesist, but I am acutely aware that many of my characteristics are second-rate. . . . Don't discount this as false modesty; you two are among the very, very few (less than half a dozen) to whom I feel safe in speaking truthfully."

Beyond This Horizon was as dense and strange as "Lost Legacy," and it was profoundly influenced by Leslyn, who casually spoke of the story as if they had written it together. If it hadn't been for their earlier confrontation, Campbell might not have taken it, but it arrived on his desk at a later stage in their partnership. Like Hubbard and Asimov, Heinlein was defining himself as a writer through his relationship with Campbell—and the careers of all four men might have unfolded very differently if they hadn't been put on hold by the disruptions to come.

IN A LETTER TO HEINLEIN, CAMPBELL HAD MENTIONED A DEPARTMENT, PROBABILITY ZERO, THAT HE was trying to launch in the magazine. The new section would consist of very short "tall stories" that hinged on amusingly impossible science: "Like that yarn about the grandfather clock that was so old the shadow of the pendulum had worn a hole in the back." He hoped that it would serve as an entry point for new writers, but he needed a few submissions from more established authors to fill it out first, and he asked Heinlein to spread the word.

Campbell had also requested a contribution from Asimov, who wrote two stories that were promptly rejected. Asimov was annoyed by this, and he decided to try just one more time. The resulting story, "Time Pussy," didn't take him long to finish, and he was done by early afternoon. Asimov turned on the radio in the apartment, keeping the volume low so that he wouldn't disturb his father, who was taking a nap in the next room. Just before three o'clock, the music cut out and was replaced by a news bulletin. It was December 7, 1941.

III.

THE INVADERS

1941–1945

In a short war, invention has no time to apply its full weight; in a long-term conflict, the role of inventive ingenuity will be powerful, if not ultimately decisive. In as thoroughly unpleasant a world as we now inhabit, there's a definite element of comfort in that. A people with the record of inventive ability that Americans have proven can, if forced to it, make of itself a most terrible enemy.

—JOHN W. CAMPBELL, *ASTOUNDING*, JANUARY 1941

7.
A COLD FURY

1941–1944

You've told me that I was your best writer—but I'm also a slightly antiquated crack gunnery officer; I ought to just fit on some slightly antiquated guns. We can afford to take a chance that guns will do a little more toward winning the war than my stories would.

—ROBERT A. HEINLEIN, IN A LETTER TO JOHN W. CAMPBELL

Campbell heard about the attack on Pearl Harbor in a phone call from Heinlein. When the telephone rang at his house that evening, he could tell from the sound of the ring that it was long distance, which told him what to expect before he even answered. As a result, he seemed so unemotional at the news that Heinlein felt obliged to say, "I'm not kidding, you know."

After Heinlein told him that he and Leslyn wouldn't be able to visit for the holidays, Campbell passed the phone to Doña, who said that it was hard to decide what affected her the most—her sadness at their canceled trip or her feelings as an American. John echoed this the next day, writing that he was "gloomy as hell" that the Heinleins weren't coming. And Doña wrote, "But do, both of you, take very good care of my daughter's only godparents. They are very precious, to all three of us."

Heinlein's call to Campbell was the second one that he had placed. The first had been to the naval personnel office in San Diego, asking to be assigned back to active duty. One of the ships struck in the attack had been the USS *Oklahoma,* on which Hubbard's father had served as an assistant gunnery officer, and where Heinlein had sailed on a practice cruise in 1927. At Pearl Harbor, the battleship, which had been believed to be unsinkable, took five torpedoes, with more than four hundred men killed or missing. As Heinlein wrote to Campbell:

> *Pearl Harbor isn't a point on a floor game to me—I've been there. The old* Okie *isn't a little wooden model six inches long; she's a person to me.... And the casualty lists at Oahu are not names in a newspaper to me; they are my friends, my classmates. The thing hit me with such utter sickening grief as I have not experienced before in my life and has left me with a feeling of loss of personal honor such as I never expected to experience.*

He was fiercely patriotic, and when the war began, he was racked with guilt at the knowledge that it had caught him as a civilian. His feelings were swiftly transformed into "a cold fury" toward the Japanese: "I not only want them to be defeated, I want them to be smashed. I want them to be punished at least a hundredfold, their cities burned, their industries smashed, their fleet destroyed, and finally their sovereignty taken away from them." He was under no illusions that he would be allowed at sea—there was scarring on his lungs from tuberculosis—but he badly wanted shore duty. In the magazine, Campbell wrote that Anson MacDonald, Heinlein's alter ego, was "somewhere in the Pacific," but this was wishful thinking. And when Ray Bradbury joked that if he were at risk of being drafted he would pretend to be gay, Heinlein was so offended that he refused to speak to him for years.

One member of the team was ready for action. Hubbard, who had been actively preparing for war, heard about the bombing from a "bum" at a cigar store on Eighth Avenue, and he was assigned to the Philippines in December. He made much of his family's naval tradition, claiming that his father had been the commander of the USS *Astoria*—in fact, he had been a supply officer—when it returned the ashes of the ambassador Hiroshi Saito to Japan in 1939. Doña wrote admiringly to the Heinleins, "He'll probably turn up in Greenland, in a typical Ron-like way."

Asimov was in less of a hurry. While Heinlein, Hubbard, and Campbell saw the war as a chance to fulfill their destinies—a rite of passage that would demonstrate that they were the equals of the competent men of their fiction—Asimov viewed it as a distraction from his chosen path. Unlike the others, he was young enough to be eligible for the draft, so he didn't need to invent a role for himself. When the war was ready, it would come for him.

But he was still emotionally affected. On the day after the attack, he took "Time Pussy" to Campbell, who accepted it "none too enthusiastically." At their meeting, Asimov told the editor that he was so furious with the Japanese that he wasn't really mad at Hitler anymore—a sentiment that struck Campbell as faintly amusing when uttered by a Russian Jew. For the next two months Asimov wrote nothing at all, and he spent much of his time riveted to the radio.

As air raid drills were conducted in New York, Campbell prepared a bomb shelter in his basement, and his family geared up for the war effort. Several years earlier, his father had been promoted to outside plant engineer in the Operation and Engineering Department of AT&T, placing him in charge of emergency stocks of materials and preparations against sabotage. His sister Laura, who had returned from Paris, was preparing to join her new husband at a diplomatic posting in Nigeria, while Doña organized a Red Cross class for women in their neighborhood.

The only one who seemed unsure of his place was Campbell himself. He wrote to Heinlein, "My own status is somewhat confusing to me now. The optimum application of my efforts would seem to be somewhere in the propaganda line—which is notoriously overcrowded. The present work is, it seems to me, a form of indirect propaganda, and probably about as useful a station as I could find anywhere." Unlike Heinlein, who had a position for himself in mind, Campbell had never come to any conclusion, although he had long mulled over his potential role in the war.

At first Heinlein sympathized with his uncertainty. He agreed that Campbell, given his age and medical history, wouldn't make good "cannon fodder," but he was ready with a counterproposal: "I suppose it has already occurred to you that there might be a spot for you in the national research program. In spite of the fact that you have been out of lab work for a number of years, it ought to be your field of greatest usefulness, and I hear they are shorthanded."

Campbell agreed that his best contribution might be as a head of research—a kind of encyclopedic synthesist. He was realistic enough about his qualifications, however, to know that his chances of landing such a position were nonexistent. Aside from his stint at Pioneer Instruments, he had minimal lab experience, and the skills that he used to generate ideas at *Astounding* were modest compared to what it would take to run projects within the military.

He was also worried that his magazines would die without him. In response, Heinlein made an extraordinary suggestion: "Of course, it would be kinda rough on Street & Smith for you to go into research or such, but, as has been pointed out a long time ago, Doña could do just as good a job of editing, if she had to, as you do. With a maid-cook at home she would keep those two books going, quality high and making money, for the duration."

Heinlein went on to propose that Leslyn and Doña run the magazines together—a remarkable acknowledgment of their uncredited roles in their husbands' careers. Campbell was less bullish, writing to Heinlein, "I doubt [Doña would] get the job, which would be stupidity on the part of S&S. She hasn't written anything, hasn't edited, has no reputation or proof of ability in that line that's official. We know—but they may not." In the margin, Doña wrote, "Ha! Such is the power of love." But she also pointed out that finding someone to watch the baby was easier said than done.

A new source of tension soon arose. After the outbreak of hostilities, Campbell had appointed himself the resident expert at the office, where he pulled out maps to explain the situation to his coworkers. In the process, he heard criticisms of the military's lack of preparedness, including some from Fletcher Pratt, who remarked that "the British once shot an admiral for a lesser dereliction of duty" than Pearl Harbor. Campbell passed his comments along to Heinlein, who became livid, saying that it came "perilously close to giving aid and comfort to the enemy."

The editor missed the hint, writing back to repeat the same points, while adding a few of his own. It prompted a pair of savage replies from the Heinleins, which Doña had the misfortune of opening first. Heinlein informed Campbell that he had written—but not mailed—a long response "to stir you up off your fat fanny," and in the letter that he did send he didn't pull his punches: "When it comes to matters outside your specialties, you are consistently and brilliantly stupid." He warned Campbell to avoid speaking in those terms to anyone in the service: "Don't write to Ron in such a vein. He has not my indoctrination and he is in the battlefield."

As he typed the letter, Heinlein began to weep. After regaining his composure, he resumed in a gentler tone. Campbell had said that he was looking into a reserve commission as a factory inspector, and Heinlein was glad to hear it, although he also revealed his earlier misgivings:

> To be frank . . . I have been slightly perturbed that you might be all out for the war effort—except of course for Astounding, Unknown, and their editor. But apparently you realize as I do that it doesn't matter if you lose your job or I my market for fiction as long as we can preserve our own way of life and make it safe from bastards like the Sons of Heaven and the Nazis.

Heinlein added that if science fiction was necessary for morale, the public could make do with what the inferior pulps were publishing, and he concluded, "By the way, talk to that young idiot Asimov—he wants to go fight. M.S.'s in physical chemistry aren't cannon fodder."

Leslyn was less accommodating. In a letter that displayed her intelligence at its most forceful, she rebuked Campbell for speaking of Pratt and his circle as if they were something other than the general public, using a devastating analogy to drive her point home: "Don't you realize what that bunch are, John? *They're an 'organized fan' club.*" She pointed out that Campbell would never permit a fan to tell him how to run his magazine, and she noted that Hubbard was one of the few in that crowd who had actually become a professional.

It was an unanswerable argument—with its unstated implication that Campbell was little more than "an organized fan" of science—and the editor wrote back to apologize, calling himself "a clumsy oaf" who was only good at shoving his foot in his mouth. He also assured them that he wouldn't dream of speaking in such terms to Hubbard. Heinlein accepted the apology, saying that the exchange of letters had provided him with the emotional catharsis that he had needed.

He also had more important news to share. A lieutenant commander named Albert "Buddy" Scoles, whom Heinlein had known at Annapolis, was the assistant chief engineer for materials at the Naval Aircraft Factory in Philadelphia, informally known as the Navy Yard. Scoles, a science fiction fan, had written to ask Heinlein if *Astounding* would be interested in publishing an article on technical problems that the military was trying to solve. In a postscript, he added, "Incidentally, how would you like to go back to active duty and go to work here in the Factory?"

It was framed as an afterthought, but it was exactly the call that Heinlein had been awaiting. He shot back a postcard to confirm his interest, and after discussing the offer by phone, he reached out to Campbell. It was only because of his stories, Heinlein wrote, that Scoles had contacted him at all, and there might be a role for Campbell as well: "You are likely to have quite a lot to do with my job—from a minimum of helping by talking with me to a maximum of possibly serving as a commissioned officer, coordinate with or superior to me."

Campbell replied that he hoped "most ardently" that it would come through. He was even more relieved that they were still speaking: "The greatest disturbance caused by your two letters last time was a very genuine fear that I might have busted up a friendship that meant a deal more to us than any single friendship should, perhaps, for our own emotional safety." Doña seconded this: "My concern lay solely in the fear that . . . a friendship very precious to us would go completely on the rocks, and all through mishandling of ideas and words on poor, unknowing John's part."

Heinlein flew out to visit Scoles in Philadelphia, where he was told that the job, if it materialized, would involve recruiting engineers. He recommended de Camp, who had applied for the Naval Reserve, and he apparently also thought of Asimov. In February, the Heinleins moved in with the Campbells for two months. Leslyn wanted to land a factory position, but she was suffering from gallstones, and she was worried for her sister, Keith, who had been on the Philippine island of Luzon with her family when the Japanese invaded.

At his friend John Arwine's apartment, Heinlein set up a meeting with Scoles, Campbell, and de Camp, who was anxious to join. Campbell's situation was less clear. He was having second thoughts about his ability to pass a physical exam, so he decided to apply to the National Defense Research Committee through a friend of his father's. He didn't want to commit himself to the Navy Yard—he still hoped to find what he saw as a more meaningful role—and there was also the problem of relocating. With a wife who had just given birth under difficult circumstances, a baby, and two vulnerable magazines, he was reluctant to leave for Philadelphia.

The men set their sights on another likely recruit. Earlier that month, Campbell had told Asimov that Heinlein was in town, and he had added enigmatically that the author should come to him first if he were at any risk of being drafted. On March 2, 1942, Asimov visited the office to see Hubert Rogers, who had painted the cover for "Nightfall," and he was surprised to find Heinlein there as well. It was the first time that they had ever met.

A week later Campbell invited Asimov to his house. On March 11, Asimov took the subway to the ferry, proceeding by train to Scotch Plains, which was a considerable journey by his standards. On his arrival, he asked a station agent how far it was to the editor's neighborhood. The agent said, "Very far."

Asimov walked as fast as he could for half an hour. When he got there, he apologized for being late, explaining that he didn't know how long the walk would be. Campbell was amazed: "Why didn't you call? I would have come and got you by car." Asimov was embarrassed to admit that he hadn't even thought of it.

Along with the Campbells and the Heinleins, the guests that

evening included Willy Ley, Hubert Rogers, and their wives. At one point Heinlein offered Asimov what looked like a cola. When Asimov asked what it was, Heinlein replied, "It's a Coke. Go ahead, drink it down."

Asimov obliged. It was a Cuba Libre, Heinlein's cocktail of choice, and his face grew red. Asimov wasn't a drinker—after accepting "one ounce of blended rye" at de Camp's apartment, he had taken the train three times around Manhattan before trusting himself to walk home—and he sank into the corner, trying to collect himself. Until then, he had been talking loudly, and Heinlein laughed. "No wonder Isaac doesn't drink. It sobers him up."

Heinlein later dimmed the lights to show slides of some nude photos that he had taken, which Asimov studied with interest. He sensed that his maturity was being tested—he was a decade younger than either Heinlein or Campbell—but he evidently passed. At the end of the month, he received a job offer from Scoles.

The Heinleins and the Campbells spent their time together as pleasantly as they could. Campbell wrote of his daughter, "[Philinda] started making eyes at Bob the day he arrived, and has been working on him ever since. She's been flirting with Leslyn very effectively, too." The couples went out on the town, and Campbell felt the pinch: "They took us to shows, but damn it, taxi fares, meals, train fare, hiring someone to stay with Peeds, six or eight times begins to mean real money. Damn these freelances; they can afford it."

But not all was well. Heinlein's application had stalled, and Leslyn's health problems made it unlikely that she would get the factory role that she wanted. Both were tense—Leslyn told Heinlein much later that she was irrationally convinced that he was trying to poison her—and Heinlein took refuge in fiction. At Scotch Plains, with Campbell's input, he wrote "Waldo" and "The Unpleasant Profession of Jonathan Hoag," framing the latter around an affectionate portrait of a married couple not unlike

the Heinleins themselves. They would be his last stories until after the war.

In April, Arwine entered the Coast Guard, and the Heinleins
moved into his apartment. Heinlein figured out that an issue in his
disciplinary file—stemming from the angry letter to the *Citizen-
News* that he had written years earlier—meant that he couldn't be
assigned to active duty, so he joined up as a civilian. On May 2, he
received his appointment as an assistant mechanical engineer, and
he and Leslyn rented a place near the Navy Yard.

Another naval officer had unexpectedly returned. Campbell
told Heinlein, "L. Ron Hubbard's in town—temporarily confined
to the Sick Officer's Quarters. He's angry, bitter, and very much
afraid—afraid he'll get assigned to some shore job." Hubbard, who
was sporting a limp, claimed to have survived the sinking of the
USS *Edsall:* "He collected a piece of Jap bomb in his thigh during the battle of the Java Sea. . . . Allied air power was not giving
adequate coverage."

The truth was much less glamorous. Hubbard had disembarked
in Brisbane, Australia, in January to await transport to Manila.
After his arrival he ran into trouble with the naval attaché, who
blamed him for rerouting a supply ship, the *Don Isidro,* without
sufficient authorization. Hubbard had sent the steamship, which
was running food and ammunition to General Douglas MacArthur's besieged troops in the Philippines, on a roundabout route
along the coast of Australia. On the way, it was attacked by the
Japanese, resulting in the deaths of twelve men.

In February, Hubbard was ordered home: "By assuming unauthorized authority and attempting to perform duties for which
he has no qualifications, he became the source of much trouble."
On the way back he fell from a ladder on a ship, which was evidently the cause of his limp, and instead of receiving disciplinary action, he was assigned to the Office of the Cable Censor. He

had been in the best position of any of them to serve, and he had blown it.

On May 11, Heinlein formally began work at the Navy Yard, asking that his pension be stopped. On the same day, Asimov was appointed a junior chemist, and soon he was on the train to Philadelphia, writing to Pohl, "Frankly, I'm scared stiff about going off to live alone."

Before long, however, he would feel differently. At the end of May, he told Pohl, "My job is really a reasonable facsimile of paradise on earth. The work is interesting, the surroundings ideal, the coworkers congenial, my room very nice—and my spirits in great shape."

And he had another piece of news. "Freddie, old man, old guy, old sock, science fiction's most eligible bachelor is engaged to be married."

EARLIER IN 1942, ASIMOV HAD BEEN INVITED TO JOIN A WRITERS' GROUP IN BROOKLYN. SOMEWHAT to his surprise, he had enjoyed himself, and he became a regular attendee. Another member was a young man named Joe Goldberger, who approached Asimov after one meeting: "Let's get together next Saturday night and go out on the town. I'll bring my girl. You bring yours."

Asimov gave the only reply that he could. "I'm sorry, Joe. I don't have a girl."

"That's all right," Goldberger responded. "My girl will bring a girl for you."

Asimov agreed with some trepidation. He had been dating more frequently, writing to Pohl of one social event, "Naturally with the dance in the evening, I'll have to spend considerable of the afternoon washing, shaving, combing, scouring, scrubbing, polishing, brushing, primping—to say nothing of delousing and deodorizing—no simple trick." But his romantic experience—as reflected by the absence of women in his fiction—was effectively nonexistent.

He worked up the courage to meet Goldberger at the Astor Hotel, although he didn't realize until later that it was Valentine's Day. Asimov was in a good mood, having just passed his qualifying exams—he had decided to stick to graduate school, rather than pursue a medical degree—but the night got off to a poor start. Goldberger had described him as "a Russian chemist with a mustache," but when his girlfriend caught sight of Asimov, she was horrified enough to apologize to the friend whom she had convinced to come along.

The girl's name was Gertrude Blugerman. Her parents were Ukrainian, and she was a few years older than Asimov—she had been born in Toronto in 1917, and she was still a Canadian citizen. She was just over five feet tall and shapely, and to his eyes, she looked exactly like the actress Olivia de Havilland.

He stared at her all evening. Their first stop was a bar, where he felt out of his depth. Asimov tried to smoke and drink, and when she noticed that he seemed uncomfortable, he explained, "I don't want to spoil things."

"You won't spoil things," Gertrude said gently. Asimov, relieved, ground out his cigarette. At the end of the evening he got up to leave, saying that he had to deliver papers at the candy store the next day. Gertrude later said that he was the only person she had ever met who made her feel wicked.

They began to see more of each other. On their third date he took her to Pratt's war game, which was evidently his idea of a good time. She was also impressed by his answer to the old question "What happens if an irresistible force meets an immovable object?" When he explained that it was a contradiction in terms, Gertrude replied, "Oh my, you *are* smart." And he was able to kiss her good night.

He began to seriously think about proposing—like Campbell,

he was ready to marry the first woman who took an interest in him—and the prospect of marriage was an important factor in his acceptance of the offer from the Navy Yard. On April 3, he raised the idea to Gertrude, going so far as to show her his bankbook. She was reluctant, but a week and a half later, they went for a stroll on the boardwalk, where he made his case as passionately as he could. Afterward, he hoped that she would take it for granted, and by the time he left for Philadelphia, she did.

Asimov's first day at the Navy Yard was May 14, 1942. Employees in the lab worked six days straight, with Sundays off, and he hoped to spend most weekends in New York with Gertrude. Because he couldn't come out during the week, there was no chance of seeing Campbell, and he had no plans to write in any case. Asimov had always seen fiction as a hobby or a way of paying his tuition, and now that he didn't need the money, he gave it up.

He was busy enough as it was. The Navy Yard was built on a stretch of swampland near the Schuylkill River, with a series of huge buildings, like airplane hangars, equipped with racks for bicycles. Its parking lot was being repaved, so everyone had to park half a mile away and continue on foot across a stretch of land that became a quagmire when it rained.

The first floor of the Materials Lab was an open shop, filled with cranes, where workers conducted noisy stress tests on aircraft. At his desk on the next level, Asimov hung a map of Europe that he used to keep track of troop movements, including a special pin for Petrovichi. Just as he had in college, he kept to his own area and didn't explore, but he saw Heinlein every day.

Most of the lab consisted of civilian engineers who checked materials—seam sealers, cleaners, soaps—to ensure that they met specifications. Asimov spent much of his time on "Mother Asimov's pies," pans of calcium chloride that he used to test plastics for waterproofness. On one occasion, he accidentally forced an evacuation after burning a substance that smelled like skunk juice. He embraced the routine, and of all the writers that he knew, he was the most content during the war, in part because he wasn't overly burdened by his own expectations.

It helped that he felt happy at home. On July 25, he and Gertrude were married in the Blugermans' living room. He was twenty-two, she was twenty-five, and as they left, her mother called out, "Remember, Gittel, if it doesn't work out, you can always come home to me." For their wedding night they rented a room at a hotel in Midtown. Both were nervous virgins, and the act of consummation wasn't particularly successful. For now, their marriage would be pleasant enough, but the one thing that they always lacked was a satisfying sex life.

The apartment in Philadelphia was cramped and hot, and Gertrude—who was unable to get war work because of her Canadian citizenship—spent most of her time alone. Asimov was afraid that she would go back to New York, but she never did. They both kept apart from the social scene. Asimov tried to join a poker game, but he left after losing sixteen cents, which prompted his father to observe, "I am greatly relieved, for you might have won sixteen cents and become a lifelong gambler."

His only friends at work were Bernard Zitin, his boss, and Leonard Meisel, a mathematician who shared their car pool. All three became conscious of an atmosphere of mild anti-Semitism, which some feared would grow worse if the war went badly. Asimov—who frequently found himself blamed for practical jokes, although he was never the one responsible—was asked to lower his profile at the lab, but he felt no obligation to change his boisterous behavior.

It came to a head in September. In the past, Jewish employees had taken off Rosh Hashanah and Yom Kippur, but under new rules the one holiday allowed was Christmas. A petition was prepared proposing that Jewish workers get time off on Yom Kippur and work on Christmas Day, and when Asimov was told that it would only be effective if they all signed it, he reluctantly added his name.

Heinlein came to see him immediately. "What's this I hear about your not working on Yom Kippur, Isaac?"

Asimov didn't know why he was asking this. "I signed a petition about working on Christmas instead."

Heinlein wasn't inclined to let the issue drop. "You're not religious, are you?"

"No, I'm not," Asimov said. He admitted that he had no plans to attend temple, and when Heinlein pressed him further, he grew annoyed. "I won't go to church on Christmas, either, so what difference does it make which day I take off for nonreligious purposes?"

Heinlein pounced. "It doesn't. So why not take off Christmas with everyone else?"

"Because it would look bad if I didn't sign. They explained to me that—"

Heinlein quickly broke in. "Are you telling me they forced you to sign?"

Asimov saw that Heinlein had trapped him, although he wasn't sure why. "No. I was not forced to sign it. I signed it voluntarily because I wanted to. But since I freely admit I intend no religious observances, I will agree to work on Yom Kippur if I am told to, provided that does not prejudice the petition."

Heinlein left, apparently satisfied. On Yom Kippur, Asimov was the only Jewish employee who came to work. He later wrote, "It was no great hardship, but I must admit that I resented Heinlein's having put me on the spot. He meant well, I'm sure, and we have stayed good friends, but I have never been able to erase the memory of his having backed me into a corner."

If anything, this was overly generous. Heinlein was administering another test, like giving Asimov a Cuba Libre or threatening to quit science fiction over his rejection from Campbell.

In both cases, he was marking his territory. A few years earlier, Asimov might have deferred unthinkingly, but they had drawn within striking distance of each other in the magazine. For now, Heinlein had established the pecking order, but it left Asimov—who remembered such slights for decades—conscious of "a meanness of spirit" in a man he otherwise admired.

On October 26, Asimov got a rare Monday off, which he used to visit Campbell for the first time in six months. Gertrude joined as well. He recalled, "I don't think they hit it off. It always seemed to me that Campbell was not at his best with women. At least, I have never heard him make a single remark in the presence of one from which one could deduce that he had noticed she was a woman. . . . It may be that I find it odd only because I never make a single remark in the presence of a woman from which one can deduce that I have even momentarily forgotten she is a woman."

In fact, this was a side of his personality that would become increasingly problematic, as his domestic life made him more secure around the opposite sex. He liked to snap their bras through their blouses, and, once, he broke the strap. It was a bad habit, he admitted, that he never lost, and it was at the Navy Yard that he began to let his fingers roam more freely.

He remained in touch with Pohl, who told him that he thought that Gertrude was "attractive and pleasingly quiet." On January 2, 1943, Pohl wrote with the news that he was divorcing his wife Leslie Perri—who had loathed Asimov—and added, "For Christ's sake, Isaac, stay married to your bride; *somebody* has to maintain science fiction's good name."

Asimov replied, "I don't know with what authority I can speak, being a married man of not quite half a year's time, but as of now I can say, with supreme confidence, that science fiction's good name is safe with me."

The exchange prompted him to think about writing again. He had always wanted to sell a piece to *Unknown*, which he loved even more than *Astounding,* so he wrote a story about a mystery writer whose fictional detective comes to life. Asimov mailed "Author! Author!" to Campbell in April. It was the first time he had sent a submission without bringing it in person, but Campbell liked it so much that he paid him his first bonus since "Nightfall."

Asimov realized that he could use the money after the war was over. At the end of the month, he visited Campbell, telling him that he wanted to write a new installment in the Foundation series. Campbell asked for a robot story as well, and Asimov understood, to his amazement, that the editor needed him, rather than the other way around. It was a profound change. A year ago, he had left as a grateful protégé, but now his apprenticeship was over.

DURING THE WAR, ONE ISSUE THAT WAS NEVER FAR FROM ANYONE'S MIND WAS THE PROBLEM OF rationing. Gertrude smoked, but neither she nor Asimov drank, and they became used to their friends asking if they had any extra liquor stamps. Their lack of interest in drinking was another quality that kept them socially apart. Asimov's idea of indulging himself after moving to Philadelphia had been to consume a huge bottle of soda on his own, which only made him sick, and Gertrude wrote to Pohl, "Try as I may, propriety and dullness must be my lot."

Another object of rationing was gas. The preferred mode of transportation at the Navy Yard was by bicycle, and Heinlein could often be seen pedaling between the buildings in his suit and tie. One day, as a joke, a coworker removed the tags from a few tea bags and stopped Heinlein in the hallway, offering to sell him some illicit gasoline stamps. After examining the paper slips, Heinlein handed them back coldly. "You're lucky they weren't real."

He wasn't inclined to make light of wartime sacrifices, and there were moments when the courtly mask that he cultivated so carefully seemed to crack. On his arrival at the Navy Yard, he had been assigned to the Altitude Chamber and Cold Room, which were used to test materials under conditions of low pressure and temperature. He supervised their construction before handing them over to de Camp, who was a lieutenant in the Naval Reserve.

Heinlein was suffering from his usual medical problems—his back and kidneys were acting up—and he felt buried by paperwork. Scoles, who admired his competence, assigned him additional administrative duties, which Heinlein accepted against his will. He wrote to Campbell, "I hate my job. There is plenty of important work being done here but I am not doing it. Instead I do the unimportant work in order that others with truly important things to do may not be bothered with it."

He derisively called himself "the perfect private secretary," but he was also good at it. Tension between civilians and officers often ran high, and Heinlein was respected by both groups, advising the inexperienced de Camp, who could irritate others, to "clip those beetling brows." De Camp recalled, "It must have irked Heinlein to be working as a civilian while I, green to Navy ways, went about with pretty gold stripes on my sleeve. But he was a good sport about it, and I am sure his advice saved me from making a bigger ass of myself than I otherwise might have."

Heinlein's basic trouble—which Hubbard shared to an even greater degree—was that he was too imaginative to fully commit himself to the work that had to be done, even as he feared that they were losing the war. He learned to deal with it, but only by consciously willing himself into the attitude of patience that came naturally to Asimov. "A war requires subordination," Heinlein wrote to Campbell, "and I take a bitter pride in subordinating myself."

This remark was aimed directly at the editor. Months after their meeting with Scoles, Campbell's status was still up in the air. Early on, he had been enthusiastic about the Navy Yard, writing to Robert Swisher that Scoles was recruiting science fiction writers "as the type of men wanted for real research today." The editor added, "I have the satisfaction of already having succeeded in contributing a suggested line of attack that yielded results on one project." He even reached out to del Rey about taking over the magazine in the event that he was drawn into war work.

Campbell remained unsure of his prospects for getting a reserve commission, however, citing a list of ailments, including bad vision in his left eye, a poorly healed appendectomy scar, an irregular heartbeat, and what he called "fear syndrome" in his psychiatric records. Ultimately, he didn't even take the physical. His attempts to find a position at the National Defense Research Committee faltered—his contact was often out of town—and it became clear that his limited lab experience made him less desirable than the most recent crop of engineering graduates.

Heinlein told him that if money were an issue, he and Leslyn would be happy to contribute a stipend for Peedee, but he conceded, "Truthfully, we aren't shorthanded enough to recommend it." But he also advised:

> I strongly recommend for your own present and future
> peace of mind and as an example to your associates that
> you find some volunteer work. . . . I predict that it will
> seem deadly dull, poorly organized, and largely useless. . . .
> I am faced with that impasse daily and it nearly drives me
> nuts.

He anticipated many of Campbell's objections: "Remember, it does not have to be work that you want to do, nor work that you approve of. It suffices that it is work which established authority considers necessary to the war." And he concluded pointedly, "But find yourself some work, John. Otherwise you will spend the rest of your life in self-justification."

Campbell never did. He found it hard to subordinate himself to duties that didn't utilize his talents, and he was disinclined to make the sacrifice that Heinlein had bitterly accepted. In the end,

L. Sprague de Camp, Isaac Asimov, and Robert A. Heinlein
at the Philadelphia Navy Yard, 1944.
Courtesy of John Seltzer and Geo Rule

he decided to stay with his magazines, a civilian role with a high priority rating because of its perceived importance to morale. Heinlein never forgave him, speaking years later of "working my heart out and ruining my health during the war while he was publishing *Astounding*."

The Heinleins still remained outwardly friendly toward the Campbells, as well as the de Camps, and they occasionally walked the two miles to visit Asimov and Gertrude. At work, their social life centered on the Navy Yard cafeteria, which was known without affection as Ulcer Gulch. Heinlein and Leslyn worked in different buildings—she had landed a job as a junior radio inspector—but they ate together every afternoon. Asimov became part of the lunch crowd when Gertrude left on a trip to clarify her immigration status, and after her return, Heinlein asked him to stay. Asimov resented the pressure, but finally consented "with poor grace."

At the cafeteria, the food was terrible, and Asimov didn't get along with Leslyn. She struck him as brittle and tense, and her constant smoking—she used her plate as an ashtray—soured him forever on cigarettes. Leslyn didn't care for him, either. His years at the candy store had left him with the habit of devouring his food in silence, and when he popped half of a boiled egg in his mouth, she couldn't contain her disgust: "Don't do that. You turn my stomach."

Asimov thought she was speaking to someone else. "Are you talking to me, Leslyn?"

When she confirmed that she was, he asked what he had done wrong—and swallowed the second half. She shrieked, "You did it again!"

His comments about the food grated on Heinlein, who decreed that anyone who complained had to contribute a nickel toward a war bond. Asimov knew that this was a message to him. "Well, then, suppose I figure out a way of complaining about the food that isn't complaining. Will you call it off?"

After Heinlein said that he would Asimov tried to think of ways to get around it. One day, as he sawed through the haddock on his plate, he asked, in mock innocence, "Is there such a thing as tough fish?"

It was another battle of wills, and Heinlein wasn't about to back down. "That will be five cents, Isaac."

This time Asimov held his ground. "It's only a point of information, Bob."

"That will be five cents, Isaac," Heinlein repeated. "The implication is clear."

Asimov was saved when another employee, unaware of the rule, took a bite of ham and remarked, "Boy, this food is awful."

Rising to his feet, Asimov pronounced, "Gentlemen, I disagree with every word my friend here has said, but I will defend with my life his right to say it." Heinlein dropped the system of fines. It was a victory, but a small one.

On September 25, 1943, the Soviets marched back into Smolensk. Two days later, a communiqué said that Petrovichi had been retaken after years under German rule. When Heinlein heard the news, he shook Asimov's hand and congratulated him gravely. For the moment, at least, they were equals.

Word finally came of Leslyn's family in the Philippines. Her sister, Keith, was interned with her two sons in Manila, but her brother-in-law, Mark Hubbard, had vanished. Until then, Leslyn had liked her job, but she began working so hard—"Just doing everything she could to shorten the misery of her sister," a friend recalled—that it affected her health. She became the personnel manager for a machine shop with six hundred employees, and although she was suited for it—she was the only administrator who made a point of wearing the same uniform as the female workers—it caused her to drink more heavily.

Heinlein was also feeling the pressure. He sometimes felt like returning to fiction, and when he mentioned this to Campbell, the editor thought that it implied that his work was either going well or "shapfu," in which the "hap" stood for "hopelessly and permanently." It was closer to the latter, and in the end, he didn't do any writing at all. He developed hemorrhoids that his doctor treated with injections, leading to an abscess "in a location where I could not see but was acutely aware of it." The Navy clearly had no intention of reactivating him, so he decided to try for the Merchant Marine, undergoing an operation to resolve his medical issues that he compared to "having your asshole cut out with an apple corer."

He was left with "no rectum to speak of," and he was recovering in the hospital in January 1944 when Leslyn heard from the Red Cross. Mark Hubbard was missing, but Keith and her sons were aboard the Swedish mercy ship MS *Gripsholm*—Leslyn had been sending money to pay for their safe passage. It took them seventy days to get from Goa to New York. After their arrival, the two boys were sent to New Jersey to live with the Campbells, where they stayed for months, until their mother had recovered. The stress led Leslyn's weight to fall below ninety pounds, and she began sleeping for up to twelve hours a day.

In late January, Heinlein underwent another operation, forcing him to wear a dressing that looked like a diaper. His convalescence would have been a good time to write again, but he could sit for only twenty minutes at a stretch with the aid of an inflatable ring. It was obvious that he would not be serving at the front in any capacity: "I'm simply going to be bored to distraction and worked to a rag doing things I don't want to do in a town I hate."

He tried to reconcile himself to his situation, but he remained envious of those who had seen action. This included L. Ron Hubbard, who was rumored to be in command of a ship. Alone of them all, it seemed, he had been given the chance to prove that he was the hero he had always claimed to be. In the magazine, Campbell wrote fondly, "Hubbard has been an adventurer all his life; he had special training of an even more directly applicable nature—he's been a fighting man and a skipper of his own ship before." And he told Heinlein:

> I imagine that the thing that would really satisfy [Hubbard's] nature . . . would be a chance to command a sub sent out to raid Tokyo harbor. I wouldn't permit him to, if I were running the Navy. He'd probably try to up ship and bombard Hirohito's hovel with his deck gun, just for the hell of it.

8.
THE WAR OF INVENTION
1942–1944

The position of America has been violently changed in twenty-four hours. The makeup of our lesser community of science fiction is of interest, if not importance. . . . L. Ron Hubbard is Lieutenant L. Ron Hubbard, U.S.N. We have a few of his stories on hand; whether he will, now, have time for more I cannot know.

—JOHN W. CAMPBELL, *ASTOUNDING*, FEBRUARY 1942

Hubbard had occupied a desk at the Office of the Cable Censor in New York since May 1, 1942. At first he did well, drawing measured praise from his superior: "Since reporting to this activity, this officer has shown a full realization of the seriousness of an assignment to duty. He has shown an increasing sense of responsibility and displayed a marked improvement in his work." But almost from the moment he arrived, he was anxious to get just about anywhere else.

Shortly after his return, Hubbard saw Campbell, who floated the notion to Heinlein of finding a place for him at the Navy Yard: "[Hubbard's] own feeling is that his direct experience with Jap weapons, methods and tactics might be his prime asset." His limp was mostly gone, but his indignation remained: "They've kidnapped him into a desk job, and he got a licking out in Java, and he wants almighty bad to get back out that way and give his red hair a chance."

What Hubbard really wanted was to go to sea. He requested an assignment to the Caribbean or Alaska, particularly the latter, "the peoples, language, and customs of which I know and of which I possess piloting knowledge." Ultimately, he was granted half of his wish. In the first of several second chances that he would receive—largely because of a shortage of personnel—he landed a post in Neponset, Massachusetts, to take charge of a trawler after it was converted to a patrol vessel. It would stick close to shore, but Hubbard seized on it as an opportunity to return to the fleet.

He was promoted to the rank of full lieutenant. Before heading to Massachusetts he found time for trips to Los Angeles and New York, and he dropped by the office to see Campbell, who noted that he seemed tickled by his new position: "He's back on sea duty, and evidently going to get somewhere near what would really suit his mentality—a chance to be a privateer." Doña agreed: "Hubbard has gone to collect a subchaser somewhere and a happier male John has never seen. That would be about as close to the old buccaneer status as he could get, wouldn't it?"

Hubbard welcomed the association with his old stories. Arriving in Neponset on June 25, he was greeted by a crew of what he later described as former convicts, "their braid dirty and their hammocks black with grime." Like one of his own heroes, he claimed to have transformed this band of outcasts into capable sailors—an achievement that existed entirely in his imagination. In reality, work proceeded smoothly, and Hubbard found time to accompany Campbell on a visit to a science fiction club in Cambridge. A month after his arrival he took the ship for a test cruise.

He would never serve at its helm again. In a remarkable repetition of his experience in Brisbane, he was relieved of his authority. There was bad blood between the men at the shipyard and those assigned to the ships, and Hubbard had an altercation with an officer whom he criticized by name to Washington. The only result was that he lost his berth, with the commandant of the Boston Navy Yard writing that he was "not temperamentally suited for independent command."

Hubbard protested in vain. He had learned nothing from his earlier mistakes, and the fact that he stumbled into a similar situation so quickly hinted at a fundamental flaw in his personality—but he was given another chance. After reporting to the Naval Receiving Station on Long Island, he successfully asked to be nominated to the Submarine Chaser Training Center in Miami. A garbled rumor of this assignment reached Campbell: "I have a feeling Ron traded his ship for a sub—a Nazi one in a mutual destruction deal. Only Ron and crew came home; the Nazis didn't."

He arrived in Miami in November. An acquaintance saw him urinating blood, which he attributed to his injury in Java, although its true cause was less heroic. He later wrote, "While training in Miami, Florida, I met a girl named Ginger who excited me. She was a very loose person but pretended a great love for me. From her I received an infection of [gonorrhea]. . . . I went to a private doctor who treated me with sulfathiazole"—which can cause bloody urine—"and so forth."

Elsewhere, he recalled his experience there more fondly: "Boy was I able to catch up on some sleep." He did passably well, telling the Campbells that he had graduated at the top of his class—he was really twentieth out of twenty-five—and landing an assignment to command a submarine chaser, the USS *PC-815*, being built in Portland, Oregon. It was close to Polly, but his marriage was effectively over, and he still feared that he had gonorrhea: "I took to dosing myself with sulfa in such quantities that I was afraid I had affected my brain."

On May 18, 1943, the *PC-815* departed for San Diego, with Hubbard left to his own devices for the first time as a commander. The calm lasted for five hours. At three in the morning, off Cape Meares in Oregon, a soundman reported something in the water about five hundred yards ahead. Hubbard slowed the engines. Over the earphones, they thought that they heard screw noises, which indicated the presence of a submarine. It was unlikely but not impossible—a Japanese sub had shelled an oil refinery in Santa Barbara the year before—and they assumed an intercept course.

When they were close enough, Hubbard ordered the crew to drop three depth charges. In his report, he wrote hyperbolically, "The ship, sleepy and skeptical, had come to their guns swiftly and without error. No one, including the Commanding Officer, could readily credit the existence of an enemy submarine here on the steamer track and all soundmen, now on the bridge, were attempting to argue the echo-ranging equipment and chemical recorder out of such a fantastic idea."

They continued to sweep the area, going on a second attack run and firing on an object that Hubbard later conceded was probably just a floating log. At nine in the morning, two blimps joined in the search, followed shortly afterward by four more ships. Hubbard began to think that they were dealing with two different subs, and the following day, he claimed, a periscope was seen by "every man on the bridge and flying bridge." When they opened fire, it vanished, and Hubbard conducted another attack before receiving the order to return.

The entire incident had lasted for sixty-eight hours. A subsequent investigation concluded that there had been no submarines there at all. The only evidence to the contrary came from the magnetic anomaly detectors in the blimps, which had probably been triggered by a natural deposit. After the war, no record was found of Japanese submarine activity in the area, and no wreckage was ever recovered. Hubbard thought that the Navy hadn't wanted to alarm the locals, and he never ceased to believe that he had sunk "two Jap subs without credit."

He avoided discipline—he had been hasty, but not reckless— and in June, the *PC-815* headed for a group of islands southwest of San Diego, where Hubbard, who was suffering from a throat infection, ordered four training rounds to be fired and anchored there overnight. It had been "a very arduous day," he explained, and he didn't trust anyone to pilot the subchaser without him. While they were holding station, he also allowed his men to shoot at a target that was tossed from the ship.

What Hubbard didn't know was that the islands were really part of Mexico. The Mexican government complained, and a board of investigation was convened at the end of the month. Hubbard said lamely, "At no time was I aware of invading Mexican territorial waters." His men lied to protect him, but he had run out of second chances. After being admonished for conducting gunnery practice and anchoring without authorization, he was transferred in early July.

Hubbard had been commander of his own vessel for a total of eighty days. A fitness report rated him below average, stating that he was "lacking in the essential qualities of judgment, leadership, and cooperation." It was his last mistake, and he was posted to the Issuing Office in San Diego until the Navy could figure out what to do with him. While there he complained of various pains—although he later admitted that he had invented them to avoid punishment—and he went to the hospital for three months. After being released in October, he was assigned to the *Algol*, an amphibious attack cargo ship, as its navigational officer.

He would never hold an independent naval command again. On some level, his life had failed to live up to his stories, but it would be even more precise to say that his fiction had been easier to manipulate than reality. Hubbard grew resigned to returning to the only career in which he had received any degree of approval:

"My salvation is to let this roll over me. . . . To pile up copy, stack up stories, roll the wordage and generally conduct my life along the one line of success I have ever had."

IF HUBBARD BELIEVED THAT HIS STINT IN THE MILITARY REPRESENTED A LOSS TO THE MAGAZINE world, he was perfectly right, at least in the eyes of his closest collaborator. After Pearl Harbor, in the February 1942 issue of *Astounding*, Campbell provided a rundown of the impact of the war on his writers. The first one he mentioned was Hubbard, followed by Heinlein, of whom he wrote, "I do not know whether he will be able to do any further writing; I greatly doubt that he will."

From the moment that war was declared, Campbell knew that the availability of his authors would present a problem. In a letter to Jack Williamson after the attack, Campbell listed the writers who he expected to lose and concluded, "That leaves de Camp, you, and van Vogt as the primary steady writers available." He was premature in naming de Camp, and after writing a few stories based on an idea from the editor about antimatter, Williamson reported for duty in New Mexico.

Many authors would be excused for health reasons—if they had been better physical specimens, they might not have been writers at all—but it didn't take long for Campbell to find that even those who escaped the draft would be hard to keep. Del Rey was classified as 4-F, but he moved to St. Louis to be close to his girlfriend, contributing just a handful of pieces while working as a metalworker at McDonnell Aircraft. Sturgeon, who was also medically exempt, left to run a hotel in Jamaica, and he wouldn't write on a regular basis for years.

Only one reliable author remained. In *Astounding*, Campbell had written, "A. E. van Vogt is a Canadian; probably his status will not be changed; if anything, his work will increase in volume." Before the war, when Heinlein was threatening to retire, Campbell had made van Vogt an unprecedented offer: "I would like to contract you to write for *Astounding*. I'm willing to buy two or three hundred dollars worth of stories a month from you. In other words, it's wide open."

Van Vogt—whose bad eyesight disqualified him from the military—had accepted the proposal. Campbell wanted stories that reflected on the global crisis, but he also had more expansive developments in mind: "I'm genuinely trying to divert the stream of science fiction a bit, and you, del Rey, and one or possibly two others are the best bets as to authors capable of making the change felt. . . . What I'm trying to do in science fiction is to turn it away from the hard, rather brittle practicality of some of the best of the stories of the last year or two."

Campbell was pleased by the results, but he continued to search for new talent. In the August 1942 issue, he told readers, "For the past several months, I've been somewhat busy. In addition to the usual job of getting the magazines together, there's been a problem of getting some new authors together, and helping some almost-but-not-quite writers into the pretty-good division." Occasionally he would make a lucky find, but he preferred to tackle the problem more systematically—by targeting writers a degree or two away from those he had already discovered.

One obvious source was the Futurians, but even if he had wanted their services, most were unavailable. Donald Wollheim, whose heart murmur had kept him out of active duty, was working for Ace Magazines, and in 1942, Cyril Kornbluth was called up. When he went to say goodbye to Pohl, they drunkenly swore an oath—slashing their hands with a razor—to kill the editor Robert Lowndes for no particular reason. The following morning, they woke up in the same bed, hungover and covered in blood. They stared at each other, pale, and Kornbluth said, "Well, I think I'd better go, Fred. So long. Have a nice war."

Campbell was more interested in the Mañana Literary Society, which had just been memorialized in the mystery novel *Rocket to the Morgue,* by Anthony Boucher. His most valued contributors from that circle were Cleve Cartmill, who was handicapped by polio, and the married writers Henry Kuttner and Catherine L. Moore, who had met through their mutual friend H. P. Lovecraft. Moore was already a respected author, while Heinlein saw Kuttner as his best replacement. Campbell eventually came to agree: "He's a homely little squirt, and looks pretty weak. I didn't see, myself, what Catherine Moore saw in him. I herewith take it back. He evidently has real character and real worth."

Even more significant was the fact that Kuttner and Moore, on the advice of the editor, had begun to collaborate, working in shifts under the name Lewis Padgett. Their run culminated in "Mimsy Were the Borogoves" and "When the Bough Breaks," two extraordinary stories with an unusual interest in marriage and the inner lives of children. It was an enormously promising line of development, but Campbell never followed up on it, in part because it seemed unrelated to the war. Yet no one else did so much to carry *Astounding* after Pearl Harbor.

Another writer from the Heinlein circle who was eager to write for Campbell was Ray Bradbury, whose eyesight made him ineligible for the draft. He had been mentored by Heinlein and Leigh Brackett, but he received his most rigorous apprenticeship from Kuttner, who jokingly threatened to kill him if he didn't stop writing so much purple prose. After selling two pieces to the Probability Zero department, which won first place in the Analytical Laboratory poll, he seemed on the verge of breaking into *Astounding,* and his timing should have been perfect.

Yet he never quite made it. In the fall of 1942, his agent submitted "Chrysalis," a superman story pitched squarely at the editor's tastes. Campbell thought that Bradbury had "mastered the mechanics of writing pretty thoroughly already," but he asked for a number of revisions. After Bradbury rewrote it with input from Moore and Kuttner, Campbell passed anyway. A year later, Brad-

THE WAR OF INVENTION 183

bury sold him a minor van Vogt parody, "Doodad," but he never placed another story in the magazine, despite giving the editor first look at such future landmarks as "The Million-Year Picnic" and "Mars Is Heaven!" Campbell turned them all down.

Even after raising rates twice, Campbell was still having trouble finding stories, and he was distracted by other problems. In a spectacular case of bad timing, *Astounding* had expanded in size shortly before Pearl Harbor, but it didn't attract new advertisers, and its placement alongside the slicks failed to increase sales. After sixteen issues, it returned to its old dimensions, and in late 1943 it shrank further. The problem was wartime rationing—the electrotyping process, which was needed for the larger pages, ate up metal, and the firm's paper allotment was repeatedly cut.

Of his two magazines, *Unknown* was the more vulnerable. Campbell had once hoped that it would exceed the sales of *Astounding*, but its circulation had turned out to be lower, making it an inefficient user of paper—it had to print the same number of display issues to fill space on newsstands, which left it with a higher percentage of returns. Playing for time, Campbell announced that its print run would be reduced, ads would be eliminated, and the next issue would be pocketbook size.

It never came. *Unknown* ceased publication after its October 1943 issue, and its paper was allocated to *Astounding*. From a business perspective, the decision was straightforward, but emotionally it was devastating. When Asimov visited the editor shortly afterward, Campbell didn't even mention it. A few weeks later, Heinlein informed Asimov that *Unknown* was gone "for the duration." Asimov wrote correctly in his diary, "I interpret that as forever."

Campbell had killed his favorite child so that the more valuable title could survive, in part because he believed that science fiction still had a role to play in the war. It was a laboratory in which his writers could work out scenarios for the future, as Anthony

Boucher wrote in response to readers who were tiring of pessimistic war stories: "The more we write about ingenious ruses by which the Axis secures victory . . . the less apt those ruses are to succeed."

The editor certainly believed it. And the death of the magazine on which he had lavished so much energy precipitated his next move, in which he was determined to prove the genre's worth once and for all.

IN THE APRIL 1942 ISSUE OF *ASTOUNDING*, IN AN EDITORIAL TITLED "TOO GOOD AT GUESSING," Campbell had quoted an unidentified contributor: "I'm doing research work of a restricted, confidential nature; other men in my lab are doing other secret work. If I write a story and, on the basis of my technical background, guess reasonably accurately, I may describe something one of those other men is actually developing. There would naturally be a feeling that it was a leakage of secret material. I'd like to write—but I'm afraid I might guess right. I'd better not."

Campbell may have been flattering himself with the notion that the magazine could stumble across an important secret by accident, but it wasn't entirely out of the question. He concluded the editorial by saying that they would restrict themselves for now to stories that were more removed from reality: "The consequence is that we will, in the future, try to be wilder guessers, place our stories further in the future, or base them on themes that can't lead to those too-good guesses. . . . For once, we're in the position of finding it wiser to guess wrong!"

It was a statement of caution, but it also reflected his faith in the genre as a proving ground for ideas, as well as the contribution that he still hoped it would make to the war effort. In the January 1941 issue, Campbell had said that America would be a terrible enemy in a conflict decided by inventive ingenuity, and he had repeated himself after Pearl Harbor: "We have the highest potential of scientific research of any nation on Earth, by far. . . . If you *must* attack America, do it with horse cavalry and war clubs—not mechanized warfare!"

At first, the Navy Yard had seemed like the chance that he had been awaiting. Campbell wrote excitedly to Swisher, "The whole setup down there is engaged in making the gadgets we've been talking about for a dozen years—plus the couple hundred more that we hadn't thought of yet." This wasn't what most of its engineers were doing—and it certainly didn't resemble the work of Asimov, Heinlein, or de Camp—but it remained his dream of what it might become.

After he failed to "crash the gate," Campbell began to think seriously about setting up something like it for himself. He felt that he would make a good head of research, and he had an existing venue for it in *Astounding*. As long as his circulation levels were acceptable, Street & Smith gave him comparative freedom, so he didn't have to report to anyone. The problem remained of pushing his ideas through the military bureaucracy, but Campbell reasoned that he could outsource this to Heinlein—who was overworked enough as it was.

One possible approach was to run technical problems in the magazine and ask readers for suggestions. This had been a key part of Scoles's pitch to Heinlein in January 1942, in which the job offer had been an aside:

> *Among the writers and readers of* Astounding *and* Amazing Stories *there must be a lot of men formerly known as crackpots who are beginning to come into their own as the "men with ideas" and possibly in the future "saviors of their country". . . . Might it not be a good idea if you wrote an article to be published in all the science fiction magazines bringing out the need for all of these ideas?*

Campbell couldn't have put it better himself, and he remained enthusiastic about the prospect long after any chance of a position at the Navy Yard had evaporated. In July, he wrote to Heinlein, "I'll have to try helping by indirection. . . . Perhaps if I knew more of the general problems, could even discuss general problems in the magazine with suggestions that the readers use imagination and see what solutions they could propose, something useful could be done."

As an example, he offered an idea of his own—filling a lab with an atmosphere of argon gas for certain kinds of industrial work, which was already being done with helium—and asked for more: "Can you suggest a list of problems, or a few, that I could at least try to mull over?" Campbell put Fletcher Pratt to work on an article on "problems of the Navy that technically minded imagination might be able to solve," and he informed Leslyn that the author had "gotten Navy authorization to write it, and is getting Navy assistance in selecting material to use."

It never appeared. Neither did "The Battle of Design," in which Campbell hoped to start a discussion of wartime engineering problems. The issue was censorship—the Navy had been receptive, but the Army rejected it as a security risk. It left the editor without a public forum, but he still wanted to play a role. At his first meeting with the fan Damon Knight, he said that he was thinking about leaving the magazine to go into research: "I'm a nuclear physicist, you know."

Campbell identified two plans of attack. In the November 1942 issue, after stating that his attempt to enlist had been "stymied," he said:

> But I'm running an unofficial recruiting office. I know
> a place where some young engineers, with engineering
> degrees and a little experience, a degree at least, are very
> badly needed. . . . It's a chance to really serve the country

*in a way that will make your training, and particularly
your trained imagination—something even rarer than
engineering training—count for a maximum result.*

As an example of the kind of problem on the table, he mentioned
the "practical, workable development" of a space suit for high
altitudes. A pressure suit project really did exist—even if none of
the writers at the Navy Yard worked on it, despite rumors to the
contrary—and the editor forwarded the responses that he received
to Heinlein, although no evidence exists that it led to anyone being hired.

Campbell's other strategy was to solicit ideas from writers in
private correspondence. Heinlein encouraged this, and he also
approached Will Jenkins, a brilliant inventor who wrote science
fiction under the name Murray Leinster. Jenkins responded with
"a very careful, long, and elaborate letter in which I listed all the
imaginative gimmicks that I thought could help win the war," and
the three men formed an unofficial triumvirate for brainstorming,
with Heinlein at the Navy Yard, Campbell at the magazine, and
Jenkins at the Office of War Information.

Jenkins, who was in contact with underground resistance
movements, was especially interested in dirty chemical tricks that
could be used by factory workers to sabotage the Nazis. Campbell
saw that this was the perfect place to get credit for something that
might be used in the field, and he pitched ways to weaken wing
struts and disable boilers, while Willy Ley contributed the "diabolic" notion of using airplanes to drop poison ivy or Japanese
beetles over Germany. The editor also bombarded Heinlein with
his own proposals, including using flares to destroy an attacking
pilot's night vision and marking submarines with magnetic bombs.
None were deemed practical.

Campbell—who had made his name with stories in which huge
engineering problems were solved overnight—was growing impa-

tient. He was unable to point to a single clear case of influence, and sending his ideas to Heinlein put him in a position of vulnerability that he had hoped to leave behind. Like Hubbard, he was burdened by an obsolete idea of heroism. While Heinlein had learned to maneuver within the bureaucracy to the best of his abilities, Campbell had gambled on finding a shortcut, but he had failed. And so had *Unknown*.

It was in this mood that he received a letter from the writer Cleve Cartmill in August 1943, pitching a story about the ghost ship *Mary Celeste*. Campbell didn't care for it, but he had another premise in mind. Ever since hearing about the cubic foot of uranium at Columbia, he had been keeping a close eye on experiments in atomic power, and he wrote to Cartmill:

> *There might be a story in this thought. . . . U-235 has—*
> *I'm stating fact, not theory—been separated in quantity*
> *easily sufficient for preliminary atomic power research,*
> *and the like. They got it out of regular uranium ores*
> *by new atomic isotope separation methods; they have*
> *quantities measured in pounds. They have not brought*
> *the whole amount together, or any major portion of it. . . .*
> *They're afraid that that explosion of energy would be so*
> *incomparably violent . . . that surrounding matter would*
> *be set off. . . . And that would be serious.*

The letter, which ran for three pages, outlined a story that paralleled the situation of the Allies and the Axis, with the latter threatening to set off an atomic bomb before it was defeated. Campbell finished, "Now it might be that you found the story worked better in allegory—the war being placed on another planet, where similar conditions prevailed. I think the story would be the adventure of the secret agent who was assigned to save the day—to destroy that bomb."

Cartmill was guarded in his response, saying that the idea was "prophecy so close to home that it may be ridiculous. And there is the possible danger of actually suggesting a means of action which might be employed." On a practical level, he wasn't sure whether he could come up with a believable alien background, and he asked a series of questions about the science, "keeping an eye, of course, on what should or should not be told for social, military, or political reasons."

Campbell's reply was two and a half pages long. He seemed confident that the alien setting would sidestep any problems with the censors: "Censorship won't give any trouble about what happens on [another planet], where they might kick somewhat about local happenings. . . . The situation will simply go along as though it were earth." Campbell advised him to study the earthlike world in "Nightfall" and to read "Blowups Happen" for approaches to the technical side, and he proposed that the hero have a prehensile tail to make it clear that he wasn't human.

Cartmill remained doubtful, but he wasn't going to turn down a sure sale. He wrote it quickly, submitting it in the first week of September, and the result, "Deadline," appeared in the March 1944 issue, which was out by February 11. Most readers didn't think highly of it—one called it "mediocre fantasy"—and it ranked last in the Analytical Laboratory poll. But Campbell had a particular audience in mind.

He had long suspected that the government was working on an atomic bomb. His earliest stories in college had revolved around the discovery of nuclear power, but when the moment finally came, it found him on the outside looking in. If he had graduated from MIT a few years later, he might conceivably have been part of the effort, but instead, he was just an "organized fan."

It led him to break his one rule. He had said that *Astounding* would refrain from publishing anything that might reveal secrets of national defense, and now he was deliberately printing a story with blatant parallels to the most important military project of all time. Campbell made no effort to clear it with the censors, as he had for similar works. It was an act of recklessness that exceeded anything that Hubbard ever did—but it was also the only bomb that he could detonate.

And its impact was felt at once. The Manhattan Project counted many science fiction fans among its workers, and word of the story rapidly spread, until employees were talking about it openly in the cafeteria of the atomic weapons lab in New Mexico. Cartmill's device bore minimal resemblance to the designs under development, but it didn't matter. Edward Teller, who would later be known as the father of the hydrogen bomb, recalled that the reaction at Los Alamos was "astonishment."

But it made its most significant impression on a man who wasn't a scientist at all. He was a security officer. As the others discussed the story over lunch, he listened quietly—and he took notes. If Campbell had wanted attention, he was about to succeed beyond his wildest expectations.

9.
FROM "DEADLINE" TO HIROSHIMA
1944–1945

Atomic physics . . . could end the war in a day, in a fraction of a second, beyond doubt—but there's considerable doubt as to whether there would then be a postwar world to worry about.
—JOHN W. CAMPBELL, *ASTOUNDING*, AUGUST 1943

Cleve Cartmill's "Deadline" was set on Cathor, a planet consumed by a global war between two factions known as the Sixa and the Seilla. Its hero was a spy whose mission is to penetrate an enemy stronghold, track down the scientist who is developing the ultimate weapon, and destroy it before it can be detonated. He succeeds, defusing the bomb and scattering the uranium inside: "It would fall, spread, and never be noticed by those who would now go on living."

The story was undeniably bad, and even the least critical readers might have found the reversals of the names "Sixa" and "Seilla" too juvenile to pass muster in *Amazing*, let alone in *Astounding*. Yet its shallowness amounted to a narrative strategy in itself. The hero's tail, the childishly coded belligerents, and even the planet without human characters—a convention that the magazine rarely used—were all clues to view it as something else. It obviously hadn't been published on its merits as entertainment, so there had to be some hidden message.

And it didn't take any scientific background to realize that the entire story was an excuse to talk about the atomic bomb, which Cartmill described using language transcribed straight from Campbell's letters, down to the line "I'm stating fact, not theory." The story noted that there were sixteen pounds of uranium in the bomb, with each pound providing an explosive yield of fifty thousand tons of dynamite, and it delved into its design at length:

> *Two cast-iron hemispheres, clamped over the orange*
> *segments of cadmium alloy. And the fuse—I see it is*
> *in—a tiny can of cadmium alloy containing a speck of*
> *radium in a beryllium holder and a small explosive*
> *powerful enough to shatter the cadmium walls. Then—*
> *correct me if I'm wrong, will you?—the powdered*
> *uranium oxide runs together in the central cavity. The*
> *radium shoots neutrons into this mass—and the U-235*
> *takes over from there.*

Decades afterward, Campbell would claim that this was the most detailed description of a nuclear device published anywhere before the trial of Julius and Ethel Rosenberg. In reality, sixteen pounds of uranium wasn't enough to set off a chain reaction—the bomb called Little Boy used one hundred and forty pounds—and the method of assembly was too slow. A real atomic bomb had to fire one mass at another using an explosive charge, while in Campbell's design, the powder in the central cavity would melt through the iron shell long before it exploded.

It wasn't the first time that U-235 had appeared in fiction, either. Just as Campbell had added superfluous touches of psychology to Asimov's "Homo Sol," he had inserted references to the fission reaction, often gratuitously, into numerous stories. But the sheer specificity of "Deadline" was enough to set off alarms in the Counterintelligence Corps—the agency responsible for security at Los Alamos—as soon as the cafeteria conversations that it inspired had been brought to its attention.

On March 8, 1944, a month after "Deadline" appeared, Agent Arthur E. Riley went to interview Campbell at the Chanin Building at 122 East Forty-Second Street, where the magazine had recently relocated. It was exactly the sort of reaction that the editor had hoped to provoke. The story wouldn't have received nearly the same degree of interest if he had simply submitted it to the censorship office, and he seemed flattered by the inquiry, answering the agent's questions as cheerfully as if he were auditioning for a role on the Manhattan Project itself.

Campbell took full responsibility, saying that he had written to Cartmill—who had "no technical knowledge whatever"—with the idea. Riley wrote in his report, "The subject of atomic disintegration was not novel to [Campbell], since he had pursued a course in atomic physics at Massachusetts Institute of Technology in 1933." As an editor with a scientifically literate audience, Campbell added, he often drew on published sources and the work of his "technically minded intimates and associates." He showed Riley a copy of a journal that talked about nuclear fission, and he even described the story line of "Solution Unsatisfactory."

If he was hoping to make a favorable impression, he wasn't entirely successful. Riley reported that Campbell was "somewhat of an egotist," a judgment confirmed when the editor stated grandly, but not inaccurately, "I am *Astounding Science Fiction*." Campbell also provided Cartmill's address and offered to suppress the magazine's Swedish edition, which seemed the one most likely to fall into German hands—and in fact, Wernher von Braun, the head of the Nazi rocket program, was allegedly obtaining it using a false name and a mail drop in Sweden, although there was no way that either man could have known this at the time.

The agent also grew interested in Will Jenkins, who had been seen having lunch with Campbell and an engineer at Bell Labs. After he was denied a security clearance, Jenkins had resigned from the Office of War Information, and he had run into trouble before. One of his efforts, "Four Little Ships," had been reworked at the request of the Navy, apparently because its plot overlapped with classified minesweeping techniques. Campbell had submitted it to the censor, as he hadn't bothered to do with "Deadline," and he may well have printed it just to see what the reaction would be.

Riley made an appointment with Jenkins, and when he arrived at the author's house, they went up to the roof to speak in private. "Tell me, have you ever read the Cleve Cartmill story 'Deadline'?"

Jenkins said that he had. When asked for his thoughts, he replied, "A pretty good story, and the science is authentic. Quite accurate."

There was a charged pause. "Well, what we want to know is, could it be a leak?"

Jenkins, unlike Campbell, was less than gratified by the attention. He later wrote, "At this point my hair stood up on end and its separate strands tended to crack like whiplashes."

On further questioning, Jenkins acknowledged that he and his daughter had "conducted experiments designed to acquire quantities of atomic copper." He had gone to Campbell's office in 1942 with ten grams of what he believed was a pure copper isotope, which he had separated using a home setup. It had clear commercial potential—Campbell had joked that he should try it on uranium—but Jenkins still had to prove that it worked. He gave the sample to Asimov for testing using the mass spectrograph at Columbia, but nothing ever came of it.

It was the first time that Riley had heard of the man whose name and rank he recorded as "Lt. Azimoff." Additional investigation alerted him to de Camp and Heinlein, the latter of whom was flagged as a person of interest because of his friendship with Cartmill. An actual leak seemed remote, but there were other reasons for concern: "In the opinion of informed persons, the story contains more than just an academic course in atomic physics, revealing as it does certain things developed since 1940." Riley concluded by advising that Campbell be reminded of the Voluntary Censorship Code, which restricted the discussion of secret weapons in print.

In California, Special Agent R. S. Killough was looking into Cartmill, who resided in Manhattan Beach, where a number of scientists on the atomic project also lived. His mail was placed under surveillance, with all of the return addresses noted down, and his mailman revealed that the author had received a letter from the editor shortly after the visit from Riley. Cartmill, the mailman added, seemed reluctant to talk about the pulps—he was more eager to discuss a story that he had placed in *Collier's*—and when asked about "Deadline," he had only said, "It stinks."

At first, Cartmill said that he had come up with the plot of "Deadline" on his own, but after being interviewed on two separate occasions by Killough and Special Agent D. L. Johnson, he revised his account. Johnson wrote, "He took the major portion of it directly from letters sent to him by John Campbell . . . and a very minor portion from his own general knowledge." At their next meeting, Cartmill showed Johnson their correspondence. The technical information in the story, Johnson noted, had been taken almost verbatim from the editor's letters.

On May 6, W. B. Parsons, the district intelligence officer at Oak Ridge, sent a memo to Lieutenant Colonel John Lansdale, the security chief in Washington, D.C. Parsons expressed concerns that the story would "provoke public speculation," and he advised that Street & Smith be told that that "such highly particularized stories on secret weapons are detrimental to national security because of the flood of rumors they begin." He also proposed that the firm's special mailing privileges be revoked, which would have been tantamount to killing the magazine.

Campbell had placed *Astounding* in a dangerous position—more dangerous, perhaps, than he ever suspected. Lansdale forwarded the memo to Jack Lockhart, an assistant director at the Office of Censorship, who was reluctant to take drastic action. He hadn't cared for "Deadline," but he felt that punishing the magazine for it would be undemocratic: "I tremble over venturing into this field. . . . I think it would be found that any such action would be more likely to lose a war than to win it."

Later that month, Parsons spoke with H. T. Wensel, a technical advisor at the United States Engineer District Office in Oak Ridge, who was of the opinion that "such articles coming to the attention of personnel connected with the Project are apt to lead to an undue amount of speculation." Like Campbell, the Counterintelligence Corps was evidently less concerned with the average reader than with the scientists of the Manhattan Project, who were so focused on the technical side that they rarely paused to consider the ethical questions.

They decided in the end to rely on the magazine's voluntary cooperation, and Lockhart asked Campbell to provide assurances that he would not "publish additional material relating to subjects involved in our special request of June 28, 1943," which restricted the discussion by publishers of "atom smashing, atomic energy, atomic fission, [and] atomic splitting." Campbell later claimed to have received an exemption from the directive, saying airily:

> We got the notice of censorship on atomic energy, along
> with a lot of other magazines, but I wrote back that
> atomic bombs had been our stock in trade for years and
> that it would look terribly suspicious if we suddenly
> dropped them—from the magazine, I mean. The Army

said they guessed so, too. They probably figured nobody would believe us anyhow.

In reality, he immediately began to censor stories. At times, he took it as a badge of honor, writing proudly to Swisher, "One of the boys guessed too good, and the resultant investigation brought a general censorship attention to [*Astounding*]. We are now censored as thoughtfully as the straight fact magazines—only more so, because we go in for 'wild' guesses." Campbell had usually been the source of this material in the first place, so it wasn't hard to remove it—he was essentially censoring himself. He even dropped a hint to readers: "The really good ideas—the ones we want to talk about and write about—have, quite literally, gone to war."

On some level, Campbell was unable to decide which narrative was more flattering to *Astounding*—that it had been granted a special release from the restrictions, or that it had guessed so accurately that it had drawn even stricter censorship. Neither version was true. No such exemption was given, while "Deadline" had only compelled him to abide by the existing rules, and in practice, he decided to have it both ways, varying the account based on who was listening.

A legend later developed that Campbell was relieved that Riley had failed to notice a map on his office wall, on which he used pins to keep track of the addresses of subscribers—including a suspicious clustering around a post office box in Santa Fe. The story is probably apocryphal, but he may well have had his suspicions. After the war, he wrote, "Every major trade journal publishing company . . . knew Oak Ridge was being built, and knew fairly well what its intended purpose was." He certainly kept an eye on the geographic distribution of sales, and a large number of copies were sold at the drugstore near Oak Ridge National Laboratory.

In any case, the gamble with "Deadline" had succeeded. Campbell had a hunch about what the government was doing, and he had successfully cast out a lure to test it. He took satisfaction in the result, and he never knew how close he had come to ruining the magazine. But after all was said and done, he was still on the outside—although he was about to get the chance to make his first real contribution.

IN LATE 1943, THE INSTALLATION AND MAINTENANCE BRANCH OF THE RADIO DIVISION OF THE Bureau of Ships realized that it had a problem. Manuals for sonar equipment—including the kind that led to Hubbard's encounter with two imaginary subs—were dangerously out of date, and some were nonexistent. The timing couldn't have been worse. Sonar was a crucial weapon in the war, with equipment being installed across the fleet, and there were no workable manuals for the men who had to use it.

A request for assistance to the National Defense Research Committee was passed along in February 1944 to the University of California Division of War Research in San Diego. For ease of access to writers, it was decided to base the project in New York, where Keith Henney, an editor at McGraw-Hill, would oversee operations. Henney, who had a background in radio, was also a science fiction fan, and when the time came to find someone to run the writing side, he contacted Campbell.

The "Deadline" inquiry was just wrapping up, and Campbell may have hoped that it would lead to just such an offer—although it was probably made in spite of the investigation, not because of it. For once, his experience was useful, and he was pleased by the fact that he had finally been approached by the NDRC, which had declined his services when the war began.

He promptly began to recruit his authors. Heinlein badly wanted to join, but the editor said that it was no use: "[We] are, as usual, unable to stick the proper pins in the proper people to get the proper reactions in anything approximating the proper reaction time." Campbell told Heinlein that he hoped to "eventually see your shining face in the slave barracks," but the transfer never came through.

Other writers were more fortunate. Heinlein came to think that Sturgeon had worked on the project—in fact, he was still overseas at the time—but Campbell did hire L. Jerome Stanton, a member of Heinlein's circle, and George O. Smith, a recent discovery from the magazine. Smith, who was born in 1911, was a radio engineer who wrote the kind of highly technical stories that Campbell liked, and the editor had invited him to spend a weekend every month in New Jersey. On these visits, Campbell—who was writing freelance articles on electronics for *Popular Science*—put Smith to work on projects in the basement, while Doña joked that he treated her "like a delicate flower instead of a husky wench."

After joining the sonar group, Smith moved into the house at Scotch Plains, where he slept on the pullout couch. Leslyn's nephews were still living there, so it was crowded, but the editor was pleased to have an electrical engineer at his disposal—and Smith also came to know Doña well. Campbell rarely drank at home, but he didn't mind when his wife had friends over for cocktails. One evening, as Smith was coming upstairs to use the bathroom, Doña asked him to join the party, and after three hours, Campbell found him still mixing drinks in the kitchen. Smith later observed, "The trouble with John Campbell is that he has no redeeming vices."

The sonar manual team eventually expanded to take up an entire floor of the Empire State Building, with a staff of four editors, ten physicists, ten engineers, thirteen rewrite personnel, four draftsmen, thirty-one clerical assistants, and a naval lieutenant to review the results. They sorted themselves into "two big and several dozen small rooms," and Campbell soon found himself up to his ears in work, shuttling between his two jobs "like a ping-pong ball with a hotfoot."

His group produced thirteen manuals, covering equipment used in antisubmarine warfare ships, destroyers, and subs throughout the Navy. Campbell was left without any vacation time, but his new job may have allowed him to print the article on military problems that he had been trying to publish for years. Titled "Inventions Wanted," it provided a technical wish list prepared by the Office of Scientific Research and the National Inventors Council. It came out too late to have any meaningful impact, but the fact that it appeared at all amounted to a minor victory.

He may have hoped that his work would lead to a more extensive research role, but it never did. Campbell resigned after half a year, before the effort was complete: "I couldn't keep up both NDRC and S&S, and the project I was on was due to fold in about five more months." Running a writing factory wasn't quite the position that he had envisioned for himself, and he was already looking ahead to the end of the war. Doña was pregnant with their second child, and he had become involved with a far more intriguing undertaking, which he owed entirely to Heinlein.

Heinlein had spent the early part of the year recuperating from his surgeries. After he returned to work, an important figure entered his life in September 1944, when Lieutenant Virginia Gerstenfeld was transferred from the Bureau of Aeronautics in Washington, D.C. Gerstenfeld, who was born in 1916, had a background in chemistry, a fiancé in the Pacific, and a fierce streak of patriotism—her only regret about serving her country was that she couldn't go into combat herself. On her first day, Heinlein gave her an amused look: "Lieutenant, your slip is showing." Gerstenfeld, mortified, ran into the bathroom to repair the broken strap.

They became good friends, despite their differences. Gerstenfeld, who went by Ginny, was smart and attractive, but she wasn't impressed by science fiction—and she was a Republican. When President Roosevelt toured the Navy Yard on October 27, she didn't even want to see him, leading Heinlein to protest, "But he's your commander in chief!" Heinlein headed over on his own, and he came away worried about Roosevelt's health. Asimov joined the crowd as well, and when he saw the president leaning out of his limousine, he found himself cheering at the top of his lungs.

Heinlein was soon pulled into another project. As the war shifted to the Pacific, the Navy became concerned by the threat of kamikaze attacks, and in the fall, he was asked by the Office of Naval Intelligence to assemble a group to brainstorm unconventional responses. Heinlein, who had trained as a gunnery officer and was familiar with the technical background of aviation, was the ideal man to organize talent and evaluate ideas. It was close to Campbell's dream, and Heinlein asked the editor to join— although he also left no doubt about who was in charge.

The core of the team consisted of Campbell, Stanton, de Camp, Pratt, and George O. Smith. Jenkins had been overruled as a full member because he had never graduated from high school, but as the most resourceful inventor of them all, he was informally consulted. Heinlein also asked Campbell to invite Sturgeon, who had returned from St. Croix in October and was suffering from depression.

Asimov was conspicuously absent. Unlike Heinlein or Campbell, he was content to keep his head down, making incremental progress on the research that he was conducting, and he lacked the technical or military background of most of the others. If he had been a regular part of Heinlein's social circle, he might have been included, but he was set apart from the others by his youth, habits, and personality, much as he had been with the Futurians.

Hubbard was also there. He had spent the first half of the year in Portland, waiting on the conversion of the USS *Algol*. As its navigational officer, he had endured an uneventful two months at sea, but his role had little in common with his fantasies of being a pirate, and his superior noted that he was "very temperamental and often has his feelings hurt." On October 4, when the cargo ship left for the Marshall Islands, Hubbard was already gone.

He made his way to Princeton, where he took part in a four-month training program at the School of Military Government, along with Heinlein's younger brother Clare. Campbell wrote proudly of Hubbard, whom he had invited to join the kamikaze group, "He'll go in with the first wave of landing craft, unarmed, but in navy officer's uniform, to take charge of civilians trapped in the newly formed beachhead." Hubbard, in turn, was spinning stories as furiously as ever. If he had failed to become a hero, it was easy enough to pretend to be one.

Hubbard wasted no time in embellishing his experiences, claiming that he had nearly been blinded in a close call with a deck gun and had taken ships up through the Aleutian Islands. He used his imaginary war wounds to explain his fragile mental state, as well as to make himself attractive to women, and his friends were happy to believe him. Campbell wrote wonderingly, "He was in command of an attack cargo carrier that helped at Saipan just before he was assigned to his present job. He's been sunk five times, wounded four. He was *the* naval officer in charge of sending ships through to MacArthur on Bataan."

Campbell, who hadn't been anywhere near the armed forces, wasn't hard to mislead, but Hubbard was never called out by any of the others, either, and he became respected as the only one of their number who had seen action. Even Heinlein—who seemed to wistfully project his own wartime hopes onto Hubbard—was fooled, writing years later, "Ron had had a busy war—sunk four times and wounded again and again." When Hubbard told him that he had broken both of his feet in combat, Heinlein felt guilty over making him walk to a neighbor's apartment to spend the night.

Around this time, Hubbard also slept with Leslyn. Heinlein evidently encouraged the affair, as Hubbard later remarked: "He almost forced me to sleep with his wife." Leslyn's thoughts on the relationship have not been recorded—although she later asserted that her husband and Hubbard had been physically intimate, an allegation that has not been otherwise corroborated. Heinlein may have pushed her into it out of pity for Hubbard, although he might have felt differently if he had known that the writer was afraid of a recurrence of his gonorrhea, or that he was sleeping at the same time with one of the couple's friends.

The group met at Heinlein's apartment every Saturday, hashing out proposals with an assortment of naval officers throughout the night, with their contact from the Office of Naval Intelligence coming by to hear their recommendations the next morning. Heinlein was pleased by the direct pipeline, which sent the most promising concepts to be tested at the Naval Weapons Station at Hampton Roads, Virginia. No hotel rooms were available, so members slept on the bed, couch, or floor, with the overflow going down the street to stay with Heinlein's supervisor.

None of the team's ideas were ever put into practice, but it was a notable success as a social gathering, and on Sunday afternoons, after its official business was over, the fun began. Hubbard and the others performed in comic skits, one of which Sturgeon, who had once wanted to be an acrobat, finished with a backflip that missed the ceiling by inches. As he watched, Hubbard said admiringly, "I can see him now, a skinny kid in a clown suit too big for him, piling out of that little car with the other clowns and bouncing straight into his routine."

Parties were also hosted by the Campbells, attended by the likes of Heinlein, Stanton, Kuttner, and Moore, at which the editor invited guests to watch the music undulating on a cathode ray screen as they crooned into the microphone. One gathering drew George O. Smith, Sturgeon, and Hubbard, who sang by the fire. Campbell recalled, "He has a low, magnificently mellow baritone voice, and he 'puts over' a song so powerfully that when he's finished . . . you have a marked feeling that the handclapping will start at any second. . . . The fact that Doña has a fairly competent singing voice does nothing to mar such an evening."

A month later, Jack Williamson, who was serving as a weatherman in New Mexico, paid a visit to Philadelphia. On December 2, the Heinleins served steak and potatoes at a dinner that was attended by Williamson, the Asimovs, the de Camps, and Hubbard. Afterward, they went back to a friend's house. Gertrude was wearing an unusually revealing dress that night, and both Hubbard and Heinlein, Asimov said proudly, "swarmed all over her."

But the real life of the party was Hubbard, who was only briefly put out by the fact that de Camp outranked him. He dominated the room, telling stories and singing "Fifteen Men on a Dead Man's Chest" on Heinlein's guitar while the rest sat "quietly as pussycats." Asimov later wrote, "In after years, Hubbard became world famous for reasons far removed from science fiction and guitar plunking, but whatever he does, I remember him only for that evening." They never met again.

Williamson, the guest of honor, came away with a rather different impression: "I recall [Hubbard's] eyes, the wary, light-blue eyes that I somehow associate with the gunmen of the old West, watching me sharply as he talked as if to see how much I believed. Not much."

In January 1945, Hubbard was transferred to the Naval Civil Affairs Staging Area in Monterey. Before his departure, he presented a box of candy bars to Heinlein, who was touched by the gift. Heinlein recommended that he seek out Jack Parsons, a rocket scientist in Pasadena whom he had met through the American Rocket Society, and Hubbard said that he would.

The plan was for Hubbard to continue to a foreign posting, but his medical issues intervened, and in April, he was diagnosed with a duodenal ulcer. Hubbard—who later described himself as "a supposedly hopeless cripple" at the time—welcomed the excuse to avoid going overseas. He was sent to Oak Knoll Naval Hospital in Oakland, and he remained on the sick list for the rest of the war.

ON CHRISTMAS DAY 1944, MARK HUBBARD, LESLYN HEINLEIN'S BROTHER-IN-LAW, WAS KILLED BY the Japanese. Three years earlier, he had been living on Luzon in the Philippines with Keith and their two sons, working as an engineer on a research expedition, when the island was taken. Dynamiting his gold mines to keep them from being taken by the enemy, he disappeared into the bush, listening to the news with makeshift radios that he fueled with alcohol that he distilled himself.

It was an example of the competent man at his best, but Mark Hubbard did not get the ending that he deserved. He caught malaria—his weight fell to below a hundred pounds—and he was handed over to the Japanese occupiers. After a protracted ordeal, he was executed at Bilibid Prison. He was later awarded the Purple Heart, and Heinlein would write one day, "This is how a man gets to Valhalla." But no one at home knew of his death for months.

In February 1945, Kuttner and Moore arrived on a visit to Philadelphia, with Asimov, the Heinleins, and the de Camps joining them at a restaurant with service so bad that it became a running joke—when one of them asked for a fork, the waiter fished through the dirty utensils at a nearby table. The Kuttners were more concerned by what they saw of the Heinleins: "Both of you seem to be strung on taut wires these days. . . . The hypertension's sneaked up on you both . . . and we are worried about it and expect you to blow up presently and suddenly."

On April 12, President Roosevelt passed away. Heinlein and Leslyn wore black armbands to work, and Asimov dropped by Heinlein's desk to share how depressed he felt at the news: "You see, I've never lost a member of my family before." But the war was entering its concluding phase. Asimov had been keeping track of troop movements on his map in the office, and on V-E Day, Heinlein took it down, replacing it with one of the Pacific Theater.

Shortly afterward, they learned that Mark Hubbard had died. Leslyn was devastated. Worn out by work and worry, she descended further into alcoholism, and Heinlein was in no condition to help. As the war wound to a close, his emotions grew overpowering. After encountering a group of marines, one with a missing leg, another with "just enough of him left to sit down," he went into the bathroom, locked the door, and cried for fifteen minutes.

When word came that an atomic bomb had been dropped on Hiroshima on August 6, one day after he had predicted it, Heinlein said, "That's the end." A week and a half later, he wrote out his resignation, citing the conclusion of the war and his health problems—but he also had another project in mind, which he described in a memorandum just before the announcement of the Japanese surrender.

The memo was titled "Tentative Proposal for Projects to Be Carried On at NAMC." Its actual subject was rockets—the deployment of atomic bombs on missiles like the ones that had rained down on London, in a terrible combination of the two weapons that had embodied the genre's greatest fears. Heinlein proposed that the Navy organize a mission to the moon, since the technical problems were largely the same, and he strongly implied that he was the one best prepared to lead the charge.

Asimov had a more pragmatic reaction to the bomb. When the news broke, he was reading a book at home while Gertrude did the ironing. Hearing the bulletin on the radio, he wasn't shocked—he had known that something like it was coming since the day that he had unwisely mentioned uranium to Harold Urey at Columbia. What he thought about instead was the draft.

He had reached a dead end at the Navy Yard. A lieutenant commander there liked to make snide remarks about his Russian ancestry, and Asimov knew that he would veto any promotion. Heinlein quietly put the officer in his place: "I sent word to him, indirectly, which let him know that Isaac had been making more money the last couple of months pulp writing than he gets paid to be a crackerjack chemist. This lunk can be impressed only by money and I know it will burn him up."

In fact, Asimov's writing had become his greatest source of pride. Campbell was eager for more Foundation stories, and Asimov was equally determined to take advantage of the new higher rates. He would have been content to stick with his proven formula, but Campbell unexpectedly asked him one day to upset the Seldon Plan, the detailed forecast of the future on which the entire series rested.

Asimov was horrified—"No, no, no"—but he wouldn't turn down a guaranteed sale. The result, "The Mule," was his finest work to date. It had one of the best twist endings that the genre had ever seen, and its titular antagonist, a mutant telepath, introduced a welcome element of chance into a series that often seemed constrained by psychohistory itself. Campbell's two best writers had pulled even.

Yet his fears about the draft persisted. The year before, the Navy Yard had announced that it was reviewing the status of all its employees, and a few days later, Asimov was classified as 1A. His first impulse was to look into becoming an officer, so he headed for the Naval Procurement Office, where he was told to remove his glasses and read the chart on the wall. He responded, "What chart?"

His eyesight was enough to get him exempted for now, but workers with "mild physical defects" were still being considered for the field. Life at the Navy Yard was winding down—employees were destroying war surplus, squashing radios in a compression machine and cutting up flight jackets with knives, and Heinlein and de Camp were preparing to leave. Asimov couldn't go anywhere yet, but he was optimistic that he would be able to return to Columbia.

On September 7, 1945, the eve of Rosh Hashanah, Gertrude telephoned him with the news that he had been drafted. Asimov knew that it wasn't as tragic as it seemed—he had been sucked into a war that was already over—but he was still miserable. He couldn't help thinking that if he had kept quiet about his real age in the third grade, he would have been twenty-six on paper when his number came up, and he wouldn't have been eligible at all.

Asimov managed to delay his induction by a month, and he and Gertrude moved back to New York. On October 15, he went to see Campbell with an idea for a story, "Evidence," about a robot that looked like a man, cautioning him that he might not be able to write it until he got out of the Army. The editor took him to lunch with some friends from Bell Telephone, who ordered steaks. Asimov, dismayed by the cost, had the pot roast instead. Campbell seemed much the same as always, and he didn't tell Asimov what few of their friends knew yet—Doña was gone.

After George O. Smith told him that the bomb had been dropped, Campbell had said, "Oh my God! It's started." He had greeted it with a grim sense of vindication. In his November 1945 editorial, he said that civilization as they knew it was dead, but he couldn't resist sounding a note of satisfaction: "During the weeks immediately following that first atomic bomb, the science-fictioneers were suddenly recognized by their neighbors as not quite such wild-eyed dreamers as they had been thought, and in many soul-satisfying cases became the neighborhood experts."

He was speaking of himself. As the atomic age dawned, Campbell was acclaimed as a prophet, a role for which he had carefully positioned himself—he had planted "Deadline" in the magazine so that he could point to it later, orchestrating the most famous anecdote of his career to illustrate the genre's ability to foresee the future. The fact that he hadn't predicted anything at all was a distinction lost on most readers, who exulted in their newfound relevance. Before long, the writer Chan Davis felt obliged to rebuke fans, "The fact that your life is in danger seems to interest you less than the fact that Anson MacDonald predicted your life would be in danger."

The calls started coming right away. When a radio station asked Donald Wollheim for comment, he referred them to Campbell, who was "the kind of man who could talk a blue streak about scientific and pseudoscientific possibilities." Both the *Wall Street Journal* and the leftist paper *PM* wanted the editor's thoughts on "the economics of atomic power," and he signed a contract with the publisher Henry Holt for a book on the bomb. He was even profiled in *The New Yorker*, in a Talk of the Town piece titled "1945 Cassandra," in which he said of the next war:

> *Every major city will be wiped out in thirty minutes. . . .*
> *New York will be a slag heap and any extensive form*
> *of government will be impossible. . . . After a big*
> *international atomic war, with atomic bombs exploded*
> *on the ground, a lot of survivors will be mutated. They'll*
> *give birth to freaks or supermen or telepaths.*

A debate about the future was looming, but he was distracted by problems at home. In 1942, his sister, Laura, had left her first husband for another officer in the Foreign Service named William Krieg. They had gotten engaged while Krieg was in Lisbon, and she had braved the Atlantic at the height of the war to join him where he was serving in Lagos, Nigeria.

What happened next, Campbell wrote, was that "she was invalided home with complete breakdown into psychotic melancholia"—or what would be known today as bipolar disorder. Laura was hospitalized, and she appears to have received electroshock therapy. Campbell wrote favorably about the treatment in the magazine, saying that it allowed patients to get the equivalent of half a year's distance on emotional trauma, but it weighed on his mind.

Doña was dealing with troubles of her own. Their second daughter, Leslyn, had been born without complications on March 22, 1945. They named her after Leslyn Heinlein, and there was no question that the Heinleins were her godparents. Between the war, her two children, and her husband's workload, however, Doña began to suffer. She had been drinking more, although only socially—she got tipsy in the afternoons with other young mothers, and she sometimes went out with George O. Smith and Stanton while Campbell watched the girls. She said of him wryly, "It must be the life I lead that has ruined his health."

But there were darker factors involved, some of which remain obscure. Sturgeon had lived with the Campbells for several weeks while Doña was pregnant, and he later hinted that it was because of a difficult personal situation—Doña was "in very real danger at the time from an outside source," and he was there to serve as her bodyguard while Campbell was at the office. Doña was also skeptical of her husband's evolving ideas, writing to the Heinleins that he was undergoing "a renovation, regeneration, or something, of personality. I await the results." She added:

> Seems like I have spent a goodly portion of these thirty-one years waiting for someone, or something, so don't be surprised if I decide to take off like one of Willy [Ley]'s rockets one day, scattering burning particles in all directions, of course, and falling to earth again with a good, solid thump.

She underwent therapy, writing to Heinlein, "I also have been the victim of a sort of postpartum psychosis. I'll let you know whether I'm working to conquer it or encouraging it." After the war, her psychiatrist told her to take a vacation, and on September 27, Doña left for Boston, leaving the girls behind, in a separation that was planned to last between four and six weeks. Campbell told Heinlein:

> *She's in violent revolt against responsibility of any kind, and determined to do what she wants to do. . . . I am in somewhat of a delicate situation in trying to get some data out of her as to her plans. The thing she resents is responsibility and "being pushed"; if I try to get her to tell me what makes* [sic]*, she automatically resents it as an effort to control her decisions—and she's supposed to be getting a rest from pressures.*

While in Boston, Doña met up with George O. Smith, who had landed a job working at the Submarine Signal Company. Two weeks after her departure, Campbell received a letter from her that was "rather impersonal, but otherwise normal." Leaving the children with Margaret, their maid, he tinkered with his record player and lost himself in work—the year before, he had been named the science editor for all of Street & Smith. Sturgeon, who was suffering from writer's block, came to stay for ten days. He finally cranked out "The Chromium Helmet," about an attempt to make the brain into an efficient machine, in Campbell's basement, with the editor reviewing the pages as they came out of the typewriter.

In November, Doña returned. Campbell wrote to Heinlein, "Doña's mood is not improved greatly, and could stand immense improvement. At present, you can't scare her with atomic bombs or any other threats. It is her deep-seated opinion that the world will be much improved by their liberal use, and [she] would like to be handy by when the first one lands." He was positioning himself for the postwar era, writing in the December 1945 issue, "May we call to your attention that the essential principles employed in the bomb were described as the arming mechanism of the atomic bomb in the story 'Deadline' in the March 1944 *Astounding*."

Doña was back, but her mood was grim. As she wrote to Heinlein, "What do you expect to do with this horrid little world and its unimportant very little people if you finally manage to save it? . . . I not only don't care if the world explodes its little self tomorrow, I hope to God it does. I prefer to be part of the splatter rather than the splattered." With her luck, she would survive the blast: "I'll die of overwork, preserving the edible portions of the animals you and John have talked to death."

TWO MONTHS LATER, THERE CAME A CURIOUS CODA. ON JANUARY 20, 1946, THE *PHILADELPHIA Record* published a story titled "Stranger Than Fiction," by the reporter Alfred M. Klein. It described a secret research laboratory at the Philadelphia Navy Yard that had been staffed by three science fiction writers, Heinlein, de Camp, and "Azimov," who had been asked to build "some of these superweapons and atom-powered spaceships you've been creating on paper."

The article, which was riddled with errors, noted that they had failed to come up with anything practical. It concluded, "Heinlein, de Camp, and Azimov, however, have been separated from the service now and have gone back to their typewriters, where it is so much easier to invent things." And the only quoted source in the entire piece was Campbell.

De Camp was furious. He called Campbell to complain, raging to Heinlein that the editor must have been "drunk, hostile, or very, very careless." Heinlein, in whom the article caused an "explosion," asked Campbell to tell the paper that he had been misquoted, and there was talk of the three authors joining in a lawsuit. De Camp contented himself with sending an angry letter, and no further action was taken after the newspaper printed his response.

Klein, the credited writer, later said that he had obtained his information from Campbell, and that his notes had been written up by a cub reporter. Campbell, in turn, blamed Klein, saying that he had only talked to him for ten minutes, distractedly, during a meeting in another editor's office. In reality, his quotes were almost certainly authentic—the article included an account of the "Deadline" affair that repeated his assertion, which only he could have made, that he had been allowed to continue printing stories about the bomb.

If he gave the rest of the story to Klein, as it seems likely that he did, it was his fantasy of what the Navy Yard might have been. Campbell still clung to the belief that science fiction could have played a greater part in the war, and he wasn't above inventing one for it out of thin air. He claimed elsewhere that the operations rooms on warships had been inspired by E. E. Smith's Lensman stories and that the magazine had "helped the Navy with more than a dozen vital little systems and gadgets." At best, these were embellishments, and at worst, they were outright lies.

It all felt a little like Hubbard, and it reflected how the war had failed to live up to either of their expectations. Hubbard had craved glory for its own sake, while Campbell—while not averse to taking credit—had wanted science fiction to rise to the occasion for which he thought it had been destined. In practice, it had turned out to be less useful than he had hoped, but after the war, he saw another chance. Before Hiroshima, he had written in *Astounding*:

> *Our present culture is finished. Either it will learn something about how men live and think and react, so it can be discarded in favor of a cultural system that can prevent warfare, or the next gross failure on its part will produce a war in which the ancient cry of "Wolf! Wolf!" will not be a false alarm—they really will have the weapon that can't be stopped.*

The atomic bomb had been a triumph of technology, but it also pointed to the fact—which Heinlein's "Solution Unsatisfactory" had foreseen—that existing social and political systems weren't up to the task of controlling it. Campbell had already moved to make sociology a province of science fiction, and the next frontier, as he had long understood, would be in the brain.

He had failed to make a direct impact on the war, but his life's work had been clarified. In the world of tomorrow, power would be based on the mind, rather than on industrial might. Campbell couldn't run a research operation on the scale necessary to produce an atomic weapon, but for a psychological breakthrough, he needed nothing but the resources that were at his disposal.

In fact, it required nothing more than two men in a quiet room. Science fiction, he decided, would save mankind from the bomb—and this time, the project would be one that he could control. As he wrote to Hubbard on November 11, 1945, "Science fiction better get stepping if it wants to lead the world!"

IV.

THE DOUBLE MINDS

1945–1951

The art [of science fiction] consists in concealing from the reader, for novelistic purposes, the distinctions between established scientific facts, almost-established scientific hypotheses, scientific conjectures, and imaginative extrapolations far beyond what has even been conjectured. The danger of this technique lies in the fact that, if the writer of science fiction writes too much of it too fast and too glibly . . . he may eventually succeed in concealing the distinction between his facts and his imaginings from himself.

—S. I. HAYAKAWA, *ETC.*, SUMMER 1951

10.
BLACK MAGIC AND THE BOMB
1945–1949

In this book it is spoken of the Sephiroth and the Paths; of Spirits and Conjurations; of Gods, Spheres, Planes, and many other things which may or may not exist. It is immaterial whether these exist or not. By doing certain things certain results will follow; students are most earnestly warned against attributing objective reality or philosophic validity to any of them.

—ALEISTER CROWLEY, *LIBER O*

At the end of 1945, the three writers who had been displaced by the war entered a world that had changed forever. Before Pearl Harbor, their careers had followed distinct trajectories—shaped in no small part by their reactions to Campbell—that had been interrupted just as they seemed on the verge of reaching the next stage. Instead, they had been diverted along other lines, and in the aftermath, they were unable to resume the lives that they had been leading before the convulsions began.

It would have been hard enough to navigate this homecoming in itself, and there were other complications. Campbell, who had brought them all together, was evolving as well. One of his authors soon found that the forces that the war had set in motion weren't quite done with him yet. Another became distracted by upheavals in the wider world and in his own life. And one had been altered in ways that neither he nor anyone else would fully understand for a long time.

ON NOVEMBER 1, 1945, ASIMOV RECEIVED A PSYCHOLOGICAL EXAMINATION AT THE ARMY INDUC-tion center in Philadelphia. He was told that he suffered from "situational tension," which struck him as the least surprising news in the world. Later that afternoon, he was sworn in by a sergeant, who asked the assembled recruits if they had any questions. Asimov felt obliged to make the traditional crack: "Yes, Sarge—how do we get out of this chicken outfit?"

The sergeant just rolled his eyes. Asimov was put on a train to Fort Meade, Maryland, and proceeded from there to Camp Lee in Virginia. When he called Gertrude, he began to cry. He learned to make a bed to military specifications and showed an unexpected talent for marksmanship, although his high score on the Army General Classification Test—an intelligence exam given to soldiers—meant that he would end up behind a desk no matter what he did.

When his furlough came, he hitchhiked to the train station in Washington and made his way to New York. On December 30, at his father's candy store, he ran into Pohl, who had just been discharged. Pohl said proudly that he had scored 156 on the intelligence test. "What was yours?"

Asimov couldn't lie. His score had been the highest anyone had ever seen. "I got 160, Fred."

"Shit!" Pohl said. It never even occurred to him that Asimov wouldn't tell the truth.

Asimov still wanted to get out of the Army. Before his departure, he had seen an article about the release of chemists engaged in research, but it would take six weeks to see any results on the application, and until then, he would be stuck wherever he happened to be. He didn't want to get stranded in basic training, so he decided to wait. In the meantime, he befriended the base librarian, who offered him a typewriter to begin a new robot story.

On February 9, 1946, he attended a USO event in Richmond, where he danced with a "very pretty girl." They arranged to meet again the next day, and he stayed in the city overnight. "I know exactly what I had in mind and I might have carried it through," Asimov recalled. "I think she was willing." When they went to her apartment, however, after making a few hesitant moves, he heard himself saying that he had to leave. The girl was startled, but she let him go. At a time when he was anxious to return to Gertrude, an affair would have been a betrayal, and as soon as he made it back to base, he submitted his request for discharge.

Rumors were circulating that he was being saved for Operation Crossroads, the atomic bomb test scheduled for Bikini Atoll in the Marshall Islands. The show would be run by the Navy, but the Army wanted to study food and equipment for the effects of exposure to radiation, and one of its "specialists" would be Asimov. He felt sick at the news, reflecting that if he had made his application in basic training, he wouldn't have been considered at all.

On March 15, Asimov arrived in Hawaii on a troopship—his first voyage at sea since his departure from Russia. Two months later, thanks to a misunderstanding over his discharge status, he escaped from Bikini with one day to spare. At a moment when Heinlein and Campbell were defining themselves through their reactions to the bomb, he was the only one who came close to being involved in nuclear testing—and he hadn't wanted anything to do with it. Campbell wrote to Heinlein, "Isaac doesn't like the atomic bomb worth a damn. Isaac, I fear, is approaching the status of one who has been successfully scared by the understanding of what the thing means."

It would be even more accurate to say that Asimov saw the bomb as a disruptive force that was keeping him away from the life that he wanted to resume. Campbell himself was an important part of that world, and on June 11, a few days into another furlough in New York, Asimov paid him a visit, bringing along his father for the first time. Afterward, he and the editor had lunch, where Asimov pitched the short story "Little Lost Robot." He couldn't write it until after his situation in the military was clarified, but he didn't like to come by without a new idea.

In July, Asimov's discharge was finally approved, and he moved back to Brooklyn, where he did his best to break the habit, which he had picked up in the service, of casually using the word "fuck." Later that summer, he received an offer to buy the rights to his story "Evidence" for $250, which Campbell said seemed fair. When Asimov learned that the interested party was Orson Welles, he agreed, delighted, but nothing ever came of it. Welles owned it in perpetuity, making it impossible to sell it again—a point that the editor, whose casual attitude toward rights outside the magazine would soon cause other problems, had neglected to mention.

On September 23, Asimov registered as a graduate student at Columbia. He continued to think of the war years as an "extraneous intrusion" on his life, lamenting to Pohl that his friends were "lost in a maze of successful agencies, editorships, and whatnots," while he was back in school as if nothing had changed. Yet he continued to flourish as a writer. Campbell paid him five hundred dollars for "Now You See It—," a new Foundation story, and at the World Science Fiction Convention the following summer in Philadelphia, Asimov was treated as a celebrity.

Another attendee was Sam Merwin, Jr., the editor of *Thrilling Wonder Stories*. Several months earlier, he had asked for a novel from Asimov, who promptly started work on *Grow Old with Me*, about a future society in which all citizens are euthanized at the age of sixty. In September, however, Merwin told him that it had to be rewritten from scratch. Asimov—who was anxious about his dissertation and his efforts to have a child with Gertrude—was furious. Picking up the manuscript, he snarled, "Go to hell!" He never submitted to Merwin again.

Campbell rejected it as well, saying that it lacked a natural breaking point for serialization—which may have been a diplomatic way of saying that it was a step down from his best work. Asimov's professional future was also up in the air. Earlier that year, he had attended a convention of the American Chemical Society, writing on his registration, "Not interested in any work having any connection to the atomic bomb." He left without any interviews. By January, he was starting to worry, but he managed to land a postdoctoral position at the last minute.

As part of his research, Asimov often had to prepare solutions of a white fluffy compound called catechol. One day, he had thought idly, "What if it dissolved just *before* it hit the water?" It occurred to him to frame the story as an academic parody, complete with references and diagrams, and when he pitched the premise—with its sidelong look at determinism, which appealed to Campbell's interest in psychology—the editor laughed: "Go try it."

Asimov wrote it up as "The Endochronic Properties of Resublimated Thiotimoline," but he worried that it would look bad if it came out before his orals, so he asked that it be published under a pseudonym. After it appeared in the March 1948 issue, he was in the lab with two other students when one said, "Hey, that was a funny satire on chemistry by you in the new *Astounding*, Isaac."

"Thanks," Asimov said. He paused. "What made you think the article was by me?"

The student pretended to consider the question. "Well, when I noticed your name on it, I thought, 'Gee, I bet he wrote it.'"

The other graduate student stared at him. "Don't tell me you put your own name on a satire on chemistry when your dissertation is coming up?"

Asimov was horrified. He called Campbell to ask why he hadn't published the article under a pseudonym, as they had previously agreed. The editor's explanation was a simple one: "I forgot."

He later wondered whether Campbell had forgotten on purpose. The article became the most popular story he had ever written, at least among the general public. Campbell claimed that readers had gone to the library to look up the fictitious sources that it mentioned, and chemists were especially tickled by it. Asimov didn't enjoy the attention—it just made him more worried about his orals.

On May 20, the day of his presentation arrived. After he was done, a professor asked, "What can you tell us, Mr. Asimov, about the thermodynamic properties of the compound known as thiotimoline?"

Asimov broke down laughing. He went outside, and after five minutes the professors emerged one by one to shake his hand. According to Gertrude, he lay awake for most of the night, giggling to himself in bed and repeating, "*Doctor* Asimov." He finally had his Ph.D.

In June, he began his postdoctoral research, on the same day that he started one of his best stories, "The Red Queen's Race," about a scientist suffering from guilt over his work on the bomb. Later that year, he visited *Astounding*'s cramped new offices in Elizabeth, New Jersey. Campbell wanted another Foundation story, but Asimov was tiring of the series. Since this would be the last installment, the editor requested that it be a long one, and he eventually took "—And Now You Don't" for a thousand dollars, which was the largest check that Asimov had ever seen.

But a new chapter of his life was about to begin. Early in 1949, he got a call from Bill Boyd of the Boston University School of

Medicine, who had recommended him for a position. Asimov, who had never considered entering academia, paid a visit to the medical school, and when he was asked if he could teach freshman biochemistry, he replied, "Certainly." He didn't tell them that he didn't know anything about it, but he figured that he could catch up later.

With help from Pohl, *Grow Old with Me* was bought by Walter I. Bradbury of Doubleday, where it was retitled *Pebble in the Sky*. Asimov had met Bradbury at the Hydra Club, a successor to the Futurians that included del Rey, Sturgeon, and Judith Merril, whom Asimov described as "the kind of girl who, when her rear end was patted by a man, patted the rear end of the patter." He was speaking from experience, but he softened the facts—Merril had actually grabbed at his crotch.

At the end of May, Asimov and Gertrude moved to Boston. For the first time ever, he was willingly leaving one life and entering another. He still didn't think that he would be able to write for a living, and he had doubts about his dependence on one editor: "There was a question in my mind as to how much of the success of my stories was mine and how much Campbell's. . . . What would happen to me, then, if something happened to Campbell? If he quit or were fired or died? Might it not be possible that I would then find suddenly that I was no writer at all?"

AFTER THE WAR, ASIMOV HAD BEEN DEPOSITED STRAIGHT INTO THE ARMY, PLUNGING HIM INTO A system that he desperately wanted to escape. Heinlein had the opposite problem. In August 1945, he had packed up his life at the Navy Yard, leaving some furniture with the Campbells, and prepared to make sense of his place in the postwar world. Before leaving, he said goodbye to Virginia Gerstenfeld. Ginny recalled, "He left me on a street corner in Philadelphia with a kiss. Our first."

Loading up their Chevy, Heinlein and Leslyn headed west.

In Santa Fe, they saw his friend Robert Cornog, a physicist who had worked on the Manhattan Project. Cornog introduced them to scientists, and Heinlein was surprised to be treated as a political authority: "The men who built the atom bomb [were] asking us quite seriously what they should do next to achieve their social aims." As a gesture of thanks, Cornog presented them with a hunk of the translucent green glass produced by the detonation of the bomb at Alamogordo. Leslyn was afraid to touch it.

On September 11, they arrived in Los Angeles, where Heinlein busied himself with letters about his rocket project. He also reconnected with Jack Parsons, an engineer who had been one of the founders of the Jet Propulsion Laboratory in Pasadena. Parsons was a member of the Ordo Templi Orientis, a group associated with the occultist Aleister Crowley, to whom he sent money. He was also a science fiction fan, and Heinlein, Williamson, and Cartmill all attended meetings of the temple, which de Camp called "a conspiracy to seize control from the extroverts."

Leslyn's health was still poor—at one point she weighed less than eighty pounds—and they went on vacation to Murrieta Hot Springs. They were joined in October by Hubbard, who was on convalescent leave from the naval hospital. Rather than go back to Polly, he had headed down to Los Angeles, and he was staying at the Eleanor Hotel when he heard that he was going to be mustered out. When they returned to Laurel Canyon, he moved in with them. Heinlein established a shared workspace, with a desk for Hubbard made out of a door and a pair of old packing crates, and charged a quarter to anyone who broke the rule of silence.

Hubbard was unable to write. He had exaggerated his injuries—if he could no longer be the most impressive person in the room, he would settle for being the most damaged—but his ulcer was real enough, and his medication had left him impotent and depressed. It combined to reveal a strain of weakness that he had previously been able to conceal, as de Camp wrote to Asimov:

"He always was that way. . . . What the war did was to wear him down to where he no longer bothers with the act."

Heinlein saw Hubbard, unquestioningly, as a wounded veteran, and he was forgiving of him, even when he snuck alcohol—which Heinlein was trying to keep from Leslyn—into the house. He recalled later, "I . . . spent weeks in '45 and early '46 trying to take care of him, trying to keep him out of trouble. I could keep him on an even keel only when I was with him constantly."

Yet he still thought highly of Hubbard as a writer, crediting him with the discovery of a plot formula, "the man who learned better," that he had used unconsciously throughout his career. There was talk of Hubbard revising *For Us, the Living,* and Heinlein put him together with his friend John Arwine to organize scientists against the bomb. Nothing ever came of it, and Hubbard returned to the hospital.

Heinlein worked diligently on his articles about atomic weapons, but he was unable to get them published, despite the efforts of his agent, Lurton Blassingame, whom he had hired on Hubbard's recommendation. Blassingame wanted him to return to fiction, agreeing with Hubbard that he was "wasted on pulp," and Campbell was asking for stories. But at the very moment that the bomb was pushing science fiction into the mainstream—and Campbell hoped to take the magazine to the next level—Heinlein had concluded that he could no longer write for *Astounding.*

The conflict revolved around the rights to his work, which had been a point of contention for years. After the war, Heinlein wanted to obtain the releases to "Blowups Happen" and "Solution Unsatisfactory" to promote his rocket project, but Campbell dodged the request, prompting Doña to demand, "What do you mean by saying that he has never been refused rights when you just refused them?" Heinlein threatened to go directly to Henry Ralston, the vice president of Street & Smith, and the ultimatum worked—but only for those two stories.

Early in 1946, Heinlein asked for a release of all ancillary rights. Campbell handled it poorly, showing their correspondence to Ralston, and he seemed unwilling to challenge his superiors. Heinlein was told that the firm wouldn't transfer any rights without a definite offer on the table, which meant that he couldn't shop his stories to the movies. This bothered him more than any personal issue, and Campbell—whom Heinlein called "a supreme scissorbill," an old term of labor slang for someone who was overly sympathetic to management—failed to understand this. Heinlein wrote to de Camp, "I hardly expect to sell to him again."

In the meantime, it occurred to Heinlein that he could earn money and reach a wider audience with a juvenile novel for boys. He conceived *The Young Atomic Engineers and the Conquest of the Moon* as a successor to the Horatio Alger and Tom Swift books that he had loved growing up, with an emphasis on the values of hard work and education, and he set certain rules for himself: "Never write down to them. Do not simplify the vocabulary nor the intellectual concepts. . . . No real love interest and female characters should be only walk-ons."

Above all else, he wanted to escape the pulps. Will Jenkins had told him that any story that was written well enough could be sold to the slicks, and Heinlein set his sights on *The Saturday Evening Post*. Like Campbell, he still believed that science fiction—which he preferred to call "speculative fiction"—could change the world: "The market is there, created by the war. . . . I can satisfy my itch to preach and propagandize, reach a bigger audience and make some dinero."

Throughout the summer, Heinlein worked on "The Green Hills of Earth," which he had once seen as his "swan song" for Campbell, who had even mentioned it in the magazine. Instead, it was bought by the *Post*. The sale was a milestone for the entire genre—Asimov was filled with "miserable envy" when he heard about it—but Heinlein was sorry that he hadn't sent it to his old friend: "I deeply regret that it should have worked out with hurt feelings, for John nursed me along a lot at the beginning." Even better, his juvenile novel, which would be retitled *Rocket Ship Galileo*, was acquired for hardcover by Alice Dalgliesh at Scribner.

Any satisfaction that he felt in his achievements was undermined by personal complications. In June, Leslyn had answered the door to find Ginny standing there with a suitcase—they had expected her to visit in the fall, but she had been demobilized in March. Her engagement had fallen apart, and Heinlein was as charmed by her as ever. In a letter that they both wrote to Ginny, he slipped in a typewritten card that Leslyn probably never saw: "I think about you all the time."

Leslyn's drinking had grown worse. At home, Heinlein emptied the liquor into the sink, and after Ginny caught Leslyn swigging from a bottle, he searched for stashes of alcohol. They were both seeing a psychiatrist—Leslyn couldn't drive, so he dropped her off at her appointments and waited until she was done—and after Ginny moved into the house, the nature of the situation became impossible to ignore. A friend recalled, "Leslyn slept in the studio whilst Bob and the femme fatale cavorted in the master bedroom. Ginny was a virgin, but she learned fast."

When Leslyn finally ordered Ginny to leave, it may have only hastened the outcome. In her first true love letter to Heinlein, Ginny wrote, "Oh, my darling, how much I miss you already—not waking with you today and not seeing you and hearing your sweet voice." Left alone with Leslyn, who was confined to her room, Heinlein despaired. He couldn't sleep, and he was feeling miserable himself: "During the past eighteen months there have been more times when I wanted to be dead than there were times when I wanted to go on living."

One day, Leslyn told Heinlein that she had tried to kill herself, in a gesture laden with symbolism, by handling the radioactive glass that they had received from Cornog. In fact, it was locked safely away, but the incident catalyzed something inside him that had been building for months. The couple made plans for a trip to Arizona, but Heinlein informed her abruptly that he intended to go off on his own. Leslyn moved in with her cousin, and Heinlein told his lawyer that he wanted a divorce. Their date of separation was given as June 20, 1947.

Heinlein expressed regret over what had happened: "I was simply a man faced with a problem which he could not solve." Leslyn, in turn, wrote to Jack Williamson, "Bob feels that I am entirely to blame, and perhaps he is right. But it has taken me some time to get used to the idea that fifteen years of habits and associations must be broken." The timing was also significant. Ginny was available, and Heinlein had made his breakthrough sales to the *Post* and Scribner. Leslyn's troubles had been holding him back, and he broke away from her as soon as he could.

Moving with Ginny to Ojai, California, Heinlein reworked *Beyond This Horizon* for book publication, removing some of the elements that he had added for Campbell. In July, he wrote a letter to Asimov that failed to mention Leslyn, and Gertrude concluded that they had split up. Asimov didn't believe her, but after de Camp confirmed it, he wrote to express sympathy over Heinlein's domestic troubles. Heinlein replied that he didn't have any. Asimov recalled, "I took it to mean that his marital problems had been solved by separation, so I said no more."

But his situation was still unresolved. Leslyn was telling others that he had been abusive, but she was also hinting at a reconciliation, and Heinlein realized that he had to stay in Los Angeles to make sure that she went through with the divorce. In the city, he kept away from his friends. He bought a caravan, the "Gopher Hole," that was so small that he had to keep his books in the trunk of his car, and he moved into a trailer park in the San Fernando Valley.

A divorce hearing occurred in September, but a year had to pass before he could remarry, and the uncertainty took its toll—he had failed to place anything new since leaving Leslyn. In 1948, there were signs of a turnaround. Fritz Lang, the director of *Metropolis,* proposed that they collaborate on a film about a voyage to the moon, and after seeing Campbell in New York, Heinlein went to Los Angeles. The partnership with Lang went nowhere— Heinlein distrusted his leftist politics—but he reached a more successful agreement with a producer named George Pal.

Heinlein felt secure enough to ask Ginny to marry him, proposing that they live in Colorado Springs, which he had visited in his teens. After writing a "drop dead" file for the movie project, which recommended Jack Parsons as a technical advisor in case anything happened to him, he reunited with Ginny in Colorado. They decided to wed out of town, to avoid a local newspaper announcement, and were married just across the border in New Mexico on October 21, 1948.

He had turned a corner. With his second juvenile, *Space Cadet,* Heinlein began to grasp that his works for younger readers were an ideal playground for his talents—he saw a technical education as a royal road to the stars, and these books, which were designed to inspire students to study science and engineering, amounted to the best propaganda imaginable. Nothing else that he ever wrote would so fully utilize his gifts or affect the future so profoundly.

The rights dispute with *Astounding* had finally been resolved, and Heinlein wanted to thank Campbell by doing a story for him. The editor was into ham radio—he would later write articles on the subject for hobbyist journals—and they used it to discuss a new idea. A few months earlier, the magazine had printed a letter from a fan claiming to review an issue from a year in the future. One of the nonexistent stories was "Gulf," by Heinlein's pseudonym Anson MacDonald, and he proposed that if they persuaded the other writers to play along, they could do it for real.

Campbell loved the notion, and Heinlein set to work. The title

"Gulf" could mean almost anything, and when Heinlein turned to Ginny for suggestions, she proposed a plot about a "Martian Mowgli," a human orphan raised by aliens on Mars. Heinlein drafted the first and last chapters and asked Campbell for feedback on potential endings: "Another solution is for him to become a messiah, either tragically unsuccessful, or dramatically successful."

The editor was intrigued, but it seemed too large for one story. Heinlein set it aside, and when he asked Ginny what else she had in mind, she reminded him of the discussion that had ensued when he asked, "What makes a superman?" She had replied, "They think better." In the meantime, a publisher wanted to put out the Future History in hardcover, and Heinlein began work on "The Man Who Sold the Moon," which would serve as a keystone for the entire series.

Another figure resurfaced in February 1949, when Heinlein received a note from Hubbard, with whom he had sporadically corresponded. Hubbard, who was living in Savannah, Georgia, wrote to ask for a loan of fifty dollars, which he needed to get to a pension hearing: "If you don't say yes, you haven't offended. But if you do, I'll name my next hero after you."

Heinlein sent the money, telling him that Ginny had taken it out of her grocery budget: "She won't turn down a shipmate. As for me, it's partly because I remember you floating around out there in that salt water with your ribs caved in." He added that he knew that he could rely on Hubbard in a pinch, which was more than he could say for some of his other friends.

On March 3, Hubbard repaid the money, adding an extra dollar. Heinlein returned it: "No son of a bitch is going to pay me interest on a personal loan and get away with it." In response, Hubbard thanked him, saying he was hard at work on the project—a book on psychology—that he had described the year before: "If it drives you nuts, don't sue. You were warned!"

WHEN THE WAR ENDED IN 1945, HUBBARD HAD BEEN UNDERGOING TREATMENT AT OAK KNOLL Naval Hospital, but it was often on an outpatient basis. When he wasn't there, he usually headed for Los Angeles, rather than to Washington, where Polly was living with their two children. On one such visit, he turned up at Jack Parsons's huge house on South Orange Grove Avenue in Pasadena, wearing dark glasses and carrying a cane, in the company of the artist Lou Goldstone. Parsons was a fan of Hubbard's fiction, and he invited the writer to move in.

The mansion had three floors and eleven bedrooms—as well as a temple for the Ordo Templi Orientis—and Parsons rented all of it out, specifying in an advertisement for prospective tenants, "Must not believe in God." Hubbard fit in at once. Seated in the kitchen, he showed off scars on his chest that he claimed were from arrows in the South American rain forest, and he was overheard saying that the best way to make money would be to start a religion—although the legend that Heinlein bet him that he couldn't is undoubtedly apocryphal.

Hubbard also left a more personal mark on the house. After his wife left him for another occultist, Parsons had taken up with her half sister Sara Northrup. Sara was eighteen and beautiful, and Parsons encouraged her to sleep with other men, including Hubbard, who later claimed that he awoke after a drunken party with her at his side. Parsons sometimes seemed jealous, but he wrote warmly of Hubbard to Aleister Crowley: "Although he has no formal training in Magick, he has an extraordinary amount of experience and understanding in the field. . . . I need a magical partner. I have many experiments in mind."

On December 5, Hubbard was mustered out for good. Instead of returning to his family, he went back to the mansion in Pasadena—he was searching for answers, and the ones that Parsons offered seemed as promising as any. Robert Cornog was living there as well, and Heinlein sometimes came by to visit. Hubbard also resumed his affair with Sara, who was seen entwined with him at the house "like a starfish on a clam." One morning, while Hubbard and Parsons were fencing, Sara grabbed a sword and lunged at Hubbard's face. Hubbard, who wasn't wearing a mask, was startled, but he fended her off, rapping her on the end of the nose.

Parsons was obsessed with creating a moonchild, the infant Antichrist mentioned by Crowley in *The Book of the Law*, which required summoning a woman to give birth in the role of the Whore of Babylon. Hubbard was enthusiastic about the project. He later referred to Crowley as "my very good friend," and although they never met, they both modeled themselves after Sir Richard Francis Burton, whom the occultist called "the perfect pioneer of spiritual and physical adventure." Hubbard always had to be the best in the room at everything, and magic, which lent itself to his talents, was no exception. Before long, he was acting as if he had fallen into one of his *Unknown* stories, which always ended with the hero's transformation.

The ritual known as the Babalon Working began at nine at night on January 4, 1946, with Parsons and Hubbard preparing magical weapons and talismans, and it continued for eleven days. One evening, Hubbard claimed that he felt something knock a candle out of his hand in the kitchen. Parsons wrote, "He called us, and we observed a brownish yellow light about seven feet high. . . . I banished [it] with a magical sword, and it disappeared. [Hubbard's] right arm was paralyzed for the rest of the night." The next day, Hubbard allegedly had an astral vision of one of Parsons's old enemies, which he drove away with a fusillade of throwing knives.

Three days later, Parsons and Hubbard went to the Mojave Desert, at the rocket engineer's favorite place for meditation, at a point where two enormous power lines intersected. Feeling all the tension leave his body, Parsons said to Hubbard, "It is done." On their return to the mansion, they found a woman named Marjorie Cameron, who Parsons later said had been in a car crash and no longer remembered who she was. In fact, Cameron—a remarkable personality in her own right—had simply been curious about the house, and she had asked a friend to drop her off.

The two men also signed an agreement for a business, Allied Enterprises, that would engage in activities of a "varied and elastic nature," with the participants dividing all proceeds, including any income from Hubbard's writings. Parsons contributed twenty thousand dollars, which amounted to most of his savings, while Hubbard added twelve hundred, and Sara, the third partner, put up nothing. As one possible venture, they discussed buying yachts on the East Coast to resell, and Hubbard left to look into the market at the end of February.

When Hubbard returned, he announced that he had experienced a mystical vision, and they commenced the second half of the moonchild ritual. As music filled the room, Hubbard, dressed in white, and Parsons, in black, prepared the altar. At the exact moment that they smashed an idol of Pan, the roof of the guesthouse caught fire. The following night, Cameron joined the proceedings, naked beneath a crimson robe. As she and Parsons had sex, Hubbard chanted, perspiring, "The lust is hers, the passion yours. Consider thou the Beast raping."

Parsons felt it had been a success, but when he informed Crowley of their efforts, the occultist replied deflatingly, "I thought I had a most morbid imagination, as good as any man's, but it seems I have not. I cannot form the slightest idea of what you can possibly mean." Crowley wrote to Karl Germer, the head of the O.T.O. in America, "Apparently Parsons or Hubbard or somebody is producing a moonchild. I get fairly frantic when I contemplate the idiocy of these louts."

Around this time, Hubbard drafted a document known as the "Affirmations," a series of notes that he evidently hoped to use to hypnotize himself with a dictating machine. The pages have been variously dated, but several entries point to the period when he was active with Parsons, of whom he wrote:

> *Any distaste I may have for Jack Parsons originated in a psychic experiment. Such distaste is foolish. He is my friend and comrade-in-arms. . . . I have only friendship for Jack Parsons. . . . Jack is also an adept. You love and respect him as a friend. He cannot take offense at what you do. You will not wrong him because you love him.*

Hubbard's fears that he would hurt his friend were far from unfounded. At the end of April, he took ten thousand dollars from their pooled funds and went to Florida with Sara, allegedly to buy a yacht. In reality, he had something else in mind. He had written to the chief of naval personnel for permission to travel to South America and China, and he had excited Leslyn's nephews over a venture involving "China, knives, guns," which irritated Heinlein: "I don't understand Ron's current activities. . . . As near as I can tell at a distance he seems to be off on some sort of a Big Operator tear, instead of straightening out and getting reestablished in his profession."

The rumors reached Crowley, who cabled Germer: "Suspect Ron playing confidence trick." Crowley had good reason to be concerned—at the time, he was living largely off funds from the Los Angeles temple—and Parsons boarded a train to Miami. On his arrival, he found that his partners had taken out loans for three boats, and he had managed to track one of them down when he received a call saying that Hubbard and Sara had sailed away. Parsons cast a magic circle in his room to conjure up a storm, forcing the couple to turn back at the Panama Canal. Magical or not, Hubbard had suffered from his usual bad luck at sea.

After reaching a settlement, Parsons returned to Pasadena, and neither Sara nor Hubbard ever saw him again. Years afterward, Hubbard asserted that he been told to investigate Parsons by the Navy, thereby "[breaking] up black magic in America," but any successes along those lines evidently went unacknowledged. Hubbard was out of money, and he threatened to kill himself if Sara—who later said that he began beating her in Miami—didn't marry him. Sara was unaware that Hubbard was still married to his first wife, and their wedding took place on August 10, 1946.

On November 25, Hubbard stayed overnight in New Jersey with Campbell, who was shocked by his appearance: "He was a quivering psychoneurotic wreck, practically ready to break down completely. When he got out of service, he had the quivers—literally. He also had several bad wounds, and was in bad physical shape. His conversation was somewhat schizoid at points, wandering in not-always lucid organization." Elsewhere, he said that Hubbard's rented room "reeked of tension and some sort of undercover activity."

They discussed some new projects, and Hubbard also tried to get back into Heinlein's good graces, "heartily and affectionately" congratulating him on breaking into *The Saturday Evening Post,* although he conceded that he was in "the Heinlein doghouse" over the misunderstanding with Leslyn's nephews. Heinlein never replied, but he made his opinion clear in a note attached to the letter in his files: "I no longer trust you. . . . I think a lot of those ribbons on your chest, even if Polly doesn't. You're an authentic hero, even though a phony gentleman. I'll give you money to get you out of a jam but I don't want you in my house."

The following year, Hubbard and Sara moved to Washington, just fifteen miles from his family in Bremerton. Sara finally learned that her husband was still married to Polly, who filed for divorce in April. From there, they headed for Ojai, where Hubbard was arrested for failing to make payments on their trailer. It isn't clear if he ever crossed paths with Heinlein, who moved to the same town in July, but their dislocated lives had taken on curious parallels—both had found new partners, and they both left Ojai to take up residence in trailers in the San Fernando Valley.

Hubbard began to work more steadily. His first major publication after the war had been "Fortress in the Sky," a cover story for the May 1947 issue of *Air Trails and Science Frontiers*, which Campbell was editing. It was credited to "Capt. B.A. Northrop," a pseudonym that the editor may well have suggested—it recalled Sara's maiden name, much as Campbell had once written as Don A. Stuart and Heinlein as Anson MacDonald. The article said that since the atomic bomb had rendered the notion of a land or naval base obsolete, the last impregnable position was the moon, and it went on to make a rather peculiar claim:

> *Here and there throughout the world many men have been thinking about rockets for some time. . . . I recall that in 1930 L. Ron Hubbard, a writer and engineer, developed and tested—but without fanfare—a rocket motor considerably superior to the V-2 instrument of propulsion and rather less complicated.*

Campbell—who failed to question the idea that Hubbard had been conducting rocket research at nineteen—provided much of the science from his unpublished novel *The Moon Is Hell*, and its discussion of the "gravity gauge," or the advantage in launching missiles from the moon to Earth, made a strong impression on Heinlein, who would draw on it in detail years later.

Even more significant was *The End Is Not Yet*, which ran in *Astounding* in 1947. In his first novel in years, Hubbard seemed to be testing alternate identities—or futures—for himself, with one character who discovers a new form of mental energy, another who becomes the world's most famous author, and a third who writes the definitive book on psychology. Campbell recalled, "I bought it quite largely because Ron, I felt, deserved a boost back onto his feet. The story . . . was mediocre. It's the only time I've ever bought a story I did not feel was one I genuinely enjoyed."

In August 1947, Forrest J Ackerman, a fan and agent in Los Angeles who had offered his services to Heinlein and Campbell, signed Hubbard as a client. Ackerman wanted him to pitch *Excalibur,* his book on psychology, to a pair of businessmen who were looking to get into publishing, but Hubbard declined: "I broke it out and then shook my head over it." His work had done nothing to address his own problems, and he wrote to the Veterans Administration to request help for his "long periods of moroseness and suicidal inclinations."

He was writing more—he cranked out a series of potboilers for *Astounding* about a character named Ole Doc Methuselah, with many of the plots proposed by Sara—and at Ackerman's urging, he began to attend meetings of the Los Angeles Science Fantasy Society. It was his first extended exposure to fans, who provided him with the audience that he had been lacking, and Hubbard showed off his skill at hypnotism, which he had studied in an effort to treat his depression. He had failed to help himself, but he was spectacularly good at it with others, with the ability to induce trances by snapping his fingers at the count of three.

Another frequent attendee was A. E. van Vogt, who had been impressed by Hubbard after meeting him at Parsons's mansion. When a fan recounted a strange dream, Hubbard said that he had caused it while "strolling in astral form." Van Vogt didn't believe it, but he began to wonder what else might have happened. Using another hypnotist, van Vogt found a man who said that Hubbard had sadistically toyed with him after implanting a posthypnotic command. It testified to Hubbard's growing reputation, even if the memory itself was a false one.

Hubbard was encouraged by these reactions, and he branched out to other treatments: "I went right down in the middle of Hollywood, I rented an office, got hold of a nurse, wrapped a towel around my head and became a swami." He later wrote that he had his subjects "writhing" as he worked on such issues as inferiority complexes, allergies, and stuttering, and he claimed to have devised a form of mental therapy that cured eight out of ten patients.

In the summer of 1948, Hubbard was arrested by the San Luis Obispo County sheriff on charges of passing a bad check. Shortly afterward, he headed to New York, where he attended meetings of the Queens Science Fiction League. He seemed to be recovering, telling Heinlein that the war had finally ended for him: "I no longer start for the bridge every time I hear a taxicab horn." Hubbard also said, falsely, that he had received a Guggenheim Fellowship for his work, and that he hoped to write "a book risen from the ashes of old *Excalibur*."

After spending Thanksgiving with the Campbells, Hubbard and Sara began looking for a change of scene, and they ended up in Savannah, Georgia, by February 1949. When he asked for his loan from Heinlein, they were living near a pulpwood plant, working on *Excalibur*. Hubbard told Ackerman that the book had information on how to "rape women without their knowing it," and that he wasn't sure whether he wanted to use it to abolish the Catholic Church or found one of his own. He concluded, "Don't know why I suddenly got the nerve to go into this again and let it loose. It's probably either a great love or an enormous hatred of humanity."

In March, Sara went to see her mother, who had suffered a heart attack, leaving him alone for several weeks. On April 13, 1949, Hubbard wrote to the American Psychiatric Association, the American Psychological Association, and the Gerontological Society in Baltimore, saying that he had treated twenty patients until they could remember events from before birth. He claimed to be working for free with criminals, orphans, and a boy who was failing his classes, and he told Heinlein that if he ever started charging for his services, "the local psychiatrists, now my passionate pals, would leave me dead in some back alley."

At the end of April, Hubbard mentioned that he was moving to Washington, D.C., for an indeterminate period. Three weeks later, he applied for a marriage license there to marry a woman named Ann Jensen, who canceled it the next day. Nothing else is known of her, although it's tempting to identify her with the girl whom Hubbard described as taking his dictation in Savannah—she couldn't spell, but she was "awful pretty." It was his last attempt to break from Sara, who represented a period in his past that he was trying to forget, much as Leslyn had for Heinlein. At one point, he sent a letter to Parsons, saying that he could have Sara back.

Hubbard was convinced that he had willed his way out of the depths of depression, and although his attempts to interest professional societies in his work had gone nowhere, one last possibility remained. In May, he contacted Campbell about his research, and the editor responded by inviting him and Sara to New Jersey. For reasons of his own, Campbell was very interested in what Hubbard had to say—and although he could have worked with him at a distance, as he had with so many other writers, he decided early on that he wanted to keep this one close.

11.
THE MODERN SCIENCE OF MENTAL HEALTH

1945–1950

Cybernetics is the big new idea of the times, and it is my opinion Hubbard . . . has got cybernetics, and got it bad; this is to say, he has got it wrong. . . . It was perhaps inevitable that the productive thinking which generated the cybernetic point of view should beget some incidental monstrosities amidst the voluminous literature accumulating in and about the field.

—YVETTE GITTLESON, *AMERICAN SCIENTIST*, OCTOBER 1950

For the December 1946 issue of the magazine *Air Trails Pictorial*, Campbell, its new editor, wrote an article titled "Bikini Balance Sheet." He provided an overview of the atomic bomb tests at the Marshall Islands and discussed matters of civil defense, with a full page devoted to a map of the aftermath of a hypothetical nuclear attack on New Jersey. At the center of the blast was Campbell's house in Scotch Plains. He invited readers to draw a similar circle on their own road maps: "The big cities may not necessarily be impact centers. Your small town may be a better aiming point."

In the years immediately after the war, Campbell occupied a

peculiar position. His career, which was thriving, was built on a threat that could annihilate him and everyone he loved in a single blinding instant. The world beyond science fiction was looking to him for his thoughts, and now that he had the role that he had always wanted, he was unable to be reassuring. A profile by Dickson Hartwell in the February 1946 issue of *Pic* caught Campbell in a typical moment:

> *If you want to know what a hell of a fix this world is in I suggest you listen for a few minutes, in a mood of deepening gloom, to Mr. Atomic. . . . It is not the way he says it so much as what he says about the future which makes Mr. Atomic the man of the hour. For it was he who scooped the world press on the atomic bomb, not by hours or weeks but by years.*

Campbell obliged Hartwell with an alarming interview—he speculated that a nuclear war might break out within the next decade—and posed for a picture in his basement, a soldering iron in one hand, a lit cigarette in the other.

He seemed to draw energy, even youth, from the forces that threatened civilization. "At thirty-five, Campbell has that peculiar feline physical makeup which makes some men look ten years younger than they are," Hartwell wrote, adding that he "seems to personify atomic power in human form." It was a comparison that Campbell liked, and he may even have suggested it. In a profile that the editor wrote for himself in *Air Trails,* he said, "Despite [his] varied activities, Campbell has managed also to acquire a wife and two children, of whom the latter two are believed by the neighbors to operate on atomic energy."

Otherwise, his family went largely unmentioned. "Questions about his personal life he dismisses in a word, if he answers them at all," Hartwell said, and Campbell referred to Doña only briefly in his own profile: "Mrs. Campbell has long since become resigned to existence over a basement laboratory which resounds to the birth pangs of divers scientific ideas." He spent most of his free time in his workshop, and Doña was feeling sidelined, which was nothing new. Referring to the photographer from *Pic,* she wrote, "I learned more about [Street & Smith's] personnel in an hour with him than I've found out in eight years from John."

Hartwell had been exhausted by hearing Campbell talk about the atomic menace over the course of a single interview, while Doña had to hear about it every day. As the map in *Air Trails* implied, their home had become ground zero in at least one respect—the bomb dominated the editor's thoughts as nothing else ever had. Like Leslyn Heinlein, Doña had been psychologically drained by the war, and her husband's fixations were hard to bear. Campbell, in turn, was bewildered that she wasn't more pleased by his current position: "I should work fifteen years toward a decent income so we can both be bitter when I get it."

If their financial stability had been created by the bomb, it only encouraged his tendency to be obsessed by it. It figured in nearly all of his editorials, and *Astounding* began to read like a trade organ for the nuclear power industry. At first, the discussion was primarily technical. Over lunch, Campbell had been told by the physicist Hans Bethe that uranium was the only nuclear fuel, but he continued to mull over the subject, resulting in an aside in the January 1946 issue:

> *The uranium reaction is reasonably potent, but another one, discovered in 1930 by Lord Rutherford, is nearly twice as powerful, pound for pound, and uses cheap lithium and ordinary hydrogen. It won't start until a temperature of several million degrees is reached, but the Hiroshima U-235 bomb would make an excellent primer to start the more violent explosion.*

Campbell anticipated not only the hydrogen bomb, but the lithium hydride method that would be utilized by the Russians seven years later. In many ways, it was the shrewdest guess that he would ever make.

Before long, however, he shifted to the social sciences and their bearing on the bomb, writing in April 1946, "Psychology must advance faster than nuclear physics." The most ambitious fictional exploration of these problems had been A. E. van Vogt's *The World of Null-A*, the first installment of which was on newsstands when Hiroshima was destroyed. It was a wild combination of Korzybski and a pulp serial, and Campbell wrote glowingly of it to Heinlein, who was less impressed: "I hate to see a man write about General Semantics who does not understand it." But he also seemed to feel a sense of proprietary irritation that he had failed to get there first.

After the war, Campbell had tried to get the band back together, with mixed success. In the February 1946 issue, he said that Heinlein and Hubbard—who had served in "Java, Australia, Alaska, Hawaii, Saipan"—would soon be available, but his hopes turned out to be premature. Heinlein would be locked out of the magazine by their dispute over rights, while Hubbard's depression kept him from writing for over a year. Campbell had no choice but to find other authors, although he no longer had the time or the inclination to develop new voices from scratch.

His one great discovery was Arthur C. Clarke, whose geographical distance—he was born in 1917 in England—kept him from being shaped by the editor to any real degree. Clarke's first sale, "Rescue Party," appealed almost by accident to Campbell's prejudices, with an encounter between mankind and an alien race that implied that humans would have the advantage. But Campbell rejected his excellent "Against the Fall of Night," an ambitious effort to extend the mood of the Don A. Stuart stories into the postwar era, and ongoing issues with foreign rights ensured that Clarke's most important work would appear elsewhere.

There were notable submissions from other writers. Will Jenkins wrote the landmark "First Contact," based on an idea from Campbell that looked ahead to the Cold War, and "A Logic Named Joe," which was one of the few stories of any era to anticipate the Internet. Catherine L. Moore, writing as Lawrence O'Donnell, produced her masterpiece, "Vintage Season," about time travelers who visit past disasters as tourists, and Campbell even published E. E. Smith's *Children of the Lens,* at the urging of a fan who argued that the magazine ought to honor one of its most beloved authors, even if his work seemed behind the times.

Other writers confronted the atomic age more directly. In 1947, at a convention in Philadelphia, the writer Judith Merril—who married Frederik Pohl the following year—tipsily cornered Campbell at a party in a hotel suite: "John, I wrote a story 'at's so good, ish mush too good for you."

Campbell was drunk as well: "You're right. If'sh that good, we don' pay enough for it." After reading her story, "That Only a Mother," he bought it, despite its bleak conclusion—it was about a woman who refuses to admit that her mutant daughter has been born without any limbs.

But he was also trying to pull back from atomic doom. Readers were having it thrown at them from all sides, and as his audience expanded, he began to look for other ways of approaching the same material. He had hoped to edit a technical magazine for years, and an opportunity arose in the form of *Air Trails Pictorial,* a model aircraft periodical devoured by hobbyists—including a teenage Neil Armstrong—who built miniature planes that flew on gasoline or rubber bands. As the model business went downhill after the war, the title grew less profitable, and it was relaunched as a science monthly with an emphasis on aviation.

Campbell had pushed hard for the change, and he landed the editorship of *Air Trails* in the summer of 1946. John Michel, a founding member of the Futurians, was working there at the time, but he disliked Campbell so much that he quit immediately. In his first editorial, the new editor informed his readers, "It is up to each of us, personally, to learn and progress with the world—or be overwhelmed and left behind." It was familiar language for *Astounding*, but a drastic shift for a model airplane magazine, which Campbell filled with psychology and the bomb: "We can already control atomic weapons—it's men who need control."

He was feeling overstretched, and at the end of 1946, he brought on L. Jerome Stanton, who had worked on the sonar and kamikaze projects, as an associate editor. Stanton later joined *Astounding*, reading the slush pile and forwarding the best stories to Campbell, while Tarrant continued to wield her blue pencil. The two men once passed along a vaguely dirty joke about "the original ball-bearing mousetrap"—the tomcat—in a story by George O. Smith, assuming that she would take it out. She didn't, and the gag famously made it into print. But it also indicated how divided Campbell's attention was becoming.

Campbell loved editing *Air Trails,* but the magazine failed to interest advertisers, and after the science angle was dropped, he bowed out in November 1947. There were rumors that *Unknown* would be revived, and Hubbard told Heinlein that he hoped that it would give him a fantasy market again: "Between you and me, I hate the hell out of gadgets." It never reappeared, and its absence only increased the pressure on *Astounding* to reflect all sides of Campbell's personality.

Yet his one surviving magazine was doing well, printing tens of thousands more copies than it had during the war. Campbell took advantage of the situation to alter the logo, with *Astounding* written in a barely visible script and *Science Fiction* in huge block letters—allowing him to achieve, in effect, the title change that he had wanted since the late thirties. A year and a half later, he arranged for advertising to be sold specifically for the magazine, rather than for all the firm's titles, enabling book publishers to reach fans directly, as well as identifying the science fiction community for the first time as a distinct demographic.

Campbell was among the first to benefit from the market for science fiction in hardcover, with collections of his work issued by several publishers, which partially made up for his one great failure. He had spent his career thinking about the atom, and his definitive statement was *The Atomic Story,* which he had written in a white heat at a low point in his marriage. He had hoped that the book would be released quickly, but it was delayed by paper and press shortages. It finally appeared in 1947, after its moment of maximum relevance had passed, and he complained that Henry Holt had "rooked" him out of thousands of dollars by postponing it.

The result was a readable work of popular science, but it ignored the personalities of the men behind the bomb, turning the story into a kind of superscience epic in which particles, not people, were the heroes. Campbell burnished his credentials with yet another account of the "Deadline" incident, and in its closing chapter, he revisited familiar territory:

> *These two incomplete sciences—psychology and nuclear physics—are now abruptly confronted with the atomic bomb. . . . Psychology has not yet advanced far enough to permit all men to live sane, balanced, and tolerant lives. That has not hitherto been essential to survival; in the not too distant future it may be.*

What was required, he wrote, was "a total reorganization of the pattern of civilization," and his final lines amounted to a prelude to dianetics: "We must learn more about atomic forces. But we'd be wise if, first, we learned more about man—the one greater force that can twist atomic energies to its will."

On April 9, 1949, Street & Smith discontinued most of its pulps to focus on slick publications like *Mademoiselle*. When Asimov was told the news, which his father had heard over the radio, he thought that his career was over. The next day, he learned that *Astounding* was the only one that had been spared. Campbell had saved it, in part because of his readers—most had college degrees, with salaries averaging four hundred dollars a month, and virtually all were male. He had their attention, and he felt that he had preserved it for a reason, even if it came at a personal cost.

And just as Sturgeon's "Microcosmic God" had served as an emblem of the magazine at the beginning of the decade, another story symbolized this moment of transition. "E for Effort" by T. L. Sherred, which appeared in May 1947, revolved around two men who develop a technique for filming the past. At first, they use it to make period epics for Hollywood, but they soon realize that the device also makes it impossible for nations to keep secrets, which is a crucial development "if atomic war is not to sear the face and fate of the world."

In short, what began as a form of escapist entertainment is transformed, with a small shift of emphasis, into a way to save mankind—which is exactly what Campbell believed science fiction could be. But the tone had changed. "Microcosmic God" had closed with its race of tiny beings surpassing all human technology. "E for Effort" ended with its heroes arrested and murdered by a government terrified of what they might accomplish—and then the war begins anyway.

IN 1949, GEORGE O. SMITH WAS DIVORCED AND WORKING AS A RADIO ENGINEER IN INDIAN QUEEN, a suburban neighborhood of Philadelphia. One afternoon, he was cleaning up at the house when his doorbell rang. When he answered it, Smith was stunned to see Doña Campbell. She had driven eighty miles from Scotch Plains, and she didn't waste time on small talk. "George, build me a good, stiff drink!"

As he listened, Doña poured out her story. Campbell, she

said, had become obsessed with Hubbard's new mental therapy, of which she deeply disapproved: "She took a dim view of anyone without academic schooling in medicine or the mind playing with what she called an 'offshoot' of psychiatry." And while this wasn't the first point of disagreement between Doña and her husband, it was the one that finally drove her into another man's arms.

Over the next year, they carried on an affair in plain sight. Every Friday, Smith took the train to Westfield, picked up Doña, and went back to Indian Queen. On Sunday, they reversed the process. Smith recalled, "John was satisfied so long as the house was clean and there was food . . . and especially happy when Doña left the place, so he could have his dianetic sessions without someone waving an admonitory forefinger from left to right while her head moved right to left in opposition."

Campbell would later say that their marriage had been in trouble for a long time, with Doña "having no interest in the future with me these past couple of years." He blamed his persistent skin problems not on overwork, but on "underwife," and said that they had agreed to end it as early as May 1949. Doña, in turn, described dianetics as "only the last straw in a very ungood situation."

But while Hubbard may not have caused the break with Doña, he certainly benefited from her absence—as well as from Campbell's other vulnerabilities. In 1948, the magazine's offices had relocated to Elizabeth, New Jersey, removing him from writers in New York. His father was in Germany, rebuilding its telecommunications system, while Laura was stationed with her husband in Venezuela. Campbell was more alone than ever—and Hubbard was ready to take advantage of it.

At the end of May, Hubbard and Sara had arrived in Elizabeth, moving into a house that the editor found for them on Aberdeen Road, just three miles from the office. Soon afterward, Campbell read *Excalibur*. He wasn't impressed, calling it "more fiction than anything else," but he was struck by Hubbard's appearance: "The sparkle was back, and it was genuine. His conversation was lucid and thoroughly organized. He was thinking again. He told me he had found the secret of the problem of the mind—but more important he had found himself."

In its latest incarnation, Hubbard's theory hinged on the idea that the brain was divided into two halves—the analytic and reactive minds. The former was perfectly rational, but it could be affected by memories, or "impediments," implanted while a person was unconscious. Such experiences were stored in the reactive mind, which took over in times of stress—a patient who heard a doctor say "He's better off dead" while under anesthesia would take it as a literal command. Hubbard's treatment, which didn't have a name yet, was designed to access these recollections, some of which dated from before birth, and erase any damaging behavior patterns.

Campbell, who had heard the doctors talking over his body during his appendix operation, was supportive, but he proved unresponsive to both hypnosis and narcosynthesis. He later gave a possible reason: "I had known [Hubbard] as a professional, accomplished liar since 1938; nothing he said could be believed without personal conscious cross-checking. That sort of barrier makes hypnosis damn near impossible!" Yet he also wanted to believe that this was the positive element that had been lacking in all his negative pronouncements about the bomb. He had been describing the problem for years, and this felt like the solution—even if his impression that Hubbard had healed himself was all that they had to go on.

They decided to involve someone from the medical side, which would allow them to present their case more convincingly. The year before, *Astounding* had published an article about endocrinology by a doctor in Michigan named Joseph Winter. Campbell had long been fascinated by the subject, which Winter extolled as the interface between the body and the mind: "It'll be a great world when endocrinology reaches its peak—no dwarfs, no sterile women, no impotent men, no homosexuals, no insanity and no unhappiness. No fooling!"

In July, Campbell wrote to invite Winter to join their new project: "L. Ron Hubbard, who happens to be an author, has been doing some psychological research. . . . He's basically an engineer. He approached the problem of psychiatry from the heuristic viewpoint—to get results." Winter was receptive. He had studied Korzybski for similar reasons, and he was intrigued by the claim that Hubbard had treated both mental illness and conditions such as asthma and ulcers.

Campbell's letter was followed by one from Hubbard: "My vanity hopes that you will secure credit to me for eleven years of unpaid research, but my humanity hopes . . . that this science will be used as intelligently and extensively as possible." Hubbard described himself as "a trained mathematician," but in a moment of uncharacteristic modesty, he also said, "The articles you suggest would be more acceptable coming from another pen than mine."

In the meantime, toward the end of July, Campbell experienced a breakthrough—the traumatic memory of his birth, with the aid of the flashing lights produced by the pyramid of mirrors on a record player. According to Hubbard, they even verified the account with the editor's mother: "The recording of her sequence compared word for word with his sequence, detail for detail, name for name." Campbell came to believe that his mother, who had passed out during the delivery, had received an impediment of her own when the doctor said, "You'll forget all about this in a little while." It had always been one of her favorite phrases.

Their work together grew more intense, with sessions often conducted by telephone. Hubbard allegedly discovered a sentence that could work as an "automatic restimulator" for anyone's impediments, and when he used it in a call to Campbell, the editor left his house at once: "[I] was barely able to hold myself under control for the seven minutes necessary to reach his place. . . . I arrived with arms and legs quivering uncontrollably, my stomach knotted up in cold fear, palpitations of the heart, heavy cold sweat, and just generally a state of acute nervous collapse."

He felt that he was benefiting from the treatment—he had lost twenty pounds, and his sinusitis seemed to be gone—and he even used it on his children. Leslyn, who had turned four, suffered from itchiness, which Campbell supposedly took away in three minutes. When Peedee, who was nine, fell off her bike and skinned both knees, he saw it as an opportunity for an experiment: "I used the technique on one knee—the worst. It healed completely about three days before the other, and all pain was gone from it within five minutes." But Doña still refused to be treated.

Campbell hoped to expand the circle, in his own version of the kamikaze team, and he began to reach out to others. He had told Heinlein about their work in July, and on September 15, 1949, he wrote excitedly:

> I firmly believe this technique can cure cancer. . . . This is, I am certain, the greatest story in the world—far bigger than the atomic bomb, because this is the story of controlling human thought, freeing it for use—and it is human thought that controls atomic energy. It is a story that must be spread, though, and spread fast. . . . But dammit, Bob, right now the key to world sanity is in Ron Hubbard's head, and there isn't even an adequate written record!

Heinlein responded cautiously, "You will appreciate that I must approach this with scientific skepticism, albeit an open mind. If he is right, he has a discovery that makes the atom bomb look like peanuts."

In the meantime, Campbell recruited a man named Don Rogers, an engineer at Western Electric with "a purple-plated doozy" of a case, and in October—the week after President Harry Truman announced that the Soviets had tested a nuclear device—Winter arrived in New Jersey. At the first session that he observed, he watched as Hubbard took Campbell back to a period before his birth. Listening to Campbell's chest with a stethoscope, Winter became concerned for his health, and he was amazed when the editor seemed to recover as soon as the memory had been discharged.

Winter concluded that the treatment was basically just a form of hypnosis, but he was willing to try it for himself. Moving in with Hubbard and the pregnant Sara, who were living in a rented cottage in the nearby town of Bay Head, he commenced treatment, lying on the couch for up to three hours a day. Like Campbell, he was a junior case—his father, Joseph Winter, Sr., had been a prominent figure in his town in Michigan—and the process was sometimes agonizing: "I had nightmares of being choked, of having my genitalia cut off."

Their work in the early days was characterized by wild experimentation. At one point, Campbell attempted to hypnotize subjects using a spiral painted on a record turntable—which was reminiscent of a device that Hubbard had mentioned in one of his Ole Doc Methuselah stories—and they tried combining scopolamine with heavy doses of phenobarbital or sodium amytal. Neither worked on Campbell. The drugs either put him to sleep, snoring, or, when the others roused him enough to conduct a session, left him awake and unhypnotizable.

They frequently argued over terminology. Years earlier, to avoid the risk of misleading associations, Campbell had proposed coining new words like "nam" and "env" to discuss mental health. Now "impediment" was replaced with "norn," after the fates of Norse mythology—in which the editor had been interested for much of his life—and then with the more clinical "engram." A "clear" was a person whose engrams had been successfully removed, leaving him with total recall and freedom from psychosomatic disease, while a patient became known as a "preclear."

Gradually, they refined Hubbard's methods, which Campbell called "rules of thumb," into a process known as auditing. A typical encounter began with the patient seated in an armchair in a quiet room. Smoking wasn't allowed, which must have annoyed Campbell. The auditor ran through the patient's memories, advancing along a "time track" of incidents, which would be relived as many times as necessary to discharge them of emotion. A special emphasis was placed on prenatal trauma, including attempted abortions, and the ultimate objective was to erase the very first engram, which had been installed shortly after conception.

It was a reasonably effective system of talk therapy, and it had as much in common with Campbell's conversational style—in which he hammered away at his listeners, asking them to question their assumptions—as with Hubbard's hypnotic techniques. Campbell compared it to figuring out a story idea, and it sometimes felt like an attempt to institutionalize his method of raising the intelligence of his readers. Hubbard himself was less good at it, and observers later noted that he rarely followed his own procedures: "Although he did a lot of talking, he couldn't audit. . . . He had to resort to a sort of black magic hypnosis."

As Campbell's confidence in the technique increased, he brought in science fiction fans to be treated in his basement, and there were even a few lighter moments. Hubbard owned a calico cat, Countess Motorboat, which the editor would always kick: "So I just simply processed the cat up to the point where the cat, every time John W. Campbell, Jr. would sit down, would go over and tear his shoelaces open." On another occasion, Campbell's daughter Leslyn rose from where she had been playing with her toys, walked across the room, and kicked Hubbard in the shins. She remembered, "I guess I didn't like being ignored."

Hubbard evidently believed in his own theories, which

amounted to a formalization of his intuitive methods of emotional manipulation. But he was also keeping his options open, and he spent the second half of the year working on the screenplay for the film *Rocketship X-M*. He said that the producers hoped to benefit from the publicity for *Destination Moon*, the movie that Heinlein was making with George Pal, and that if it did well enough, there might even be a film based on Ole Doc Methuselah. Hubbard also produced several short stories and a serial, *To the Stars*, writing to Heinlein in July, "Nothing of real interest. Campbell happy. Field calm. Track muddy."

Throughout this period, the assumption within the group was that they were preparing a paper for a professional journal, with Campbell hoping to run a piece in *Astounding* as well. The first hint of an article appeared in the December 1949 issue, in which Campbell wrote:

> *It is an article on the* science *of the mind, of human thought. It is not an article on psychology—that isn't a science. It's not General Semantics. It is a totally new science, called* dianetics, *and it does precisely what a* science *of thought should do. . . . The articles are in preparation.*

It was the first attested use of the word "dianetics," which was allegedly derived from the Greek for "through the mind." Campbell, notably, failed to mention Hubbard by name—although the announcement ran across from the author's story "A Can of Vacuum"—and he didn't state specifically that the articles would run in *Astounding*, which indicated that authorship and placement were still under discussion.

Shortly afterward, Winter went home to Michigan for Thanksgiving. His son Joey—another junior case—was six years old, and after seeing a play that featured a ghost, he developed a fear of the dark, refusing to go upstairs by himself: "That's where the ghosts are."

Winter decided to put his new skills to use. "Why should you be afraid of ghosts?"

"They choke you," Joey said. Winter told him to lie down, shut his eyes, and describe the ghost. "He has a long white apron, a little white cap on his head and a piece of white cloth on his mouth."

The boy began to squirm. When Winter asked for the ghost's name, Joey answered, breathing hard, "Bill Short." It was the name of the obstetrician who had delivered him. Winter told him to repeat the story a dozen times, and Joey relaxed. His fear of the dark never returned.

After Winter came back to New Jersey, they prepared for publication. Winter submitted a paper informally to the *Journal of the American Medical Association,* which turned it down for lack of evidence, saying that it might be a better fit for a psychotherapy journal. It was dutifully revised for the *American Journal of Psychiatry,* which rejected it on similar grounds.

Astounding was their last remaining option. Campbell evidently feared that printing it there would make it harder for readers to take it seriously—he cautioned a correspondent years later against publishing research in a science fiction magazine, which would stamp it with that label for decades. He decided against presenting himself as a coauthor, a decision that would have important consequences, and asked Hubbard to obtain a rebuttal that could run alongside the article.

In response, Hubbard said that he couldn't get any doctors to listen to him, so he and Winter composed a fake reply, "A Criticism of Dianetics," credited to the nonexistent Dr. Irving R. Kutzman, M.D. Hubbard claimed that it consisted of comments from four psychiatrists he had consulted, which he had "played . . . back very carefully" using his own perfect memory. He also described setting up "a psychiatric demon" to write the article, which referred to the notion that a clear could deliberately create mental delusions for his own amusement.

It was an unexpectedly straightforward piece—Hubbard said that "it is in no sense an effort to be funny and it is not funny"— that anticipated many objections that would later be raised against dianetics, including the charge that it merely repackaged existing concepts. "Kutzman" argued that Hubbard had just thirteen months of data—which was actually a generous estimate—and that there was no evidence that any improvements would be permanent.

The article was never published, and no actual rebuttal ever materialized, which indicated the extent to which Hubbard had given up on collaborating with the establishment. Campbell had yet to abandon that hope, and he worked hard to find a reputable publisher. He finally succeeded with Art Ceppos of the medical publishing firm Hermitage House, and a contract was signed around Christmas. They hoped to release the book by April— Hubbard cranked out a draft in a month—but it was delayed by the addition of fifty thousand words of new material.

Anticipation within fan circles was growing, stoked by Campbell's announcements, and it seeped into the wider culture. On January 31, 1950, the columnist Walter Winchell wrote, "There is something new coming up in April called Dianetics. A new science which works with the invariability of physical science in the field of the human mind. From all indications it will prove to be as revolutionary for humanity as the first caveman's discovery and utilization of fire."

On March 8, Sara—who later claimed that Hubbard had kicked her in the stomach in an attempt to induce an abortion—gave birth to a daughter named Alexis Valerie. Winter was the doctor at the delivery, which was conducted in silence, to avoid implanting any engrams. Hubbard proudly said that the world's first dianetic baby was unusually alert, and Winter concurred, "There was a greatly accelerated rate of development. . . . This child had a much more even disposition and was less given to startle reactions and temper manifestations than the average child."

Hubbard had reason to be pleased, but Campbell was less happy. Without attribution, he had written an appendix to the book, "Advice to the Pre-Clear," in which he laid out the challenges that the patient faced:

> *Anyone attempting to stop an individual from entering*
> *therapy either has a use for the aberrations of that*
> *individual—on the "push-button" order—or has*
> *something to hide. . . . Wives with children may have*
> *a fear that therapy will eventually be applied to the*
> *children, in which case much information might come to*
> *light which the husband or society "should never know."*

Campbell was speaking from experience. His wife still refused to support dianetics, and she had resisted auditing for herself and their children. In the terms that the Church of Scientology would later use to describe its enemies, Doña Campbell was the original Suppressive Person.

"TERRA INCOGNITA: THE MIND," WHICH MARKED THE INAUSPICIOUS DEBUT OF DIANETICS IN PRINT, appeared not in *Astounding* but in the Winter/Spring 1950 issue of *The Explorers Journal,* the official periodical of the Explorers Club. In a brief article, Hubbard provided the first public description of dianetics, including the claim that he had developed it as a way for expedition leaders to screen team members for mental problems, as well as a form of emergency medicine in the field.

The piece testified to how malleable the principles of dianetics could be, depending on its intended audience, but it was also important to Hubbard that it appear there first. It was friendly territory, independent of Campbell, where he could frame his work in terms of how he liked to see himself—as an adventurer and man of action. It aroused no perceptible response, but it shed light on the readership that he was hoping to reach. Hubbard wanted to attract explorers and men of the world. Instead, he ended up with science fiction fans.

But its most intriguing sentence offered a glimpse into the therapy's origins: "While dianetics does not consider the brain as an electronic computing machine except for purposes of analogy, it is nevertheless a member of that class of sciences to which belong General Semantics and cybernetics and, as a matter of fact, forms a bridge between the two." In reality, neither field had played any significant role in Hubbard's work before his arrival in New Jersey, and their inclusion here betrayed how deeply his ideas had been shaped by Winter and, above all, by Campbell.

The connection to General Semantics was natural enough. Hubbard later wrote, "Bob Heinlein sat down one time and talked for ten whole minutes on the subject of Korzybski to me and it was very clever. I know quite a bit about Korzybski's works." He had also encountered it in *The World of Null-A,* writing, "[Van Vogt] with his null-A is going to be an awful surprised young man!" Sara had read *Science and Sanity* in the late forties, and she recalled that her husband was excited by it: "He became a big follower of Korzybski."

Hubbard, like Campbell, was unable to finish any of Korzybski's books, and he relied mostly on Winter and Sara for his knowledge of General Semantics, which anticipated dianetics in several ways. Korzybski had written that painful memories could be restimulated by events in the present, and that treatment might consist of reliving such incidents under therapy. Hubbard also alluded to what Korzybski had described as the confusion between a mental map and the underlying reality: "The analytical mind computes in differences. The reactive mind computes in identities."

Even more profound was the influence of cybernetics. As a

discipline, it had arisen in the work of Norbert Wiener, Campbell's old professor at MIT, who had designed antiaircraft guns during World War II. Wiener found that one prototype would swing wildly while locking on to its target, which one of his colleagues compared to "purpose tremor," the involuntary trembling that can occur during fine motor activity. It led Wiener to look into the phenomenon of feedback, in which the difference between an intention and its result generates information that is fed back into the system—a concept that was first developed at Bell Labs.

Wiener began to study servomechanisms, or machines that used negative feedback to correct themselves, such as thermostats or naval steering systems. In 1948, he coined the term "cybernetics," after the Greek word for navigation, and defined the field in the subtitle of his landmark *Cybernetics, or Control and Communication in the Animal and the Machine*. Campbell was undoubtedly familiar with Wiener's research—as well as in contact with Bell Labs—and he would have eagerly read the book soon after its publication. When Hubbard arrived in Elizabeth, a piece on cybernetics was already in the pipeline at the magazine.

And its impact was felt at once. A fascinating detail about *Excalibur* was preserved in the "Affirmations": "There was one error in that book and you have psychically willed it into nothing. It was the electronic theory of the workings of the human mind. Human, material minds do work this way and you were right. Your own mind does not work this way." An "electronic theory" was evidently present at an early stage of Hubbard's work, but it troubled him, and in its intermediate versions, it disappeared entirely. In a letter to Heinlein on March 31, 1949, Hubbard focused instead on what he called the tone scale, an elaborate hierarchy of human emotion, and he wrote proudly of its benefits, "I'm up to eight comes. In an evening, that is."

What he didn't mention was any relationship between the brain and a computer. Four months later, when Campbell wrote to

Heinlein, this analogy was suddenly at the forefront. After mentioning that he had attended a lecture by Warren McCulloch, one of Wiener's collaborators, he stated, "Basically, the brain is a relay-computer of the type that the ENIAC is." In a subsequent letter he repeated this point—"The human mind is a calculating machine, a binary digital computer, of immense complexity, and absolutely unrealized capability"—and only after discussing it at length did he write, "Now we take off on Ron's work."

Campbell's distinction strongly implied that the computer analogy was his own contribution, even if it was only a return to the "electronic theory" that had been previously discarded. In a letter to Winter, Hubbard named psychoanalysis, hypnosis, and Christian Science as his major influences, while Campbell provided an expanded list to Heinlein: "Christian Science, Catholic miracle shrines, voodoo practices, native witch doctor work, and the witch methods of European tradition, as well as modern psychology's teachings." Cybernetics was nowhere to be found.

Less than a year later, it was all over the book. The term "dianetics" itself, which was coined in the fall of 1949, evoked cybernetics, while the word "clear" was an analogy to "clearing" an adding machine. Both theories drew parallels between the brain and a computer—Wiener pictured "anxiety neuroses" as circular processes that drained the mind of its capacity, while dianetics evoked the "demon circuit," a parasitic memory that depleted the brain of its life force. Yet there is no indication that Hubbard had read Wiener before coming to New Jersey, if he ever read him at all. In "A Criticism of Dianetics," he referred to him as "Dr. Werner."

Any cybernetic elements in dianetics emerged, in short, during the period in which Campbell was working with Hubbard to position it for his readers. His primary role was to add a layer of science over what was already there, as he had with so many other writers. He effectively edited the book *Dianetics,* and his impact on it was just as meaningful as it was on the fiction that he published. Sara later said of Campbell, "He was a marvelous editor."

If the cybernetic angle came primarily from Campbell, it was motivated largely by his sense of how the therapy could be presented. On May 30, 1950, he wrote to the managing editor of the journal *Psychiatry* about "a new, logical theory as to why there are two levels of mind in man," but he didn't mention Hubbard for nearly three pages. Instead, he summarized an article in *Astounding* that defined a perfect computer, moving from there to dianetics, which he described as a separate development from "the cybernetic suggestion" that led to "precisely similar conclusions."

In reality, the relationship was tenuous at best, which didn't prevent him from claiming otherwise. He either willfully misunderstood cybernetic ideas or saw them as a rhetorical entry point to persuade skeptics, and he persisted in treating dianetics as a kind of practical cybernetics. Campbell even reached out to Wiener himself, writing that his former professor would "be greatly interested" in dianetics "as suggesting a new direction of development of the work from the cybernetics side," and concluding, "Further study of dianetics will be of immense aid in your projects."

He also contacted his neighbor, the mathematician Claude Shannon, who had founded the field of information theory at Bell Labs. Shannon encouraged Warren McCulloch to meet Hubbard: "If you read science fiction as avidly as I do you'll recognize him as one of the best writers in that field. . . . [He] has been doing some very interesting work lately in using a modified hypnotic technique for therapeutic purposes. . . . I am sure you'll find Ron a very interesting person . . . whether or not his treatment contains anything of value." McCulloch was traveling, so he was unable to arrange a meeting, but he wrote to Hubbard, who thanked Shannon for the introduction.

Hubbard tolerated Campbell's contributions, and he eventually appropriated them for himself. Writing to Heinlein on March 28,

1950, he referred to electronic demons: "They are parasitic and use up computer circuits." Elsewhere, he said that dianetics was a return to "the electronic computer idea" that he had conceived in the thirties, but he also sounded a cautionary note: "The concept of the electronic brain was not vital but only useful to dianetics and it could be swept away as well—dianetics would still stand." He was right. Cybernetics was less an integral part of the theory than a form of branding, and he would ultimately remove nearly all of it.

Campbell's hand was visible in the book in other ways. He was responsible for several key sections, including a long footnote in which he used a computer analogy to explain how the analytic mind could be free of error, and he wrote an appendix on the scientific method, signing it "John W. Campbell, Jr., Nuclear Physicist," and thanking the engineers of Bell Labs. Campbell also composed the appendix "Advice to the Pre-Clear," of which Hubbard said years later, "You can tear that out. . . . I didn't write it in the first place. Written by John W. 'Astounding' Campbell, Jr., who the older he gets the more astonishing he is."

The editor even figured anonymously in at least two case studies. One was an account of his birth, while the other was a memory of his grandmother watching him while he was sick. It concluded:

> *Now with this engram we have a patient with sinusitis*
> *and a predisposition to lung infections. It may be that he*
> *was luckless enough to marry a counterpart of his mother*
> *or his grandmother. . . . And even if the wife thinks that*
> *sinusitis and lung infection are repulsive enough to lead*
> *to divorce, the reactive mind keeps that engram keyed-in.*
> *The more hatred from the wife, the more that engram*
> *keys-in. You can kill a man that way.*

It was an unsettling glimpse into Campbell's state of mind at the time. When this passage was written, his marriage was already over.

THERE ARE TWO DIFFERENT VERSIONS OF HOW DOÑA FINALLY LEFT CAMPBELL. ACCORDING TO George O. Smith, he had arrived on the train for their weekly rendezvous when Doña told him that it was time to confront her husband. They headed for the house in Scotch Plains, where Campbell seemed surprised to see them. "Shouldn't you be on your clandestine way to Philly?"

"We should," Doña said. "But this business has to come to some sort of finish sooner or later."

Campbell pretended to absorb this. "And what do you want me to do about it?"

Doña wouldn't be dissuaded. "John, I want a divorce. I want to marry George."

If she had wanted a scene, Campbell was unwilling to provide one. "And has George been asked about it?"

"John, it's only in those silly romantic novels of the Victorian period where the man throws himself on his knees, places one hand on his heart, and supplicates his lady love to give him her hand in holy matrimony."

Campbell glanced at Smith, who had remained silent. "Okay, if that's what you want, but I don't think it will work."

"John, if it doesn't work, it will be our fault, and ours alone," Doña said. "And outside interference isn't going to help."

Her husband looked at his watch. "It's too late to call Bruce"—the family lawyer—"this evening, but I'll get in touch with him and see what can be worked out. Now, get along to Philly, and please, don't stop in New Hope on your way. It makes me nervous when people drive after a couple of quick ones."

Campbell provided a very different account. On March 9, 1950, he wrote to Heinlein, "Doña sort of blew her top." In his version, Doña had decided to leave him at the beginning of February, and he recalled her saying, "If I don't get out of here, I'll go mad, mad, mad." On reading that statement in print, Doña dryly remarked, "This shows the word rate influence."

According to Campbell, Doña drove to Boston with Peedee and Leslyn on February 7. A few days later he went to see her, returning with the car and the girls, and when he told Peedee what had happened, he was afraid that she might have a nervous break-down. Fortunately, Hubbard was available, and he audited her to remove the emotional charge, although she continued to walk around muttering, "That George!" When Leslyn figured it out, Campbell gave her the same treatment.

In his mind, Doña's refusal to be treated was inseparable from the end of their marriage, and he believed that she was afraid of what might be revealed if the girls were audited: "I'd like to know just what the living hell she did to Peeds and Leslyn that she feels must never, never, never come out." Campbell warned Heinlein that if he wrote to Doña, "you'll also get a long discussion of how I'm playing God, I put pressure on her, dianetics is untried, dangerous, deadly, and drives people crazy." It was the first recorded attempt—but not the last—to cast doubt on a critic of dianetics, and the same letter included the chilling passage:

> *So it works out that the only way we could get her straightened out would be to use force; i.e., tie her down, put a nitrous oxide mask over her face, knock her out, and work on her in deep trance therapy. In a few hours' work that way we could break loose the commands that keep her from accepting dianetic therapy. From then on, we'd be able to straighten her out.*

Campbell wrote to Robert Swisher in a similar vein, "If the situation had seriously disturbed me, it wouldn't have worked that way, I suspect. It's quite easy to install engrams to produce a desired effect." He never acted on it, but it revealed a side of his personality that was close to Hubbard at his worst.

In any event, his old life was over—the price, perhaps, that he had to pay to save the world, although Doña saw the separation as "the obvious move for a relatively rational person in an intolerable situation." She went to live with Smith, while Campbell hired a housekeeper to watch his daughters. Every evening, after tucking in Peedee and Leslyn, whom he saw as his compensation for his unhappy marriage, he worked on dianetics until midnight. Like Hubbard and Heinlein, he was entering a new phase, but unlike them, he would do it alone. And he had no way of knowing that the golden age that he had inaugurated was about to come to an end.

12.
THE DIANETICS EPIDEMIC
1950–1951

If anyone wants a monopoly on dianetics, be assured that he wants it for reasons which have to do not with dianetics but with profit.

—L. RON HUBBARD, *DIANETICS*

When "Dianetics: The Evolution of a Science" appeared at last in the May 1950 issue of *Astounding,* Campbell's first order of business was to convince his audience that it wasn't a joke. This was partially his own fault. The success of "The Endochronic Properties of Resublimated Thiotimoline" had inspired a series of hoax articles by other writers, leading to some mild confusion among readers, and Campbell had decreed that such stories would be called "Special Features" in the future.

But it left him in an awkward position when it came to dianetics. In his announcement in the December 1949 issue, Campbell had written, "This is *not* a hoax article." He felt obliged to repeat himself when the article was published: "I want to assure every reader, most positively and unequivocally, that this article is *not* a hoax, joke, or anything but a direct, clear statement of a totally new scientific thesis." Joseph Winter emphasized this point yet again in his introduction: "[Campbell] wanted to make certain that you readers would *not* confuse dianetics with thiotimoline or with any other bit of scientific spoofing. This is too important to be misinterpreted."

These repeated disavowals weren't entirely successful—many fans still thought that it was a gag—and the article itself turned out to be short on specifics. It opened with a line apparently calculated to appeal to the magazine's core readership: "The optimum computing machine is a subject which many of us have studied. If you were building one, how would you design it?" From there, it specified thirteen attributes that an ideal computer would possess, closely paralleling a list of seventeen items that Campbell sent to Heinlein on November 29, 1949, in which he strongly implied that he had written this section himself.

At that point, Hubbard took over, claiming to have spent eleven years on observations of "the medicine man of the Goldi people of Manchuria, the shamans of North Borneo, Sioux medicine men, the cults of Los Angeles, and modern psychology. . . . Odds and ends like these, countless odds and ends." The article reflected this hodgepodge of influences, comparing the analytic mind to "a well-greased Univac," alluding to demon circuits, and quoting Claude Shannon and Warren McCulloch. Hubbard provided no real description of the therapy itself, but he concluded with what might have been the motto of the postwar *Astounding:* "Up there are the stars. Down in the arsenal is an atom bomb. Which one is it going to be?"

The issue also carried an advertisement for *Dianetics: The Modern Science of Mental Health,* which was scheduled to be released by Hermitage House on April 19. It was delayed until May 9—Campbell wrote that the publisher was "straining a gut" to meet its deadline—and when readers finally got their hands on it, they were confronted by a truly weird book, alternately compelling and incomprehensible, with an inconsistent tone that reflected its rushed writing and production.

It was dedicated, inexplicably, to the historian Will Durant, a favorite of Heinlein and Asimov with no previous connection to dianetics. Those who ventured further were rewarded with the first comprehensive account of auditing, as well as a fixation on attempted abortions and a level of sexual explicitness that must have taken many readers by surprise: "Mother is saying, 'Oh, I can't live without it. It's wonderful. It's wonderful. Oh, how nice. Oh, do it again!' and father is saying, 'Come! Come! Oh, you're so good. You're so wonderful. Ahhh!' "

At times, Hubbard seemed to be channeling Campbell: "Dianetics addresses war because there is in fact a race between the science of mind and the atom bomb." In another section, he spoke from personal experience: "Sometimes soldiers in the recent war have come home pretending they had been wounded and, when in therapy, are afraid the auditor will find out or give them away to their people. This soldier might not have been wounded in the war, but an engram will be found which contains sympathy for the injury of which he complains. He is asking for sympathy with a colorful story and believes he is telling a lie."

Compared to its subsequent incarnations, however, the text as a whole was relatively restrained. Hubbard called it a provisional theory, open to revision, and he ended by predicting its obsolescence: "In twenty or a hundred years the therapeutic technique which is offered in this volume will appear to be obsolete. Should this not prove to be the case, then the author's faith in the inventiveness of his fellow man will not have been justified." And his last line was a ringing call to action: "For God's sake, get busy and build a better bridge!"

In fact, the book was conceived as the beginning of an ongoing scientific revolution. The year before, Hubbard had tried to found an organization called the American Institute of Advanced Therapy, but its real debut came with the incorporation of the Hubbard Dianetic Research Foundation in April 1950. Its offices were Hubbard's cottage in Bay Head and Campbell's house in Scotch Plains, and its board included Hubbard, Sara, Don Rogers, Art Ceppos, and C. Parker Morgan, a lawyer and former FBI agent who had been treated by Campbell. Winter, who had sold his practice and moved to Union, New Jersey, with his family, would serve as the medical director, and the treasurer would be Campbell himself.

The foundation's first order of business was to generate publicity. At the end of May, after the book had been out for a few weeks, the board members gave a presentation to an audience in Washington, D.C. Winter didn't think that it had gone well: "The professional people evidenced an interest in the philosophy of dianetics; their interest was repelled, however, by the manner of presentation of the subject, especially the unwarranted implication that it was necessary to repudiate one's previous beliefs before accepting dianetics."

But word was spreading. Within two weeks, they received two thousand letters, with hundreds more pouring in every day—only three of which, Hubbard claimed, were totally unfavorable. As a space for patients, the foundation rented the house on Aberdeen Road in Elizabeth where Hubbard and Sara had lived on their arrival. When his landlord complained about the cars parked out front, Hubbard cabled back, "Happily for me, if unhappily for you, I have a book on the bestseller lists."

Later that month, after taking out a loan of ten thousand dollars, the foundation leased the top floor of the Miller Building on Morris Avenue, which was divided into eighteen consulting rooms furnished with "surplus army cots, surplus navy lecture-hall chairs, and some twenty-dollar sheet metal auditor's desks."

A second office was established at 55 East Eighty-Second Street in New York. An associate membership cost fifteen dollars a year, while a full course of treatment came to six hundred dollars, and everyone who applied was accepted.

Campbell threw himself into his new cause. As one of just four trained auditors in the world—by his reckoning, he had undergone more hours of free auditing than anyone else alive—he felt obliged to give it everything he had. Leaving his daughters with the house-keeper, he arrived at the foundation at eight in the morning to teach, followed by hours of therapy and "bull sessions," and didn't return home until after midnight. Unlike Hubbard, he didn't draw a salary, and although he was spending just two days a week at the magazine, he began to feel overextended.

Yet he thought that he had found his life's work, and he gen-uinely believed that dianetics could achieve miracles: "Why, for God's sake, do you think I thought dianetics was so important? Hell, man, because I *knew* it was, because I tried it, and it helped." His letters were filled with descriptions of the successful treatment of "homosexuals, alcoholics, asthmatics, arthritics, and nympho-maniacs." Even before the foundation was established, he had written to Heinlein, "We have case histories on homos. One we worked on for ten days got married three months later. A fifteen-year record of homosexuality behind him, too."

He also served as the public face of the foundation, participat-ing in debates at colleges—including Rutgers, which was said to be looking seriously into dianetics—and promoting it to his readers. After the article was published, an advertisement proclaimed, "It is not the first, nor will it be the last time, *Astounding Science Fiction* precedes science generally." In a response to a letter, Campbell explained why the piece had appeared in the magazine at all, rather than a scientific journal, while avoiding any mention of the fact that they had failed to place it elsewhere:

*The professional journals would normally take two to
four years of cautious experimentation and consideration,
particularly when material so revolutionary was
involved. . . . The publication of the article now has, thus,
saved a considerable number of lives—and a considerable
number of minds from prefrontal lobotomy and the like.*

He hoped to start a dedicated periodical for dianetics, but there
was no question that the attention had benefited *Astounding*. In
1949, its circulation stood at 75,000. The following year, it approached 100,000. Sales of the book were accelerating as well, and
by the summer, it was selling over a thousand copies a day.

Not surprisingly, the first major center of activity outside New
Jersey was Los Angeles, where it came to focus on A. E. van Vogt,
who began to get daily calls from Hubbard. His phone would ring
at seven in the morning, and Hubbard would talk for an hour before excusing himself: "Well, I've got to go. I'm teaching a class."
Hubbard encouraged him to get involved, but van Vogt demurred:
"I'm not interested in anything but being a writer."

Then the checks started coming in. Hubbard had given van
Vogt's address to prospective applicants, and he received five
thousand dollars in fees. After eighteen days, he was convinced.
Obtaining a copy of *Dianetics,* he read it through twice. For his
first test subject, he chose his wife's sister, who shrieked at the
touch of the forceps during a memory of her birth. Next on his
couch was Forrest Ackerman, who experienced a cathartic sense
of grief over the death of his brother in the war.

Dianetics benefited greatly from the targeted advertising that
Campbell had recently introduced in the magazine, and within
the fan community, it was universally seen as the event of the year.
Auditing was becoming a parlor game. Unlike psychoanalysis, it
was simple enough to be practiced by anyone, and it positioned
itself as a response to legitimate concerns over shock therapy and

lobotomy. Like many social epidemics, it took advantage of an existing group of receptive readers, and the treatment, which required a partner, encouraged them to recruit others. In the language of a later generation, dianetics had gone viral.

Despite these triumphs, Campbell remained bitter about Doña's departure, writing to Heinlein, "If you can get a *reasoned* explanation of why she wants to give up a fine pair of kids, a good home, financial security, and a husband who has never touched her in anger, or even bawled her out particularly, I shall be much interested." Heinlein, who was "sorry as hell but not surprised," offered to take the editor's daughters off his hands, and Campbell raised the possibility of a visit to Peedee as her reward for completing dianetic therapy: "If she is cleared, you will probably be seeing her this summer." In the end, the girls never made it to Colorado Springs.

As for Doña, she was in the Virgin Islands, where she had to remain for six weeks to secure a divorce on grounds of "incompatibility of temperament"—a popular choice for unhappy couples in those days. At her hotel on St. Thomas, she found herself surprisingly content: "I fully expected to come down here and wallow in misery and brood but there hasn't been much time." She remained wary of dianetics, warning the Heinleins that the therapy, while potentially helpful in certain cases, would be dangerous "in the hands of a couple of crackpot world-savers."

By the end of June, Doña was back in town. As a treat for the girls—who would live with their father—she and Campbell took them to see *Destination Moon,* the movie that Heinlein had written for George Pal. At the theater, where the doorman was dressed in an orange space suit, a teenage fan in the row behind them tapped Campbell on the shoulder to say hello. His name was Robert Silverberg.

Campbell had also met a figure who would play an even more significant role in his life. Winter's older sister Margaret Kearney, who was known as Peg, had arrived earlier that month in New Jersey. Peg, who was born on March 15, 1907, had grown up with her brother in Negaunee, Michigan, where their father had been a bank president and served three terms as mayor. She attended high school in Ironwood, where she was nicknamed "Irish" on account of her reddish hair and blue eyes.

At the University of Wisconsin, Peg obtained a master's degree in English literature and philosophy with a minor in educational psychology, and she briefly taught remedial English before marrying Everett Kearney, the owner of a flour and feed company. During the Great Depression, she organized local housewives into a lucrative business embroidering crewel ski sweaters for such companies as Brooks Brothers and Abercrombie & Fitch. They had two teenage children, Joe and Jane, but their marriage was unhappy, and they had recently separated.

In New Jersey, Peg became involved with the movement at once, teaching classes and investing five thousand dollars in the foundation. She also became Campbell's auditing partner. Peg was heavy and rather plain, with dark braids pinned to the top of her head, but also strikingly intelligent. When he made a crack about the female mind, she replied, "You don't know anything about that, and you never will. You've never been a woman, you aren't a woman, and you never will be. I'm talking about something you don't know anything about, so just sit back and listen."

Campbell did. Peg's abilities as an auditor, he marveled, made Hubbard look like a kindergartner, and he was eager to question all his assumptions. The end of his marriage was about to become public knowledge. Word of the split had been spreading—Asimov had heard about it from de Camp in April—and it became generally known at the Hydracon convention in New York in July, to the point that many fans were under the impression that it had happened there. On August 19, Doña married George O. Smith in Millbourne, Pennsylvania.

Even if it was partially a matter of timing, Campbell came to believe that Peg was the partner he had always wanted. He wrote later that the ideal auditor was someone "with a stable, wise, honest, and intelligent personality," and he added, "That's a little difficult to find, of course—and if you do find such a personality in a woman, you'll rather naturally want to make the relationship more extensive than merely 'auditor!'" And he told another correspondent, "If you start cross-auditing with a woman, and your cross-auditing team has even moderate success, there's about a .999 probability you'll be married within a year."

CAMPBELL ENVISIONED THE FOUNDATION NOT JUST AS A PLACE IN WHICH DIANETICS COULD BE practiced and taught, but as a think tank for the enlightened minds that the therapy produced. The "clears" were the embodiment of the genre's persistent dream of an exclusive society of geniuses, as foreshadowed by the Foundation series and, even more strikingly, by the novella "Gulf," which Heinlein had written for the November 1949 prophecy issue of *Astounding*.

Heinlein's story described an organization of "new men" who develop a form of mental engineering to increase their brainpower, which they use in their fight against a weapon called the Nova Effect—a veiled allegory for science fiction and the bomb. It was his response to *The World of Null-A,* but also to Hubbard, who had written approvingly of a future in which only the clear had civil rights. When a character in "Gulf" makes a similar argument, the hero replies, "I confess to a monkey prejudice in favor of democracy, human dignity, and freedom."

Campbell, by contrast, was untroubled by the prospect, telling George O. Smith, "The next president will have to be a clear." Any nation that failed to take dianetics seriously was doomed to fall behind the ones that did, and the first step was the foundation, which he had willed into existence out of the pages of the magazine. Campbell had always seen *Astounding* as "a good bull session," and he hoped to take it to the next level in Elizabeth, as long as he could convince Hubbard that the best approach was to throw out as many ideas for discussion as possible.

He was staking all the goodwill that he had accumulated since the war, and his next move was to recruit his own writers. One of the first to feel the force of his enthusiasm was Alfred Bester. A brilliant, versatile author, Bester had also worked for DC Comics—where he wrote the most famous version of the Green Lantern oath—and for radio and television. In late 1949, he finished a story, "Oddy and Id," that was heavily influenced by Freud. Bester sent it to Campbell, who called early the next year to invite him to discuss a few revisions in person.

The author was glad to make the trip, although he was chagrined to discover that the magazine was located in the "boondocks" of Elizabeth. He found Campbell seated with Tarrant in their tiny office. When the editor got up for a handshake, he impressed Bester as both physically huge and oddly distracted—Doña had recently left him, and Campbell was in a sour mood. "You don't know it, you can't have any way of knowing it, but Freud is finished."

Bester stared at him. "If you mean the rival schools of psychiatry, Mr. Campbell, I think—"

Campbell cut him off at once. "No, I don't. Psychiatry, as we know it, is dead."

"Oh, come now, Mr. Campbell," Bester said uncertainly. "Surely you're joking."

"I have never been more serious in my life. Freud has been destroyed by one of the greatest discoveries of our time." When Bester expressed confusion, the editor told him about dianetics. "It was discovered by L. Ron Hubbard, and he will win the Nobel Peace Prize for it."

Bester couldn't quite believe what he was hearing. "The peace prize? What for?"

"Wouldn't the man who wiped out war win the Nobel Peace Prize?" Bester was still lost, so the editor fished out the proofs for Hubbard's article, which hadn't yet appeared. "Read this."

Bester looked at the pages. "Read them here and now? This is an awful lot of copy."

Campbell only turned back to his work. As Bester began to read, he grew bored, but he took his time, not wanting the editor to realize that he was only skimming each sheet. When he set the pages down, Campbell looked at him expectantly. "Well? Will Hubbard win the peace prize?"

Bester, who wanted to be tactful, asked if he could take the galleys home for further study. The editor refused: "You're blocking it. That's all right. Most people do that when a new idea threatens to overturn their thinking."

"That may well be, but I don't think that's true of myself. I'm a hyperthyroid, an intellectual monkey, curious about everything."

"No," Campbell said. "You're a *hypothyroid*. But it's not a question of intellect. It's one of emotion. We conceal our emotional history from ourselves, although dianetics can trace our history all the way back to the womb."

Campbell took him downstairs to the cafeteria, a windowless space that echoed with the sound of lunch orders. Bester sat down across from the editor, who launched into an impromptu auditing session: "Think back. Clear yourself. Remember! You can remember when your mother tried to abort you with a buttonhook. You've never stopped hating her for it."

If Campbell seriously hoped to audit Bester, he had picked a location that was utterly unlike the surroundings in which treatment usually took place. As the writer tried to keep from laughing, he began to tremble, and a way out finally occurred to him: "You're absolutely right, Mr. Campbell, but the emotional wounds are too much to bear. I can't go on with this."

"Yes, I could see you were shaking," Campbell said. After

lunch, they went back to the office, where the editor asked Bester to remove all references in his story to Freud. The author agreed, recovering afterward with three double Gibsons. He never submitted anything to Campbell again, and the magazine was deprived of one of the greatest voices in the genre's history.

Around the same time, Campbell had a similar interaction with Pohl. When the editor fed him the line about his mother trying to abort him with a buttonhook, Pohl replied, "Actually, that may be so, but I just don't have the memory of it, and that's not a problem for me."

Campbell asked if he ever had migraines. When Pohl said that he didn't, Campbell continued unfazed, "Most people do, and I know how they're caused—they're caused by the fetal memory. Because in the womb of the mother, there are these rhythmic sounds. There's this slow one"—the editor hammered it out on his desk—"and a rapid one, which is her heartbeat."

Right on cue, Pohl began to feel a pounding headache. "You've done it, John."

Campbell seemed satisfied. "Aha, now I will fix you up. How old are you?"

"Forty-five." In fact, he was just thirty, which the editor must have known. When Campbell asked him what had happened when he was forty-five, Pohl responded, "John, I don't know. It hasn't happened yet."

Campbell pressed on. "What happened to you when you were forty-five months? Forty-five days? Forty-five minutes?"

The attempt at auditing was unsuccessful, and Pohl left with his head still throbbing. Shortly afterward, he wrote to Campbell, "Incidentally, my dianetics-induced headache didn't go away until I woke up the morning after I saw you. That's powerful stuff you've got there!"

After the publication of *Dianetics,* Campbell went after his authors even more aggressively. He wrote to Jack Williamson to offer treatment on a contingent payment plan: "I *know* dianetics is one of, if not the greatest, discovery [*sic*] of all man's written and unwritten history." Williamson—who had more experience with psychoanalysis than anyone else in the editor's circle—hadn't forgotten his negative impression of Hubbard in Philadelphia. Dianetics, he felt, was a "lunatic revision of Freudian psychology," and he declined to get involved.

Eric Frank Russell was more diplomatic. He joked in a letter to Campbell that Hubbard could use his discoveries to destroy all religion, but he took a rather flippant stance toward the treatment itself: "If I concentrate hard enough I can concoct a picture of my mother breast-feeding me. . . . However . . . I suspect it of being pure imagination. Evidence in favor of imagination—I can equally well picture Rita Hayworth or Myrna Loy doing the same."

Other writers were opposed. De Camp felt that it was ridiculous, although Campbell thought that he was just envious of Hubbard, while Willy Ley broke away entirely, which deeply saddened the editor. When del Rey was warned that he wouldn't sell to Campbell again because he had criticized dianetics in print, he promptly brought in a new submission. At the office, Campbell greeted him warmly: "I guess we're not going to talk about dianetics, are we?" And he bought the story.

Campbell also failed to interest Norbert Wiener, who instructed his lawyer to ask the foundation to stop listing him as an associate member: "I have no connection [with] dianetics nor do I approve the fanfare of claims which Mr. Hubbard makes. If he has used any part of my ideas, he has done so at his own responsibility, and I do not consider myself involved in any way in his ideas." Wiener later referred to dianetics as "detrimental to my standing as an honest scientist."

Not all writers were doubtful. Will Jenkins was merely amused by it, and authors who became interested in dianetics to some degree included Ross Rocklynne, Katherine MacLean, Nelson S.

Bond, James Schmitz, Robert Moore Williams, and James Blish. One of its most enthusiastic adopters was Raymond F. Jones, who wrote to Campbell about guiding his wife through a memory of her birth: "Brother, you're not kidding about dianetics being wonderful."

Apart from van Vogt, the writer who took dianetics the most seriously was Sturgeon, who was audited by Campbell himself. Sturgeon, who had suffered from depression during the war, became a trained auditor, and he continued to defend its core ideas for decades, stating that it was a "synthesis rather unlike anything done before, and totally practical stuff that really and truly worked. And the thing, the blueprint behind it, was solid and reasonable."

But the real prizes were Heinlein and Asimov. Of the two, Heinlein seemed like the more obvious bet—he had been involved with General Semantics for years, and he had repeatedly asked Hubbard about his work: "If it does you that much good, it ought to be good for me. In my own way I came out of this war battle-happy myself—from *not* having been shot at." He had also been receptive to Campbell's accounts: "I have heard from [Hubbard] several times about such activities . . . but *your* letter has been a dern sight more informative than *his* letters."

Campbell responded with a hard sell, and he didn't avoid making grandiose claims: "I most solemnly assure you that, with the knowledge I now have, I could turn most ordinary people into homicidal maniacs within one hour, or produce a certifiable insanity equally rapidly." But he also committed a tactical error by casually dismissing Korzybski, referring to General Semantics as a game that undervalued the importance of the unconscious.

Heinlein wouldn't have taken kindly to this, although he remained sympathetic: "I am most anxious to know more about it and to learn of data gathered by persons other than you and Ron." On more than one occasion, he asked Campbell—who didn't respond—how it was helping his sinusitis, his eyes, and his "unallocated fear," and he even tried to get the military to look into it. Campbell, in turn, recognized the impact that Heinlein's endorsement would have: "You, for instance, could do a far, far better job [than Hubbard] of presenting dianetics."

His involvement was limited by distance. Heinlein had gone to Hollywood to serve as a consultant on *Destination Moon*, which he had sold as a screenplay in 1949. He failed to get along with his coauthor, but he respected the director, Irving Pichel, who threw out most of what the other screenwriter had written—although he retained the comic sidekick from Brooklyn, who annoyed Asimov when he saw it. The result was flawed, but it signaled the migration of science fiction into movies for a mass audience, and Heinlein had reason to be pleased after he left in February 1950.

When the dianetics movement caught fire, he had been back in Colorado Springs for months, building a house with sufficient privacy to allow for nakedness—he was an enthusiastic nudist. He was also working on the juvenile *Between Planets*—the outline of which included a supporting player based on Hubbard, whom he called "Captain Dianetic"—and on *The Puppet Masters,* a novel about alien parasites that featured a character with affinities to Campbell: "His unique gift was the ability to reason logically with unfamiliar, hard-to-believe facts as easily as with the commonplace. . . . I have never met anyone else who could do it wholeheartedly."

After Ginny warned him not to do anything with dianetics for five years, Heinlein told Campbell that he didn't have a choice: "I would love to experiment a bit, but I have no one, literally no one, as a partner." He wrote to Robert Bloch, who became famous years later as the author of *Psycho,* "I tried lying down on the couch and asking myself questions, but nobody answered." Heinlein may well have been too skeptical—and too familiar with Hubbard—to embrace it, but it might also have appealed to his longing for control, and the outcome might have been different if he had delayed his departure from Los Angeles by just a few months.

Asimov was more resistant, although the themes of dianetics were far from unknown to his work. With input from Campbell, the Foundation and robot stories had been vehicles for exploring the notion of an exact science of psychology, and *Pebble in the Sky*, his first novel, included a machine, the synapsifier, that could be used to turn ordinary people into geniuses. But he was also naturally cautious, and when Campbell first told him about "Hubbard's dabblings in amateur psychiatry" on September 16, 1949, he listened "cold and untouched."

Like Heinlein, Asimov, who was busy conducting cancer research at Boston University, benefited from his fortuitous removal from the fan scene. On April 13, on a trip to Philadelphia, he went over the article with de Camp: "Neither Sprague nor I were in the least impressed. I considered it gibberish." A few days afterward, he saw Campbell, who became so frustrated by his resistance that he finally said, "Damn it, Asimov, you have a built-in doubter."

Asimov's reply was a simple one: "Thank goodness I do, Mr. Campbell."

In June, Asimov relished a speech at a convention in which del Rey "lambasted dianetics very rationally and without stint." Campbell, he noted, wasn't in the audience. Yet he avoided directly engaging the editor, with whom he still had the closest partnership of any writer of the time. A few years earlier, when Pohl had asked if he could serve as an agent for his stories to *Astounding*, Asimov had declined: "I want to maintain my loving relationship with Campbell."

He eventually accepted the offer, although he still wrote to Pohl in January 1950, "All stories that go to magazines go to Campbell first. That is a must." But the landscape of the genre was changing.

Just a month earlier, Anthony Boucher and J. Francis McComas had launched what became known as *The Magazine of Fantasy & Science Fiction*, an audacious melding of *Astounding* and *Unknown*, and Ray Bradbury's *The Martian Chronicles* announced the rise of a major talent who had developed in the absence of any support from Campbell.

Asimov himself had benefited from the movement of science fiction into the mainstream. Martin Greenberg of Gnome Press had contracted to do a collection of his robot stories, proposing that it be called *I, Robot*. When Asimov replied that this was impossible—Eando Binder had published a story of that title in the thirties—Greenberg responded, "Fuck Eando Binder." Asimov was also feeling envious of Heinlein's success: "It was like having a stomachache in the mind, and it seemed to spoil all my fun in being a science fiction writer."

But another significant player was about to appear. Asimov heard that Horace Gold, whose work in *Unknown* he had enjoyed, was founding a magazine called *Galaxy*. Gold wanted to buy a story from Asimov, who went to visit him at his apartment. The two men were chatting pleasantly when the editor abruptly excused himself. Asimov thought that he had gone to the bathroom, and he was confused when Gold's wife, Evelyn, said that he might have to leave. "Have I done something?"

"No. He's not well." Evelyn explained that Gold suffered from agoraphobia as a result of trauma in the war, which left him unable to go outside or talk to strangers for long. Asimov, mortified, was about to make his departure when the phone rang. Answering it, Evelyn held out the receiver. "It's for you."

"Who knows I'm here?" Taking the phone, Asimov found that it was Gold, who was calling from the next room. They talked for another hour. Asimov learned that this was the only way in which Gold could speak comfortably, and he began to dread the editor's interminable calls—although he may have also seen it as a distorted reflection of his own fondness for enclosed spaces.

If nothing else, it was another market, as well as a reminder that he was still an important name in science fiction. In August, Pohl told him that Gold wanted to serialize his novel *The Stars, Like Dust*. Asimov worried about what Campbell would think, but after reflecting that *Astounding* was currently filled with dianetics, he finally agreed. And that was when Campbell lost him—not entirely, but to an extent that would forever alter their partnership.

On August 31, Asimov drove to Elizabeth to have lunch with Campbell and the artist Hubert Rogers, who told the editor that dianetics was nonsense. Asimov recalled, "I kept my mouth shut, since Rogers clearly needed no help." Later that day, he saw Gold, who handed him a copy of the debut of *Galaxy*. It was the most impressive single issue of any science fiction magazine that he had ever seen.

Heinlein also heard from Gold. After sending him the first two issues of *Galaxy*, Gold bought an article that had been rejected by *Cosmopolitan,* and he later agreed to serialize *The Puppet Masters*. Heinlein wasn't pleased by the experience—Gold was a "fusser and tinkerer," as well as chronically late with payments, and the author was horrified by how his story was rewritten.

Yet this was the most revealing point of all. Despite Gold's personal issues and heavy editorial touch, both Asimov and Heinlein were willing to work for him. *Galaxy* had approached Campbell's two best authors at a time when their relationship with their longtime editor was vulnerable, and *Fantasy & Science Fiction* was waiting in the wings. They would peel off his most popular writers one by one, in an accident of timing as significant as the one that had put Campbell in charge of *Astounding* in the

L. Ron Hubbard in Los Angeles, 1950.
Courtesy of UCLA Library Digital Collections

first place. It meant that he would enter the next phase of his life largely without Heinlein or Asimov—and he was about to lose Hubbard as well.

WHEN HUBBARD FLEW BACK TO LOS ANGELES IN AUGUST 1950, HE CARRIED THE AURA OF A RETURN-ing hero. No one had been more surprised by the success of his work than Hubbard himself, but he threw himself into its promotion. He had recently finished *Masters of Sleep,* one of his few pieces of fiction from that period, which featured a depraved psychiatrist who "had neglected to read anything about dianetics." At the end of the story, the villain is lobotomized.

On August 10, Hubbard held a rally before an unruly audience of six thousand at the Shrine Auditorium. He had considered presenting Sara as the world's first clear, but the honor fell on Sonya

Bianca, a physics major from Boston, who was said to have "full and perfect recall of every moment of her life." When the floor was opened up for questions, however, she was unable to remember even the color of Hubbard's tie. Afterward, Forrest Ackerman felt disappointed, but Hubbard just clapped him on the shoulder: "Well, Forry, I'm dragging down Clark Gable's salary."

The Los Angeles foundation formally opened its doors several days later at the Casa, a former governor's mansion on South Hoover and Adams Boulevard. Van Vogt rose at the crack of dawn each morning to open the office, with Hubbard showing up after an hour to meet with the instructors. When the students arrived at eight, Hubbard lectured and conducted demonstrations for audiences that numbered in the hundreds. He was a fine speaker, with a smooth delivery that rubbed some people the wrong way, as Campbell noted to Heinlein: "When Ron wants to, he can put on a personality that would be a confidence man's delight."

Hubbard enjoyed the attention, as well as its financial rewards. One day, van Vogt got a call from a bank manager who said that Hubbard wanted a cashier's check for $56,000. Van Vogt replied, "He's the boss." On another occasion, when Sara admired the cars on display at a Lincoln dealership, Hubbard bought one for her on the spot. He had achieved everything that he had ever wanted—money, fame, respect—but unlike Campbell, who regarded the foundation as his true calling, he behaved as if it were a lucky break that could end at any time.

Before long, branches had opened in Washington, D.C., Chicago, Honolulu, and Kansas City. In Elizabeth, which Hubbard visited in October, the money was being spent as quickly as it came in, with its founder writing in a memo, "Funds received by the foundation have been expended to the best of the foundation's ability." Campbell, the treasurer, seemed unconcerned. Despite his admiration for executives, he had always left the administrative side of the magazine to Tarrant, and he came off as detached from the practical end—a visitor found him "cold and uncordial."

Campbell was also preoccupied by what he saw as a break-through in his sessions with Peg, in which they were departing from orthodox techniques to concentrate on emotion and instinct. Much of the remaining workload fell on Winter, who grew concerned after two patients developed psychoses. The only real research being conducted was a study of "guk," a mixture of vitamins and amphetamines that was believed to facilitate auditing. Winter called it "a dismal, expensive failure."

In the end, Winter decided that he had no choice but to resign, followed in short order by Art Ceppos of Hermitage House. Their departures marked the first public defections from the foundation, and Hubbard, who was becoming paranoid, responded by claiming that he had pushed them out when they tried to grab power. He believed that he was being watched by the American Medical Association and the CIA, and in Los Angeles, he had told Barbara Klowden, an employee with whom he was having an affair, "You don't know what it's like to be a target."

His visit to New Jersey lasted less than a week. After returning to California, he was arrested for leaving his baby daughter Alexis alone in his car, which he blamed on Sara. They also met the writer Aldous Huxley, who recalled them as "stiff and polite" when they brought coffee and cakes to his house. Huxley and his wife were audited, apparently to negligible effect: "I have proved to be completely resistant—there is no way of getting me onto the time track or of making the subconscious produce engrams. . . . Maria, meanwhile, has had some success."

But the issues at the foundation persisted. Van Vogt was struggling with its finances—it had spent a million dollars and was heavily in debt—and slashed its head count to stay afloat. On his return, Hubbard hired new people, putting them right back where they had started. Van Vogt remained loyal, and dianetics took him out of writing at the very moment when authors like Heinlein and Asimov were breaking into the mainstream, forever diminishing his status in the genre.

Hubbard's personal life was also imploding. On the suspicion that his wife was cheating on him, he arranged a double date with Sara, Klowden, and an instructor named Miles Hollister. The plan, whatever it was, backfired, and Sara and Hollister began an affair of their own. Hubbard hated Hollister, who was handsome and intelligent, and fired two of his friends on suspicion of being communists. Campbell was more than supportive. When Hollister visited Elizabeth to accuse the trustees of enriching themselves, they laughed at him, and he left, Campbell wrote, "when the group decided he was in need of some intensive processing himself."

After Hollister's departure, however, Campbell took it upon himself to get to the bottom of the rumors, and the foundation established a board of ethics. There was concern over "black dianetics," which twisted the therapy into a form of mind control, but the investigation was primarily an extension of Hubbard's accusations about communism. The editor began "a simple process of getting all the gripes I could, airing them in the meetings, and back-checking on the information until we found where it started," with the assistance of the former FBI agent C. Parker Morgan, whose investigative methods included "desk-prying [and] wastebasket studying."

Campbell informed Heinlein, "The thing blew sky-high with a horrible stench at that point." He encouraged an atmosphere of suspicion, with offenders sent away for intensive auditing, and it ended with Morgan approaching the FBI with the allegation that Art Ceppos had tried to use the foundation's mailing list to disseminate communist propaganda: "Many clubs have been formed, and [Morgan] believes they would be a fertile source for communist infiltration on a national scale, inasmuch as they have already been set up on an organizational plan."

There was also a growing debate over past lives. Dianetics had always encouraged its subjects to think back to the moment of conception, which Campbell accepted as a valid line of inquiry, noting that his daughter had been born two months prematurely: "What's magic about the instant of birth?" After some subjects went back even further, retrieving memories that seemed to come from previous incarnations, the board voted to discourage such research, but Hubbard was receptive, advertising for a volunteer to run past lives at the end of the year.

But the real turmoil was back in Los Angeles. Hubbard told Klowden that his wife had swallowed an overdose of sleeping pills—although Sara later said that Hubbard had forced her to take the medication—and around Christmas, he allegedly strangled her so violently that she ruptured a tube in her ear. In January 1951, the New Jersey Board of Medical Examiners filed suit against the foundation for teaching medicine without a license. Hubbard asked two students, including Ernest Hemingway's son Greg, to drive his belongings to California, and he arranged for Countess Motorboat, the cat that had attacked Campbell's shoes, to be shipped by air express.

In Palm Springs, he was joined by Sara, Alexis, and his assistant Richard de Mille, the nephew and adopted son of the director Cecil B. de Mille—another early example of his fondness for famous last names. He remained abusive toward Sara, and she finally left with the baby. Hubbard, who was drinking heavily, ranted that he had seen evidence of a conspiracy between Hollister, Winter, and Ceppos to take over the foundation. He had managed to hold himself together for just long enough to found a movement, and now he was falling apart. As the imaginary Dr. Kutzman had noted, there was no evidence that any improvement would last.

On February 24, John Sanborn, one of the students who had

driven Hubbard's possessions across the country, was watching Alexis at the Casa. Around ten at night, Alexis, who was eleven months old, awoke. When Sanborn tried to comfort her, she looked up and whispered, "Don't sleep."

Feeling a chill, Sanborn put her back to bed. An hour later, there was a knock at the door. When he answered, he found himself looking at Frank Dressler, one of Hubbard's aides, who seemed to be carrying a gun. "Mr. Hubbard's coming," Dressler said. "He's here to get Alexis."

Hubbard arrived, took the baby, and left. After depositing Alexis at the Westwood Nurses Registry in Palm Springs, he went to Sara's house and forced her into the car. As they pulled away with de Mille behind the wheel, Sara shrieked at her husband, who shot back, "If you really loved me, you would kill yourself." When they halted at a red light, she tried to jump out, but he wrestled her inside by the throat. After dropping off Dressler, they continued to San Bernardino, where Hubbard tried unsuccessfully to find a doctor who would declare Sara insane.

As Sara threatened to call the police, they crossed the border into Arizona. Finally, at Yuma International Airport, Hubbard said that he would let Sara go if she signed a statement saying that she had gone with him willingly. Sara agreed, weeping. Hubbard got out with de Mille, leaving behind a note with the name of the agency where the baby was being kept, and Sara drove back to Los Angeles.

Hubbard went immediately to a phone booth, where he called Dressler, ordering him to pick up Alexis before Sara arrived and find a couple to drive the baby to New Jersey. He then flew to Chicago, where a psychologist gave him a clean bill of health, which pleased him enormously. Hubbard also found time to phone Sara, who recalled, "He said that he had cut [Alexis] into little pieces and dropped the pieces in a river and that he had seen little arms and legs floating down the river and it was my fault, I'd done it because I'd left him."

After visiting a local FBI office to denounce Hollister as a communist, Hubbard took a plane to New York and continued by taxi to Elizabeth, where he and Campbell had one last encounter. Campbell later claimed that he resigned in February, around the time of this visit, in what was evidently an attempt to revise the date of his departure. In fact, he gave no indication that he was planning to leave. Instead, he discussed his work with Peg, who was watching the girls two days a week—*Astounding* had moved back to the city—and seeing patients in New York. As soon as her divorce was settled, they hoped to get married.

In Elizabeth, Hubbard filled the editor's ears with allegations of communist activity at the Los Angeles foundation, to which he added an even more startling accusation: "Joe [Winter] had been spreading rumors, while in California, that he, Ron, was homosexual." Campbell took these assertions at face value, and he failed to raise any objection to Hubbard's proposal that members sign a loyalty oath to the United States and have their fingerprints sent to the FBI.

On March 6, Campbell wrote to Heinlein, "Privately, for your close-held information, dianetics appears to have been attacked by a communist group that was not playing for marbles." The editor expressed his belief that six people had conspired against Hubbard and that the primary target of their efforts had been Sara: "Three times she was drugged and beaten." He betrayed no trace of concern over Hubbard's instability. In the founder's absence, Campbell was effectively in charge in New Jersey, and he persisted in thinking that he could continue his work in peace.

While in Elizabeth, Hubbard wrote to the FBI with the names of fifteen suspected communists, including Hollister and Sara, and offered to submit the fingerprints of all members for analysis. The response, over J. Edgar Hoover's signature, concluded blandly, "I wish to thank you for the information you have made available to this Bureau." Four days later, Hubbard told an agent that Art

Sara Hubbard at a custody hearing, April 1951.
Courtesy of USC Digital Library

Ceppos was organizing a rival organization called the Caduceus Foundation. His interviewer concluded that Hubbard was "a mental case."

As soon as Alexis arrived in Elizabeth, Hubbard flew down to Tampa with de Mille. They went from there to Havana, where two local women were hired to watch the baby, keeping her in a crib covered in chicken wire. On April 12, Hubbard learned through the papers that Sara had filed a complaint for the return of their daughter. It was far from good publicity, as Heinlein dryly noted: "The story about Ron and another man 'kidnapping' Sara . . . would lead me to think that dianetics had not made the founder thereof into a stable personality."

Hubbard's ulcer was acting up, which he claimed was the result of hypnosis that had been performed by Winter and Sara. After his wife filed for divorce on April 23, accusing him of "systematic torture," he saw just one way out. He sent a telegram to Don Purcell, a wealthy supporter in Wichita, Kansas, who immediately dispatched a plane with a nurse. Hubbard boarded with Alexis, telling de Mille to stay behind to finish transcribing the dictation for his new book.

The following month, Hubbard wrote a letter to the U.S. attorney general, describing himself as "a scientist in the field of atomic and molecular phenomena." He referred to Winter as "a psycho-neurotic discharged officer of the U.S. Army Medical Corps," hinting that he might have been responsible for the death of a medical director at the foundation, and intimated that Greg Hemingway was part of the plot. Hubbard also claimed that Sara had been intimate with scientists from "Los Alamo Gordos"—an apparent reference to Robert Cornog.

A year after it was founded, the Hubbard Dianetic Research Foundation was in ruins. Campbell was gone as well. The date of his resignation is unclear, although it could have been no earlier than the second week of March. Toward the end of May, he summed up the situation:

> The original group has sort of moved off in various directions, each developing one aspect of dianetics further. . . . Hubbard's trying to develop the professional auditing business end; Dr. Winter is researching psychosomatic difficulties, and I'm doing my own research on the philosophical development of dianetics. . . . The result is that the original Hubbard foundation is sort of scattered.

But Campbell's faith in dianetics, if not in Hubbard, remained unshaken. The following week, he wrote to Heinlein, "I can tell you, Bob, that you're inevitably going to have to take up dianetics; it's inescapable for a man of your mental bent. For one thing, you won't be fully, consciously aware of the methods you are already using in writing until you have actually explored your own mind, to find what those techniques you use are." Hubbard may have been gone, but Campbellian dianetics—on which he was still working with Peg—was very much alive.

What had been lost was the foundation, which Campbell had played no small part in destroying by his encouragement of Hubbard's paranoid fantasies. Campbell later admitted that he hadn't been prepared for the responsibility: "I wasn't yet competent for the job. The result was that I failed to make Ron Hubbard realize his own limitations." Afterward, he framed his resignation as the product of his discomfort with "extreme mismanagement" and Hubbard's dogmatism: "I departed from Hubbard's ideas . . . when he started mistaking himself for The Second Coming—a delusion he doesn't seem to have abandoned."

While these may all have played a role, they minimized the extent to which Campbell enabled Hubbard's worst tendencies. He had been insulated by distance from Hubbard's excesses, and it wasn't until they became impossible to overlook that he left. Ultimately, he hadn't been in charge. It was Hubbard's name on the book, and although Campbell had hoped to run the foundation on his own authority, he became just as frustrated as he had during the war. As always, the magazine was the only place where he had ever been in control—and even his sinusitis was back.

But he had also been shown a way forward. He would take the hard, unsparing look at the mind that Hubbard had been unwilling to attempt, and he and Peg could do it alone. Campbell wrote to Heinlein, "Peg and I have advanced almost as far beyond Ron and his book as that is beyond standard psychiatric techniques." And in the years that followed, he would drag the entire genre, willingly or otherwise, into the strange land that was unfolding before him.

On May 28, 1951, Campbell told Asimov that he had broken

with Hubbard. Asimov was less than surprised. He later recalled, "I knew Campbell and I knew Hubbard, and no movement can have two Messiahs."

IN JUNE, HUBBARD'S DIVORCE FROM SARA WAS FINALIZED. AS PART OF THE SETTLEMENT, SARA HAD signed a document stating that everything she had said about her husband in public was false: "I wish to lead a quiet and orderly existence with my little girl far away from the enturbulating influences which have ruined my marriage." The word "enturbulating" didn't appear in any standard dictionaries, but it could often be found in Hubbard's writings.

Hubbard remained convinced that Sara would come back to him, as soon as whatever spell the communists had cast over her was broken. After leaving the courthouse, he took her to pick up Alexis, but as they were driving to the airport in Wichita, Hubbard said that he didn't want to give them up. "You're going to get on that plane and go away, aren't you?"

"Well, I have to follow their dictates," Sara said. "I'll just go to the airplane."

After parking at the airport, Hubbard told her that he hated the idea of abandoning her to the psychiatrists. "I'm not going to let you go."

Sara simply jumped out. Leaving her suitcase and Alexis's clothes in the car, she ran across the airfield, carrying nothing but her daughter and her purse. Finally, she made it to the plane, leaving Hubbard behind forever. Alexis, the world's first dianetic baby, had lost one of her shoes.

V.

THE LAST EVOLUTION

1951—1971

*The average [science fiction] author is more stage
magician, a creator of convincing illusions, than
scientist or serious prophet. In practice, once you're
into the process of actually writing a work of fiction,
the story itself gets to be more important than
futurology. . . . You may find yourself even opting
for the* least probable *event rather than the most
probable, simply because you want the unexpected.*

—JACK WILLIAMSON

13.
A FUNDAMENTAL ATTACK ON THE PROBLEM

1951—1960

Man molded the machine, but the machine is going to mold Man. . . . He's darned well got to learn to escape cruising machines. And he's got to learn to control machines, or be smashed up.

—JOHN W. CAMPBELL, IN A LETTER TO *ASTOUNDING*, APRIL 1938

On May 21, 1951, Campbell was driving from Westfield to Elizabeth when he picked up three teenage hitchhikers who were on their way to see *The Thing from Another World*. None of them had a pen for an autograph, and they later said that their parents would never believe that they had been given a ride to the movie from the man who had written its original story. Campbell, for his part, didn't bother telling them that its monster had been inspired by his own mother.

In 1950, the rights to "Who Goes There?" had been bought for $1,250 by Winchester Pictures—the production company of the director Howard Hawks—at the urging of the writers Ben Hecht and Charles Lederer. Van Vogt had hoped to write the script, but the assignment went to Lederer, with uncredited contributions from Hawks and Hecht. The direction was by Christian Nyby, but Hawks was always on set and claimed most of the director's fee, leading to much subsequent disagreement over who was responsible for the finished product.

The film threw out nearly all of Campbell's story, shifting the setting from Antarctica to Alaska. Hawks was more drawn to his favorite theme of a group of men in danger, and he took a greater interest in the types that he understood—the pilot, the girl, the reporter—than in the scientists, who were reduced to thankless foils. But there were striking images—the burning letters of the opening titles, the crew standing in a circle on the ice to reveal the outline of a flying saucer, the shock reveal of the alien in the doorway, and the final warning to the world: *"Watch the skies."*

Asimov thought it was one of the worst movies ever made. Campbell was more generous: "I think they may be right in feeling that the proposition in 'Who Goes There?' is a little strong if presented literally in the screen." Elsewhere he wrote, "I have an impression that the original version directed and acted with equal restraint would have sent some ten percent of the average movie audience into genuine, no-kidding, semi-permanent hysterical screaming meemies." When Asimov commiserated over his lack of financial participation, the editor only replied, "It helps spread science fiction among the outsiders. That's all that counts."

Even as *The Thing* played in theaters nationwide, Campbell was turning inward, with the help of the most loyal partner he would ever have. On June 15, 1951, he married Peg Kearney, who wore pearls, a corsage, and a gray dress. Their wedding took place despite what Campbell called his mother's "utmost desire to drive Peg away from me before we were married," which led to such a bitter argument at the house one night that he had to send her home. Peg, his mother realized, couldn't be pushed around—which was precisely what her son wanted in a wife.

Peg Campbell on her wedding day, June 15, 1951.
Courtesy of Leslyn Randazzo

In the fall, they moved into 1457 Orchard Road in Mountain-side, New Jersey, a newly built ranch house with cedar siding and a spacious basement that was big enough for Campbell's electronics workshop and Peg's workroom—she later started a business that sold embroidery supplies by mail. They needed the space. Along with Peedee and Leslyn, who were eleven and six, Campbell now had two teenage stepchildren. Joe was seventeen, Jane sixteen, and they were thrown even closer together after Peg's first husband died in October.

At first, the blended family seemed off to a promising start. Campbell told Heinlein that the two teenagers had "accepted me completely," which proved to be overly optimistic. Later that year, Joe left for Williams College, and when he returned, they frequently argued. Joe suffered from asthma that was worsened by stress—Campbell thought that he was using it to dramatize his emotions—and when he majored in political science, his stepfather saw it as an act of revolt, since he openly doubted that there was anything scientific about such fields at all.

Campbell's skepticism toward the social sciences was reflected in his work with Peg. At first, they approached it as an extension of their research at the foundation, and they even sent monthly updates to an independent dianetics newsletter in Florida. In the October 1951 issue of *Astounding,* the editor took pains to distance himself from Hubbard, while also taking partial credit for what had worked. Dianetics, he wrote, was "much less than Hubbard believed it to be—but . . . considerably more than he realized. . . . It needs a tremendous amount of development."

Of Hubbard himself, Campbell said privately, "He's now operating in a not-so-good condition, with a conviction that Joe Winter, I, and the others who originally backed him are his worst enemies." As far as their personal history was concerned, Campbell wrote to Winter, "Peg's cordially hated Ron . . . because he experimented on my mind, and on other people's minds." When van Vogt paid a visit, he asked if Campbell thought that Hubbard had used hypnosis to convince him to promote dianetics. If anything, Campbell said, he had hypnotized himself into believing it.

Before long, however, he and Peg had moved off in their own direction. In the magazine, he had written, "But the deep self-understanding that must be achieved for full happiness can be achieved only with the help of someone who is strongly, warmly, personally-emotionally attached to the individual." It was a statement that arose directly from his private life. After the successive implosions of his marriage and the foundation, he was ready to tear down everything that he knew, and Peg was more than willing to help him rebuild his personality from scratch.

It was, Campbell said, "a kind of suicide pact." For fifty hours a week, they confronted their most painful memories, especially from their first marriages, generating ten pages of typewritten notes every other day. Campbell talked about turning it into a book, but apart from some essays that he wrote for his own use, no usable manuscript ever emerged. He preferred to drop hints in conversation, in editorials, and in his increasingly long letters to writers, all of which radiated out from his evenings with Peg, who influenced the second half of his career—and thus science fiction as a whole—as profoundly as Doña had shaped the first.

They conducted sessions in the den every night, working after Campbell's daughters, who adored their new stepmother, had gone to bed. As Peg stitched at her embroidery, Campbell sat on bolsters with his legs crossed, and they talked until two in the morning. Later, he started off with twenty milligrams of Benzedrine, which had been used by the dianetics group to aid the auditing process. Their discussions left him feeling as if he had been worked over with a baseball bat, and afterward he slept like a log. On several occasions he was left so "mentally twanging" that he feared that he might be psychologically crippled, or even die.

Peg was uniquely capable of standing up to Campbell—Asimov called her "the velvet glove around the iron fist"—and their work centered on a question that she had asked him after their marriage: "How do you think?" Campbell spent the next decade convinced that he was on the verge of a breakthrough, with a messianic belief in his abilities that was not unlike Hubbard's, and their ideas came to sound oddly alike. One night, Campbell sat up in bed "with bright and gladdened face," transfixed by the revelation that he was the repository of two billion years of genetic memory, and proclaimed, "Peg—I am an Immortal Essence!"

It soon led him into strange places. Since logic had failed to prevent his old life from falling apart, Campbell began to focus on intuition, which he felt was only the surface manifestation of a vast subterranean continent of unexplored powers. The term "psionics" had first appeared in a story by Jack Williamson in 1950, but the editor's interest in telepathy and clairvoyance went back years.

The dianetics group had taken them seriously, and in Hubbard's absence, Campbell started to study them more closely. He wrote to Eric Frank Russell, "I know the general concept of teleportation, levitation, and a few other spontaneous psi phenomena—also telekinesis, etc. In addition, I know the general basic laws which can permit precognition."

Campbell also thought that he had the power to impose his will on others. At the office one day, he told Asimov that he wouldn't be able to raise his hands from his chair. A look of panic crossed the writer's face: "He could not move his arms. He tried, and unlike a hypnotized subject, he was *consciously trying to break the spell*. He was fully aware of his condition. He was *not* hypnotized; he was enchanted—in the old, fear-tingling magical sense." Finally, the editor gave him permission to lift his arms again, and Asimov—who never spoke of the incident—managed to free himself. Campbell was equally shaken: "It scared the hell out of me."

In 1952, Campbell began to drop hints about his interest in psionics to "various authors and key fans" at the Worldcon in Chicago. Soon afterward, he mentioned the term for the first time in his editorials, arguing that science fiction possessed an advantage in the study of paranormal powers, which would only introduce noise into conventional experiments. Just as he had with dianetics, however, he wanted to present it in a form that his readers would accept: "Until I can demonstrate the phenomena myself, and communicate the exact nature of the mechanisms involved, with demonstrations of each step, I'm not ready to talk."

He confided his plans to an unlikely correspondent. In May 1953, his father, who had retired to Sarasota, Florida, had suffered a stroke, partially paralyzing him on his left side. At the urging of his stepmother, the two men began to correspond on a regular basis for the first time in years. Campbell's letters were often emotional—he still resented how he had been treated as a child—but he also made an effort to impress his father with his new interests: "I'm in this for blood; it's not a game, or a hobby. Somebody's going to be a new Newton, or a new Edison; the field is untapped. I've got the neatest little research organization for high-power thinking anybody ever dreamed up: the science fiction readers and authors."

His primary project, which he planned to call Serendipity Inc., had arisen from an unexpected source. Gerald Smith, the head of Street & Smith, had left the firm after a long battle with cancer, and Arthur Z. Gray, his successor, was surprisingly open to unconventional ideas. Not only did he encourage Campbell's interest in psionics, but he introduced him to a group of businessmen who wanted to invest in it, and in 1954, he told him about a man named Welsford Parker.

Parker was an inventor in Belleville, Ontario, who had spent two decades working on what he described as a gold-finding machine. Its most significant test had occurred a few years earlier, when the treasure hunter Mel Chappell hired Parker to use his equipment on Oak Island, the speck of land off Nova Scotia rumored since the nineteenth century to be the site of a pirate hoard. The expedition failed, and Chappell lost more than thirty thousand dollars.

In the spring of 1954, Campbell and Gray traveled to Belleville to conduct an investigation of their own. Campbell examined Parker's machine, which was a box with dials on the outside, various "condensers, vacuum tubes, electrical wiring, batteries," and a pair of rods that were held by the operator. When a mineral sample—or even a photograph of where a deposit might be found—was brought nearby, the rods were allegedly drawn in that direction.

Campbell was convinced: "Parker is not a fool; he's a brilliant pragmatic experimenter. He has stumbled onto a new, basic principle of the universe." The editor theorized that it tapped into an "urge field" present in all human beings, which meant that the operator, not the machine, was the real detector. Its best commercial application, he thought, would be as a substitute for radio. They just had to build one device that could detect another, which he estimated could be done within two years.

He was willing to put his own money on the line. Gray's investment group had sunk $150,000 into various avenues of research, and Campbell invested as well, buying ten thousand shares of stock in the Parker Universal Contact Co., Ltd. He wanted to become rich, not just for the obvious reasons, but as proof of his legitimacy. Campbell had spent most of his career as an editor earning just sixteen thousand dollars a year, and he told his sister, "[A] larger-scale crackpot has to be a millionaire to be a genius, and I'll be a millionaire."

Parker's device seemed like the great discovery he had been seeking, but an even more important test was just around the corner. Campbell was about to see Heinlein for the first time in six years, and it would be no ordinary reunion. Heinlein was still the best writer he had ever known, and Campbell wanted to recruit him as badly now as he once had for dianetics—not for the Parker Machine, which he was reserving for his fellow investors, but for the research program that he had undertaken with Peg. And this meeting would be the best chance that he would ever have.

Heinlein and Ginny had recently returned from a trip around the world. After dinner with Asimov in New York, Ginny, who was feeling ill, caught a flight back to Colorado Springs, and Heinlein headed to Mountainside the following day "for the express purpose of giving John a chance to tell me what he was doing." Campbell had described his research in letters, but Heinlein found it hard to understand: "I don't know your methods, I don't know how you work, I don't know what you are driving at—you are going to force me to come east just to find out!"

On May 26, 1954, when Heinlein arrived at the house, it was empty—Campbell had arranged for Peg and the girls to be away.

This was striking in itself. Heinlein had never met Peg, and he hadn't seen his goddaughters in years, but Campbell didn't want any interruptions. He ushered the writer into the basement, and instead of asking about the trip, he launched into the lecture that he had prepared, subjecting Heinlein to the full weight of his obsessions at once.

Heinlein couldn't make head or tail of it. When the editor said that he was working on a new definition of distance, Heinlein challenged him, only to be told that he didn't know enough mathematics to understand it—although Campbell later claimed that Heinlein had made the same accusation to him: "He said I had no right to say I was a nuclear physicist, because I hadn't had enough higher math." Campbell vaguely alluded to the Parker Machine, but when Heinlein asked to hear more, he was informed that the details were confidential.

They also rekindled their disputes over General Semantics, which Campbell later said he dismissed "in about five minutes." The discussion became heated, and Heinlein—who felt that the editor hadn't seriously studied the subject—responded at one point by objecting, "I didn't say that, Korzybski did." Campbell shot back, "A magnetic tape recorder would show that your voice said it, not Korzybski's. Aren't you responsible for any authority you quote?"

Back in the kitchen, Campbell tapped Heinlein on the chest, telling him that this work was as important as the race for the bomb, and that he lacked serious social purpose because he didn't have children. This was a low blow. Heinlein wanted kids, but Ginny had learned from their doctor that her husband was sterile. She never told him, but it left a gap in their lives to which Heinlein, who returned to issues of fatherhood compulsively in his fiction, never reconciled himself.

It was the last straw. Four hours was the equivalent of a single session with Peg, but it was more than Heinlein could handle. He wrote to their friend G. Harry Stine, who was working on rockets in New Mexico, "I got preached at, had verbal paradoxes hung under my nose and then snatched away, was told repeatedly that I did not understand, and that I lacked the patience for the sort of difficult work he was doing, and was told again and again how important and revolutionary it was."

They parted on bad terms. Heinlein told Stine, "After four hours of bullyragging I felt insulted—not only my intelligence insulted by prime damfoolishness, but personally and emotionally insulted by being told repeatedly that I did not understand simple statements—and then told I was a slacker because I did not drop everything and follow him!" Campbell, in turn, informed Stine, "In the course of the evening, I learned a lot; he, on the other hand, successfully resisted learning."

As Stine saw it, Campbell was "mashing Bob's face in," and in the process, he left no doubt that it had to be all or nothing. Revealingly, he never delivered the pitch with the same intensity to Asimov, who lacked a comparable sense of mission. Heinlein disliked the pressure: "I wish John would just let it be an ordinary friendship without insisting that his friends be his disciples." And in another letter to Stine, he vented his frustration: "As for space flight, who is actually sweating to achieve it? You and the boys with you, eating sand and wind . . . ? Or John Campbell sitting on his fat buttocks back in Jersey and laying down the law from his easy chair?"

EARLIER THAT YEAR, CAMPBELL HAD READ *THE LIVING BRAIN* BY THE NEUROPHYSIOLOGIST W. GREY Walter, who described how strobe lights could cause epileptic seizures. It reminded him of his experience with the mirrors, and he built a "panic generator" in his basement with a flickering fluorescent tube. When he tried it on his family, Peg's throat tightened, Joe felt asthmatic, and Peedee got a headache—but it bothered

Campbell for only ten seconds. He was, he proudly noted, "immune."

Campbell was less impervious to his own mother, who remained as hard to handle as ever. After one of her visits left him seething, he decided to take action. His sessions with Peg encouraged him to cultivate a brutal honesty, as he had with Heinlein, and he wrote a startlingly savage letter to his mother and stepfather that ran for nine pages: "I will judge Mother as one adult judging another. I judge her unreliable." He informed her that she had made him miserable as a boy, told her that she had no friends, and called her a "a vicious harridan."

It was October 1954. The following week, just before his mother's sixty-sixth birthday—her twin had passed away six years earlier—Hurricane Hazel tore through New Jersey. At her house, the lights and telephone went out, and she felt sick. Her husband drove her to the hospital, where she died of what was later diagnosed as coronary thrombosis and arteriosclerosis. In a letter to Theodore Sturgeon, however, Campbell offered another theory:

> The trigger that caused her death by heart attack was,
> I believe, my interdicting her efforts [against Peg]. . . .
> I clipped her wings three successive times, each time
> cutting her down harder. . . . The fourth time I went a
> step further; I showed mother why she was driven to act
> the way she did, in a particular instance. She died a week
> later.

Campbell seemed to genuinely believe that he had caused his mother's death, as if he had finally discovered her one weakness, as his heroes had done with the monster that she had inspired in The Thing.

His sister was passing out of his life as well. In 1952, while stationed in Guatemala, Laura had converted to Christianity. She became highly devout, and Campbell, a lifelong agnostic who had only recently taken to describing himself as "a deist," needled her newfound faith: "You have found The Light, and know I speak from the Outer Darkness, so what I say must have but little value." Elsewhere in the same letter, he wrote more bluntly, "Christianity has failed."

After her conversion, Laura read the novel *The Lion, the Witch, and the Wardrobe* to her son Laurence, who was troubled by the thought that he loved Aslan, the lion, more than Jesus. Laura reached out to C. S. Lewis himself, who wrote back to reassure her: "He must be a corker of a boy." Laurence later corresponded with Lewis, whom he saw as a mentor for the rest of his life. He was less close to his uncle, although both Campbell and Lewis were writers of speculative fiction who used their position to advise their readers on how to live—and both would have their convictions tested in middle age by unexpected tragedy.

On June 6, 1955, Joseph Winter, who was in his forties and overweight, lifted a heavy motorboat engine by himself onto the back of a truck. He felt chest pains, but he failed to seek treatment, and by the time it became clear that he had suffered a heart attack, it was already too late. He passed away two days later in Englewood, New Jersey, leaving behind his wife and children. Years afterward, Hubbard wrote of his death, "There are men dead because they attacked us—for instance Dr. Joe Winter. He simply realized what he did and died."

It came as a shock to Campbell and Peg, and it led them to take a course of action that they had long postponed. For more than a decade, the editor had effectively treated Heinlein as a godfather to Peedee and Leslyn, and this informal arrangement had remained in place even after the Heinleins divorced. On the day after Winter passed away, Campbell called the artist Frank Kelly Freas, a close

Joe Kearney in 1955.
Courtesy of College Archives and Special Collections, Williams College

friend, saying that he wanted him to be the guardian for his children if anything happened to him or Peg.

A week later, on Friday, June 17, Joe Kearney rose early at his stepfather's house in Mountainside. Joe had received his bachelor's degree from Williams College the week before, and he had reason to feel optimistic about his future. He had graduated sixteenth in his class, Phi Beta Kappa, with a Ford Foundation scholarship to study sociology in the fall at Harvard, and he had impressed Asimov two years earlier as "a very charming and intelligent young man."

After breakfast, Joe set off in his Plymouth sedan for Chicago, where he would meet up with his fiancée and take summer classes at Northwestern. Peg was grieving for her brother, but she took comfort in her son, whose graduation she had attended. Campbell wrote to a friend, "It was a very good thing for Peg; part of her world might be gone, but another part was doing mighty well."

It was a clear, bright morning, and Joe made decent time on the road. Five hours after his departure, around noon, he was on the Pennsylvania Turnpike, passing through the small town of New Baltimore. He was driving at the legal limit of seventy miles per hour. Directly ahead of him, moving slightly more slowly, was a trailer truck loaded with twenty tons of slag, the glassy waste material left over after metal has been smelted from its ore.

Joe plowed into it at high speed. The truck bed cleared the hood of the Plymouth and smashed into the windshield, leaving him with just enough time to take his left hand from the steering wheel and fling it in front of his face. His skull was crushed, but his only other injuries were a broken arm and some scrapes—if he had thrown himself down onto the passenger seat, he might have lived. No skid marks were left on the pavement, which indicated that he had never even hit the brakes.

His accident occurred near the Carmelite monastery of St. John the Baptist Church, known informally as the Church of the Turnpike, which stood overlooking the highway. A set of concrete steps led down the hillside to the road, and a few of the monks hurried to help, along with a passing physician. Joe never regained consciousness, but he survived for another ten minutes, until the bleeding spread to the motor areas of his brain to stop his heart and lungs.

The day before, Joe had received a routine medical checkup—one of his classmates had been diagnosed with leukemia, prompting him to schedule an exam. A prescription for vitamins was found among his belongings, and after his doctor was notified, he called the Campbells.

When the telephone rang, Peg was out shopping for groceries. On her return, she took one look at her husband's face, which had gone gray, and knew that something had happened.

She asked what was wrong. Campbell stared at her for a long moment. "You've really had it, kid. Better sit down first."

Peg's mind immediately went to the unimaginable. "What? Not Joe? An accident?"

Campbell told her as bluntly as he could. "Killed instantly on the turnpike. He hit a truck."

"No," Peg said. Her first, disbelieving instinct was to deny it. "It can't be—"

Through his own shock, Campbell had been thinking of how to break the news, and he deliberately delivered it as a flat statement. By giving it to Peg directly, he hoped to push her into denial, which he compared to a slippage mechanism—like the clutch in an automobile—that could prevent greater damage. In a letter recounting the day's events, he compared its effects to those of science fiction itself: "It lets you consider the problem before the problem hits you."

Later that afternoon, a doctor gave Peg a sedative. Campbell recalled, "It didn't make Peg sleepy, but sort of slightly euphoric. . . . It made everything seem much less important." In the days after the accident, Peg spent much of her time with Jane, who had been a student at Wellesley with Joe's fiancée. The worst moment was when her son's personal effects arrived from Bedford, Pennsylvania, including his steel watchband, which had been twisted and crushed. Campbell wrote, "It threw Peg; she hadn't worked her way through as yet. It did not throw me; it fitted into a completed visualization I already had worked out."

But Campbell had been through an ordeal of his own. For three days, he obsessively relived the crash, as if he had been the one who had died: "The experience ran through from driving along the highway, through the truck coming in the windshield, the emotional shock of realization, the physical shock of the impact—and back to the driving along the highway." He became nervous in his own car: "I was afraid to make the familiar drive down to the railroad station, because I now knew that some hitherto unsuspected danger was lurking."

And the more he thought about the accident, the harder it seemed to understand. The official explanation was that Joe had dozed off, but Campbell refused to believe it. While packing the night before, Joe had mentioned the risk of becoming tired on a long drive, and he had slept for eight hours. The Plymouth had been checked prior to the trip, and after the crash, Joe's heart had kept beating, which implied that he hadn't been incapacitated at the wheel.

The unavoidable conclusion was that the crash had been caused by some external factor, and within a day of the accident, Campbell became convinced of what it was. Joe had been killed by highway hypnosis—a waking trance produced by the act of driving itself. The sound of the wheels, the drone of the engine, and the monotony of the landscape had all created the conditions for disaster.

As soon as Campbell arrived at this explanation, his fear of driving disappeared—but it led to a deeper crisis of conscience. In figuring out the problem of highway hypnosis, he had drawn on information that had been available to him before the accident, which pointed to a terrible conclusion: "*I could have warned Joe. I could have saved his life. The fact that I did work out the problem proved that I could have weeks before.*" And he decided that he would never be at peace until he was able to say calmly to himself, "I am guilty of Joe's death."

It wasn't a rational statement, but it also pointed the way forward. Campbell would take his revenge on the unseen danger that had killed his stepson, personifying it like the villain in a story: "I am, as you see, seeking vengeance against the killer that got Joe." He later wrote to Asimov, "Joe Kearney was sacrificed; we're exploring the relationship between the present human mental mechanism and the operation of high-energy, high-performance, extreme-endurance machines. Joe summoned a demon too powerful to handle; it destroyed him."

Campbell had been preparing for this fight his entire career, and he immediately began seeking allies: "I'm trying to rally the tribe to go on the warpath to avenge Joe's death." He reached out for help from all sides, including the county legislature, the highway department, the big three auto companies, and his own authors, including Will Jenkins—although he pointedly failed to involve Heinlein. He worked hard on an article, "Design Flaw," to mobilize his writers and readers, and when it appeared in the October issue, Asimov thought that it was the most powerful piece that Campbell had ever written.

In a twist worthy of one of his own stories, Campbell argued that highway hypnosis disproportionately affected people of high intelligence—the greater one's ability to focus, the higher the risk of falling into a trance, which meant that it killed "the Good Joes." To overcome it, psychology had to submit to the discipline of engineering: "No real solution to the problem can be achieved until the basic mechanisms of the mind involved are elucidated. . . . We do not care in the slightest who solves it—whether it's a psychologist, an information theory expert, or an African witch doctor; the sole consideration is that *it must be solved*."

He had rarely allowed himself to appear so vulnerable in the magazine, and after the article was published, letters poured in with possible fixes. Campbell welcomed the discussion, but he cautioned readers against missing the big picture: "The pragmatic, trial-and-error approach to a solution is necessary—but must not be allowed to make a fundamental attack on 'What is hypnosis?' unnecessary." He had known that the project would require the synthesis of numerous subjects, from automotive design to highway planning, and now he suspected that a concentrated assault on the nature of thought itself would be needed before work could even begin.

And then, slowly but inevitably, he started to back away. Six weeks after the accident, Campbell wrote to a friend, "I've sort of slowed down on the anti-hypnosis campaign, for a reason. There is no point in trying to get Somebody To Do Something, until you have some idea of what to do that will be effective. As of now, so little is known about hypnosis that efforts to Do Something would be purely trial and error." The questions involved seemed almost unfathomable: "Define 'reality' so that we can distinguish between 'reality,' 'hallucination,' 'delusion,' and 'illusion.' That involves a fundamental attack on the problem of the nature of the process 'to think.' "

It was typical that he became distracted from his campaign almost at once—he lacked the patience to be a true scientist, and he tended to drop projects abruptly in favor of the next tempting possibility—but Joe's death was too painful for him to abandon it entirely. The answer, he decided, was psionics, which could serve as a source of objective data on the brain. From there, it was a short step to "the basic mechanisms of the mind," which would illuminate the causes of his stepson's death. It was a turning point in the history of the genre, and although Joe was never mentioned again, he provided its unspoken motivation, haunting it to the end like a ghost.

The Parker Machine had turned out to be a bust—Parker had refused to provide crucial details about his work, and after a second trip to Belleville, the scheme petered out to nothing. Shortly after his stepson's accident, Campbell received a more promising lead from Colonel Henry Gross, a member of a group in Pennsylvania that hoped to sell psionic machines. Gross alerted him to the work of Galen Hieronymus, a Florida inventor who had developed what sounded at first like another mineral detector—but unlike Parker, he had actually patented the design.

Without contacting Hieronymus, Campbell assembled the device for himself. It took the form of a flat box with a pickup coil on one end, a knob in the middle, and a touchplate sandwiched over a spiral of copper wire. According to the instructions in the patent, you placed a mineral sample—Campbell used a chunk of lead—near the coil. You then turned the knob, which rotated a prism, while stroking the touchplate with your free hand. When the prism lined up with the radiation that the sample was allegedly emitting, the touchplate was supposed to feel sticky.

After Campbell was finished, he called in his youngest daughter, Leslyn, who was ten years old. The girls were used to helping him out with his home experiments, and this one seemed like more of the same. "You stroke this plastic gimmick here. Tune it till the plastic feels different."

"Feels different?" Leslyn asked her father. "What do you mean? Different how?"

"Well, that's for you to tell me," Campbell replied. "Maybe it'll feel furry, like a kitten, all of a sudden, or maybe it will feel as though it turned into a bowl, instead of being flat. But you tune it and tell me."

Leslyn did as instructed. After a minute, she said, "It feels like—sort of like tar. If I pushed on it, my fingers would get stuck."

Campbell grew excited. He called Hieronymus in Florida, and the two men cooked up another test. Like Parker, Hieronymus claimed that the machine worked on photographs, and that it could be used to kill pests from a distance. Campbell sent him a snapshot of a cherry tree, along with a twig with a few leaves, and was amazed by the result: "All the tent caterpillars dropped out of it, dead, within three days, precisely as he predicted." Years later, he described it to the author Poul Anderson as the moment that he began to take psionics seriously: "I got shown."

He prepared for publication, even as he privately ventured into weirder territory. Hieronymus revealed that the machine ceased to work during nuclear tests, which intrigued Campbell, but the strangest discovery of all was one that the editor made on his own—the machine functioned even when unplugged. This led to a series of experiments, of which he obscurely wrote, "I have a Campbell Machine, derived from the Hieronymus Machine, that works, too. Only it's based on something so insane that it makes the Hieronymus Machine look as conventional as a shovel."

But he wasn't ready to reveal this yet. Instead, he continued to invite writers to try the Hieronymus Machine, including the one author who was the least likely to be receptive to it. On March 28, 1956, Asimov delivered his novel *The Naked Sun* to the editor's house, where he was asked to test the machine. He would have refused, but he felt obliged to humor Campbell, although he later admitted, "I no longer trusted the rigidity and integrity of his judgment."

Asimov twisted the knob, but he failed to feel any sticky sensation. After a while, however, his fingertips became sweaty. He said hesitantly, "Mr. Campbell, the plate feels slippery."

"Aha!" Campbell made a note of the reading on the dial. "Negative stickiness!"

In the June 1956 issue, Campbell described the Hieronymus Machine in detail, saying that he hoped to publish similar pieces in the future: "The articles we run are going to be exceedingly unauthoritative, untrustworthy, incoherent, and misinterpreted." He drew the line, however, at studies of extrasensory perception, which was too unreliable to be tested. A device, by contrast, could be built by anyone, with the magazine serving as a clearinghouse of experimental data.

The following year, in the February issue, he unveiled the Campbell Machine, which he had been secretly developing since before the first article appeared. It was a "symbolic" Hieronymus Machine that used no electronic parts whatsoever, aside from a meaningless switch and a pilot light on the outside of the box. In place of the remaining components, Campbell drew a circuit diagram with ink, made a "touchplate" out of a piece of paper, and linked all the pieces together with nylon thread from Peg's sewing basket. And it still worked.

Campbell concluded that it was the relationship between the parts that mattered, not the mechanism itself, and he was pleased by how insane this sounded. Yet he never conducted obvious tests on either version, and he resisted calls to do so, insisting that he was just an amateur: "I am not compelled to defend my hunches, or perform any experiments you think I should perform." It was exactly the attitude that had infuriated him in Parker, and his refusal to be pinned down undermined any attempts to investigate the subject seriously.

Many were skeptical, and when a fan asked Campbell whether the Hieronymus Machine was a hoax, like Asimov's articles about thiotimoline, the editor seemed horrified by the implication. There were inquiries from Bell Aircraft and the RAND Corporation, and Claude Shannon offered to test it, although the timing never worked out. Campbell soon moved on to other causes, and Hieronymus himself felt that the editor had set back acceptance of his work by a century. The symbolic machine, he said, functioned because the ink conducted lines of force, but when it came to serious research, it wasn't worth "a tinker's damn."

AS *ASTOUNDING* BECAME DOMINATED BY ARTICLES AND STORIES ABOUT PSIONICS, THE QUALITY OF the magazine suffered. At times, Campbell seemed detached from fiction—he was more interested in his contacts at Bell Labs, the Harvard Computer Lab, and MIT—but he continued to give ideas to writers. He pitched a premise to Asimov about a man who can levitate, which appeared as "Belief," and they reunited again with "The Micropsychiatric Applications of Thiotimoline," which presented a method of turning psychology into "an exact science." It was a conscious parody of dianetics, and Campbell may have published it as a subtle act of revenge.

The early fifties saw the appearance of several classics, including Hal Clement's *Mission of Gravity*, but the decade's most famous story was Tom Godwin's "The Cold Equations," in which a pilot was forced to jettison a stowaway, a teenage girl, to prevent his rescue spacecraft from crashing. Godwin's first draft ended with her surviving, and the editor responded harshly, "You gypped me. I accepted that your ship could not land with the stowaway—you stated that as the condition—and then you hornswoggled me and did what you said couldn't be done." He had Godwin rewrite the conclusion repeatedly until the girl died.

Campbell occasionally thought about returning to fiction— *The Moon Is Hell* had finally seen print, and he wrote his first new story in years, "The Idealists," for an original anthology—but he preferred to hand out ideas to others. In his search for reliable writers, he came to know an unlikely pair. Robert Silverberg was now a student at Columbia University, and in 1955, the author Harlan Ellison introduced him to a neighbor named Randall Garrett, who proposed that they write a serial together. They tailored the outline to Campbell's prejudices about humans and aliens, and when they were done, Garrett said that they would pitch it in person.

To his amazement, Silverberg found himself in the editor's office on East Forty-Fifth Street, with its view of the United Nations, where Garrett announced, "This is Robert Silverberg, a great new science fiction writer." After hearing their idea, Campbell proceeded to invert the premise—the hero shouldn't be the human scientist, but the alien—and ordered them to turn it into a series of novelettes. When Silverberg came back with the first installment, Campbell bought it on the spot.

Silverberg reminded the editor of another Jewish prodigy from Columbia, and Campbell realized that he could be just as useful:

"Bob Silverberg is a kid, a nice kid, whom I like, just as I did Ike Asimov. . . . Bob needs time and experience; Ike did, twenty years ago." For his part, Silverberg couldn't believe his good luck: "I was so excited at the thought of having sold a story to John Campbell. . . . I couldn't sleep all night, just revolving that notion."

Within a year, Silverberg and his partner were practically making a living by writing up the editor's ideas, and Randall Garrett became a frequent guest at the house in Mountainside. It was hard to imagine anyone less like Campbell than Garrett, a bearded Texan who was known within the science fiction community as a drunk and a sexual predator, but the two men grew surprisingly close—and on one of his visits, the author got to know Jane Kearney.

When Garrett began to date Campbell's stepdaughter, it was a startling development, and their courtship was remarkably rapid—

Jane Kearney in the early fifties.
Courtesy of Leslyn Randazzo

they met when Jane was back from college for the summer, and she fell for him in about two weeks. At first, Campbell approved. Despite his interest in the mind, he was blind to Garrett's personal problems, and when they announced their engagement, with a wedding scheduled for the following August, he seemed delighted by the match.

In private, Garrett was shockingly frank about his intentions. He boasted to Silverberg about the liberties that he had taken with Jane, and he openly mocked her appearance—she was skinny, verging on bony, with what Campbell casually described in a letter as a "lack of breast development." Garrett said that he was willing to overlook such shortcomings for the prestige of marrying into the editor's family, which he cynically regarded as his big break.

On a visit to MIT in the fall of 1956, Campbell told Asimov about the engagement, expecting to be congratulated. Instead, Asimov fell silent. They were seated in a darkened car, and Campbell couldn't see his expression. "What's the matter, Isaac? Don't you approve?"

Asimov was torn. He liked Garrett, with whom he traded jokes at conventions, but he was finally swayed by his loyalty to Campbell. "I don't think I approve, actually. Randall is a brilliant fellow, generous and kind to a fault, but I don't know if he would be right for your daughter."

These words turned Campbell against Garrett, or made him realize what should have been obvious all along, and he became opposed to the engagement overnight. When the writer promised to change his behavior, Campbell took it on as his new project, and for three and a half months, he treated Garrett at the house. Some of these sessions were recorded, and the editor insisted on playing a tape for Asimov, who protested in vain that it wasn't any of his business. Campbell also told him that Garrett had "guessed" that

Asimov had spoken of him disparagingly, and as a result, the two writers were estranged for years.

When it ended, the engagement was over, although Campbell blithely reached out to Garrett a few months later with a story idea: "It's been so long since I've heard from you I don't know whether you've quit writing, or what." Jane left for the Bay Area, where she married John Allen, the son of the head of the biochemistry department at the University of California, Berkeley. They eventually divorced, and Campbell remarked afterward that Jane had fallen for the first two intellectually stimulating men she met, one of whom was a "slob" and the other a "complete bum."

From his perspective, he had better luck with Peedee and Leslyn. Of the two, Peedee, who was headstrong and impulsive, was harder to manage. She had trouble in school and with her weight, and Campbell wasn't always the most patient teacher, although he could be amusing. After she used the word "damn," he told her that she couldn't say it again until she was tall enough to touch the top of the door frame. Six years later, reminding him of their deal, she demonstrated that she could reach it. Campbell replied, "Well, by damn—so you can." She failed to take any interest in his various causes, however, and she finally left for Ohio State University.

Leslyn, whom Campbell described as "the brightest and kindliest" of his daughters, was his favorite, although she wasn't a fan of science fiction—she loved horses instead. On April 4, 1958, she was sitting bareback on a friend's horse in a field by the highway, with a line of brush and brambles between them and the road. Without warning, her horse leaped over the barrier into traffic and was hit by a car, rolling over the hood and severing one of its legs. Leslyn tumbled back over a concrete divider, and if she had fallen badly, the accident might have been fatal.

Instead, she landed on her feet, leaving her with a broken ankle and "an Italian sunset color display" on her buttocks. When

Campbell arrived at the hospital, he barged into her room and demanded without any preamble, "What happened?" He forced her to tell him every detail of the incident until it bored her, using a technique that he had learned from Hubbard, and it apparently worked—the next morning, the pain in her ankle was almost gone.

"Leslyn got started right," Campbell once wrote, by which he only meant that she had fewer aberrations to overcome from her mother. Doña had moved with George O. Smith to the Jersey Shore, where they had a son named Douglas in 1952. In a weirdly misguided gesture, Heinlein had sent all of her letters—including those about her marriage—to Campbell, in a breach of trust that she never forgave. Campbell disapproved of their bohemian lifestyle, and he disliked being reminded of the circumstances of their divorce. When the skeptic Martin Gardner wrote that Doña had left him over dianetics, the editor accused him of intellectual fraud: "He hasn't creative ability enough to be a scientist, so he has made himself a genuflecting acolyte of science."

His eagerness to push beyond the limits of the magazine had taken him into unfamiliar territory. In his search for "a stick of dynamite to blast off the rigidity of thought," he continued to explore psionics, faith healing, and other forms of pseudoscience, and he clashed with his more skeptical acquaintances. When de Camp told him that the famous medium Eusapia Palladino had been exposed as a fake, Campbell shouted back, "Bullshit!" An attempt to host a radio anthology series, *Exploring Tomorrow,* went nowhere—Campbell lectured his listeners, rather than expressing his ideas in dramatic form, and the show was canceled after less than a year.

He made much the same mistake in his most determined effort to reach past his existing audience. After Russia launched the satellite Sputnik on October 4, 1957, Campbell responded with the Interplanetary Exploration Society, a research organization for "gentleman amateurs." It was another effort to found a movement that he could oversee in the real world, and it may have been partially inspired by Hubbard, whose efforts along those lines had been ridiculously successful. Asimov was persuaded to attend its inaugural meeting at the American Museum of Natural History on December 10, 1958, and when he arrived, he found just fifty attendees in a room with capacity for four hundred.

After providing a few introductory remarks, Asimov wound up seated next to F. Darius Benham—a public relations expert who had partnered with Campbell—as the editor launched into his speech. As usual, Campbell had no idea how to speak to outsiders, and after a minute, Benham whispered loudly, "What's all this? He's killing the club. This isn't what we're here for." Asimov flushed, but Campbell had no choice but to continue. There was never another event in New York, but Asimov went to four meetings of a chapter in Boston, which quietly folded after an event at an arboretum in which nobody was able to find anybody else.

Campbell was left with the magazine, a fallback option that often dissuaded him from taking greater risks. Yet he was still searching for a change in direction, and another opportunity seemed to arise in 1959, when Street & Smith was bought by Condé Nast. Its new owner, Samuel I. Newhouse, was more interested in *Mademoiselle,* but he kept *Astounding,* which was modestly profitable, and the acquisition encouraged Campbell to make a decisive break from the past.

He had been mulling it over for a long time, and there had been hints of it in his correspondence. Years earlier, he had written to Heinlein, "You—and many another—have attacked my use of analogs in discussion." Campbell had always been fond of the idea of science fiction as an "analog simulator" for the future, and in the January 1960 issue, he announced without warning that the title of the magazine was changing from *Astounding* to *Analog Science Fact & Fiction.*

The new title amounted to a statement that what fans believed was central to the genre—its sense of wonder—wasn't what mattered, and the response was resoundingly negative. Campbell wrote the following month, "I've already received a number of comments, ranging from howls of anger to gentle wails. To date, no compliments on the change." He argued that the previous title was "unhelpful," and that a new name would clarify what the magazine really was:

> Now Analog *is a term most men-in-the-street don't know. With that title, we will, for once, be able to tell* him *what the magazine is, before our title tells him . . . and gives him a wrong answer. . . . The science fiction we run in this magazine is in actual fact a good analog of the science facts to come. . . . We've earned the title* Analog; *having earned it—we have a right to wear it!*

Not everyone agreed with his reasoning. Asimov felt that the editor had thrown away "a name of memories and tradition," and he wrote much later, "I have never quite managed to forgive Campbell for the change."

14.
STRANGERS IN A STRANGE LAND
1951–1969

Under extreme environmental pressure, [animals] can go into panic behavior, acting with great violence and determination in a manner entirely different from the normal behavior patterns of the organism. This applies all the way up to and including man. . . . When the probability of survival is zero on the basis of all known factors—it's time to throw in an unknown.

—JOHN W. CAMPBELL

Campbell's three most significant collaborators spent the fifties in transition, after a decade in which they had worked closely with the man who had been as responsible as anyone else for the shape that their careers had taken. They were also entering uncharted territory. It amounted to a test, conducted in real time, of science fiction's central assumption—that the skills that it developed in its writers and readers would prepare them for an unknown future.

For all of Campbell's flaws, his presence had been a corrective and a goad, and Hubbard, Heinlein, and Asimov had developed in large part along the lines that he laid down. In his absence, they became authority figures to distinct circles of their own, leading to a cycle in which they were encouraged to become more like what they already were. They retreated into isolation while holding sway over separate slices of the world—and the real question was what they would do with it.

IN APRIL 1951, HUBBARD HAD EMERGED FROM A PLANE IN WICHITA, DRESSED IN A TROPICAL SUIT. Files and furniture—some of which belonged to Peg Campbell, who had to sue for compensation—were shipped from Elizabeth to Kansas, which had been chosen, a spokesman claimed, as "one of the most central points, geographically, in the United States." Hubbard's upcoming book, *Science of Survival,* threw out most of the cybernetic material that Campbell had contributed, replacing it with an emphasis on the tone scale. He was redefining dianetics on his own terms.

Don Purcell, his new benefactor, had made a fortune in oil and real estate, and Wichita became the headquarters of the second foundation. Later that summer, however, a newcomer disrupted the dynamic. Mary Sue Whipp, a nineteen-year-old from Houston, had been persuaded to make the trip by a friend who had read about dianetics in *Astounding,* and she became Hubbard's lover and auditing partner. His other favorite auditor was Perry Chapdelaine, a science fiction fan who later grew convinced that a man named Ron Howes was the world's first true clear. When this was perceived as a challenge to Hubbard's authority, the two men split off on their own.

In the meantime, Purcell reached out to Campbell, who didn't want to get involved. Hubbard, for his part, wrote in 1951, "Two of the early associates, John W. Campbell and J. A. Winter, became bitter and violent because I refused to let them write on the subject of dianetics, for I considered their knowledge too slight and their own aberrations too broad to permit such a liberty with the science." Elsewhere, he called van Vogt, who had sacrificed so much for the foundation, "a heavy foe of dianetics . . . for years, although pretending to be involved in it."

Hubbard was happy to be the sole authority in Wichita, with Purcell serving as little more than a source of cash. When the businessman belatedly realized that he was vulnerable to claims from creditors, he decided that he had no choice but to file for bankruptcy. In response, Hubbard resigned to set up a competing Hubbard College across town, while Purcell acquired the foundation's assets—including the rights to the term "dianetics"—for just over six thousand dollars.

The college lasted for six weeks. Its high point was a convention at which attendees were shown the E-meter, a metal box hooked up to two tin cans that had been devised by Volney Mathison, another pulp author, after hearing Hubbard mention the need for it in a lecture. The device measured emotional stress by tracking the galvanic skin response of the subject, who held a can in each hand—much like a lie detector that van Vogt had described in *The World of Null-A*.

It was exactly what Hubbard had wanted. In Elizabeth, electroencephalograph readings had been taken during auditing sessions, but this was much easier to use, and Hubbard touted it as a tool for measuring subjective mental forces. It was strikingly similar to the impulse that would make psionics attractive to Campbell, who wrote of the E-meter, "It works magnificently for therapists who have the sensitivity and wisdom to interpret its readings."

Hubbard also announced that dianetics had been superseded by a theory called Scientology, which he said had been its original name—the term "dianetics" had been forced on him by his publisher. The change was partially inspired by the group's legal situation, but it marked a genuine shift in direction. Even after the trademark dispute was resolved, dianetics—which, with its echo of cybernetics, may have been too reminiscent of Campbell—was deemphasized, and in April 1952, the Hubbard Association of Scientologists was established in Phoenix.

Scientology came to focus on the concept of the individual as a "thetan," which made its first known appearance in a session that Hubbard conducted in April with his new wife, Mary Sue. A thetan—derived from "theta," a form of life energy—was an immortal entity that occupied countless bodies over time. Unlocking its power would lead to such abilities as telepathy, levitation, and full access to memories of past lives, which had moved decisively to the center of the founder's teachings.

It was a pivotal change, and it arose directly from the men and women with whom Hubbard was surrounded. He had never much cared for science fiction, but his followers did, and the disciples who joined him in Phoenix unconsciously drew on the genre's conventions when audited about their previous lives—which even Hubbard conceded might be "fantasies built upon reading and imagination." They gave him material, and he fed it back to them in an amplified form, in an editorial role that resembled Campbell's relationship with his writers.

Not surprisingly, his theories quickly evolved to appeal to the only audience that he had available. In *What to Audit,* Hubbard wrote that disembodied thetans reported to implant stations on Mars, and several years later, he published a dozen case studies of past lives with science fiction elements, which his followers evidently provided of their own accord. He even claimed to have audited E. E. Smith, whose novels were reinterpreted as actual events—except that Hubbard was reaching into the past, not the future, resulting in a cosmology that stretched back for millions of years.

One of Hubbard's most faithful supporters was Helen O'Brien, the head of the Philadelphia branch, where he delivered a series of lectures. Hubbard spoke highly of the book *Twelve Against the*

Gods by William Bolitho, which he had first encountered in his days with Jack Parsons, and he paid close attention to the chapter on Muhammad, whom he followed Bolitho in calling a "small-town booster" who founded a religion for practical reasons. He may also have been struck by one line: "The lever of his position is now his own converts, his own past, the picked fanatics."

On April 10, 1953, Hubbard wrote to O'Brien—whom he had asked to build a machine that induced hypnosis using sound, which recalled one of his Ole Doc Methuselah stories—about another development:

> *I await your reaction on the religion angle. . . . A religious charter would be necessary in Pennsylvania or [New Jersey] to make it stick. But I sure could make it stick. We're treating the present time beingness, psychotherapy treats the past and the brain. And brother, that's religion, not mental science.*

Recasting the movement as a religion also offered potential tax and legal benefits, and his work was undeniably inching into mystical territory. Churches were soon incorporated in New Jersey, California, and Washington, D.C., and Hubbard asked existing branches to begin the process of conversion.

It was a crucial moment, and the reasoning behind it was more complicated than it might seem. According to multiple witnesses, over the previous decade, Hubbard had uttered some variation on the statement "If you want to get rich, you start a religion." Yet he had made no serious effort along those lines for years. He had described dianetics as a new science of the mind, and his initial goal had been to win over the medical establishment. If founding a religion had been his plan from the beginning, he had approached it in a very roundabout way.

Years later, Campbell remarkably stated, "It was, as a matter of fact, I, not Ron, who originally suggested that it should be dropped as a psychotherapy, and reconstituted as a religion. Because *only religions are permitted to be amateurs.*" This claim—a mirror image of Hubbard's assertion that he had introduced real characters to science fiction, with each man taking credit for the other's innovations—is impossible to verify, although the editor had pitched the notion of a cult of scientists in stories ranging from *Sixth Column* to the Foundation series itself.

The decision to franchise paid off almost immediately. Scientology benefited from the same cultural forces that drew people to such controversial movements as Transcendental Meditation and the Unification Church, and as its membership continued to grow, a tenth of all revenue was channeled to Hubbard. He was also furiously producing new books, including *All About Radiation*, in which he concluded, like Campbell, that the prevention of nuclear war lay in "better controls" and a "change of status of man and his national governments."

With his newfound wealth, Hubbard purchased Saint Hill Manor, the former estate of the Maharajah of Jaipur in Sussex, England, where he took up residence in 1959. By all indications, he believed in his work. In his study, Hubbard and Mary Sue— with whom he had four children—held sessions for hours every day, in a version of the research group that Campbell had always wanted. The resulting theories appealed to the writer William S. Burroughs, who told Allen Ginsberg, "Of course Scientology attracts all the creeps of the cosmos. You see *it works.*"

At times, Hubbard seemed paranoid. All staff members had to be checked with the E-meter, and at worst, an offender could be declared a Suppressive Person. In August 1962, Hubbard wrote to President Kennedy offering to train astronauts using the principles of Scientology, and he came to believe that the letter inspired a raid on the church the following year. He indicated that he was willing to meet the president about the situation, with one provision: "If

President Kennedy did grant me an audience to discuss this matter that is so embarrassing to the government at home and abroad, I would have to have some guarantee of safety of person."

In his more generous moods, he thought about his former collaborators. On October 29, 1964, Hubbard wrote to Campbell, saying that he had seen the editor's picture in an advertisement in *Analog.* After asking him to say hello to Tarrant, he concluded, "Things go well. We keep winning." Campbell himself saw Scientology as "intellectual garbage," and criticism of the church was growing. In 1965, the Australian Board of Inquiry called it "evil," stating in its report, "Some of [Hubbard's] claims are that . . . he has been up in the Van Allen Belt, that he has been on the planet Venus where he inspected an implant station, and that he has been to Heaven."

Hubbard was thinking about pulling up stakes. After a failed attempt to gain influence in Rhodesia—he believed that he had been Cecil Rhodes in a previous life—his thoughts turned to the sea, which had always been his first love. Rumors circulated of a mysterious Sea Project, and in September 1966, he clarified his plans. Resigning publicly from the church, which he continued to control in secret, Hubbard announced that he was becoming an explorer again, buying a ketch, the *Enchanter,* that was followed by a trawler and a motor yacht.

He flew to Morocco, with a crew of nineteen sailing after him early in 1967. Hubbard was drinking heavily, taking pills, and working on the most audacious—and lucrative—story of his career. It became known as OT III, for Operating Thetan, or "The Wall of Fire," the writing of which had been so dangerous, Hubbard said, that he had broken his knee, leg, and back: "It is carefully arranged to kill anyone if he discovers the exact truth of it. . . . I am very sure that I was the first one that ever did live through any attempt to attain that material."

The handwritten pages, which remained a closely guarded secret, revolved around the figure of Xenu, the tyrannical dictator of the Galactic Confederation. Millions of years ago, Xenu, faced with an overpopulation crisis, took hordes of his own people, injected them with a mixture of alcohol and glycol, and shipped them to Earth, which was then known as Teegeeack. After throwing them into volcanoes, he blew them up with atomic bombs, leaving them in the form of disembodied thetans that cling to the present day to unsuspecting humans.

Between two lines in the manuscript, squeezed in like an afterthought, Hubbard added his own comment on what he had written: "Very space opera." It was startlingly unlike his published fiction. In his old stories, galactic empires had rarely played any significant role, except as a kind of painted backdrop. Now he was embracing these images wholeheartedly, in a logical culmination of the cycle of influence that had arisen from his circle of followers. If they wanted science fiction, Hubbard was typically determined to outshine them all.

For now, the contents of the OT III documents remained confidential, although members of the church—including William S. Burroughs—would pay dearly for decades to learn their secrets. Yet they rippled outward in visible ways. As he sailed around the Canaries on the *Enchanter*, Hubbard regaled his crew members—who had signed contracts of a billion years for what became known as the Sea Org—with tales of his past existence driving race cars in the Marcab civilization, a society exactly like that of America in the fifties.

Hubbard, who called himself the Commodore, had achieved his dream of captaining his own fleet, but science fiction refused to let him go. The crew went in search of treasure that he had buried in his previous lives, although none was ever found, and there were rumors of a hidden space station in the mountains in Corsica. In practice, Hubbard was growing increasingly abusive—offenders as young as five were punished by being sent belowdecks to the chain locker, while other wrongdoers were "overboarded" into the water, where some nearly drowned.

His search for a safe harbor, which had been his original mission, turned into an aimless voyage that would last for years. The Sea Org became a way of life, but on land, his fantasies assumed a more lasting form. At the Los Angeles headquarters of the Church of Scientology, staff members dressed in white uniforms with silver boots, in imitation of Xenu's Galactic Patrol, and gathered on the roof every night to look for enemy ships. They were watching the skies. As Bolitho had said of religious adventurers: "They have lived on this little earth like an island, and made up their night fires to scare away the noises of the interstellar dark."

ON JUNE 17, 1952, JACK PARSONS HAD RECEIVED AN ORDER FOR A BATCH OF AN EXPLOSIVE FROM a pyrotechnics company that provided special effects for the movies. While working in the coach house that he used as a lab, he dropped a coffee can in which he was mixing chemicals, and the explosion shattered his legs and tore off his right arm. Hours after he was declared dead, his mother, Ruth, committed suicide by swallowing a bottle of sedatives. Parsons was thirty-seven years old.

Heinlein heard the news from a mutual friend. The following year, he attended a party hosted by Ron Howes, the man whom Perry Chapdelaine had hailed as the world's first clear. Howes—who made his greatest mark, years later, as the inventor of the Easy-Bake Oven—had established a group called the Institute of Humanics in Colorado Springs, and he spent the evening auditing his guests. Also present was van Vogt, who had distanced himself from Hubbard, but was still interested in dianetics. Heinlein noted that this was a pattern among the people he met that night: "Ron is a jerk, Ron is a nut—but nevertheless he is the prophet of the One True Faith."

He was feeling detached from the science fiction community,

in part because of geographical distance. Aside from occasional visits from their friends—including George O. and Doña Smith—he and Ginny were largely on their own in Colorado. In 1953, they left on a trip around the world, proceeding from South America to Africa, with a stop at the isolated island of Tristan da Cunha, where Heinlein sent a letter to Hubbard for the sake of the unusual postmark. They continued on to Singapore, Jakarta, Sydney, and New Zealand, the socialist economy of which Heinlein dismissed as "a fake utopia." In a world defined by the Cold War, he was losing patience with the economic ideals to which he had devoted himself as a young man.

The trip also insulated him from the worst of McCarthyism, which he absorbed from newspaper accounts overseas. Like Asimov and Campbell, Heinlein had no sympathy for Joe McCarthy, whom he called "a revolting son of a bitch," but he felt that the outrage on the left was overblown, given the treatment of dissidents in other nations: "I thank heaven that I live in a country so free that the worst an innocent man has to fear is slander, bad publicity, tarnished reputation and, under some circumstances, possible loss of employment through taking refuge in the Fifth Amendment."

Elsewhere, he referred to the witnesses who had exercised their right against self-incrimination as "traitors" and "custard heads." It was a strangely unfeeling response, especially since the victims of the Red Scare included Irving Pichel, the director of *Destination Moon;* Dalton Trumbo, who had gone uncredited for the script for *Rocketship X-M;* the science fiction writer Chan Davis; and Bernhard J. Stern, whose work had inspired Asimov's "Trends." After his return, Heinlein withdrew from friends, including Anthony Boucher, whose politics were to the left of his own.

On May 26, 1954, he had his confrontation in Mountainside with Campbell. After the argument, the editor sent him a peace offering—a record by Tom Lehrer—but they would never fully reconcile. Heinlein was also annoyed by Alice Dalgliesh at Scribner, who had asked for revisions to his juveniles. Lurton Blassingame, his agent, pointed out that she was just trying to publish books that would be acceptable to schools and libraries, but Heinlein had trouble making this distinction. It made for a notable contrast to Asimov, who was informed by his own editor: "Isaac, your books are so proper that librarians are confident enough to buy them without reading them, and we don't want to do anything to upset them."

Asimov accepted this logic, while Heinlein hoped one day to ignore editors altogether, even as they provided a measure of control that he badly needed. Yet he kept writing juveniles, including *Tunnel in the Sky,* perhaps the best of his novels for young readers, about a school trip to another planet that becomes an ordeal of survival. Campbell turned it down, but he bought *Double Star,* a slight but engaging serial that won a Hugo Award. When the Heinleins spent a week in New York, however, the two men failed to meet up, and the author was tired of Campbell's provocations: "Half the time at least, I don't know what the argument is all about."

He was also distracted by his former wife, who was sending what he saw as "poison pen" missives to their friends. After moving to Stockton, California, with her new husband, Leslyn had suffered a series of strokes that confined her to a wheelchair. Her most virulent letters—including several to Doña—all dated from this time, which meant that she would be judged by posterity for the worst period of her life. Heinlein was more concerned for his own safety: "The only thing that really worries me—and this scares the hell out of me—is that someday she might get out of bed, hop a bus, and show up here."

In 1956, Heinlein wrote *The Door into Summer,* an adult novel about time travel that ranked with his best work, and *Citizen of the Galaxy,* a juvenile about a young slave who becomes a spy. Campbell rejected the former, but bought the latter, taking the opportunity to share a few thoughts on the institution of slavery itself. Dalgliesh, in turn, worried that its treatment of religion would pose problems for book publication, causing Heinlein to recoil more than usual: "Two changes, admittedly easy and unimportant, threw me into [a] spin and lost me ten days' working time."

In fact, it was Heinlein who was changing. He felt that the juveniles were his most important work, a sense that was under-lined by Sputnik, which left him "very shook up." His concerns for the future resulted in the lovely *Have Space Suit—Will Travel,* in which a boy represents humanity in an interstellar court. It was as strange and moving a novel as he ever wrote, and Campbell was tantalized by it, but passed. When Dalgliesh asked Heinlein to tone down its violence, his response indicated how his feelings had evolved: "I do not think we have better than an even chance of living, as a nation, through the next five years. . . . I don't ever want to pull my punches again."

His resolve was about to be tested. On April 5, 1958, Hein-lein was shaken awake by Ginny, who showed him a newspaper advertisement calling for a unilateral halt to nuclear testing. Hein-lein saw it as an act of spineless capitulation to the Soviets, and he wrote his own ad in response, "Who Are the Heirs of Patrick Henry?," in which he implied that the ban's proponents, including Eleanor Roosevelt and the psychiatrist Erich Fromm, were instru-ments of communist propaganda: "Consciously or unconsciously they prefer enslavement to death."

Ginny warned him, "You do realize, if we run this ad, we're going to lose half our friends in town?" Heinlein sent copies to everyone he knew, but the response was lukewarm. Campbell was skeptical of the whole approach, while Asimov was in favor of the ban. One of his articles had influenced a paper by Linus Pauling that later contributed to the suspension of atmospheric nuclear testing, prompting Asimov to write, "I therefore played a very small part in bringing about the nuclear test ban—and I'm delighted." He never discussed the issue with Heinlein, whose campaign succeeded only in putting a few hundred signatures on Eisenhower's desk.

Yet it marked a change in his outlook. Heinlein quickly wrote up the time travel story "—All You Zombies—," but his thoughts were elsewhere. Brooding over the liberal resistance to his efforts, he conceived of a novel in which military service was a condition for full citizenship. It inspired some of his best work—the sections on boot camp were the strongest sustained sequences he would ever write—but the argument was also deliberately slanted. The enemies were alien bugs, and if they had been human, with less of an absolute sense of good and evil, the impact of *Starship Troopers* would have been very different.

But it was meant to get a rise out of readers, and Heinlein had a good idea of what the reaction would be, although he may have underestimated its fury. Scribner rejected it, while Campbell objected less to the thesis than to its presentation. Writing for once with unusual prescience, he told Lurton Blassingame, "I fear Bob's going to induce considerable anti-patriotism in a lot of readers by telling a story from the viewpoint of a hundred-percent dedicated patriot."

Starship Troopers was published by Putnam shortly after the death of Heinlein's father, and it divided readers as none of his previous novels ever had. Heinlein wasn't surprised, saying that "the pious critic will allow any speculation at all, on any subject— as long as it conforms to the unwritten assumptions of the new orthodoxy." Deep down, however, he felt that the response proved that other writers secretly hated him—but it also won him a second Hugo Award.

The controversy freed up something inside him. He returned to his Martian Mowgli story, which he had repeatedly failed to finish over the last decade, despite the fact that it was "the best setup for a novel I ever had in my life." Heinlein filled it with his advice on how to live, "ignoring length [and] taboos," with a picture of a religious movement that reflected the watchful eye that he was keeping on Hubbard. It came as close as any science fiction novel ever would to awakening real possibilities in the lives of its readers, and when *Stranger in a Strange Land* won the Hugo the following year, Heinlein was greeted at the ceremony with thunderous applause.

Although he insisted that he was only trying to raise questions, his fiction was growing undeniably more didactic. His next effort, *Podkayne of Mars,* was only superficially a juvenile—it was really a message to parents, culminating in the heroine's death, although he grudgingly revised it to save her life. He was less inclined to compromise with *Glory Road,* a deconstruction of Hubbard's yarns about an ordinary man in a world of fantasy, as if Heinlein were determined to show once and for all how it was done. Campbell felt that it broke its contract with the reader: "I thought I was getting a saga—and I got a sermon. Nuts." Heinlein believed that he knew better, and the disagreement led to a long gap in their correspondence.

At the beginning of his career, Heinlein had been attracted to science fiction as a vehicle for his politics, and now this impulse returned to the forefront. *Farnham's Freehold* was conceived in part as a response to Campbell's opinions on slavery, while his libertarian views, combined with the gravity gauge from Hubbard's "Fortress in the Sky," resulted in *The Moon Is a Harsh Mistress,* which introduced a catchphrase into the wider culture: "There ain't no such thing as a free lunch." It was an exciting story, but Campbell felt that it was too long for a serial, and in his last known letter to Heinlein, he reluctantly rejected it. The novel won a record fourth Hugo, cementing its author's status as the most acclaimed science fiction writer alive.

As far as his political convictions were concerned, Heinlein liked Barry Goldwater, whom he saw as a liberal who had evolved: "The central problem of today is no longer individual exploitation but national survival . . . and I don't think we will solve it by increasing the minimum wage." He claimed that his views had remained consistent, while the rest of the country had moved to the left, but this was disingenuous at best—his priorities had indeed changed, and in the absence of other strong personalities, as Asimov noted, his beliefs became more like those of his wife.

Heinlein was also willing to overlook problematic positions— such as Goldwater's vote against the Civil Rights Act—if they were packaged with the security policies that he favored. He was guardedly sympathetic toward the John Birch Society, which picketed a talk by Linus Pauling that Asimov had attended: "I think Bob Welch's methods are puerile and I do not find it worthwhile to support him. But if I am ever forced to a choice between the John Birch Society and its enemies, I know which side of the barricades I belong on. I'll be on the same side the John Birch Society is on— because my enemies are on the other side."

In 1965, the Heinleins left Colorado Springs. Ginny thought that her health problems, which Campbell had casually suggested were "psychogenic," were caused by the high altitude, and they moved to the college town of Santa Cruz, California, bringing them into contact for the first time with the counterculture. Heinlein dismissed it as "a parasitic excrescence to the 'square' culture," and although he had sampled marijuana in his youth, he called LSD "as much of a failure as other drugs in producing any results of any value other than to the user." But the hippies embraced *Stranger in a Strange Land,* which saw a spike in sales in the late sixties.

It was a vindication of the risks that he had taken, and he would never submit to the control of editors again. Since he had no children, his newfound prominence seemed like his best chance to affect the future, although he had mixed feelings about being seen as a guru. In *Stranger in a Strange Land,* he had coined the term "grok" to describe a form of empathy so deep that it was inexpressible, but in practice, he was wary of misinterpretation. His most famous novel was taken as a statement about free love, but he wrote to one reader, "If a male and a female each loves the other, it is almost a certainty that they will also feel physically attracted—in which case, if they choose to do something about it, the safest arrangement is contractual marriage."

ON APRIL 22, 1953, ASIMOV HAD LUNCH AT HOWARD JOHNSON'S WITH A WOMAN HE HAD MET AT Boston University, who invited along a girlfriend. As usual, Asimov flirted shamelessly, and he was startled when the second girl calmly parried him "innuendo for innuendo." After he dropped his friend off at her next appointment, the woman he had just met asked him to drive her home to Cambridge. He agreed. When they got to her place, she invited him up.

"What it amounts to is that she then seduced me," Asimov later wrote. It was a sexual awakening of the kind that Heinlein had experienced as a young man on the train with Mary Briggs—except that it had happened to Asimov in his thirties. In the aftermath, he was eager to make up for lost time. One day, Pohl met him at a hotel near Boston Common, where Asimov "looked around, grinning, and volunteered that this was the place where he used to take his girlfriends." And when he informed a woman at a party that he didn't drink or smoke, she asked, "Well, what the hell do you do?" Asimov replied, "I fuck an awful lot, ma'am."

His extramarital activities made him more confident, but he wasn't about to leave Gertrude, who had given birth to their first child, David, on August 20, 1951. Asimov was working hard, taking on nonfiction projects and following Heinlein into juveniles with a series about the space ranger David "Lucky" Starr, whom he named after his son. His status was less clear with Campbell, who bounced two submissions, in his first rejections in nine years.

Asimov recalled, "I was having a stronger and stronger impulse to stay away from him, but the ties of love, and the memory of all he had done for me, kept me from ever breaking with him."

His first three novels, which had been written with minimal input from Campbell, had felt like a retreat from his best work, but he was slowly coming into his own. When Horace Gold suggested that he write a mystery about a detective with a robot partner, the result was *The Caves of Steel*, which Asimov set in an underground city that reflected his own preference for enclosed spaces. It was a major advance, and he followed it with *The End of Eternity*, his single best novel, as well as a secret repudiation of the Foundation series—it described a similar organization of scientists as a collection of "psychopaths." Campbell turned it down.

After Pohl closed his literary agency, Asimov was left without representation, and he didn't particularly think that he needed it. On May 25, 1954, however, he spent the evening with the Heinleins, whom he hadn't seen in years, and Lurton Blassingame. At one point, Heinlein—who was one day away from his confrontation with Campbell—quietly confided that his income under Blassingame had quintupled. Asimov was tempted, but fate intervened at dinner, when the agent's wife took one of the shrimp from his plate and ate it. He always regarded his food as his special property, and he decided then and there that he would never sign with Blassingame.

In 1955, Gertrude gave birth to their daughter Robyn—Asimov called her "Robbie," like his most famous robot, although he said that this was just a coincidence—and he was promoted to an associate professorship at Boston University. Yet cracks in their marriage were showing. Gertrude frequently mentioned divorce—they often quarreled over money in front of friends—and he hated that she smoked. Asimov began to think of their life together as a failure: "In all those years I had not made her happy and I didn't see how I could make her happy in the future."

He channeled this dissatisfaction into his work. In 1956, they moved to West Newton, Massachusetts, where Asimov decorated his office with images of rocket ships and stickers that read "Genius at Work" and "Great Lover." He wrote to Heinlein, "Gertrude complains that she doesn't lay eyes on any part of me but the back of my neck when I'm typing." Elsewhere, he confessed that he was "miserably unhappy" whenever he wasn't writing: "I like it in the attic room with the wallpaper. I've been all over the galaxy. What's left to see?"

Asimov was still selling stories to Campbell, but an exchange about race—to be explored later—had left him deeply uncomfortable, and he was looking for alternative markets. The editor Robert Lowndes agreed to his terms: "I would write one for him, just as though I were writing it for *Astounding.* In return, if he liked it, I would expect him to pay the *Astounding* rate of four cents a word." Asimov rewarded Lowndes with "The Last Question," in which he proposed an unforgettable solution to the problem of a dying universe. It became his favorite of his own short stories, and he no longer cared where it appeared.

As he worked on science books for teenagers and articles for *Astounding,* he began to realize that he could support himself with writing and public speaking alone. His relationship with the director of the medical school had degenerated, and he finally proposed that he remain on the faculty without teaching or taking a salary—although he insisted on keeping his title, knowing that losing it would disappoint both his father and Campbell, who loved having a professor among his writers.

This departure coincided with a break in his career. Campbell rejected "The Ugly Little Boy," which became one of Asimov's personal favorites, and his own interests were changing, particularly after Sputnik: "I berated myself for spending too much time on science fiction when I had the talent to be a great science writer." He shifted his focus to nonfiction, and as one book followed another, he began to effectively define the emerging genre of popular science.

And his life was about to change in other ways. On May 1, 1959, Asimov attended a dinner of the Mystery Writers Association, where he shared a table with a woman with an elfin face, glasses, and a tiny chin. Years before, they had met at a convention, where she had asked him for an autograph. Asimov, who was suffering from gallstones, had felt terrible. "What's your name?"

"Janet Jeppson." She spelled it. When he asked her what she did, just to make conversation, Janet—who had studied at Stanford and New York University Medical School—told him that she was a psychiatrist.

Asimov handed the book back. "Good. Let's get on the couch together."

He had said it reflexively—he certainly wasn't in an amorous mood—but the line, as well as his unpleasant appearance, had left a bad impression. That night, however, the dinner passed enjoyably, and when it was over, Asimov turned to Janet. "There's no need to end the evening, I hope."

Janet, who was thirty-two and unmarried, was surprised. "Wouldn't you rather stay with your friends here?"

"At the moment, you're my only friend," Asimov said. They went back to her apartment, where they talked past midnight. Afterward, they exchanged letters, and he called her whenever he was in New York.

He had grown closer to his other editors, but he still crossed paths with his old mentor. At the World Science Fiction Convention in Detroit in 1959, Asimov was heading to breakfast when he ran into Campbell and Peg, who told him, "I am glad to see that at least one other person keeps sensible hours."

Asimov had been up all night, "telling jokes and laughing and pinching the girls," but he didn't want to disillusion her. "I always do, Peg."

Yet he was also more aware of Campbell's shortcomings. He once told the paleontologist George Gaylord Simpson, "Suppose you meet a man who asks you what your field of endeavor is and you tell him that you are the world's greatest living vertebrate paleontologist, which is, of course, what you are. And suppose that, on hearing this, the man you meet fixes you with a glittering eye and proceeds to lecture you for five hours on vertebrate paleontology, getting all his facts wrong, yet somehow leaving you unable to argue them. You will then have met Campbell."

Asimov wrote occasional articles for *Astounding,* but he was growing confident in his ability to do good work on his own. His skills and personality—his memory, his dislike of travel, his preference for enclosed spaces, and his ability to rewrite material from other sources—all combined to make him exceptionally productive, and he began to dream of publishing one hundred books. When he mentioned this to Gertrude, she objected, "You'll regret all the years you wasted just so that you could write a hundred books, and it will be too late."

"But for me, the essence of life is writing," Asimov replied. "In fact, if I do manage to publish a hundred books, and if I then die, my last words are likely to be, 'Only a hundred!' "

His writing also affected his relationship with his children. As a toddler, David would bring a toy typewriter up to the attic and pretend to work, but as he grew older, he didn't care for his father's books: "They just sound too much like you." David had trouble getting along with other kids—his parents consulted psychiatrists and neurologists—and after he was sent to boarding school in New Haven, Connecticut, Asimov channeled his paternal impulses toward a series of younger protégés, including Harlan Ellison. Even Robyn, whom he adored, sensed that his loyalties were divided. She asked him one day, "Suppose someone said you had to choose either me or writing? Which would it be?"

"Why, I would choose you, dear," Asimov said. But he had hesitated, and she saw it.

As Heinlein broke through to the counterculture, Asimov was becoming a celebrity in the mainstream. He began to affect glasses with black frames and bushy sideburns, growing the face that he would wear for the rest of his life, and when he met John Updike, the novelist just grinned: "Say, Asimov, how do you manage to write all those books?" Asimov was still beloved by fans, and he mastered an informal style that made readers feel that he was confiding in them. At a time when the genre was expanding, he made it seem as close and intimate as it had been in the thirties.

But there was also a less attractive side to his fame. He was still pinching women's bottoms, prompting a friend's wife to snap, "God, Asimov, why do you always do that? It is extremely painful and besides, don't you realize, it's very degrading." Yet he did nothing to change his behavior. Before the World Science Fiction Convention in 1962, he was invited by Earl Kemp, the chairman, to deliver a talk on "The Positive Power of Posterior Pinching." Kemp said cheerfully, "We would, naturally, furnish some suitable posteriors for demonstration purposes." Asimov declined, but he added, "Of course, I could be persuaded to do so on very short notice, even after the convention began, if the posteriors in question were of particularly compelling interest."

And it wasn't just a joke. In his younger days, Judith Merril said, Asimov had been known as "the man with a hundred hands. . . . When it went, occasionally, beyond purely social enjoyability, there seemed no way to clue him in." Decades later, Asimov wrote in the parody *The Sensuous Dirty Old Man*, "The question then is not whether or not a girl should be touched. The question is merely where, when, and how she should be touched." And Harlan Ellison remembered, "Whenever we walked up the stairs with a young woman, I made sure to walk behind her so Isaac wouldn't grab her tush. He didn't mean anything by it—times were different—but that was Isaac."

Asimov also had the habit of "hugging all the young ladies" at his editors' offices, prompting Tim Seldes of Doubleday to tell him affectionately, "All you want to do is kiss the girls and make collect calls. You're welcome to that, Asimov." At another publisher, the women found excuses to leave the building whenever he was scheduled to visit, while the editor Cele Goldsmith said that he chased her around a desk. Asimov thought that it was generally agreed that he was "harmless," and that his attentions toward fans were usually welcome: "I kiss each young woman who wants an autograph and have found, to my delight, that they tend to cooperate enthusiastically in that particular activity." An attendee at a convention in the late fifties recalled with wonder, "Asimov . . . instead of shaking my date's hand, shook her *left breast*."

When Pohl questioned his actions, Asimov replied, "It's like the old saying. You get slapped a lot, but you get laid a lot, too." At times, he seemed to sense that he had crossed a line, writing to the author Mildred Clingerman to apologize for his "unbearable convention manners." But if his treatment of women was often inexcusable, or worse, it did little to diminish the affection in which he was held by other men, or his position as an ambassador for the genre. He wrote the novelization of the movie *Fantastic Voyage*—passing on the chance, to his regret, to meet Raquel Welch—and was interviewed on camera for *2001: A Space Odyssey*, which Arthur C. Clarke was writing with Stanley Kubrick, although his footage never made it into the finished cut.

He was no longer close to Campbell, but he remained conscious of his debt. At a convention where the editor was the guest of honor, Randall Garrett, with whom Asimov had reconciled, said of the Three Laws of Robotics, "Isaac says John made them up and John says Isaac did, and I say they're both right. The laws were invented in symbiotic cooperation." Asimov agreed, and a few years later, when the Foundation trilogy won a special Hugo Award as the best series of all time, he simply said in his speech, "I would like to thank Mr. John W. Campbell, Jr., who had at least as much to do with the Foundation series as I had."

Asimov's stature continued to grow—he was even briefly investigated by the FBI on suspicion of being a communist spy, although no evidence for the allegations ever materialized. But it was his work as a science writer that provided his wealth and fame, and he depended on his reputation for rationality. When Robyn told him one night that she had seen a flying saucer, Asimov went outdoors, where he was horrified to see a metal disk hanging in the sky. After it turned out to be the Goodyear blimp, he was unspeakably relieved. Robyn remembered, "He nearly had a heart attack. He thought he saw his career going down the drain."

His own father was proud of him, and he loved to show off his son's books, although he wouldn't let anyone touch them. When his parents retired to Florida in 1968, Asimov, who refused to fly, had the feeling that he would never see his father again, and he never did. Judah Asimov died on August 4, 1969.

Gertrude and Robyn were in Europe, and David was away at school. Asimov—who had spent his life trying to live up to his father's example, approaching each day as if he were still at the candy store—didn't want to bother them, so he drove alone to New York for the funeral.

On August 11, Asimov was feeling miserable when he got a call from Janet Jeppson, who agreed to join him for lunch. They went afterward to Sleepy Hollow Cemetery in Concord, where they paused before the grave of Emerson, who had written over a century earlier, "If the stars should appear one night in a thousand years, how would men believe and adore."

Two months later, Asimov, who was not yet fifty, published his hundredth book.

IN MARCH 1969, HEINLEIN FLEW WITH GINNY TO A FILM FESTIVAL IN RIO DE JANEIRO, WHERE HE met the director Roman Polanski. Later that year, he attended the launch of the Apollo 11 mission, which he called "the greatest spiritual experience I've undergone in my life," telling the anchorman Walter Cronkite, "This is the greatest event in all the history of the human race. . . . Today is New Year's Day of the Year One."

It was a moment in which reality and science fiction seemed close enough to touch. Asimov and Pohl participated in a television panel moderated by Rod Serling of *The Twilight Zone*, and *Analog* sent a press representative to Florida. One man who wasn't alive to see it was Willy Ley, who had spent his life dreaming of rockets, but died three weeks too soon. Campbell attended his funeral, filled with regret over the fact that they had never reconciled over dianetics.

The editor himself watched the moon landing at home. Campbell called it "the greatest show ever staged," observing that no writer had ever predicted that it would be televised, and told readers, "There's [a] considerable sense of fulfillment for someone who, like myself, has been discussing, considering, imagining, and visualizing this event for some forty years."

On July 24, Neil Armstrong, Buzz Aldrin, and Michael Collins returned to Earth. The following day, as the papers carried coverage of the splashdown, Charles Manson ordered three of his followers to rob Gary Hinman, a California drug dealer, whom they stabbed to death. On August 9, the actress Sharon Tate—who was married to Roman Polanski—was killed by the Manson Family, along with four other victims. She was eight months pregnant.

Two months later, Heinlein received a letter from a woman named "Annette or Nanette or something," who claimed that police helicopters were chasing her friends. Ginny was alarmed by its tone, and she warned her husband to be careful: "Honey, this is worse than the crazy fan mail. This is absolutely insane. Don't have anything to do with it." It was evidently from Catherine

"Gypsy" Share, a member of the Manson Family who used the alias Manon Minette.

On January 8, 1970, the *San Francisco Herald-Examiner* ran a story on the front page under the headline "Manson's Blueprint? Claim Tate Suspect Used Science Fiction Plot." Later that month, *Time* printed an article that began:

> *In the psychotic mind, fact and fantasy mingle freely. . . .*
> *In the weeks since [Manson's] indictment, those connected*
> *with the case have discovered that he may have murdered*
> *by the book. The book is Robert A. Heinlein's* Stranger in
> a Strange Land, *an imaginative science-fiction novel long*
> *popular among hippies.*

Manson subsequently denied having read the novel, but it was undeniably familiar in his circle. When his son was born in 1968, his mother named him Valentine Michael, after the man from Mars, and Heinlein received at least two other letters from members of the Manson Family.

Years earlier, Manson had been exposed, to a far more significant extent, to the work of another science fiction writer. At McNeil Island Federal Penitentiary, Manson gave his religion as "Scientologist," saying that he was looking for insights from "the new mental health cult known as Scientology." In his memoirs, Manson wrote, "A cell partner turned me on to Scientology. With him and another guy I got pretty heavy into dianetics and Scientology. . . . There were times when I would try to sell [fellow inmate Alvin Karpis] on the things I was learning through Scientology."

Manson received about one hundred and fifty hours of auditing. In 1968, he visited a branch of the church, where he asked the receptionist, "What do you do after 'clear?'" Some of his followers were audited as well, although the prosecutor Vincent Bugliosi dismissed any connection, and Heinlein's and Hubbard's superficial influence on Manson was largely a testament to the cultural position that they had attained. As an attorney representing Leslie Van Houten, another disciple, said of his client, "That girl is insane in a way that is almost science fiction."

Yet it also cut deeper. Manson represented the psychopathic fringe of an impulse toward transformation in the face of overwhelming cultural change, and science fiction provided it with a convenient vocabulary—as it would, decades later, for the Aum Shinrikyo cult in Japan, which was partially inspired by Asimov's Foundation series. But the Manson Family seemed indifferent to its more transcendent manifestations. At the ranch where they were living, a woman had remarked, "There's somebody on the moon today." And another replied, "They're faking it."

15.
TWILIGHT

1960–1971

For each human soul, there is a unique, constant value of "a." The imaginary index "b," however, is continuously variable. . . . At end of life, the soul abandons its complex eigenvalue and assumes a new wave form whose eigenvalue is real. . . . This change is known to be accompanied by conformal transformation, but . . . there's disagreement about the details.

—JOHN W. CAMPBELL, "ON THE NATURE OF ANGELS"

In the December 1959 issue of *Astounding,* just before the title change was announced, Campbell dropped a tantalizing hint to readers: "I've seen some pictures of a gadget." It was the brainchild of Norman L. Dean, an executive specializing in mortgage appraisal, who had built a device in his spare time that he had actually patented in 1956. Despite his best efforts, however, he had failed to convince NASA, the Office of Naval Research, or the Senate Space Committee to even look at the invention of which Campbell wrote, "By all the physics I ever learned, it's nonsense."

It would be the editor's last great provocation. When Dean

sought him out in the fall of 1959, Campbell was intrigued, and after studying pictures of the mechanism, he drove down to Washington, D.C., to see it in person. It was "a contraption of rotating eccentric weights, solenoids, and clutches," driven by the motor from an electric drill. By continuously shifting the center of gravity of each weight, Dean claimed, the whole assembly would rise, and when it was placed on a bathroom scale and switched on, the reading on the dial seemed to go down. With six pairs, it could supposedly lift itself off the ground, although a working model no longer existed.

Upon further investigation, Campbell convinced himself that Dean had invented a reactionless space drive—a device that could fly without throwing away fuel as a propellant. He knew that he had something outrageous on his hands, and he devoted a long article to it in the June 1960 issue. Before diving into the details, he spent seven pages arguing that it wasn't just a technical problem, but an emotional and political one. The fact that nobody had tested the Dean Drive was the real scandal, although the editor also made his own views clear: "I believe the true space drive has been discovered, tested in models, and patented."

Asimov—who met Dean at the editor's house—was doubtful, and according to such skeptics as John R. Pierce of Bell Labs and the roboticist Marvin Minsky, it was more likely that the device resonated with the springs of the scale, which made it look as if its weight had decreased. After a test by the military failed, Campbell said that it proved his point—the government had conducted a lynching, and now it was belatedly holding the trial. At a convention, he was giving a speech on the subject when he saw de Camp in the front row. "Now, Sprague!"

De Camp glanced up. He had an uncomfortable sense of what was coming. "Yes?"

"You know about strain gauges, from having worked at the Navy Yard," Campbell said. "Well, the strain gauge is a sophisticated, modern device, isn't it? And the Navy, instead of testing the drive with this accurate modern device, used a crude, simple hookup like a rope, a couple of pulleys, and a spring scale. That proves that they never intended to get favorable results, doesn't it?"

De Camp could have told him that the spring gauge was used for forces that couldn't be measured directly, and that an ordinary scale would have been fine for the Dean Drive. But Campbell had already moved on.

In the years that followed, Campbell continued to defend both the Dean Drive and the new principles of physics that it seemed to demonstrate. Few others were impressed, and even the most meticulous attempts to build working models repeatedly failed—the drive tended to fly apart at the exact moment when it seemed on the verge of doing something interesting, and Campbell suspected that the inventor was keeping aspects of the design to himself. Like Welsford Parker, Dean refused to play by the rules, and like Campbell, he resisted being put to any definitive test.

As Campbell moved on to such fixations as dowsing and astrology, he began to badly trail Pohl, who had taken over as editor of *Galaxy*. Between the two of them, Campbell was having more trouble developing new voices—his discoveries tended to stay within *Analog,* which increasingly emphasized nonfiction— and Pohl no longer felt any of his former awe. Yet there were also moments when it seemed as if no time had passed at all. One day, as they were flying home from a speaking engagement, Campbell touched Pohl's shoulder and said, "Fred, you did real good for science fiction." And Pohl found himself blushing.

Campbell was also isolated from the New Wave, a generation of experimental authors who took his innovations for granted. He insisted that readers wanted heroes—his publication of Anne McCaffrey's Dragonrider series felt like an effort to recover ground that had been lost to fantasy—and he rejected stories that depicted psionics in a negative light, which annoyed Philip K. Dick:

"[Campbell] considered my writing not only worthless but, as he put it, 'nuts.'" Dick sold just one story to Campbell, who never published such rising stars as Richard Matheson, Ursula K. Le Guin, or even Larry Niven, who recalled, "He liked his ideas better than mine."

The editor was also losing touch with established writers. As early as 1957, he had written, "Sprague de Camp can't make the magazine any more; Jack Williamson's pretty much out. Bob Heinlein still hits about thirty percent of the time. Ike Asimov is about the only one who's been able to grow fast enough to keep leading the field." Not even Asimov was exempt, with Campbell referring to him privately as "a book-learning follower; he's a sucker for propaganda." He lamented in public, "The Great Old Authors . . . aren't gonna be told what they should write by that dictatorial, authoritarian, uncooperative Campbell. . . . They hate me for shoving new concepts and new ideas at them—and damn me for *their* lack of a Sense of Wonder!"

He was particularly disillusioned by Heinlein, who he felt had "rejected discussion of his ideas" with fans for decades. Campbell thought that Heinlein was frightened of the implications of his own work, writing to E. E. Smith:

> *He's scared blue-with-chartreuse-spots of psi, and he's got precognition and doesn't-for-God's-sake want to know it. It was all right writing "Solution Unsatisfactory" until the damned thing came true. Now he wants to stay way, way, way away from anything that might turn out to be true!*

Campbell told another correspondent that if he had been offered *Stranger in a Strange Land*, he would have rejected it: "[Heinlein is] much more concerned with selling his philosophy of sexual promiscuity than in writing science fiction tales." If he tried to give Heinlein any ideas, Campbell added, the author would view it "as an effort to confine his artistic creativity," and he was probably right—Heinlein was dismissive of his old editor, telling Blassingame that he was tired of wading through "ten pages of his arrogant insults, explaining to me why my story is no good."

Campbell also had "really bitter" arguments with Sturgeon over genetics, taking him into a private room during a convention, closing the door, and letting him have it with both barrels. They never saw each other again after the late fifties. He had even fallen out with Silverberg, in whose eyes he had "invalidated" himself as an editor. In 1967, Silverberg was walking through a convention around midnight when he saw Campbell sitting alone in his hotel room with a bottle of scotch. Campbell, who seemed depressed, poured him a drink and asked why he, Asimov, and Sturgeon no longer wrote for him. Silverberg didn't mince his words: "I can't speak for Isaac or Ted, but I don't feel comfortable with your thoughts any more."

Almost by accident, however, Campbell had stumbled across the most famous story that he would ever publish. In 1957, Frank Herbert, a journalist who had contributed occasionally to the magazine, began researching a serial called "Dune World." Six years later, he submitted it to Campbell, who bought it. The editor wasn't particularly interested in its philosophy or the ecology of the desert world of Arrakis. Instead, he saw it as a superman story, with his comments concentrating on the teenage clairvoyant Paul Atreides, who resembled an "adolescent demigod" of whom he had mused about writing years earlier.

In his acceptance letter, Campbell told Herbert, "Congratulations! You are now the father of a fifteen-year-old superman!" After repeating his favorite point that it was impossible to imagine how a superior being would act or think, he complimented Herbert for following the approach that van Vogt had used in *Slan,* which showed the superman before his development was fully complete. For the sake of future stories, he advised him to limit

Paul's gifts, but Herbert pushed back, and his hero's powers remained mostly unchanged.

Campbell and Herbert never met in person, but they frequently discussed the story in letters or over the phone. The editor reviewed Herbert's proposals for later installments, buying "Prophet of Dune," and requested small changes and clarifications. In a piece of advice that had a pivotal impact on the series, he suggested that they save Paul's younger sister Alia, who died in the first draft: "Sorry to see her go, by the way; did she have to be eliminated?"

In general, though, the serial remained essentially as Herbert conceived it. Campbell offered ideas for sequels, including the proposal that Paul be challenged by an alien race, which Herbert declined to use. When *Analog* won a Hugo the following year, Herbert accepted it in the absence of the editor, who noted that the win was mostly due to the enthusiastic reception of *Dune*.

When Herbert submitted *Dune Messiah* in 1968, however, Campbell objected to the treatment of its protagonist: "Paul was a damn fool, and surely no demigod; he loused up himself, his loved ones, and the whole galaxy." After a revision, he remained unconvinced:

> In this one, it's Paul, our central character, who is a
> helpless pawn manipulated against his will, by a cruel,
> destructive fate. . . . The reactions of science-fictioneers,
> however, over the last few decades have persistently
> and quite explicitly been that they want heroes—not
> antiheroes.

In the end, the sequel went to *Galaxy*, ending Campbell's chance to influence the career of a writer whose novels would pave the way for science fiction's invasion of the bestseller lists.

The editor took comfort in his eight Hugo Awards, which he proudly displayed in his office, and in the fact that the sales of his magazine were still the highest in the field. As always, Campbell retained what Heinlein called his "slightly open-mouthed adoration" of businessmen—he loved Ayn Rand's *Atlas Shrugged,* although he suspected that its author was "somewhat of a lesbian"—and it was widely perceived that his views had grown more entrenched after the acquisition by Condé Nast. In practice, he was unaffected by the change in ownership, and he joked that he employed the company to get his ideas out, rather than the other way around.

Campbell had once told his father that the magazine was "carefully expurgated to suit the most prudish—while I'm busy sawing away at the piling on which the whole crazy structure is resting." Yet he took capitalism at face value, and in the Graybar Building on Lexington Avenue—where he might have crossed paths with Diana Vreeland of *Vogue*—he identified with his corporate superiors. When a fan told him that he had written a story but wasn't sure whether it was right for the magazine, Campbell drew himself up: "And since when does the Condé Nast Publications, Incorporated pay you to make editorial decisions for *Analog*?"

But a more troubling aspect of his personality was becoming harder to overlook. In 1968, the World Science Fiction Convention was held at the Hotel Claremont in Berkeley. The building sweltered, and antiwar protesters were demonstrating nearby—when the wind was right, fans could smell tear gas. One of the attendees was a college senior named Alan Dean Foster, who saw Campbell holding forth in favor of the Vietnam War. The editor's position on it had evolved—he had once argued that Vietnam wasn't ready for democracy, but he later signed a statement in support of American intervention—and after the discussion, he smiled and offered to switch sides, much as del Rey had seen him do after the Nazi invasion of Russia.

Also in search of Campbell was Gregory Benford, a postdoctoral fellow at the Lawrence Radiation Laboratory who had written a paper on tachyons—hypothetical particles that travel faster than light—and proposed an article on the subject. Campbell had written dismissively of tachyons in the magazine, but Benford tracked him down at the hotel bar, where he pitched the idea again. To his dismay, Campbell didn't seem to grasp the physics involved, and Benford himself was in a puckish mood. After the editor mentioned that he had studied German in college, Benford switched to the other language. Campbell only stared at him.

Benford was more impressed by the fact that over the course of their conversation, Campbell smoked five cigarettes and ordered two martinis with lemon—he was drinking more heavily in public now, although this left him no more receptive to Benford's proposal. After the convention, Benford sent him a copy of his paper on the subject with a note attached: "Perhaps this will make it clearer." Campbell didn't respond. A year later, Benford tried again, and the editor replied that tachyons were "a bit too esoteric" for *Analog*.

But Benford was even more struck by another statement that he had made. The year before, Campbell had cast a disapproving eye on the riots in Newark, saying that it was an example of blacks wanting "something for nothing." And at Berkeley, in reference to the unrest outside, the editor had said, "The problem with this country is that it doesn't know how to deal with the niggers."

IF ASKED, CAMPBELL MIGHT HAVE EXPLAINED THAT HE HAD A PARTICULAR DEFINITION OF THE word in mind. Two years earlier, he had written in a letter, "There is such a thing as a nigger—just as there are spicks and wops and frogs and micks. A bum of Italian ancestry is a wop; a bum of Jewish ancestry is a kike—and a bum of Negro ancestry is a nigger." And it was in the sixties that his attitudes about race, which until then had formed an unspoken backdrop to his work, rose poisonously to the surface.

His racial views had begun to harden decades earlier at Duke. He once wrote to Poul Anderson:

*All human beings are not equal. When the Southern
white says "Negroes aren't human!" he is speaking from
experience. I've been there, Poul; they are not human-
in-the-normal-sense-of-the-term. They're low grade
morons and high-grade idiots. . . . The competent Negro
moves North or West to an area where he can achieve
something.*

Campbell added that there were young black girls "that I would
not allow in my house in any role but that of serf labor, the role
of pure slave. . . . They are to be dealt with as one deals with a domestic animal."

His feelings grew more pronounced in response to the civil rights
movement. When Asimov told him that he was against segregation,
Campbell wrote back, "If you deny the existence of racial differences, the problem of racial differences cannot be solved." He then
transitioned into what verged on a personal attack: "Why *should* all
races be alike, Isaac? Simply so you wouldn't have to think so hard
to understand a different kind of intelligent entity? Simply so that
you wouldn't have to work out more than one set of right-wrong
values? Simply so that people can identify the Good Guys from the
Bad Guys without the trouble of making basic evaluations?"

On some level, Campbell was needling Asimov's progressiv-
ism, as he had taken contrarian stances on so many other issues,
but he was also expressing his true feelings. Toward the end of
1955, he wrote to Asimov:

*The result is that the old question "Would you want your
daughter to marry a Negro?" is a very good philosophical
question indeed. The only answer I can give, now, is "I
know too little about genetics to be able to give a reply
based on understanding; I cannot compute the risks and
benefits involved for the next few generations."*

In another letter, Campbell considered the question of whether he would "condemn" a man for the color of his skin: "Essentially, I am forced to answer, 'Yes.' His skin color is genetically determined; it is not something he chose. But *his mental-emotional patterns are also genetically determined.* . . . If he can't choose one—why expect him to be able to choose the other?"

For a man who took pride in questioning the beliefs of others, Campbell's opinions on race were horrifyingly unexamined. He had always believed that intelligence was the paramount factor in human life, and, by that logic, if a group was disadvantaged, it had to be due to statistical inferiority. Asimov's patience with such views could only go so far. Less than two years after his break with Heinlein, Campbell was risking a breach with his most loyal author, who later wrote, "I think [Campbell] saw himself as fulfilling Socrates' function as gadfly. . . . There were times when I feverishly wished I had a cup of hemlock handy—for him, of course."

Peg saved them. After they had traded blows for a few months, she stepped in: "Any more and the friendship will be destroyed, and this argument is not worth a friendship." They called a truce, which saved Campbell from alienating Asimov forever—although it also made it easier for the author to write for other editors at a crucial point in his career. And their differences occasionally resurfaced. Writing to Asimov in 1957, Campbell indulged in a twisted kind of psychohistory, saying that Africans were the only race never to develop "a high-order civilization," despite the presence of nearby Egypt: "The Negro does not learn from example."

Campbell's views also began to infect the magazine. In 1955, he had published the serial *The Long Way Home,* by Poul Anderson, which featured a slave who refused to be freed, arguing that she was better off the way she was now. Anderson saw this as a minor plot point, but the editor seized on it as "a new heresy," writing to Heinlein in their discussion of *Citizen of the Galaxy,* "Slavery is a useful educational system; it has a place in the development of a race, just as the tyranny of parents has a place in the educational development of an individual."

Heinlein responded that he didn't have the time to answer Campbell's "interesting letter" at length. Unlike Asimov, he knew better than to take the bait. Yet he never forgot it, and it inspired a novel, *Farnham's Freehold,* that was conceived in part as a response. Its characters—including the protagonist's alcoholic wife—are thrown by an atomic bomb into a future in which blacks enslave whites, underlining the absurdity of the notion that slavery could be preferable for anyone. Unfortunately, his black ruling class also engages in cannibalism, distracting from whatever point he wanted to make, and the book as a whole was a frustrating misfire.

If Heinlein's experience pointed to the fine line that the genre had to walk with regard to race, Campbell was untroubled by it, and racial issues began to appear frequently in his editorials. In 1960 he offered readers his own definition of slavery: "Slavery is a system in which one group of individuals, the slaves, are forced by another group, the masters, *to learn something they do not want to learn.*" Before long, he was arguing that blacks and whites had different bell curves for intelligence. On a visit to the office, the author Harry Harrison found himself shouting in exasperation to Campbell and Harry Stine, "Gentlemen, you can't reduce everything in life to a bell-shaped curve!" In response, they said, "Yes, you can!"

Campbell's sense of oppression throughout his life made him unsympathetic to calls for social justice, and as the sixties unfolded, he grew even more reactionary. In 1962, he editorialized for eight pages about being given an unfair traffic ticket. Three years later, his views on the police were strikingly different:

> *The police have as their function the imposition of discipline on those who lack self-discipline. . . . To one*

who denies that discipline should exist, this is torture. It's
deliberately inflicted pain—emotional pain of frustration
at the very least. Therefore, the police are clearly being
brutal. . . . Statistically speaking, the Negroes lack self-
discipline.

This is incredibly painful to read, and the question of how Campbell's views affected the fiction he published is central to any consideration of his legacy. He certainly lacked any interest in diversity: "Think about it a bit, and you'll realize why there is so little mention of blacks in science fiction; we see no reason to go saying 'Lookee lookee lookee! We're using blacks in our stories! See the Black Man. See him in a space ship!' " The implication was that protagonists should be white males by default—a stance that he might not even have seen as problematic.

Campbell argued elsewhere that he had no idea what a writer's race might be when he read a submission: "If Negro authors are extremely few—it's solely because extremely few Negroes both wish to, and can, write in open competition." He often touted the high sales of the magazine in black neighborhoods, which he attributed to its policy of "minimizing race problems," but it never occurred to him that the dearth of minority writers might be caused by the lack of characters who looked like them, or that he had any ability or obligation to address the situation as an editor.

These assumptions affected his treatment of Samuel R. Delany, the most important black writer the genre had ever produced. Campbell rejected several stories from Delany, but he had high regard for his talents, repeatedly stating, "The guy can write, and he has a lot of brilliant ideas." In 1967, after winning his first Nebula Award, Delany—who had briefly met Campbell at a convention—submitted his novel *Nova*. He recalled of its rejection, "Campbell . . . didn't feel his readership would be able to relate to a black main character. . . . Otherwise, he rather liked it."

Campbell expressed similar views about other minorities. In 1966, at the World Science Fiction Convention in Cleveland, he encountered a young fan named Joe Haldeman, who had risen early to smoke a cigarette. Seeing his University of Oklahoma sweatshirt, Campbell went off on a speech about Native Americans—unlike blacks, he believed, they couldn't be enslaved, so they died instead. In the thirties, he had written in the magazine, "The aboriginal race of Australia are . . . useless beggars without self-respect hanging on the fringes of the white man's civilization."

On the subject of homosexuality, Campbell shared the casual homophobia of his era, and his letters were peppered with such terms as "queer," "fairy," and "pansy." He wrote to Asimov in 1958:

> And Ike, my friend, consider the case of a fairy, a queer. They can, normally, be spotted about as far off as you can spot a mulatto. I'll admit a coal-black Negro can be spotted a bit further than a fairy can, but the normal mulatto can't. Sure, I know a lot of queers don't look that way—but they're simply "passing."

In his editorials, Campbell stated that homosexuality was a sign of cultural decline, and he had thought that it could be cured by dianetics, approvingly citing "successful" cases to Heinlein: "My God! You should hear the things that actually lie behind homosexuality—what sort of unspeakable violence it takes to aberrate the sexual drive in human beings that badly."

When it came to women, Campbell was dismissive of feminists, saying that they demanded equal rights but refused to give up their "girlish special privileges." He believed that men and women thought in inherently different ways, and that a woman's greatest contribution was to ask, "Are you sure, dear?" He wrote elsewhere, "No woman has ever attained first-rank competence in literature in any Indo-European language." But he also published such authors as Leigh Brackett, Catherine L. Moore, Jane Rice, Judith Merril, Wilmar H. Shiras, Katherine MacLean, Kate Wilhelm, Pauline Ashwell, Anne McCaffrey, and Alice Bradley Sheldon, whom he knew as James Tiptree, Jr.

Campbell admired Islam, but his feelings toward the Jews were more complicated. Asimov wrote firmly, "He never, *not once,* made me feel uncomfortable over the fact that I was Jewish." Yet the editor also referred to Mort Weisinger in passing as "a fairly decent little Jew-boy," and he famously asked Milton A. Rothman to write as Lee Gregor. As a joke, Randall Garrett once proposed that Silverberg use the pseudonym "Calvin M. Knox," on the assumption that the editor preferred gentile names, without telling him that the middle initial stood for "Moses." When Silverberg revealed this fact years later, Campbell replied, "You ever hear of Isaac Asimov?"

When he tried to demonstrate a lack of prejudice, it didn't always go as intended. At lunch one day with Philip Klass, who wrote as William Tenn, Campbell saw a military pin in his lapel and asked if he had seen a concentration camp. Klass replied that he had. Campbell was clearly impressed, and before they ordered, he covered Klass's hand with his own: "Phil, I want you to know something I've always believed. I've always believed the Jews are *Homo superior.*"

"I wish you hadn't said that," Klass said. When Campbell asked why, he explained, "Because it's racism. And at the moment I don't want to hear any—I can't live with any kind of racist formulation."

Campbell didn't get it. "You didn't understand me. I said *superior—Homo superior.*"

Klass informed him that it was racist either way, but the editor didn't get the point. Campbell later recounted his own version of the conversation in Klass's presence: "The man didn't hear the prefix. I said *superior*. He didn't hear the prefix." And he never understood why Klass might have been offended.

His most fraught relationship with a Jewish writer was, inevitably, with the combative Harlan Ellison. Ellison had written to the editor in the late fifties to complain about the excess of psionics in *Astounding*, but he also asked him years later to contribute a story to his groundbreaking anthology *Dangerous Visions*. Campbell declined, saying that he had a "shocker" that he couldn't write himself, and even if he did, he would want to save it for his own magazine.

Ellison thought that Campbell disliked him because he was Jewish, while their mutual friend Ben Bova felt that their differences were more temperamental. In *Dangerous Visions*, Ellison mocked the editor's submissive circle of writers and referred to "John W. Campbell, Jr., who used to edit a magazine that ran science fiction, called *Astounding*, and who now edits a magazine that runs a lot of schematic drawings, called *Analog*." Campbell dismissed Ellison in turn as a "destructive, rather than constructive" genius: "He needs a muzzle more than a platform."

Bova finally persuaded Ellison to submit their collaboration "Brillo" using a pseudonym, but it was accidentally sent under both of their names. Ellison was convinced that it would be rejected, and after hearing that the editor was taking it instead, he became ecstatic: "He's *buying* it?" Bova later thanked Campbell: "Harlan's always wanted to win your approval." Yet the author's suspicions might not have been entirely off the mark. In 1966, Campbell wrote of Ellison:

> *I don't know whether it's the hyper-defensive attitude of the undersize or what, but he's an insulting little squirt with a nasty tongue. He's one of the type that earned the*

appellation "kike"; as Einstein, Disraeli, and thousands of others have demonstrated, it ain't racial—it's personal.

As the decade wore on, Campbell's political stances continued to harden, with his reflexive contrarianism colliding with the progressive tendencies of many of his readers. Asimov argued that he was on the wrong team, comparing civil rights to other causes that Campbell had defended:

In fact, John, I think you're on my side and as soon as you get it through your head that the Negroes are the way-out people facing the authoritarianism of Big Whitedom, you're going to come charging out to fight on the side of the Negro, as you have staunchly borne the standards for everything from dianetics to Krebiozen.

If Asimov truly hoped that Campbell would take up civil rights with the same enthusiasm that he had shown toward Krebiozen— an alternative cancer treatment that briefly caught his eye—he was disappointed. In 1968, Campbell complained in an editorial that Democrats and Republicans had become indistinguishable, closing with the startling announcement that he was voting for George Wallace: "I want a chance to vote for a different approach!" In private, he defended his right to cast a protest ballot, although he also conceded that Wallace was "a terrible choice."

His last years were spent attacking such targets as the protesters at Kent State and the ecologist Rachel Carson, and his contrarianism, which had once been an engine for generating stories, began to limit what he could say or publish. The writer Michael Moorcock saw him as the editor of "a crypto-fascist deeply philistine magazine," which, given Campbell's lifelong war against the establishment, was profoundly ironic. Despite his belief in new modes of thought, he was hostile to change that he couldn't control. The counterculture shared his interest in transformation and alternative viewpoints, but not in supermen or psionic machines.

As the country around him underwent the seismic upheavals that he had long prophesized, he dug in his heels, losing his chance to participate seriously in the most important social conversations of his time—and the question of whether his statements reflected his true feelings is secondary to the damage that they caused. In his novel *Mother Night*, Kurt Vonnegut, Jr., told the haunting story of an American secret agent posing as a Nazi propagandist, concluding, "We are what we pretend to be, so we must be careful about what we pretend to be." And he gave the character a name that must have resonated with many readers: Howard W. Campbell, Jr.

Campbell was reducing his audience at a time when it was already slipping away, and he began to alienate even fans who admired him. One was Barry Malzberg, a volunteer editor for the Science Fiction Writers of America. Malzberg, who was twenty-nine, had adored Campbell for most of his life, and he decided to use his position as an excuse to visit the editor on June 18, 1969.

Their conversation, which lasted for three hours, was a disaster. Malzberg and Campbell spent most of it arguing within earshot of Kay Tarrant, who had remained the one constant at the office. Several years earlier she had suffered a heart attack, taking her out of work for months, which only underlined how indispensible she was—it took five others to do what she handled alone.

As Tarrant listened, she tried not to smile. Malzberg asked Campbell to sympathize with his critics, who were concerned by the dilemmas that technology presented: "These are the issues that are going to matter in science fiction for the next fifty years. It's got to explore the question of victimization."

The editor refused to budge. "I'm not interested in victims," Campbell said calmly. "I'm interested in heroes. I have to be. Science fiction is a problem-solving medium. Man is a curious animal who wants to know how things work and, given enough time, can find out."

"But not everyone is a hero," Malzberg said. "Not everyone can solve problems."

"Those people aren't the stuff of science fiction. If science fiction doesn't deal with success or the road to success, then it isn't science fiction at all. Mainstream literature is about failure, a literature of defeat. Science fiction is challenge and discovery." Campbell's face lit up. "We're going to land on the moon in a month and it was science fiction which made all of that possible. Isn't it wonderful? Thank God I'm going to live to see it."

"The moon landing isn't science fiction. It comes from technological advance—"

Campbell broke in. "There's going to be a moon landing because of science fiction. There's no argument."

Malzberg saw that the conversation hadn't gone as he had hoped, and he stammered that he had to leave. Standing up, he shook the editor's hand, nodded at Tarrant, and fled. In the corridor, as he pressed the button for the elevator, a sinking sense of the encounter washed over him, and he began to tremble.

A second later, Campbell came around the corner, probably on his way to the bathroom. For an instant, the two men simply looked at each other. At last, the editor's eyes twinkled.

"Don't worry about it, son," Campbell said gently. "I just like to shake 'em up."

EVEN AS *ANALOG* LOST GROUND TO ITS COMPETITORS, THERE WAS A GROWING SENSE THAT THE future of science fiction might not lie in the magazines at all. On September 8, 1966, NBC aired the series premiere of *Star Trek*, which in many ways was an extension of the tradition embodied by Campbell. Gene Roddenberry, its creator, had been turned on to science fiction in his teens by the *Astounding* of the Tremaine era. He provided pulp covers from his own collection as inspiration to his art directors, counted Asimov and Heinlein among his influences, and turned to the existing ranks of science fiction writers when it came time to hire a writing staff.

To some extent, this was just common sense, but on another level, Roddenberry was positioning himself as the successor to Campbell—an organizer and arranger of the talents of others, in a medium that had the potential to reach an even wider audience. The names on his list of potential writers included Heinlein, Asimov, and Ellison, who went on to write the classic "The City on the Edge of Forever." He signed Robert Bloch, Sturgeon, and van Vogt, who wrote outlines but was unable to work within the confines of television, while the plot of "Arena," in which Kirk faced an alien in a fight to the death, was credited to the *Astounding* story by Frederic Brown.

Roddenberry was laying the groundwork for a fundamental shift in the genre's center of power, although this development wasn't immediately obvious. At the World Science Fiction Convention in 1966, he presented a preview of the episode "The Cage." As the screening began, a man in the front row failed to quiet down, and Roddenberry spoke up: "Hey, fellow, stop talking. That's my picture they're starting to show." The speaker fell silent, and it was only then that Roddenberry was informed that he had scolded Isaac Asimov. He tried to apologize, but Asimov quickly admitted that he had been the one in the wrong.

Asimov wasn't particularly impressed: "No breath of prescience stirred within me." A few months later, in *TV Guide,* he made fun of an error in one episode, leading to a flood of angry letters from fans, including Janet Jeppson. After taking another look, he wrote a more positive take, and he corresponded with Roddenberry, who asked for advice on how to make better use of William Shatner. Asimov responded, "It might be well to unify the team of Kirk and Spock a bit, by having them actively meet various menaces together with one saving the life of the other on occasion." Roddenberry wrote back, "I will follow your advice. . . . It will give us *one* lead, the team."

Heinlein was also drawn into the orbit of *Star Trek*, although much less willingly. After reviewing the teleplay for an episode by David Gerrold, "The Trouble with Tribbles," the studio's research firm noted a similarity between the tribbles—a species of furry alien that multiplied rapidly—and the "flat cats" in Heinlein's *The Rolling Stones*. Heinlein agreed to waive any claim, but after the script arrived, he felt that he had been "overly generous, to put it mildly." All the same, he admitted that he had lifted the basic notion from Ellis Parker Butler's "Pigs Is Pigs," and there was a certain similarity to a "very fecund" creature that Campbell had described in the Penton and Blake story "The Immortality Seekers."

As rumors of cancellation swirled in 1967, Roddenberry drafted a telegram to go out over Asimov's name, saying that the space program "desperately" needed the publicity that the series provided. Roddenberry was also looking into securing the rights to *I, Robot,* and he approached Asimov about writing a spin-off novel. Of the show's threatened end, Asimov wrote, "My major sadness is for the science fiction writers who see an adult market close for them. I'm sure they can write for other programs, but certainly not with equal satisfaction." It was a measure of the extent to which Roddenberry was filling the role that Campbell had once occupied in print.

For now, the show survived, and Campbell became involved as well. On January 23, 1968, he wrote to Roddenberry, "I'm joining in the campaign to promote *Star Trek*, naturally—it's the world's first and only true science-fiction program, and it averages really high in quality. . . . I'm writing a few letters—but I also thought of something that might help otherwise." He proposed that winter caps with felt Vulcan ears be sold for kids, and Roddenberry passed the concept along to marketing: "Too often they've taken old space toys and simply slapped a *Star Trek* label on them."

The two men, a decade apart in age, continued to correspond, with Campbell pitching a story about the problems of trade between aliens from different planetary environments. After the Berkeley convention in 1968, he went down to Los Angeles to pay a visit to Desilu Studios, touring the lot on a day when the show wasn't filming. He later dropped by Roddenberry's apartment, where he admired the producer's collection of mobiles and offered to send him a kalliroscope, a pane of heated glass that could create colored patterns.

Their political differences often surfaced. In October, Roddenberry wrote that he had been invited to tour the aircraft carrier USS *Enterprise,* which filled him with mixed feelings:

> *Well, for that week . . . I will not wear my Peace medal, I will not mention Vietnam and the Nuremberg trials in the same breath, and when the mess boy brings me my coffee I will be delighted the Philippine Islands produced this race of pleasant little brown men for my comfort.*

Campbell, in typical fashion, responded with a long letter in which he expressed his opinion that slavery, under certain circumstances, could be beneficial. Like Heinlein, Roddenberry sidestepped the argument: "I can see no signs that the institution [of slavery] has vanished."

After *Star Trek* was banished to the Friday night "death slot," Roddenberry stepped back from everyday involvement, writing to Campbell, "Time, I think, to wash *Star Trek* out of my hair."

Campbell lamented that the series could no longer tell the difference between fantasy and science fiction, thereby "lousing up the one good science fiction show that ever hit the air." He thought that the network was trying to kill it deliberately, and he informed Roddenberry, "I'm afraid I can't use *Analog* to support *Star Trek* again, as we did before—it's simply moved out of the field of science fiction in nearly all the shows." It was a sign of the degree to which the genre was becoming too large for any one man—even Roddenberry—to control.

The editor was in no position to assume that role himself. He liked to think of himself as stronger than average—his fiction had always linked mental ability with strength, and he had embraced Hubbard's contention that most illness was due to the mind. Walking down Madison Avenue one day with Sturgeon, he had asserted that he had so much control over his cellular structure that he wouldn't die. As Campbell aged, this stance became harder to maintain. He was diagnosed with severe hypertension, and he suffered from gout, which left him with painful tophi—deposits of uric acid in his feet—that were the size of a raspberry.

At home, he scooted around on a stool on wheels, and he put a chair on the landing from the basement, since he was no longer able to make it all the way up without resting. He and Peg began living on the ground floor, but he still commuted to New York twice a week. After experiencing pain in one arm, he was diagnosed with arthritis of the spine, caused in part by his heavy briefcase of manuscripts, which he just switched to his other hand. He was unable to manage the walk to the subway from the train at Fulton Street, so he hailed a cab for a single block. At the convention in Berkeley in 1968, Benford saw him fall down in the lobby, and at their final meeting, Poul Anderson found him so crippled that he needed help putting on his coat.

Many of his health issues were due to cigarettes. Campbell was doubtful of the link between lung cancer and smoking, arguing that tobacco might even suppress cancer, and that those who were susceptible to it smoked instinctively. At last, in the July 1969 issue, he wrote:

> *Tobacco is not habit-forming, and discontinuation causes no withdrawal symptoms whatsoever. . . . Last year, my family, friends, physician, and neighbors finally gave up trying to argue me into stopping. Since I had finally been granted freedom of choice—I decided to try quitting. So I did. I now smoke about two a day—I find I genuinely enjoy one after breakfast, and sometimes after dinner.*

He later clarified that his provocative assertion that smoking wasn't "habit forming" in his case meant only that further research was required. But he also understated the situation. His doctor had ordered him to quit or die, conceding that two cigarettes a day wouldn't damage his lungs any further, and he had trouble sticking to the regimen. In the short film *Lunch with John W. Campbell,* Campbell was seen discussing a story at the Hotel Commodore with Harry Harrison and Gordon R. Dickson. He had a cigarette in his hand the entire time.

When it came to most other drugs, Campbell was a skeptic, although he experimented with marijuana, which he believed should be legalized. As his illnesses left him in pain, his drinking increased—although he maintained a reputation as a teetotaler— and his poor health left a mark on his personality. He wrote to Frank Herbert, "Patience, tolerance, and forgiveness are hard-won attributes in anyone with a roaring gout attack." And much of his final decade—his alcohol use, his estrangement from his writers, the tone of his editorials—reflected his physical decline.

He sometimes struck others as lonely. In March 1970, he traveled by himself to Cape Canaveral to attend a satellite launch. The hotel was fully booked, so he ended up staying with the writer Joseph Green, who worked in the education office of the Kennedy Space Center. Campbell looked sick, but finally, after reluctantly climbing a set of stairs, he viewed the takeoff from an observation platform, watching as the rocket ascended toward "the distant, dark horizon."

At Mountainside, readers paid occasional pilgrimages to the house, and he remained an idol to the likes of Roger Ebert, who pitched him an article in college and referred to him as "my hero." At conventions, he still hosted fans in his suite, serving up beer and pretzels while Peg knitted in the corner. But he often seemed forgotten. At Lunacon in 1971, the fanzine editor Arnie Katz saw Campbell wander into the room. He asked a circle of younger fans if they had seen Sam Moskowitz, and when they said that they hadn't, he drifted off. No one had recognized him.

Although their nightly sessions on the nature of the mind were long over, Campbell's relationship with Peg remained vibrant. A visitor to the house once asked how long they had been married, and after hearing the answer, he exclaimed, "My God, you talk together as though you'd just met!" But it was often just the two of them. Campbell's father had died in 1959. Jane had married Ian Robertson, a printmaker in the graphic arts department at Colby College in Maine, where their son Justin was born. They moved from there to Chicago and finally to Alabama.

In 1962, Peedee, who now went as Lynn, married James Hammond, a billing manager at a tire company. She taught remedial reading in Ohio, where she gave birth to their daughter Margaret. Leslyn enrolled in a secretarial program at Dean Junior College on the advice of her father—who pointed to Tarrant as a role model— and landed a job as an executive secretary, marrying Jasper Randazzo in 1970. The following year, they visited Mountainside. When Leslyn left to see Doña, her father and husband were deep

John W. Campbell and his daughter Leslyn Campbell.
Courtesy of Leslyn Randazzo

in conversation at the kitchen table. When she returned after a few hours, she found that they were still talking.

A week later, on July 11, 1971, Campbell felt unwell, with pain in his back and stomach, although a visit from his doctor in the afternoon revealed nothing unusual. At a quarter to eight, instead of eating dinner, he settled into an armchair with a plate of cookies and a glass of milk to watch his favorite television show—professional wrestling on the local Spanish channel.

Peg went downstairs to her workroom. After about fifteen minutes, concerned by the lack of noise, she called for him. There was no response. Going up, she found that Campbell had passed away. It was the first time in their marriage that he had failed to hold up his end of the conversation.

Campbell was sixty-one years old. He had died of an aortic aneurysm—the dangerously thin walls of his abdominal aorta had burst, leading to massive internal bleeding, which was one of the expected outcomes of extreme hypertension. According to Peg, he had been "a walking time bomb."

Earlier that night, Sam Moskowitz had driven by the house with his wife, a doctor, who later said that she had felt a premonition that she should check on Campbell. The editor may have also sensed that the end was coming. He usually turned in his editorials just before deadline, but shortly before his death, he handed three of them at once to Tarrant, and he quietly built up enough inventory to last the magazine through the end of the year.

The day after he died, Tarrant was back in the office, typing up letters to notify correspondents of his passing. Word was spreading quickly, but Asimov, revealingly, heard it secondhand from Lester del Rey's wife, Judy-Lynn. He had last seen Campbell at a convention in April, where the editor held forth on psychiatry as Peg crocheted in the corner: "It never occurred to me when I shook hands in farewell that night that I would never see him again. . . . He was the fixed pole star about which all science fiction revolved, unchangeable, eternal."

On July 14, Asimov picked up the del Reys, Gordon R. Dickson, and Harry Harrison, who had slept on the floor of Dickson's room at the Algonquin, and they drove to Westfield for the memorial service. When they arrived, Harrison wondered where Campbell was, and after being told that he wasn't there, he asked, "I know he's not *here,* but where is he?"

He had been cremated. The service was attended by a throng of science fiction luminaries, including Asimov, de Camp, del Rey, Dickson, Harrison, Hal Clement, Frank Kelly Freas, Philip Klass, and George O. Smith. Asimov recited the twenty-third psalm, Smith gave another reading, and Harrison, who had edited a collection of Campbell's editorials, read from "one of the nasty ones."

Afterward, the mourners crowded into the house in Mountainside for dinner. As they sat in folding chairs, Peg played a recording of Campbell's voice, allowing him to deliver his own eulogy—even in death he had to have the last word. Leslyn's husband said that he was sorry that he hadn't gotten to know him, and someone replied that no one had ever really known him at all.

Before long, Asimov, back in his usual mode, was telling a dirty joke about a parrot. When he was finished, he suddenly remembered where he was. Growing red, he managed to choke out, "I'm sorry, Peg."

"Please go on, Isaac," Peg said gently. "I don't want this to be an unhappy occasion."

Fandom slowly began to realize what it had lost. On hearing of his death, the writer Laurence Janifer said to Barry Malzberg, "The field has lost its conscience, its center, the man for whom we were all writing. Now there's no one to get mad at us any more." The Society for Creative Anachronism, a medieval reenactment group to which Campbell had given money, paid tribute to him with a march for the honored dead. But Heinlein and Hubbard were conspicuously silent.

Campbell wasn't entirely gone—the headlong momentum of his career kept the ideas coming even after he died. He had written numerous unsent letters, including a rejection of the story that became Joe Haldeman's *The Forever War,* and they continued to trickle out with cover notes from Tarrant. At the time of his death, the page in his typewriter included a typical line: "One never can tell when some weirdo problem makes what looks all wrong the right answer."

He also made his posthumous farewells in the magazine. The September 1971 issue featured the short story "On the Nature of Angels," the last piece of fiction that he ever wrote. Campbell proposed that the soul was a complex number in which the variable b stood for the level of sin. No one knew the exact level at which a spirit became good or evil after death, so it would be best, he said, "to keep our soul's *b* value as close to zero as possible."

His own legacy rested on his achievements of twenty years before, which was not the ending that he would have wanted—but he never ceased to believe in its importance. In a conversation a few months before his death, Campbell had stretched his arms wide: "This is science fiction. It takes in all time, from before the universe was born, through the formation of suns and planets, on through their destruction and forward to the heat death of the universe, and after." Then he put his hands an inch apart. "This is English literature—the most microscopic fraction of the whole."

His final editorial, on quasars, appeared in the December 1971 issue. It ended, "You know—things can go into a black hole, but nothing ever comes out. All roads lead to it only."

A FEW WEEKS AFTER THE FUNERAL, ASIMOV WAS INTERVIEWED OVER THE PHONE BY A RADIO SHOW in Dayton. Afterward, he took questions from listeners. A woman called to ask, "Who, in your opinion, did most to improve science fiction?"

Asimov was tempted to go for an easy laugh and say, "Me." In the end, however, he spoke the truth. "John Campbell."

"Good," the young woman said on the other end of the line. "He was my father."

Epilogue
BEYOND THIS HORIZON

The very act of trying to look ahead to discern possibilities and offer warnings is in itself an act of hope. . . . Our tomorrow is the child of our today. Through thought and deed, we exert a great deal of influence over this child, even though we can't control it absolutely. Best to think about it, though. Best to try to shape it into something good. Best to do that for any child.

—OCTAVIA E. BUTLER

On December 4, 1972, the ocean liner SS *Statendam* sailed from New York to Florida, where its passengers would witness the launch of the final manned mission to the moon. The guests included Asimov, Heinlein, Pohl, Sturgeon, Harry Stine, Ben Bova, Marvin Minsky, Norman Mailer, Katherine Anne Porter, and the newscaster Hugh Downs, who served as the master of ceremonies. Also present were members of the press, many of whom, on account of the title of Porter's most famous book, felt obliged to refer to the cruise as "a ship of fools."

The enterprise was the brainchild of a science lecturer named Richard C. Hoagland, who would become notorious years later as a conspiracy theorist with an obsession with the Face on Mars. A ticket for the combined cruise and conference cost upward of a thousand dollars, and it was soon clear that the venture known as Voyage Beyond Apollo was already a financial failure—there were only a hundred paying passengers on the ship, and Holland America, which operated the *Statendam,* would end up losing a quarter of a million dollars.

At first, the experience hardly seemed worth the price. On the second night, during a screening of *2001,* a rough sea sent people vomiting over the railing, and events were so disorganized that the guests openly wondered what they were supposed to be doing. But there were memorable moments. One panel featured Mailer and Asimov, two Jewish writers from Brooklyn who had crossed paths before. Asimov had been riding an elevator in New York when his eye was caught by the man beside him: "Did anyone ever tell you, sir, that you resemble Norman Mailer in appearance?"

The most famous author in America had offered a deadpan response. "Yes, I get told that now and then."

Now they faced off on the subject of space. Mailer complained that NASA had turned the greatest achievement in human history into a "monumentally boring" spectacle. Like Campbell, he was intrigued by the possibility of communication that didn't involve the electromagnetic spectrum, and he said that the astronauts should have conducted experiments in telepathy on the moon.

Asimov's response was diplomatic. "When you apply the scientific method to the supernatural, then it automatically becomes natural."

Mailer replied by expounding on his theory of the "thanatosphere," a layer of the atmosphere populated by the souls of the dead. In another talk, he noted that the public was starting to view space travel with indifference, rather than as a form of adventure—which may have been his most insightful remark.

On the evening of the Apollo 17 launch, the *Statendam* held station in the water near Cape Canaveral, waiting beneath a darkened sky crossed by distant lightning. A series of holds postponed takeoff until after midnight, but at last, the rocket ascended. As Mailer and Downs smoked a joint with a pair of stowaways, the sky brightened to a dull copper and the stars disappeared.

Glancing back, Pohl saw Asimov, Heinlein, and Sturgeon standing together with their faces lit by the flare. A sound like thunder caused the hull of the ship to vibrate. Heinlein compared it to an atomic explosion, while Asimov was more struck by the reaction of the underground publisher Rex Weiner, who was gazing up behind him, stoned out of his mind: "Oh, shit. Oh *shi-i-i-it.*"

The ship continued on to the Virgin Islands, where Mailer disembarked, taking some of the air out of the proceedings—the press was more interested in him than in any of the science fiction writers on board. Carl and Linda Sagan took his place, and the second half of the trip passed pleasantly. Heinlein gave a speech, but he was told just beforehand that he could speak for only fifteen minutes, or half as long as he had expected. Asimov felt that the talk was "rather wandering."

Voyage Beyond Apollo was more aptly named than any of its participants could have known. While Mailer sparred with Asimov, the journalist Tom Wolfe was in Florida, trying to persuade the astronauts to open up about their experiences—and, in retrospect, the week marked a high point in the dialogue between science fiction and the intellectual establishment. It was the final act of the drama in which the genre had made its most profound impact on the imagination of the world, and some of the writers there had reason to wonder if they would live to see what came next.

IN JANUARY 1970, HEINLEIN HAD ENTERED THE HOSPITAL WITH AN UNTREATED CASE OF PERITONI-tis. After a colectomy, in which he was given blood transfusions from five donors, he was left nauseous and weak. He knew that his new novel *I Will Fear No Evil*—about a dying billionaire whose brain is transplanted into the body of his female secretary, with a minor player named Judge McCampbell—had to be cut by thirty thousand words, but he was too exhausted to revise it. As published, it was a repellent combination of radical weirdness and smug complacency, with the barest hint of what it might have been if the reader had been able to care about the characters.

By the end of the year, Heinlein felt well enough to try for a comeback, conceiving of an ambitious novel, *Time Enough for Love,* to close out his Future History. It centered on Lazarus Long, the effectively immortal protagonist of *Methuselah's Children,* whose superhuman fecundity—women beg to have his children—came off as a wishful reaction to the author's own childlessness. The result was his last major work, and it included a few nostalgic nods to Hubbard, whom he had never ceased to see as a war hero. Lazarus uses the pseudonym "Lafayette Hubert, M.D.," and he refers to another Lafe, a naval officer, with some familiar qualities:

> *He had hair so red that Loki would have been proud of it. Tried to choke a Kodiak bear to death. . . . Lafe tackled him with bare hands . . . and mind you, when he had no need to. I would have faded over the horizon. Want to hear about Lafe and the bear and the Alaskan salmon?*

Heinlein put more of himself into it than perhaps any other story, and it became his first bestseller in hardcover.

The world had caught up with him, and as fans of *Stranger in a Strange Land* sought out his other books, a lucrative chain reaction ensued. Much of his newfound wealth went toward his medical bills, as well as those of his mother, who died in 1976. He also assisted with the hospital expenses of Philip K. Dick, who wrote to him with awe, "I am trembling as I write this, to address a letter to you. . . . You made our field worthy of adult readers and adult writers."

Despite such testimonials, Heinlein felt wounded by criticism from fans, and he was distracted by other causes. He credited the transfusions that he had received during surgery for saving his life, and he spent the better part of a year researching an article on blood sciences, seeking advice from Asimov, whom he admiringly described as a renaissance man: "If Isaac doesn't know the answer, don't go look it up in the *Encyclopedia Britannica,* because they won't know the answer either." On a visit to the Jet Propulsion Laboratory—which must have reminded him of Jack Parsons—for the launch of the Viking spacecraft, the writer Jerry Pournelle informed him that half of the scientists there had been drawn to their profession by his stories.

He was one of the undoubted big three authors in science fiction, along with Clarke—whom Heinlein criticized for having never written a memorable character—and Asimov. When Asimov jokingly suggested that one of them should die to make room for their successors, Heinlein replied, "Fuck the other writers!" But he

Robert A. Heinlein, L. Sprague and Catherine de Camp,
and Isaac Asimov at the Nebula Awards in 1975.
*Courtesy of the Jay Kay Klein estate. Used by permission of Special Collections &
University Archives, UCR Library, University of California, Riverside.*

had trouble maintaining his old levels of productivity. In 1978, he suffered a blockage of blood to the brain, and his doctor ordered him to quit smoking. Heinlein, who was holding an unlit cigarette at the time, slid it quietly back into the pack.

After a carotid bypass, he improved, returning to *The Number of the Beast,* a metafictional fantasy that owed something to Hubbard's *Typewriter in the Sky.* The novel—with a villain who uses the alias "L. Ron O'Leemy," an anagram of Heinlein's pen name Lyle Monroe—was bought by Fawcett for half a million dollars, which he needed to pay for his operations. Its appearance also led to an exchange of letters with Hubbard, who wrote to him fondly, "Now they're accusing us old-timers of being society's fortune tellers. I'm glad they've come to that, actually."

Heinlein had become a statesman for the genre, testifying before the House Select Committees on Aging and Science and Technology on applications of space technology for the elderly—he said that he hoped to stay alive until he could buy a commercial ticket to the moon. He was also positioning his work for future readers. In the autobiographical material in the collection *Expanded Universe,* he minimized his relationship with his editors, stating that Alice Dalgliesh had "disliked" him, but liked the sales of his books, and that *Sixth Column* was "the only story of mine ever influenced to any marked degree by John W. Campbell, Jr."

When the writer George R. R. Martin asked him to contribute an introduction to a volume in honor of Campbell, Heinlein called back to refuse, saying that the editor had never taught him anything. It was in sharp contrast to Asimov, who agreed to write an essay for Martin, even if his private feelings were more conflicted than the ones that he expressed in print: "It sometimes seems to me that if I weren't so insistent on speaking of Campbell in my own writings, he would vanish forever from the minds of people—and in that same way, I often think, my own name will vanish too after the first flurry of regret when I die."

Heinlein denied Campbell's influence with equal intensity—although the issue hardly could have mattered to most readers—and his statements carried a trace of personal bitterness. Although he had achieved greater acclaim than any other science fiction writer, living or dead, he felt underappreciated. He distanced himself from the pulps, saying that he had sliced up his novels for serialization solely for the money, and at times, he resembled Hubbard, who insisted that he wrote science fiction only to finance his research and systematically erased all collaborators from his life story.

There was also a dispute with Campbell's successor. After the editor's death, a search had begun for his replacement at *Analog,* with rumored candidates including Harry Harrison, Poul Anderson, and Fred Pohl. Asimov recommended del Rey, who was closest "in ability and character" to Campbell, but the publisher wanted someone younger. His second choice was Ben Bova, who landed the job. Bob Lapham, a vice president at Condé Nast, later said that he had read stories by all the contenders, and Bova's was the only one that he could understand.

Bova had big shoes to fill. After he took over *Analog,* he met with Will Jenkins, who remarked, "Here we've had a good lunch and we haven't come up with one single brilliant idea for a story." In time, he rose to the occasion, and it was under his guidance that a sense emerged of what the magazine might look like without Campbell. He left in 1978, handing the reins to Stanley Schmidt, and accepted a position as the editor of *Omni.* It seemed like a natural home for Heinlein—but when he saw the draft of a negative review of *Expanded Universe,* he told Bova that unless it was pulled, he would never work for him again. It wasn't, and he never did.

On April 13, 1981, Leslyn Heinlein, who had suffered a stroke, died in Modesto. Her ashes were scattered at sea. Heinlein hadn't been in touch with her for decades, and he might not even have known. If he had, he might have reflected that with both Leslyn and Campbell gone, no firsthand witnesses remained to the earliest stages of his development as an author.

The most memorable episode of his twilight years didn't involve writing at all. Jerry Pournelle was chairing the Citizens Advisory Council on National Space Policy, a loose consortium of writers, scientists, and public figures who prepared white papers on strategic defense for President Ronald Reagan. It was as close as anything ever came to Campbell's dream of a direct pipeline to the halls of power, and Heinlein joined in avidly—he admired Reagan, who reminded him of Barry Goldwater, and he had registered for the first time as a Republican.

Within two years, the council's work seemed to pay off. On March 23, 1983, Reagan delivered a speech proposing a defensive shield to guard against missile attacks: "I call upon the scientific community who gave us nuclear weapons to turn their great talents to the cause of mankind and world peace—to give us the means of rendering these nuclear weapons impotent and obsolete." The program's official name was the Strategic Defense Initiative, but in a nod to its evident fictional precursors, it soon became known as Star Wars.

The announcement and the first round of tests led to heightened tension, both on the international stage and within the genre. One prominent skeptic was Asimov, who said, "I don't think Star Wars is feasible and I don't think anybody takes it seriously. It's just a device to make the Russians go broke. But we'll go broke, too. It's very much a John Wayne standoff." On September 17, 1984, Arthur C. Clarke told the Senate Foreign Relations Committee that the principles behind Star Wars were "technological obscenities." Heinlein was furious.

Events came to a head when both writers attended a meeting at Larry Niven's house. Clarke had written a critical article on the subject for *Analog*, arguing that an orbiting laser station could be destroyed by "a bucket of nails," and when the aerospace engineer Max Hunter brought it up at the gathering, he replied lightly, "But Max, I learned everything I know about celestial mechanics from you."

"I didn't teach you enough, Arthur," Hunter responded. Clarke found himself facing a hard line of questioning from the other attendees, and he conceded a few technical errors. The discussion remained cordial and focused on the science, however, and Clarke stuck to his political views.

Heinlein was less willing to let it drop. After the formal session had broken for lunch, Heinlein—who had remained silent—told Clarke, in a tone that shocked the others, that he had no business giving advice to Americans. Clarke recalled, "He accused me of typically British arrogance, and he really was vicious. It really hurt me. I was very sad about it."

When Clarke responded that he had a moral objection to the program, Heinlein advised him to avoid getting involved in matters in which he didn't have a stake. Clarke felt that the issues in question affected everyone on the planet, but he ended on a conciliatory note, telling Heinlein, "I can't help the British, but I'll try to do something about the arrogance."

He never changed his position, and the encounter effectively ended their friendship. Clarke made a few attempts at reconciliation by mail, sending Heinlein a picture of two fighting bull elephants with the note "Does this remind you of anything?" He later remembered, "Though I felt sad about this incident, I was not resentful, because I realized that Bob was ailing and his behavior was not typical of one of the most courteous people I have ever known."

This may have come closest to the truth. Heinlein's health had forced him to summon all his physical courage, while draining him of energy that he had used to keep other parts of himself under control, much as the war had revealed a strain of weakness in

Hubbard that had been present all along—or as Campbell's darker side had been exposed by gout and hypertension. Asimov drew a telling contrast:

> [*Heinlein*] *had a definite feeling that he knew better and to lecture you into agreeing with him. Campbell did this too, but Campbell always remained serenely indifferent if you ended up disagreeing with him, whereas Heinlein would, under those circumstances, grow hostile. . . . I do not take well to people who are convinced they know better than I do, and who badger me for that reason, so I began to avoid him.*

And there was no doubt as to where Asimov's own sympathies fell. When he heard what Heinlein had said to Clarke, he became enraged—and he banished all of Heinlein's books from his library.

LIKE HEINLEIN, HUBBARD HAD SPENT MUCH OF THE LAST THREE DECADES BROODING OVER THE threat of nuclear war, and he seemed equally unable to separate it from the ups and downs of his own career. An associate recalled, "If [his enemies] caught up with him they would cause him so much trouble that he would be unable to continue his work, Scientology would not get into the world, and there would be social and economic chaos, if not a nuclear holocaust."

Hubbard had sailed the Atlantic for years. Whenever they had to welcome "wogs," or outsiders, onto the ship, his portraits were turned to the wall and materials relating to Scientology were hidden. He insisted that he was no longer connected to the church—which sent him fifteen thousand dollars a week—but he was just as involved as always. Wherever he went, he was followed by his "messengers," a squadron of teenage girls in blue uniforms who conveyed his orders and lit his cigarettes. He never touched them sexually, but he took obvious satisfaction in their loyalty. During a family argument, he told one of them to spit in his daughter Diana's face.

He also rebuffed Alexis, his daughter with Sara Northrup, whom he had already excised from his official biography. When Alexis reached out to him, Hubbard dispatched two agents with a letter, which had been written on a typewriter that was discarded after a single use to prevent it from being traced. They informed an astonished Alexis that Hubbard had married the pregnant Sara only out of pity, with the strong implication that her real father was Jack Parsons. The letter was signed "Your good friend, J. Edgar Hoover." Alexis never tried to see him again.

His attempts to find a safe haven had failed. In 1972, after a rumor arose that France would seek his extradition for fraud, he took off for New York, where he went into hiding with a pair of staff members in Queens. Remarkably, he also found time for at least two visits to the house of George O. Smith in Rumson, New Jersey. The magician James Randi, who encountered him there at parties attended by science fiction writers, recalled that the other guests ignored Hubbard, who sat drinking by himself in the corner: "He was a mess."

One day, Hubbard asked an assistant to look up the names of the Seven Dwarfs. In a secret order written on April 28, 1973, he laid out his plans for what he called the Snow White Program, with projects for different countries named after characters from the Disney movie. It was part of a larger effort to go after the church's enemies—including journalists—more aggressively, and it would ultimately succeed in planting spies in the Drug Enforcement Administration, the Department of Justice, the Federal Trade Commission, and the Internal Revenue Service.

By September, the prospect of extradition seemed to have faded and Hubbard went back to his fleet. Any hopes of a turning point were dashed after he was hurt in a motorcycle accident in the Canary Islands—a bad skid on gravel left him with cracked ribs and a broken arm. Until then, it had occasionally seemed possible for him to enjoy his wealth, but now his most sadistic tendencies took hold, amplified by a closed world in which he had total authority, with nothing to prevent him from becoming the worst possible version of himself.

He established an internal gulag—the outcasts wore black coveralls and were fed on food scraps—that expanded to encompass a third of the crew. After an unfortunate incident at a port in Madeira that ended with rocks being thrown on both sides, he decided to go to South Carolina. As they were nearing shore, they received a frantic message from the church's intelligence arm, warning him that federal agents were waiting on the dock. Hubbard made for the Caribbean, where he was visited by his aging father. Harry Ross Hubbard, whose wife had died in 1959, had "a wonderful trip," and he passed away soon afterward.

Hubbard's own declining health and the rising price of oil made it seem advisable to seek a permanent base, and his attention was drawn to the town of Clearwater, Florida, the name of which carried an obvious resonance. He hoped to take control of the local government, but he indiscreetly let his identity slip to his tailor, a science fiction fan. The word spread, and Hubbard, spooked, fled to Washington, D.C. A regional Scientology office was nearby, and he was handed fliers for the church in the street, to his considerable amusement.

Under the direction of Mary Sue, the Snow White Program was going strong, but its agents grew reckless, and when their activities were exposed, Hubbard had no choice but to vanish again. Looking for a place to hide from process servers, they settled on Olive Tree Ranch in La Quinta, California. Quentin, their son, was growing visibly unstable: "He was talking about people coming from outer space and what we were going to do about it." After admitting to a staff member that he had faked auditing results for a friend, he left the ranch.

On October 28, 1976, Quentin was found behind the wheel of a white Pontiac parked outside McCarran Airport in Las Vegas. The engine was running, and a vacuum cleaner hose ran from the exhaust pipe to one of the windows. Quentin was alive, but he never regained consciousness, and he died in the hospital two weeks later. He was twenty-two years old. When his parents heard the news, Mary Sue screamed for ten minutes, while Hubbard was furious: "That stupid fucking kid!"

After Quentin's suicide, the mood grew darker. Mary Sue's dogs, which were said to be clear, allegedly snarled at anyone who had negative thoughts about their owners, while Hubbard became obsessed with a system for cleansing the body of drugs, hinting that only those who underwent it would survive the coming nuclear holocaust: "And *that* poses the interesting probability that only Scientologists will be functioning in areas experiencing heavy fallout in an atomic war."

On July 8, 1977, federal agents with sledgehammers conducted raids on the Church of Scientology in Los Angeles and Washington, D.C., in a clear act of retaliation for the Snow White Program. Hubbard saw that he had to put distance between himself and his wife. A week later, he snuck out of La Quinta by night, accompanied by three messengers, and ended up in Sparks, Nevada. As he had with Polly and Sara, Hubbard was ready to cast off Mary Sue as soon as she became inconvenient, and he no longer had to wait for a replacement.

In his isolation, he returned for the first time in years to fiction. A key factor was the release of *Star Wars*, which became one of his favorite movies. It was the ultimate invasion of the genre into the mainstream—even if it owed more to Joseph Campbell than to John—and Hubbard felt that he was in a better position than anyone to supply the culture with the material that it wanted. He commenced work on a novella, later adapted into a screenplay, titled *Revolt in the Stars*, which combined the Xenu story with a blatant attempt to capitalize on George Lucas's space opera.

After Hubbard tried unsuccessfully to shop the script around to studios, it occurred to him to make it himself. In early 1978, he returned to La Quinta, where he shot a series of training films. They allowed him to indulge in his fondness for gore—the actors were so covered in fake blood that their clothes had to be cut off after filming—but he always found something wrong with the result, and few of the movies were screened. One of the camera operators was a teenager named David Miscavige, who became one of the only men whom Hubbard trusted.

On August 15, 1978, a grand jury in Washington, D.C., indicted Mary Sue and eight other Scientologists on twenty-eight counts relating to the Snow White Program. Shortly afterward, Hubbard suffered a pulmonary embolism, collapsing while filming in the desert. A senior case supervisor was brought out to treat him, and during their auditing sessions, Hubbard confessed that he had been driven by "an insatiable lust for power and money."

Hubbard began to improve, but after another agent of the church went to the FBI, he disappeared again. Under cover of darkness, he traveled with a small staff to a town in the San Jacinto Mountains, where he settled in March 1979. At his new house, he audited himself every morning and regaled his followers with accounts of his past lives, some of which were drawn from his old stories.

In October, the defendants pled guilty to a single charge each, and Mary Sue was sentenced to five years in prison and a fine of ten thousand dollars. Hubbard moved into an expensive Blue Bird mobile home, living on the road until 1983, when he bought a ranch in Creston, California, that had once belonged to the ac-tor Robert Mitchum. He seemed outwardly detached from the church, restricting himself to statements on his birthday and at the beginning of each year.

Yet he maintained control from a distance. On his orders, Miscavige, who had risen rapidly in the ranks, embarked on a vast restructuring, deposing Mary Sue, expelling her children, and overseeing a mass expulsion of offenders. The church, which had once consisted of fifty thousand members, saw its numbers reduced by half. Miscavige had studied Hubbard closely, and it was through him that the Sea Org's culture of paranoia grew into something that would outlive its founder.

Incredibly, many of those who were driven out refused to blame Hubbard, whom they thought was either dead or imprisoned. In fact, he was "deeply involved" with Miscavige's actions, dispatching weekly orders designed primarily to increase the flow of money into his private accounts. But he was still effectively isolated, and he responded by focusing on his writing, much as Asimov had dealt with his troubles by plunging into solitary work. Both men defined themselves as monsters of productivity, and Hubbard returned to fiction with a vengeance.

He had continued to rework *Revolt in the Stars,* but after it became clear that a movie was unlikely to materialize, he channeled his energy in another direction. Over a period of eight months, he wrote a massive novel of close to half a million words, based on seven hundred pages of handwritten notes. Its title was announced as *Man: The Endangered Species,* but it was ultimately published by St. Martin's Press as *Battlefield Earth: A Saga of the Year 3000,* with a muscular figure on its cover who bore a distinct resemblance to Hubbard himself.

No less an authority than Mitt Romney would later call it his favorite novel, and although Hubbard's reclusiveness and health problems have led to speculation about ghostwriters, any doubts that the book was written by him were dispelled by its first section, which was close to a straight rewrite of *Buckskin Brigades.* Its protagonist was the latest incarnation of Yellow Hair, living in leather and moccasins with the last vestiges of humanity, which had been devastated a millennium earlier in an invasion by greedy aliens called Psychlos. Their unseen rulers were the Catrists, making the real villains the "Psychlo Catrists."

In the introduction, Hubbard alternately built Campbell up and tore him down, often in the same sentence, and the entire book played like a frenzied exorcism of the editor's influence. Van Vogt couldn't finish it, but he provided a blurb calling it a "masterpiece," while Heinlein wrote in a letter, "It's a great story, Ron. I hope it sells a million copies in hardback." St. Martin's Press had similar hopes. The church pledged to buy fifty thousand copies, and after it hit the bestseller lists, John Travolta, a devoted Scientologist, expressed interest in starring in the movie.

Hubbard wasn't quite done yet. After finishing *Battlefield Earth,* he plunged immediately into an even more bloated novel, which Miscavige personally delivered in a banker's box to Author Services, the affiliate of the church that handled the founder's literary work. *Mission Earth* weighed in at more than a million words, and its editors were reluctant to touch it, aside from carving it up at random into a hideously distended "dekalogy" of ten books.

Its first volume, *The Invaders Plan,* went on sale in October 1985. As before, Scientologists bought copies by the armful, which would be recycled back to stores, sometimes with their price tags still attached. Hubbard was never informed of these tactics, and he took genuine satisfaction in the knowledge that he had written another bestseller. Three months later, he was dead.

ON FEBRUARY 13, 1970, ASIMOV HAD TAPED AN APPEARANCE ON *THE DICK CAVETT SHOW.* SEATED beside him on the couch was an attractive English actress, and Asimov was his usual self. When Cavett jokingly told him that he was a romantic, Asimov replied, "Yes, I am." He turned to the starlet. "And talking of romantic, dear, what are you doing tonight after the show?"

Cavett played along with the bit: "Come, come, Isaac, don't get horny on my time." There was laughter from the audience, but afterward, Asimov began to worry. After the taping, he phoned Gertrude about it, hoping that she wouldn't be offended when it aired the following night, but it didn't work. Before long, she was talking about leaving him again.

The week after the telecast, Gertrude went on a visit to her mother, implying that she might not be coming back. She had made similar threats before—she was suffering from arthritis, which darkened her moods—but this time, he decided to take her seriously. Going to his lawyer, he prepared a formal letter stating his intention to seek a divorce. The decision was seemingly abrupt, but it reflected a conviction that had been growing inside him for years, much like Heinlein's break from Leslyn—except that it had taken Asimov the better part of a decade.

It was no accident that he made his choice soon after publishing his hundredth book, a personal milestone that Gertrude had dismissed. Yet it was still a drastic move for a man who hated change. Asimov couldn't obtain a divorce in Massachusetts without alleging wrongdoing, so he moved into a hotel in New York, where Janet Jeppson was waiting for him. As they unpacked, she said hesitantly, "You know, my apartment isn't far away, and you're perfectly welcome to spend time there over the weekend, if it gets too lonely for you out here."

He gladly accepted, and he eventually moved in with her, using the hotel only as an office. Asimov had worried that he would have trouble writing, but Campbell, who was still alive, bought the first story that he finished in the city, offering him the same kind of encouragement at the end of their partnership that he had at the beginning. When Janet met the editor, who lectured her on her own field of psychiatry, she thought that he was "exasperating—but fascinating."

After Campbell's death, Asimov made a triumphant return to science fiction with *The Gods Themselves*, a novel that gave him more pleasure in writing than he had felt in more than a decade. Mindful of his reputation for avoiding sexual content, he decided that the central section would be all about sex—but for a species with three sexes, not two. His experiences with Campbell had left him reluctant to deal with extraterrestrials, but now he resolved to create the best aliens that anyone had ever seen. When set alongside *I Will Fear No Evil*, it made a strong case that Asimov, after trailing Heinlein for most of his career, had finally pulled ahead.

It also reflected his newfound personal contentment. By the summer of 1972, he was referring to Janet as his fiancée, and in November of the following year, shortly after his mother passed away, his divorce from Gertrude—which cost him a staggering fifty thousand dollars in legal fees—was finalized. He and Janet got married, moving into a luxurious apartment with a beautiful view of Central Park—although Asimov, with his fear of heights, rarely ventured onto the balcony.

One of his finest stories, "The Bicentennial Man," soon followed, and his career continued to flourish—he discussed projects with the likes of Woody Allen, Paul McCartney, and Steven Spielberg. In 1976, the publisher Joel Davis told him that he wanted to launch a science fiction magazine with a famous name. *Isaac Asimov's Science Fiction*, with his face prominently featured on the cover, was a success, and Davis later doubled down by buying *Analog*.

Asimov remained close to his daughter, but not to his son, who was set up with a trust fund after he declined to go to college. They spoke only rarely on the phone, and Asimov devoted his attention to younger men to whom he could more comfortably serve as a mentor. As far as women were concerned, Janet was conscious of his behavior, which she tolerated. When he joked to her once that he had been caught kissing a woman by the *New York Post*—it was actually Janet herself—she simply said, "I keep telling you to be careful."

The only sore point was his health. In May 1977, he felt chest pains, but he insisted on walking to a medical checkup. Paul Esserman, his doctor, was furious, and an electrocardiogram revealed that he had suffered a coronary earlier that month. "If it hadn't been a mild one," Esserman said, "you would have died some time in this last week, probably as you ran up the stairs to my office."

Asimov was on the mend, but mortality was on his mind. When the novelist Martin Amis met him in 1980, he reported, "I expected cheerful volubility, but Asimov gives off an air of irritated preoccupation, as if silently completing a stint of mental arithmetic." He was an institution by now. Gene Roddenberry asked for his advice on *Star Trek: The Motion Picture*, which listed him as a special consultant. When Asimov saw his credit in the theater, he clapped wildly, prompting someone to remark in the aisle, "There's Asimov, applauding his own name."

After the success of *Star Wars*, the studios had begun to look more seriously at science fiction. When the director John Carpenter was offered a chance to remake *The Thing from Another World*, he became enthusiastic about returning to the premise of "Who Goes There?," and the makeup artist Rob Bottin devised unsurpassed practical effects to put its horrors on-screen. On its initial release in 1982, *The Thing* was poorly received—Harlan Ellison dismissed it as a "pointless, dehumanized freeway smashup of grisly special effects *dreck*"—but its reputation grew over time, and it became more responsible than any other work for keeping Campbell's name alive.

As for Asimov, it was his science fiction, not his nonfiction, that remained perpetually in print. His publishers wanted more, and he was offered a large advance for a new Foundation novel, which he had to tackle for the first time without Campbell. *Foundation's Edge,* which played down the concept of psycho-history and emphasized his own ideas, was a comeback that gave him his first bestseller, as similar efforts had for Heinlein and Hubbard—and in his case, no one had to be ordered to buy it. Science fiction had always favored the young, and all three men wanted to prove that they still mattered.

Over the next nine years, Asimov passed two hundred books through his word processor, including more Foundation and robot novels. His arteries had narrowed, forcing him to ask those around him to walk more slowly, which left him in more of a rush on the page. Years earlier, Barbara Walters had asked him what he would do if he had only six months left to live. He had replied, "Type faster."

In 1983, he was advised to undergo a triple bypass. On the day of the operation, he told Paul Esserman, "Listen, I must have plenty of oxygen for my brain. I don't care what happens to my body, within reason, but my brain mustn't be in any way disadvantaged. You'll have to explain to everybody involved in the operation that I have an unusual brain that must be protected."

The doctor reassured him, and the bypass, he was later told, had been perfect. When Asimov opened his eyes in the recovery room, Esserman asked him to recite a limerick to test his faculties. Asimov began:

> *There was an old doctor named Paul*
> *With a penis exceedingly small—*

Esserman broke in to say that he seemed fine. The following day, however, Asimov came down with a fever, and it seemed that he might not survive. Within a few days, it passed. His doctors, who thought that it was postsurgical inflammation, didn't realize that it was a symptom of something worse. Asimov had received a blood transfusion during his operation, and he was infected with HIV.

IN 1973, THE INTERNATIONAL ASTRONOMICAL UNION APPROVED A PROPOSAL TO NAME A CRATER on Mars after John W. Campbell. By honoring such figures as Campbell, H. G. Wells, Edgar Rice Burroughs, and Stanley Weinbaum, Carl Sagan said, they were acknowledging "a debt to science fiction that scientists have now in part repaid." The Campbell Award for Best New Writer was inaugurated by the World Science Fiction Society, along with the Campbell Memorial Award for Best Science Fiction Novel by the Center for the Study of Science Fiction at the University of Kansas.

A year later, George O. Smith retired after decades of work in the electronics industry. He was looking forward to spending more time with Doña, but twelve days after their shared retirement began, she underwent a sudden decline and was hospitalized. She died on May 25, 1974.

After Campbell's death, Peg sold her crewel business and the house in Mountainside, moving to Alabama to be close to Jane. She passed away in her sleep, of cardiac arrest, at their vacation home in Maine on August 16, 1979.

Kay Tarrant left *Analog* in 1973 and retired to Hoboken. She died on March 1, 1980. A few years before her retirement, she reportedly said to a startled group of writers at lunch, "Personally, I don't give a fuck what you write, but we have teenagers who read the magazine."

ON JANUARY 19, 1986, HUBBARD SENT A FINAL MESSAGE TO HIS FOLLOWERS. HE PROMISED THAT the Sea Org would always exist, "no matter that we may leave the surface of this planet," and concluded, "I'll be scouting the way and doing the first port survey missions. I expect your continuing backup. You've got a little under a billion left on your current hitch, and it is hoped you will sign up again—veterans are valuable!" It was signed "L. Ron Hubbard, Admiral."

Hubbard had suffered a stroke three days earlier. Knowing that he was dying, he had revised his will, muttering in his nightgown, "Let's get this over with! My head is hurting!" He died in his Blue Bird mobile home on January 24, attended by a few followers, with the cause of death given as a cerebral vascular accident. His ashes were scattered at sea, in accordance with his teachings, which stated that the dispersal of remains in water would liberate the thetan from its host.

On January 27, before a crowd at the Hollywood Palladium, Miscavige delivered the news in front of a portrait of Hubbard: "L. Ron Hubbard discarded the body he had used in this lifetime for seventy-four years, ten months, and eleven days. The body he had used to facilitate his existence in this universe had ceased to be useful and in fact had become an impediment to the work he now must do outside its confines. The being we knew as L. Ron Hubbard still exists. Although you may feel grief, understand that he did not, and does not now. He simply moved on to his next step."

Hubbard's obituary ran on January 28, 1986, on the day of the explosion of the *Challenger* shuttle, which delivered a devastating blow to the American space program. In his will, he left millions of dollars to the church, with smaller amounts for Mary Sue and some of his children. L. Ron Hubbard, Jr., and Alexis got nothing, although they later settled with the estate.

His true legacy lay elsewhere. At three remote compounds, plans were made to preserve his writings—including his fiction—in underground vaults designed to withstand a nuclear blast. Written on steel plates or archival paper and encased in titanium capsules, they might conceivably outlast most of the works that human civilization has produced. Future generations may well read Hubbard, assuming that he is all that survives. But they might be the only ones who will.

ON JULY 26, 1986, GINNY HEARD A NOISE IN THE BATHROOM. GOING INSIDE, SHE FOUND HEINLEIN, who had been diagnosed with emphysema the year before, bleeding heavily from his nostrils—it had flowed down his chest to stain the front of his pajamas. After a series of hospitalizations, he underwent surgery to tie off the artery in his nose. It seemed to go well, and Ginny wrote, "Now all there is to worry about is hepatitis and AIDS from the transfusions."

They moved to Carmel, which was closer to hospitals, but it was clear that Heinlein—who had published several late novels, including *The Cat Who Walks Through Walls*, which featured Colonel Colin "Killer" Campbell and his uncle Jock—would never write again. Before they left, Ginny asked if he ever regretted not having any children. Heinlein reassured her that he didn't, although the fact that she raised the question at all indicated that it was never far from their minds.

Settling into his new house, Heinlein contemplated a campaign to recruit the diplomat Jeane Kirkpatrick, whom he regarded as tougher on communism than George H. W. Bush, to run for president. For the most part, however, he focused on his recovery, and when he learned of a treatment for emphysema that removed the carotid bodies in the neck, he impulsively decided to try it without consulting his doctor: "I'm just going to do it." It was his last attempt at control.

On January 5, 1988, he underwent the operation in Los Angeles. At first, his breathing seemed easier, but he began to weaken, until he was so tired that he couldn't get out of bed. Three weeks later, he showed signs of congestive heart failure. More hospitalizations followed, leaving him wearier than ever. As his medical bills mounted, he returned to the hospital for a fifth time in April, using a walker and breathing through tubes in his nose.

After eating breakfast at home on May 8, Heinlein said that he wanted to take a nap. Ginny left to work on their correspondence at her desk, where she was informed by their nurse that her

Isaac and Janet Asimov in 1987.
Courtesy of Stanley Schmidt

husband was no longer responsive—he had died in his sleep at the age of eighty. As he had wished, his ashes were scattered in the Pacific with full naval honors. Afterward, Ginny wrote him a letter: "Now you know the answer to the great mystery, but I don't. Will you be waiting at the end of that tunnel, as you promised me, or is there just nothing out there?"

Ginny also told Heinlein that the tributes were pouring in from all over, including one from Asimov, who "spouted off in his usual fashion." Later, however, she remembered, "When Robert died, I never heard a word from Isaac—not a note, not a phone call—nothing."

AFTER HIS TRIPLE BYPASS, ASIMOV TOOK TO READING THE OBITUARIES IN THE PAPER MORE CLOSELY. Many of the writers he had known were gone. Theodore Sturgeon had died in 1985, followed two years later by Catherine L. Moore.

After an attack of encephalitis, Randall Garrett spent much of the last eight years of his life in an unresponsive state, and he passed away on December 31, 1987.

Asimov himself was slowing down. For most of his life, he had relied unthinkingly on his energy, but now his legs and feet were swollen from his kidney problems. He suffered "wipeouts" in which he was unable to leave his bed, and he began to think of how nice it would be to fall asleep and never wake up—although he was worried about how Janet and Robyn would feel.

The world continued to make demands on his privacy, which he protected with varying degrees of guardedness. At a meeting with the film producer Brian Grazer, Janet broke in after ten minutes: "You clearly don't know my husband's work well enough to have this conversation. This is a waste of his time. We're leaving." But when Marilyn vos Savant, the woman with the highest recorded intelligence in history, asked him to walk her down the aisle at her wedding, he agreed, although they knew each other only casually through the society Mensa.

In December 1989, after an appearance at which he spoke and signed books for three hours, he found that he could barely move the next morning. He spent three weeks in bed, his legs like tree trunks, and he had to wear slippers to walk. In January, he told his doctor, Paul Esserman, that he wanted to die in peace. Esserman booked him a hospital room instead, explaining, "Well, you might have been ready to die, but I wasn't ready to let you."

Asimov spent the rest of the winter in the hospital or in bed at home. His heart murmur resulted in circulatory problems, shortness of breath, and kidney trouble, and his mitral valve appeared to be infected, which led to a discussion about whether to operate. In the meantime, Janet had become concerned by another possibility. She had been reading about HIV for years, and she wondered if it might be responsible for her husband's medical issues.

When Asimov was tested, it came back positive, and the valve surgery was canceled. At first he wanted to go public, but his doctors warned him against it. There was widespread prejudice against AIDS—caused in part by the Reagan administration's unfeeling response to the crisis—and he decided to keep his condition a secret, motivated largely by concern for Janet, who had tested negative. For the next two years, he slowly declined. During one hospital stay, he said to Ben Bova, "I'm seventy-one and a half years old, and I don't like it."

In 1990, Asimov learned that Gertrude had died of breast cancer. He was no longer close to his son, of whom he said in his memoirs, "David's great hobby is to tape the television shows he likes and to build up an enormous library of such things." David eventually moved to Santa Rosa, California, where he lived off a stipend from Asimov's estate. In 1998, after his father's death, he was arrested for possession of "the biggest child pornography collection in Sonoma County history," with thousands of videos found in his home. After pleading guilty to two counts, he was sentenced to three years' probation.

EARLY IN 1992, AFTER FINISHING *ASIMOV LAUGHS AGAIN,* ASIMOV GREW MORE WITHDRAWN. HE was seventy-two, and he was convinced that he wouldn't live longer than his father, who had been one year older when he died. In a farewell essay in *Fantasy & Science Fiction,* Asimov wrote, "It has always been my ambition to die in harness with my head face down on a keyboard and my nose caught between two of the keys, but that's not the way it worked out." His final book published in his lifetime, *Our Angry Earth,* was a collaboration with Pohl, who had been there from before the beginning—and now it was almost after the end.

The last months of his life were spent in and out of the hospital. As his kidneys failed, he slept a great deal. He once dreamed about going to heaven, where he asked, "Do you have a typewriter I can use?" When he was awake, he was often in pain, but in contrast to

Campbell, Hubbard, and Heinlein, whose sufferings had revealed so much of what they had tried to hide, his sense of humor remained intact. On the day before his death, Janet told him, "Isaac, you're the best there is." Asimov smiled and shrugged, and finally, raising his eyebrows, he nodded.

A day later, Asimov was in too much agony to speak, and it hurt to breathe. He was given medication for the pain, and Janet and Robyn were with him when he passed away on April 6. Like the others, he was cremated, and his ashes were scattered. His last words had been "I love you, too."

By his own count, he had published more than four hundred books, as if the ambition that had driven him and the others throughout their lives had crystallized into a visible form. Unlike Campbell, he had never wanted to create a new kind of man, but he had. More than any single story or idea, Asimov would be remembered for embodying the kind of human being who could live in the future, even if it required sacrifices in the present that few would ever understand.

He had wanted to live to see the next millennium, and although he fell short, he made it further than the rest. If he ever paused to consider the future in which he had found himself, he would have seen that it strangely mirrored the landscape of his dreams. What had once been the closely held secret of the pulps—the ideas and images of science fiction—had penetrated into every corner of the culture, both in its inner life and in its inescapable reality. As Asimov himself had once remarked, "We are now living in a science fictional world."

And the explanation was so incredible that it transcended even the claims of psychohistory. Science fiction had set its stories in the future or in space because that was where the action was, and *Astounding* had begun to take itself seriously as prophecy only after its core assumptions were already in place, with its best guesses arising mostly by chance. With so much wild speculation, some of it was bound to be correct—even if the man at the helm had often steered in the wrong direction.

Yet if the future—from atomic energy to the space race to the computer age, which would threaten the existence of the very magazines from which it had emerged—felt like science fiction, it was largely because the prophecy had fulfilled itself. It had inspired countless readers to enter the sciences, where they set themselves, consciously or not, to enacting its vision. Space, which had begun as a backdrop for stock adventure stories, came to seem like humanity's destiny. Campbell and his authors had been the men—and women—who sold the moon.

They hadn't predicted the future—they had made it. And Asimov knew that he was his most astounding creation. In his last week at home, he awoke one day in an agitated state: "I want—"

Janet tried to understand what the matter was. "What do you want, darling?"

"I want—" He managed to force out the words. "I want—Isaac Asimov!"

"Yes," Janet responded gently, knowing that it wouldn't be long. "That's you."

An expression of triumph spread slowly across his face. "I *am* Isaac Asimov!"

Janet never forgot the note of wonder in his voice. She spoke softly to her husband. "And Isaac Asimov can rest now."

ACHNOWLEDGMENTS

I knew more about Isaac Asimov than I knew about anyone else alive. What could there be left to add?

—MARTIN AMIS, *VISITING MRS. NABOKOV*

"It's becoming increasingly obvious that we need a long, objective look at John W. Campbell, Jr.," the author and critic Algis Budrys once wrote. "But we're not likely to get one. . . . Obviously, no one who knew him well enough to work for him at any length could have retained an objective view of him; the most we can hope for from that quarter would be a series of memoirs which, taken all together and read by some ideally situated observer, might distill down into some single resultant—which all its parents would disown." In writing this book, I've done the best impersonation that I can of Budrys's "ideally situated observer," although I soon found that any history of science fiction requires countless compromises. No single volume can cover everything, and I'm painfully aware of the perspectives that this one omits, even when it comes to Campbell himself. But to the extent that I managed it at all, it was due entirely to the help that I received along the way.

I am profoundly grateful to Leslyn Randazzo, John Hammond, Katea Hammond, Justin Robertson, and Doug Smith. For insight, advice, and encouragement, I thank John Joseph Adams, Charles Ardai, Jon Atack, Astrid Bear, Greg Bear, Chuck Beatty, Gregory Benford, Ben Bova, Jennifer Brehl, Damien Broderick, Emanuelle Burton, Michael Cassutt, Hank Davis, Samuel R. Delany, David Drake, Richard Fidczuk, Alan Dean Foster, Jim Gilbert, Matthew Giles, James Gunn, Marie Guthrie, Gay Haldeman, Joe Haldeman, Bill Higgins, Michael Kurland, Rachel Loftspring, Shawna McCarthy, Barry N. Malzberg, George R. R. Martin, Jess Nevins, Annalee Newitz, Larry Niven, John O'Neill, Tony Ortega, Chris Owen, Alexei Panshin, Jason Pontin, Mark Pontin, the late Jerry Pournelle, Manny Robalino, Samantha Rajaram, James Randi, Mike Resnick, Cheri Lucas Rowlands, Jamie Todd Rubin, Yashar Saghai, Robert Silverberg, Sam Smith, Harriet Teal, Gordon Van Gelder, Lydia van Vogt, Sheila Williams, Rex Weiner, Ted White, Ed Wysocki, and many others. I owe a special debt of gratitude to Trevor Quachri and Emily Hockaday of *Analog*.

In 1966, Campbell wrote in response to a request for his papers from Syracuse University, "Any scholarly would-be biographers are going to have a tough time finding any useful documentation on me! I just didn't keep the records!" Fortunately, this prediction turned out to be wildly off the mark. The efforts by the late Perry Chapdelaine to preserve Campbell's correspondence were my indispensible starting point, and I received valuable aid from Pilar Baskett and Wendy Mackey at Texas A&M University; John Betancourt; Gene Bundy at Eastern New Mexico University; Alessia Cecchet, Julia Chambers, Nicolette A. Dobrowolski, Kelly Dwyer, and Jacklyn Hoyt at Syracuse University; Zayda Delgado and Jessica Geiser at UC Riverside; Katie Fortier, Jane A. Parr, and Laura Russo at the Howard Gotlieb Archival Research Center at Boston University; Colleen Garcia at UC San Diego; Jake Gardner at Brown University; Salomé Gomez Upegui and Susan Halpert at Harvard University; Nathaniel Hagee at MIT; the Heinlein Prize Trust; Julianna Jenkins at UCLA; Madeline Keyser at Indiana

University Bloomington; Katie Nash at Williams College; Carol Orloski at Advanced Data Solutions; Debbie Rafine at the Oak Park Public Library; Michael Ravnitzky; Robert C. Ray at San Diego State University; Jean Ross at Duke University; Geo Rule at the Heinlein Archives; John Seltzer; Arley Sorg at *Locus;* and Ann Williams at Blair Academy.

My greatest hope is that this book will inspire a larger conversation about the history of science fiction. Innumerable studies and biographies have yet to be written, and many will be about important figures who look nothing like John W. Campbell. What I've attempted here reflects just one aspect of the story, but it seemed like a necessary step toward any comprehensive reckoning, and it owes its existence largely to three people. One is Stanley Schmidt, who bought my first submission to *Analog* more than fifteen years ago. Another is my agent, David Halpern, who encouraged me to tackle a nonfiction project and supported my work at every step of the way. The third is my editor, Julia Cheiffetz, who brilliantly recognized what it could be. My thanks as well to Kathy Robbins, Lisa Kessler, Janet Oshiro, and everyone else at the Robbins Office; Carrie Thornton, Lynn Grady, Sean Newcott, Eliza Rosenberry, Tom Pitoniak, Victor Hendrickson, Renata De Oliveira, Mary Brower, and the rest of the staff at Dey Street Books and HarperCollins; Jon Cassir at CAA; and Ploy Siripant and Tavis Coburn for their astounding cover. As always, I'm thankful for my friends and family, especially my parents, my brother, and all the Wongs; Wailin, the best of wives and best of women; and my daughter, Beatrix, in whom I see the future.

NOTES

For many events and details of the lives of Heinlein, Hubbard, and Asimov, I am particularly indebted to the books *Robert A. Heinlein: In Dialogue with His Century* by William H. Patterson, Jr.; *Bare-Faced Messiah* by Russell Miller; and *In Memory Yet Green, In Joy Still Felt,* and *I. Asimov* by Isaac Asimov. To keep the notes to a manageable length, I have cited these indispensible works primarily in cases of direct quotation or when the original source might be unclear.

My primary sources of correspondence were *The Complete Collection of the John W. Campbell Letters* on microfilm, the originals of which are held at San Diego State University, and the Heinlein Archives at the University of California, Santa Cruz. In quoting letters, I have generally corrected and standardized the spelling and punctuation. For quotations from novels and short stories, because of the large number of variant editions, I have refrained from citing specific page numbers except when the works in question are obscure, out of print, or otherwise unavailable.

A few short passages relating to Hubbard's writing career have been adapted from my earlier essay "Xenu's Paradox: The Fiction of L. Ron Hubbard and the Making of Scientology."

PROLOGUE: ASIMOV'S SWORD

1 *"My feeling is that as far as creativity is concerned"* Asimov's essay, which was privately written and circulated in 1959 for a group funded by the Advanced Research Projects Agency, was first published in *MIT Technology Review*, January/February 2015, https://www.technologyre view.com/s/531911/isaac-asimov-asks-how-do-people-get-new-ideas (accessed December 2017).

Conference on Education for Creativity in the Sciences "Creative Chat," The Talk of the Town, *The New Yorker*, June 15, 1963, 24–25.

2 *"That world will be more complex than it is today"* Jerome B. Wiesner, "Education for Creativity in the Sciences," *Daedalus*, Summer 1965, 537.

One of the attendees was Isaac Asimov Asimov, *In Joy Still Felt*, 313–14.

"I just dropped it somewhere" Ibid., 313.

3 *"there is no possibility of pretending to youth at forty"* Ibid., 185.

"Wars are different these days" Asimov, "The Sword of Achilles," 17.

4 *"What we need is a simple test"* Ibid.

"good science fiction" A decade later, Asimov might have used the term "hard science fiction" for works with an emphasis on technical accuracy, as opposed to the "soft" social sciences. The term, which became popular in the seventies, first appeared in a review by P. Schuyler Miller of JWC's *Islands of Space* in the November 1957 issue of *ASF*, and it is sometimes used interchangeably with "Campbellian science fiction," although the stories that JWC actually published resist any such categorization.

5 *"that branch of literature"* Asimov, *Asimov on Science Fiction*, 76.

6 *"the most powerful force"* Asimov, *I. Asimov*, 73.

7 *the golden age of science fiction* "There is one golden age of science fiction that has actually been institutionalized and frozen in place, and that is the period between 1938 and 1950, with its peak years from 1939 to 1942." Asimov, *Gold*, 212. This book follows the convention of dating it to the July 1939 issue of *ASF*, which is "sometimes considered by fans of the period to have marked the beginning of science fiction's 'Golden Age,' a period stretching through the 1940s." Asimov, *In Memory Yet Green*, 242.

"the brain of the superorganism" Asimov, *Asimov on Science Fiction*, 196.

"the single most important formative force" Ellison, *Again, Dangerous Visions*, 9.

Neil Gaiman Neil Gaiman, foreword to Doctorow, *Information Doesn't Want to Be Free*, viii.

"The Campbell that influenced me" George R. R. Martin, comment on blog post "Next Year's Hugos," August 31, 2015, https://grrm.livejournal .com/440444.html (accessed December 2017).

8 *Hermann Göring* JWC to Robert Swisher, February 11, 1937.

8 *the Shadow* Dickson Hartwell, "Mister Atomic," *Pic,* February 1946, 20. In a letter to RAH dated May 27, 1951, JWC claimed to have plotted stories for *The Shadow* in collaboration with Walter B. Gibson and John Nanovic.

he was hated Kingsley Amis called JWC "a deviant figure of marked ferocity," while the writer John Lafferty thought he was "the *worst* disaster ever to hit science fiction." Amis, *New Maps of Hell,* 98, and Lafferty, "The Case of the Moth-Eaten Magician," in Greenberg, *Fantastic Lives,* 68.

10 *"In the essential characteristics"* Asimov, *In Memory Yet Green,* 201.

"the hand of John Campbell's mind" Algis Budrys, quoted in Bova, "John Campbell and the Modern SF Idiom."

"[it] carried in it the seeds" Virginia Heinlein, "Science Fiction and John W. Campbell," biographical essay in the RAH Archives, UC Santa Cruz.

11 *"The real golden age of science fiction is twelve"* Hartwell, *Age of Wonders,* 13. The earliest version of this quote is attributed to the fan Peter Graham.

Albert Einstein "As to sending Dr. Einstein a reprint of the December *Astounding*—not necessary. He's a subscriber." JWC to Robert D. Dooley, M.D., January 5, 1953.

the scientists of Bell Labs "And you know at that time one of the things we did [at Bell Labs] was to read *Astounding Science Fiction.* Even some of us wrote for it." Philip W. Anderson, oral history interview with Lillian Hoddeson, May 10, 1988, https://www.aip.org/history-programs/niels -bohr-library/oral-histories/30430 (accessed December 2017).

12 *"A glance at the cover"* Sagan, *Broca's Brain,* 161.

Paul Krugman "I grew up wanting to be Hari Seldon." Seldon was the inventor of the science of psychohistory in the Foundation series. Paul Krugman, "Asimov's Foundation novels grounded my economics," *The Guardian,* December 4, 2012.

Elon Musk "[Musk] was influenced, he says, by Isaac Asimov's Foundation series, a science fiction saga in which a galactic empire falls and ushers in a dark age." Rory Carroll, "Elon Musk's mission to Mars," *The Guardian,* July 17, 2013.

Newt Gingrich "While Toynbee was impressing me with the history of civilizations, Isaac Asimov was shaping my view of the future in equally profound ways. . . . For a high school student who loved history, Asimov's most exhilarating invention was the 'psychohistorian' named Hari Seldon." Gingrich, *To Renew America,* 24.

13 *"We have called for a Campbellian revolution"* Vox Day, "Racists vs. Child Rapists," May 21, 2015, http://voxday.blogspot.sk/2015/05/the -campbell-delany-divide.html (accessed December 2017).

This book is not a comprehensive history of the genre It also omits any discussion of the artists whose work was a vital part of *ASF,* including Hubert Rogers, Charles Schneeman, H. W. Wesso, Frank Kelly Freas, and many others. As Freas observed, "There are fewer tales about [JWC's] artists only because there have been fewer artists—it took a certain amount of resiliency in an artist to keep from being worn down to a mere nub on the grinding wheel of the Campbell brilliance." Frank Kelly Freas, in *Locus,* July 12, 1971, 9.

13 *one man was thought to oversee it* JWC is sometimes quoted as saying: "Science fiction is what I say it is." The closest approximation to this statement in his published work was his proposal for a "general definition" of science fiction: "The kind of stories I personally like to read when I want to read 'science fiction.'" JWC, Brass Tacks, *ASF,* August 1952, 132.

14 *"I even told myself stories"* Asimov, *In Memory Yet Green,* 102n.

PART 1: WHO GOES THERE? (1907–1937)

15 *"You may have had troubles"* JWC to Asimov, December 2, 1955.

CHAPTER 1: THE BOY FROM ANOTHER WORLD (1910–1931)

17 *"Do not take on a Junior"* LRH, *Dianetics,* 305.

trouble remembering his childhood JWC to Dr. W. Grey Walter, unsent, May 1, 1953.

no visual memory JWC to RAH, November 4, 1949.

18 *"The prize case in difficulty"* LRH, *Dianetics,* 343.

"a permanent—but useful!—scar" JWC to William R. Burkett, Jr., July 1, 1968.

They decided to try drugs JWC described their use of drugs in letters to G. Harry Stine, March 1, 1953, and Eric Frank Russell, July 11, 1953.

Four mirrors were arranged JWC recounted the experience in letters to G. Harry Stine, March 1, 1953; Raymond F. Jones, April 29, 1953; Eric Frank Russell, July 11, 1953; Bill Powers, November 4, 1953; and Gib Hocking, February 24, 1954.

19 *"I'd been scared before in my life"* JWC to Raymond F. Jones, April 29, 1953.

they never used it again JWC to Gib Hocking, February 24, 1954.

his brain's alpha rhythms Ibid.

electroshock therapy or the use of drugs JWC to Dr. W. Grey Walter, unsent, May 1, 1953.

"Do I know things" JWC to RAH, November 4, 1949.

"The cord is caught around his neck" JWC to RAH, September 15, 1949.

20 *salt water to make him sick* JWC to RAH, November 4, 1949.

drowned at age three ... swallowed morphine pills JWC to RAH, September 15, 1949.

20 *"a shrew"* JWC to Susan Douglas, November 9, 1954. Susan was the daughter of JWC's aunt Josephine and Samuel B. Pettengill.

Harry Strahorn An article in the February 17, 1888, issue of the *Chicago Tribune*, "Hyde Park Society Astonished: Clifford Strahorn's Secret Marriage All Forgiven," implies that Laura Harrison eloped with Strahorn, who was at least six years her junior, after "passing the winter at the Strahorn mansion." JWC later suggested to his cousin Susan that their grandmother had gotten married "in a hurry." JWC to Susan Douglas, November 9, 1954.

"somewhat involved" JWC to Dwight Wayne Batteau, November 20, 1954.

21 *His ancestors* "[William W. Campbell's] Scotch forebears went to New England during the colonial period, and many of its members served in the French and Indian Wars and in the Revolution. One of his ancestors fell at Saratoga during the Burgoyne invasion, another died at Fort Edwards, and others were at the battle of Bunker Hill. . . . His grandfather, Horace Campbell, was born in Connecticut and married Sallie Martin, who was from the original *Mayflower* stock in direct line." Winter, *A History of Northwest Ohio*, 1201. JWC added in a letter to Ron Stoloff on May 1, 1969: "One of my great-grandfathers was an M.D. in the Union Army. One hadn't left Germany at that time. One was a Vermont legislator and active abolitionist, and one was a minister operating an Underground Railway station."

both sides of the Salem witch trials "My father was amusedly interested in genealogy, and discovered with delight that one ancestress was tried and condemned as a witch in Salem—by a judge who was also, on another line, an ancestor!" JWC, Brass Tacks, *Analog,* February 1965, 92.

Irish, Dutch, Hungarian, English "My ancestry is typically American; that is, it's a mixture of Irish, Dutch, Hungarian, English, French, German, and some indeterminate North European stocks." JWC to Sten Dahlskog, February 14, 1956.

16 Treacy Avenue Moskowitz, *Seekers of Tomorrow*, 36. Moskowitz incorrectly gives the street as "Tracey," stating that it bordered the "fashionable Clinton Hill section," although it was actually part of the West Side neighborhood.

"Every individual starts out in life" JWC to RAH, November 4, 1949.

Bell Telephone John W. Campbell, Sr.'s career is described in detail in *The Michigan Alumnus*, January 29, 1949, 232.

a religious conservative JWC to Gotthard Gunther, June 11, 1953.

22 *"Mentally speaking, I was brought up in hellfire"* JWC to Raymond F. Jones, August 13, 1953.

two women in the neighborhood JWC to Gib Hocking, May 8, 1954.

22 *his father learned to leave the house* JWC to Laura Krieg, October 20, 1952.

a legendary arguer in the courtroom JWC to James C. Warf, July 29, 1954.

"It is necessary" Moskowitz, *Seekers of Tomorrow*, 37.

"The boy stood on the burning deck" JWC to Laura Krieg, October 20, 1952.

"a good and sincere guy" JWC to Dwight Wayne Batteau, July 27, 1955.

a crowbar from a thread JWC to Laura Krieg, November 12, 1957.

"I feel there must be a wise creator" Ibid.

23 *his father reviewed his homework* Moskowitz, *Seekers of Tomorrow*, 38.

to solve math problems in two different ways JWC to Perry Chapdelaine, February 24, 1970.

"a good beginner" JWC to John W. Campbell, Sr., June 11, 1953.

"Well, it was a good idea, John" JWC to Bernard I. Kahn, December 15, 1957.

"a would-be aesthete" Ibid.

Episcopalian upbringing Sam Moskowitz, handwritten notes for *Seekers of Tomorrow*, Sam Moskowitz Collection, Texas A&M University, Series VIII: Subject Files, Box 3-150, "Campbell, John W."

Campbell compared to brainwashing JWC to Bernard I. Kahn, August 6, 1957.

Laura learned to independently verify JWC to John W. Campbell, Sr., November 28, 1954.

who identified as agnostic JWC to "Pease," February 10, 1953.

"She was a very brilliant woman" JWC to "Spring," June 19, 1957.

24 *"a failure in human living"* JWC to Gotthard Gunther, September 29, 1953.

"They clawed each other viciously" JWC to Bernard I. Kahn, October 8, 1954.

"cordially detested" JWC to Kenneth Pecharsky, April 12, 1971.

she was afraid of reptiles JWC to Susan Douglas, November 9, 1954.

the single most famous anecdote Moskowitz, *Seekers of Tomorrow*, 37.

25 *she introduced him to science fiction and fantasy* Bretnor, *Modern Science Fiction*, 3.

Campbell turned to books for escape Moskowitz, *Seekers of Tomorrow*, 38.

either a genius or a criminal JWC to John Scott Campbell, March 2, 1964.

25 *"[I was] the damn fool"* JWC to Raymond F. Jones, October 28, 1953.

"Kids who don't get angry" JWC to RAH, October 5, 1951.

"I was unpopular with local kids" JWC to Eric Frank Russell, May 9, 1958.

"heart set on dismemberment" JWC to Gotthard Gunther, November 24, 1954.

26 *he built a catapult in his yard* JWC, "Meet the Authors," *Air Trails Pictorial,* December 1946, 17.

He loved his Meccano set Dickson Hartwell, "Mister Atomic," *Pic,* February 1946, 21.

a radio receiver JWC, "It's been a long, long time," *Analog,* February 1966, 158.

he put together his first car JWC to G. Harry Stine, October 11, 1953.

his basement chemistry lab Moskowitz, *Seekers of Tomorrow,* 38.

an eavesdropper JWC to Welsford Parker, July 27, 1954.

"The old son of a bitch" JWC to Joseph Winter, January 27, 1953.

"mental beating technique" JWC to Susan Douglas, November 29, 1954.

"My childhood battles with her" JWC to Gotthard Gunther, October 12, 1954.

Lemon Grove Avenue JWC to RAH, February 26, 1940.

"had her so thoroughly scared" JWC to Susan Douglas, November 9, 1954.

Kittatinny Campground JWC to Dorothy (Campbell) Middleton, October 9, 1954.

27 *"Everybody is trying to be nice to me"* Ibid.

"I'd have gotten a higher score" JWC to "Mrs. McCormick," September 18, 1955.

to correct his teachers in class Moskowitz, *Seekers of Tomorrow,* 38.

joined no teams or societies Ann Williams, Blair Academy, e-mail to author, October 31, 2017.

"hiking" Ann Williams, Blair Academy, e-mail to author, November 1, 2017.

In tennis ... When he played chess JWC to Gotthard Gunther, November 24, 1954.

Campbell plowed through two years of French JWC to John Arnold, April 21, 1953.

28 *"I've felt a vast need for love and affection"* JWC to Joseph Winter, June 21, 1953.

an unassuming appliance salesman JWC to Susan Douglas, November 9, 1954.

28 *"You and Mother between you"* JWC to John W. Campbell, Sr., June 18, 1955.

29 *Cambridge* JWC lists his address as 38 Bigelow Street in Cambridge in a letter to *Amazing Stories,* May 1930, 89. His roommates included Rosario Honore Trembley and Richard Rush Murray, the latter of whom published a few stories in *Amazing.* Moskowitz, *Seekers of Tomorrow,* 38, and Bleiler, *Science-Fiction,* 304.

"a little, dingy town" JWC, "Invaders from the Infinite," *Amazing Stories Quarterly,* Spring/Summer 1932, 193.

"I found a bunch of rather bewildered men" JWC to John Arnold, November 29, 1952.

the department of physics Nathaniel Hagee, MIT Office of the Registrar, e-mail to author, September 2, 2016.

a course in analytical chemistry JWC to Gotthard Gunther, November 24, 1954.

to prove a professor wrong JWC to Gotthard Gunther, April 10, 1959.

"dearest antagonist" Wiener, dedication to *The Human Use of Human Beings.*

the worst teacher he had ever seen JWC to Nils Aall Barricelli, April 16, 1970, and Bud Herrmann, January 21, 1971.

dirty limericks JWC to Gib Hocking, February 24, 1954.

chemicals on locker room benches JWC to Joe Poyer, April 27, 1966.

"Anything that can go wrong, will" JWC to Gunther Cohn, August 11, 1969.

30 *rowed crew, played tennis* JWC to Asimov, July 24, 1958. There is no mention of him in any of the team rosters in yearbooks from MIT.

a fan of the pulps since high school Moskowitz, *Seekers of Tomorrow,* 39.

Campbell's decision to major in physics JWC, "Meet the Authors," *Air Trails Pictorial,* December 1946, 17.

"I owe you a good education" JWC, "In Memoriam," *Analog,* August 1968, 177.

Incredibly, it was accepted Moskowitz, *Seekers of Tomorrow,* 39.

31 *Campbell decided to visit the editor* Ibid., 39–40.

"material energy" Ibid., 40.

a thousand times greater Sam Moskowitz, handwritten notes for *Seekers of Tomorrow,* Sam Moskowitz Collection, Texas A&M University, Series VIII: Subject Files, Box 3-150, "Campbell, John W."

33 *"I'm waiting anxiously for all comments"* JWC, letter to *Amazing Stories,* November 1930, 764.

prostituting his talents JWC to Gotthard Gunther, April 10, 1959.

William Chace Greene, Jr. JWC to Mark Clifton, October 3, 1952.

"Green" is mentioned in Sam Moskowitz's notes for *Seekers of Tomorrow*.

33 *The only professor who ever helped him* Sam Moskowitz, handwritten notes for *Seekers of Tomorrow*, Sam Moskowitz Collection, Texas A&M University, Series VIII: Subject Files, Box 3-150, "Campbell, John W."

"It isn't The Saturday Evening Post" Ibid.

eight hours on twisty roads Budrys, *Benchmarks Continued*, 62.

His grades had been good but unexceptional JWC to John Arnold, April 21, 1953.

"constitutionally opposed to math" JWC to Gib Hocking, October 20, 1953.

he failed to pass after three tries JWC to John Arnold, April 21, 1953.

34 *the repressed memory of the doctor* "I dimly remember a bit about some engram concerning the German language that was giving you trouble." Jesse Bruce Hopkins to JWC, September 12, 1958.

"If das Haus means 'the house'" JWC to Jane Kearney, May 4, 1954.

an unclassified student Nathaniel Hagee, MIT Office of the Registrar, e-mail to author, September 2, 2016.

CHAPTER 2: THREE AGAINST THE GODS (1907–1935)

35 *"The adventurer is an outlaw"* Bolitho, *Twelve Against the Gods*, 4.

36 *Swope Park in Kansas City* RAH told this story in a speech, "The Future Revisited," at the 19th World Science Fiction Convention in 1961, reprinted in Kondo, *Requiem*, 178–80. He also recounted it in an address at Annapolis in 1973, reprinted as "The Pragmatics of Patriotism" in *Expanded Universe*, 469–70.

"This is how a man lives" RAH, "The Future Revisited," reprinted in Kondo, *Requiem*, 180.

William Tanner was killed Hagedorn, *Savage Peace*, 335–36.

37 *a high school debate on shipping regulations* JWC to Laura Krieg, September 25, 1954.

38 *he had nightmares about the beatings* Virginia Heinlein, "The Years at the Naval Academy," biographical essay in the RAH Archives, UC Santa Cruz.

"a grandmother" RAH to Poul Anderson, September 6, 1961.

39 *"Had you not been engaged"* RAH to Mary (Briggs) Collin, August 6, 1962.

40 *"sexually adventurous"* Patterson, *Learning Curve*, 113.

"poisonous, like mistletoe" RAH to Cal Laning, August 1, 1930, quoted in Patterson, *Learning Curve*, 129.

Leslyn MacDonald In addition to Patterson, *Learning Curve*, 144–46, the most comprehensive account of Leslyn's early life appears in James, "Regarding Leslyn" and "More Regarding Leslyn."

40 *Theosophy* For references to Theosophy in RAH's "Lost Legacy," see Patterson, "The Hermetic Heinlein."

42 *"totally and permanently disabled"* Patterson, *Learning Curve,* 170.
Old Tom Madfeathers Wright, *Going Clear,* 25–26.
learned to ride before he could walk Atack, *A Piece of Blue Sky,* 47.

44 *"Whenever I sat down"* LRH, *Early Years of Adventure,* 39.
"They smell of all the baths they didn't take" Miller, *Bare-Faced Messiah,* 47.

45 *"to escape the Naval Academy"* LRH, "Affirmations." This document can be viewed in its entirety at http://www.lermanet.com/reference/Ad missions.pdf (accessed December 2017).
"[He said] I should study engineering" Atack, *A Piece of Blue Sky,* 60.
"the first American class" "Who Was L. Ron Hubbard?" Church of Scientology International, http://www.scientology.org/faq/scientology -founder/who-was-lronhubbard.html (accessed December 2017).
"smiling woman" "If I was trying to find the ground through the heart of a thunderstorm, and feared a fatal crash, and looked out to see a smiling woman sitting on one of my wings, I knew I would come through. She was always there, and visible, when I knew myself in great trouble." Burks, *Monitors,* 99.
Flavia Julia "Only Flavia Julia and then the All Powerful have opinions worth inclining toward." LRH, "Affirmations." Jack Parsons later stated that LRH referred to his guardian as the Empress, which also points to Saint Helena, who was the mother of the emperor Constantine. Miller, *Bare-Faced Messiah,* 120.
"strongholds and bivouacs of the Spanish Main" Miller, *Bare-Faced Messiah,* 56.

46 *Hubbard hung in effigy by his passengers* Wright, *Going Clear,* 31.
"Despite these difficulties" Miller, *Bare-Faced Messiah,* 59.
dismissed his mother as a "whore" Ibid., 170.

47 *marking troop movements with pins* Asimov, *In Memory Yet Green,* 5.
"A few miles south of Smolensk" JWC, The Analytical Laboratory, *ASF,* November 1941, 58.
"as the only way of getting rid of him" Asimov, *In Memory Yet Green,* 24.

48 *He learned the alphabet from a jump-rope rhyme* Asimov, *Before the Golden Age,* 5.

49 *"Junk! It is not fit to read"* Asimov, *In Memory Yet Green,* 71–72.

50 *a paskudnyak* Asimov, *Asimov Laughs Again,* 93.
"Science fiction? Like Jules Verne?" Asimov, *Treasury of Humor,* 245.

51 *"Well, Isaac"* Asimov, *In Memory Yet Green,* 96.
"It was just enough of a slipping of bonds" Ibid., 169.

51 *he didn't like it* Asimov, *Before the Golden Age*, 794.

"Astounding Stories *as a whole"* Asimov, letter to *Astounding Stories*, February 1935, 157–58.

52 *fantasized about running a newsstand* Asimov, *In Memory Yet Green*, 124.

long walks in the cemetery Ibid., 131.

CHAPTER 3: TWO LOST SOULS (1931–1937)

53 *"No one should be a freelance writer"* JWC to Ben Bova, January 18, 1965.

Durham, North Carolina Their address is given as 1501 Watts Street on the cover page of Doña Campbell's unpublished story "Beyond the Door." John W. Campbell compositions, Houghton Library, Harvard University, folder "Beyond the Door."

his first close encounter with the unknown JWC to Cal Laning, July 21, 1959.

54 *his grandmother's house in Ohio* JWC to Asimov, February 17, 1958.

reported the incident to a physics professor JWC to Theodore Cogswell, January 3, 1962.

"My one advantage" JWC to RAH, January 11, 1955.

55 *childlike and "stupid"* JWC to William H. Burkett, Jr., March 30, 1966.

"the city where every pimp" Ibid.

"Paris itself is fine" Ibid.

his intended occupation Duke University registration record for JWC.

His performance in his first semester Ibid.

Joseph B. Rhine JWC to Joseph B. Rhine, November 23, 1953.

56 *runs with the Zener cards* Ibid.

"the evil eye" JWC, letter to *Amazing Stories*, May 1933, 182.

"You can generally smell them" JWC to A. Spurling, May 18, 1970.

he took no science classes at all Duke University registration record for JWC.

57 *a rebuke in print* "If [Campbell] has left out any colored rays, or any magical rays that could not immediately perform certain miraculous wonders, we are not aware of this shortcoming in this story. . . . We were tempted to rename the story 'Ray! Ray!' but thought better of it." Hugo Gernsback, "Reasonableness in Science Fiction," *Wonder Stories,* December 1932, 585.

he didn't even attend his graduation ceremony JWC to John W. Campbell, Sr., June 11, 1953.

During a visit home JWC to Raymond F. Jones, August 13, 1953.

he came to despise Roosevelt In a letter to Robert Swisher on November 12, 1936, JWC referred to Roosevelt as "F(ool) D(olt) R(abblerouser)."

58 *Doña Louise Stewart Stebbins* Doña's birth date and state appear on the birth certificate of her son Doug Smith, who confirmed her full name and the names of her parents in an e-mail to the author, September 9, 2016.
a Latin high school in Waltham Moskowitz, *Seekers of Tomorrow*, 44.

59 *"We were two lost souls"* Leslyn Randazzo, e-mail to author, July 21, 2016.
"I quit MIT at twenty-one" JWC to Asimov, May 5, 1957.
she disapproved of his writing JWC to Susan Douglas, November 9, 1954.
"When his wife Doña was new" Catherine de Camp, quoted in Moskowitz, "Inside John W. Campbell," 113.
Boston School of Cooking Leslyn Randazzo, e-mail to author, July 31, 2016.

60 *"were walking in about two feet of water"* JWC to Curtis Upton, July 19, 1957.
"She considered the proper thing to do" JWC to John Clark, May 14, 1963.
"Beyond the Door" The story, which was ten pages long, revolved around a method for returning the dead to life, which its inventor is forced to use on his girlfriend after she drowns. John W. Campbell compositions, Houghton Library, Harvard University, folder "Beyond the Door."
to retype his stories JWC to Robert Swisher, April 2, 1937.
"sounding board . . . that science was for **people**" LRH, "An Introduction to Science Fiction," reprinted in LRH, *Writer: The Shaping of Popular Fiction*, 154.
The Red Gods Call Algis Budrys, "Paradise Charted," in Hartwell and Wolff, *Visions of Wonder*, 313.

61 *a backlog of his unsold manuscripts* "In 1934 . . . [JWC] came to me with a stack of short stories from his morgue, and unsmiling told me he wanted one cent per word for them—double our usual rate. I told this to Gernsback and also noted that these stories must have been rejects from his childhood, as none of them were any good. I had the dubious duty of returning stories to John W. Campbell, Jr. He hated me ever after." Charles Hornig, interview in *Galileo*, November 1979, 23.
The Mightiest Machine Moskowitz, *Seekers of Tomorrow*, 46.
"And Now Campbell!" F. Orlin Tremaine, *Astounding Stories*, October 1934, 38.

62 **Arthur C. Clarke would later borrow** Clarke, *Astounding Days*, 103.
to use a pseudonym Moskowitz, *Seekers of Tomorrow*, 47.
"almost overnight" F. Orlin Tremaine, *Astounding Stories*, February 1935, 106.

63 *"a dirty, underhanded crack"* JWC, introduction to *Cloak of Aesir*, 10–11.

63 *"I'm doing some work now"* JWC, as "Karl Van Campen," letter to *Astounding Stories,* February 1935, 157.

MacKenzie Motors Moskowitz, "Inside John W. Campbell," 3.

64 *Robert Swisher* Ibid., 7–8.

Their apartment in Cambridge The building was at 6 Agassiz Street. Ibid., 7.

"Always a Breeze" Moskowitz, *Seekers of Tomorrow,* 45.

The Moon Is Hell *"The Moon Is Hell* was written about 1935 and relatively little modernizing and rewriting was done before it was published." JWC to Arthur C. Clarke, July 2, 1951. The draft preserved in the John W. Campbell compositions at Harvard is identical to the published version, apart from a few minor revisions. Its original title, crossed out in the manuscript, was *Frozen Hell,* which JWC later reused for the story that became "Who Goes There?"

a series of articles on the solar system The articles ran in *Astounding Stories* from June 1936 through November 1937. Asimov mentioned them approvingly in a letter to *ASF,* July 1938, 158, and RAH recommended them in his speech at the Third World Science Fiction Convention, Denver, 1941, reprinted in Kondo, *Requiem,* 165.

65 *"a factory town . . . a terrible hole"* Doña Campbell to Robert and Frances Swisher, April 1, 1936.

"Experimental Engineer" JWC to Robert Swisher, March 26, 1936.

"Poor John" Doña Campbell to Robert and Frances Swisher, April 1, 1936.

the couple was evicted JWC to Robert Swisher, April 9, 1936.

66 *"rejection of an up-till-then idea"* JWC to Reginald Bretnor, June 6, 1953.

Samuel B. Pettengill JWC to Robert Swisher, April 23, 1936.

a beer garden in New York JWC to Robert Swisher, June 11, 1936.

"with a nasty little sneer" JWC to Robert Swisher, July 29, 1936.

"I'm beginning to get restless" Doña Campbell to Robert Swisher, June 1, 1936.

Pioneer Instrument Company JWC to Robert Swisher, July 29, 1936.

"tweezer dexterity" JWC to RAH, July 21, 1942.

Carleton Ellis JWC to Robert Swisher, September 11, 1936.

he left anyway JWC to Robert Swisher, March 1, 1937.

67 *"no man in all history"* JWC, "Invaders from the Infinite," *Amazing Stories Quarterly,* Spring/Summer 1932, 216.

"The total capacity of the mind" JWC, "The Story Behind the Story," *Thrilling Wonder Stories,* August 1937.

rewritten as a horror story JWC to Robert Swisher, May 15, 1937.

"Frozen Hell" The five false starts and the original manuscript of "Fro-

zen Hell," which JWC also considered titling "Pandora," were discovered by the author in the John W. Campbell compositions, Houghton Library, Harvard University, folders "Untitled" and "Pandora." Its deleted opening section recounted the discovery of the alien spacecraft.

68 *Richard Byrd* JWC to Robert Swisher, May 15, 1937.

"too frightful to mention" JWC to Robert Swisher, May 26, 1936.

"Doña says I clicked" JWC to Robert Swisher, May 15, 1937. In a letter to Swisher on June 21, JWC wrote that he was hoping to submit the story to *Argosy*.

"M, my friend" JWC to Reginald Bretnor, June 6, 1953.

an attack of appendicitis Doña Campbell to Robert Swisher, July 2, 1937.

rumors at Street & Smith JWC to Robert Swisher, September 15, 1937.

"But Tremaine" JWC to Robert Swisher, October 4, 1937.

69 *to fill a gap in inventory* Ibid.

"Hiya, Bob!" JWC to Robert Swisher, October 5, 1937.

Isaac Asimov saw with approval Asimov, *In Memory Yet Green*, 189.

Astounding Science Fiction Technically, the title was *Astounding Science-Fiction*, with a hyphen, which it retained until November 1946. For the sake of consistency, the hyphen will be omitted throughout this book.

CHAPTER 4: BRASS TACKS (1937–1939)

73 *"There are times of evolutionary stress"* JWC, as "Arthur McCann," letter to *ASF*, April 1938, 152.

"a tall, rather thin" JWC to Robert Swisher, August 9, 1939.

an ancestor on his mother's side JWC to Eric Frank Russell, June 20, 1957.

74 *"The conditions [man] tries to adjust to"* JWC, as "Arthur McCann," letter to *ASF*, April 1938, 151.

several older structures Frederik Pohl, "Astounding: The Campbell Years," December 3, 2009, http://www.thewaythefutureblogs.com/2009/12/astounding-campbell-years (accessed December 2017).

John Nanovic Ashley, *The Time Machines*, 83.

the copper ashtray Pohl, *The Way the Future Was*, 43.

"a continuous very mild sniffle" JWC to Robert Swisher, March 25, 1938.

75 *the covers for all thirteen magazines* Harry Bates, in Rogers, *A Requiem for Astounding*, ix–xi. In a response to a question from the author, Richard Fidczuk, a publishing production director, suggested that the extra covers from magazines with smaller print runs were simply discarded, and the editor Sheila Williams confirmed in an e-mail on November 10, 2017, that this remained the case until recently at Dell.

75 **"scientifiction"** The term first appeared in Hugo Gernsback, "Thought Transmission on Mars," *The Electrical Experimenter,* January 1916, 474.

"Ninety percent of science fiction is crud" The law made its earliest appearance in print in Theodore Sturgeon, "On Hand: A Book," *Venture Science Fiction,* March 1958.

76 **"If Weinbaum had lived"** Asimov, *Asimov on Science Fiction,* 211–12.

a single story worth remembering Asimov, *Before the Golden Age,* 16.

a series of frantic innovations Most of these features appeared in the final Clayton issue of *Astounding Stories of Super-Science,* January 1933.

77 *the pulp publisher Street & Smith* Ashley, *The Time Machines,* 82.

Desmond Hall Hall left *Astounding* in 1934 to edit *Mademoiselle* for Street & Smith, and he was succeeded as associate editor by R. W. Happel. Ibid., 105.

"thought variant" F. Orlin Tremaine, *Astounding Stories,* December 1933, 69.

a circulation of fifty thousand Ashley, *The Time Machines,* 85.

the climax of his infatuation with the genre Asimov, *In Memory Yet Green,* 198n.

78 *more lousy science fiction than anyone else* JWC to Terry Carr, June 17, 1968.

twelve hours a day on manuscripts alone Bova, "John Campbell and the Modern SF Idiom."

offering notes for writers "I never sent [JWC] a story after 1938 because I had to revise that one. First, to suit John's idea, and then to suit John's wife's idea. *That* was a little hard to do, so I never sent John any more stories." Edmond Hamilton, interview with Dave Truesdale and Paul McGuire III, April 1976, https://www.tangentonline.com/interviews -columnsmenu-166/1270-classic-leigh-brackett-a-edmond-hamilton -interview (accessed December 2017).

"At present my eyes feel" Doña Campbell to Robert Swisher, April 18, 1939.

Catherine Tarrant The description of Tarrant is based largely on an e-mail to the author from Robert Silverberg, September 20, 2016. Malzberg gives her hiring date as 1938 in *The Engines of the Night,* 72.

R. W. Happel Happel was associate editor at least through the end of October 1937, when he was the guest of honor at the Third Eastern Science Fiction Convention in Philadelphia. Moskowitz, *The Immortal Storm,* 117. JWC also refers to "Happle" as one of the usual readers of his stories—along with Doña, Robert Swisher, L. Sprague de Camp, and John Clark—in a letter to Swisher on November 8, 1938.

79 **"Campbell's editing Astounding"** JWC to Robert Swisher, October 30, 1937.

79   *dividing submissions into two piles* Frederik Pohl, "Campbell Gets the Magazine," October 24, 2011, http://www.thewaythefutureblogs.com /2011/10/campbell-gets-the-magazine (accessed December 2017).

"about fourteen months ago" JWC to Robert Swisher, February 11, 1938.

selling to himself In a letter to Robert Swisher dated November 8, 1938, JWC mentioned that he was revising an old story, "Empire," with an eye to publishing it in *ASF,* and that he hoped to try his other rejects in England.

"Stuart, I'm afraid" JWC, Brass Tacks, *ASF,* May 1939, 157.

it was Don A. Stuart who was really editing **Astounding** JWC to Jack Williamson, October 7, 1941, quoted in Williamson, *Wonder's Child,* 134.

"I'm thinking up ideas at a furious rate" JWC to Robert Swisher, October 30, 1937.

"The future doesn't happen one at a time" Scithers, *On Writing Science Fiction,* 117.

80   *the same premise to multiple writers* Pohl, *The Way the Future Was,* 87.

"Television will never replace radio" Ibid., 86–87. JWC's editorial on television, "Communication and Noncommunication," appeared in June 1945, which suggests that his first conversation with Pohl must have been on a different subject—although the dynamic between the two men was presumably much the same.

"I've never liked him" Memo from Catherine Tarrant to JWC, June 8, 1951.

81   *Pohl obtained free magazines* Pohl, *The Way the Future Was,* 88.

Mort Weisinger Budrys, *Benchmarks Revisited,* 242n.

to write stories around paintings One example was "Lunar Landing" by Lester del Rey, which JWC commissioned to go with a painting by A. von Munchhausen. Del Rey, *Early Del Rey,* 270.

he hoped to change the title Ashley, *The Time Machines,* 146.

"The discoverer of the secret of atomic power" JWC, "Fantastic Fiction," *ASF,* June 1938, 21.

Enrico Fermi JWC to John W. Campbell, Sr., August 29, 1953.

82   *the first "mutant" story* JWC, In Times to Come, *ASF,* March 1938, 4.

"an ace of the pulps" "Burks of the Pulps," The Talk of the Town, *The New Yorker,* February 15, 1936, 12.

a premise about a replication machine JWC to Robert Swisher, December 4, 1937. The story was serialized as *Jason Sows Again* in *ASF,* March and April 1938.

"An **editor** *does"* Panshin, *The World Beyond the Hill,* 257.

82 *writers submitting to the revived* **Amazing** JWC to Robert Swisher, February 11, 1938.

just one out of every fifteen submissions JWC to Robert Swisher, February 7, 1938.

a meeting with Tremaine and Blackwell LRH, "An Introduction to Science Fiction," reprinted in LRH, *Writer: The Shaping of Popular Fiction*, 151.

83 *come up with the plot in his sleep* LRH to Jim Higgins, reprinted in LRH, *Literary Correspondence*, 63.

"A story jammed and packed" LRH, "Suspense," reprinted in LRH, *Writer: The Shaping of Popular Fiction*, 78.

"a country almost as large as the United States" LRH, "Five Mex for a Million," *Top-Notch*, November 1935.

84 *"I guess L. Ron Hubbard"* Leo Marguiles, *Thrilling Adventures*, October 1934.

"The morgue is open to you anytime" Widder, *Master Storyteller*, 36.

analyzing the percentage of stories that sold LRH, "The Manuscript Factory," reprinted in LRH, *Writer: The Shaping of Popular Fiction*, 19–21.

85 *switching the envelopes* Wright, *Going Clear*, 40.

"Because of her coldness" LRH, "Affirmations."

"a remarkable young man" De Camp, "El-Ron of the City of Brass," *Fantastic*, August 1975.

The Secret of Treasure Island This description is based on scenes available on YouTube at https://www.youtube.com/watch?v=FxjHf4Af_tY (accessed December 2017).

"an executive named Black" LRH, "An Introduction to Science Fiction," reprinted in LRH, *Writer: The Shaping of Popular Fiction*, 151.

86 *"was mainly publishing stories about machines"* Ibid.

"He was going to get people *into his stories"* Ibid.

"the effort to get the best stories" JWC, In Times to Come, *ASF*, August 1938, 124.

"Hubbard Snubbard" JWC to LRH, April 5, 1938.

"quite ignorant of the field" LRH, "An Introduction to Science Fiction," reprinted in LRH, *Writer: The Shaping of Popular Fiction*, 151.

he repeatedly asked his friends and family JWC to Robert Swisher, June 19, 1938.

his note on the upcoming issue JWC, In Times to Come, *ASF*, June 1938, 135.

it placed first in fiction The Analytical Laboratory, *ASF*, September 1938, 87. First place overall went to L. Sprague de Camp's nonfiction article "Language for Time Travelers."

87 *"a weird or occult mag"* JWC to Robert Swisher, November 15, 1937.

he spread a rumor JWC to Robert Swisher, October 25, 1938.

the magazine . . . had been founded expressly for him "[Campbell] got the fantasy I wrote out of *Astounding* by starting a brand new magazine to accommodate it—*Unknown*." LRH, interviewed in Platt, *Dream Makers Volume II*, 182.

After receiving a requested rewrite Moskowitz, *Seekers of Tomorrow*, 137–38.

the best story that he had read in a decade JWC, "Unknown," *ASF*, February 1939, 72.

88 *he began to pay visits to the editor's home* JWC to Robert Swisher, October 4, 1939.

"Ron can do almost anything" JWC to Robert Swisher, November 1939.

a university science department LRH, "An Introduction to Science Fiction," reprinted in LRH, *Writer: The Shaping of Popular Fiction*, 154.

New Year's Day, 1938 Wright, *Going Clear*, 35.

"I was dead, wasn't I?" Miller, *Bare-Faced Messiah*, 137.

89 **The One Command** LRH refers to the manuscript under this title in the "Affirmations."

Penn Station Wright, *Going Clear*, 37.

the first six people who read it went insane Ibid.

"Foolishly perhaps" Miller, *Bare-Faced Messiah*, 85.

"It was the strangest book I ever read" Burks, *Monitors*, 99.

"I didn't tell John" LRH, "Science Fiction and Satire."

"Give me the L. Ron Hubbard fairy tale" Asimov, letter to *Unknown*, August 1939, 140.

"With Hubbard . . . I consider anything below perfect" Asimov, letter to *Unknown*, September 1939, 143.

90 *annoyed with his wisecracks* Moskowitz, *Seekers of Tomorrow*, 253.

"When we want science fiction" Asimov, letter to *ASF*, September 1938, 161.

"Let me point out" Asimov, letter to *ASF*, February 1939, 160.

92 *"Mr. Campbell will see you"* Asimov, *In Memory Yet Green*, 194.

"It was the nicest possible rejection" Ibid., 201.

93 *"I've got to skim over these"* Ibid., 206.

"a sound, and pretty fair piece of work" JWC to Robert Swisher, October 25, 1938.

he considered the magazine "trash" Asimov, *Before the Golden Age*, 883.

the author Clifford Simak JWC to Robert Swisher, October 25, 1938.

"hackneyed" Asimov, *In Memory Yet Green*, 223.

"definitely improving" Ibid., 224.

⁹⁴ *"I am of medium height"* Asimov, "Meet the Authors," *Amazing Stories,* March 1939, 126.

"properly banged up" Asimov, *In Memory Yet Green,* 382.

"Isaac, a check!" Ibid., 229.

⁹⁵ *"Yes, it was impossible"* Ibid., 202.

"sat in adoring admiration" Ibid., 290n.

"the fan who's been trying to be a writer" JWC to Robert Swisher, October 25, 1938.

"I could endure him" Gunn, *Isaac Asimov,* 21.

⁹⁶ *"On this point"* Asimov, *The Early Asimov,* 78.

"Next month, **Astounding** *introduces a new author"* JWC, In Times to Come, *ASF,* June 1939, 44.

"A university equipped" JWC, "Addenda," *ASF,* July 1939, 7.

the university was **Columbia** A description of the important work underway at Columbia appears in Rhodes, *The Making of the Atomic Bomb,* 268–71.

Campbell would later visit the cyclotron JWC, as "Arthur McCann," letter to *ASF,* March 1940, 160–62.

⁹⁷ *"Mr. Campbell, how can you bear not to write?"* Asimov, *Asimov on Science Fiction,* 194.

"When I give an idea to a writer" Ibid.

"That was the way he saw us all" Ibid.

*"***Astounding** *will find and develop"* JWC, In Times to Come, *ASF,* September 1939, 32.

CHAPTER 5: THE ANALYTICAL LABORATORY (1938–1940)

⁹⁹ *"[Science fiction] writers"* Knight, *The Futurians,* 240.

"fairly interesting" Ibid., 30.

¹⁰⁰ *"double carfare"* Asimov, *In Memory Yet Green,* 208.

"That's all right" Asimov to Frederik Pohl, September 15, 1938. Correspondence between Pohl and Asimov can be found in the Frederik Pohl papers, Special Collections Research Center, Syracuse University, Box 1.

Science fiction fandom The most comprehensive account of this period appears in Moskowitz, *The Immortal Storm,* on which much of the following material is based.

"any fan from the field" Moskowitz, *The Immortal Storm,* 126.

¹⁰¹ *"Better than I expected"* Ibid., 146.

¹⁰² *lunch with Sykora and Wollheim* Ibid., 175–76.

"I intend to write for [the magazine]" Knight, *The Futurians,* 31.

¹⁰⁴ *opposed "like hell"* Ibid., 33.

Welles's intrusion on his turf "So far as sponsoring that *War of Worlds* thing—I'm damn glad we didn't! The thing is gonna cost CBS money, what with suits etc., and we're better off without." JWC to Robert Swisher, November 8, 1938. He later wrote that he felt that the incident only showed "a need for wider appreciation of science fiction." JWC, "A Variety of Things," *ASF*, January 1939, 6.

104 *picking out "The Internationale"* Knight, *The Futurians*, 35.

he actually smoked two cigarettes Ibid., 36.

ejected for talking too loudly Ibid., 32.

"Have I been blackballed out?" Asimov to Frederik Pohl, December 19, 1938.

"I got very panicky" Knight, *The Futurians*, 32.

"Now you see the world's worst" L. Sprague de Camp, "Isaac and I," *Isaac Asimov's Science Fiction*, November 1992, 5.

"in accordance with certain suggestions" Frederik Pohl to Asimov, February 3, 1939.

"Campbell is a good friend of mine" Asimov to Frederik Pohl, February 6, 1939.

"Campbell once remarked to me" Frederik Pohl to Asimov, February 7, 1939.

"Through your acquaintance with Campbell" Frederik Pohl to Asimov, March 20, 1939.

105 *deny knowing anything about Marx* Asimov, "Asimov's Guide to Asimov," in Olander and Greenberg, *Isaac Asimov*, 203.

"You call yourself a communist" Frederik Pohl to Asimov, March 20, 1939.

he might not need the money Asimov to Frederik Pohl, March 31, 1939.

Finally, he agreed Asimov, *In Memory Yet Green*, 237.

"much against her will" JWC to Robert Swisher, March 18, 1939.

Pohl had also written to complain Frederik Pohl to JWC, June 23, 1938. Correspondence between Pohl and JWC can be found in the Frederik Pohl papers, Special Collections Research Center, Syracuse University, Box 2.

"Maybe he didn't like the story?" JWC to Robert Swisher, June 21, 1938.

he occasionally tossed a coin Warner, *All Our Yesterdays*, 20.

106 *the first World Science Fiction Convention* The following account is based primarily on Moskowitz, *The Immortal Storm*, 213–24, and Asimov, *In Memory Yet Green*, 243–45.

Forrest J Ackerman Ackerman preferred to omit the period after his middle initial.

freshly shaved and wearing a new suit Asimov, *Asimov on Science Fiction*, 230.

"ruthless scoundrels" Moskowitz, *The Immortal Storm*, 215.

"I thought you just stated" Ibid., 216–17.

107 *"But the core of the group"* Ibid., 217.

107   *"No one tried to stop me"* Asimov, *In Memory Yet Green*, 244.
Williamson, whom he had met Williamson, *Wonder's Child*, 117.
Williamson came out to see them Ibid., 118.
Campbell tried to persuade Sykora Rich, *C.M. Kornbluth*, 387.

108   *Campbell delivered a talk* Moskowitz, *The Immortal Storm*, 220–21.
"How about Asimov?" Asimov, *In Memory Yet Green*, 245.
"the worst science fiction writer unlynched" Ibid.

109   *"I wanted to make sure he remembered me"* Knight, *The Futurians*, 116n.
the only game fit for adults Patterson, *Learning Curve*, 194.

110   *"a grisly horror"* RAH to Robert Bloch, March 18, 1949, quoted in Patterson, *Learning Curve*, 198.
"The map is not the territory" The term first appeared in Korzybski's paper "A Non-Aristotelian System and its Necessity for Rigor in Mathematics and Physics," December 28, 1931. RAH and Leslyn met Korzybski in 1939. Patterson, *Learning Curve*, 236.

111   *"for plot twists and climaxes"* Leslyn (Heinlein) Mocabee to Frederik Pohl, May 8, 1953. Frederik Pohl papers, Syracuse University.

112   *"I hope you won't need it"* RAH to JWC, April 10, 1939.
"How long has this racket been going on?" Patterson, *Learning Curve*, 231.
"I am a retired naval officer" RAH to JWC, May 1, 1939.
"I think if you would amputate" JWC to RAH, May 16, 1939.
"Your work is good" JWC to RAH, May 31, 1939.

113   *the novel* **Babbitt** Hutchisson, *The Rise of Sinclair Lewis*, 53.
"I work very slowly" RAH to JWC, March 2, 1940.
"the mass of small details" JWC to RAH, August 25, 1939.
"Cultural patterns change" JWC, introduction to *The Man Who Sold the Moon*, ix–x.
"one of the strongest novels" JWC, In Times to Come, *ASF*, January 1940, 29.

114   *"a definitely warmish subject"* JWC to RAH, August 25, 1939.
"my pet" RAH to JWC, August 29, 1939.
he bought it as an experiment JWC to RAH, September 11, 1939.
he also wrote Heinlein directly In one of Asimov's early letters, now lost, he joked that God had all the good press agents, while Satan "wasn't getting a fair shake," which RAH credited decades later as the inspiration for his novel *Job: A Comedy of Justice*. RAH to Asimov, August 8, 1984.
the apparently unused structures of the brain RAH to JWC, December 1, 1939. The item appeared in *Unknown*, April 1939, 124.
"It's good. It should be great" JWC to RAH, December 6, 1939.

115   *irritated by the final version of "Requiem"* Leslyn Heinlein to JWC, January 27, 1941.

115   *"They'll nearly all go mad"* JWC to RAH, January 15, 1940.

"I hope that both Don A. Stuart" RAH to JWC, January 20, 1940.

"Heinlein taught me human beings" Weller, *The Bradbury Chronicles,* 99.

"The trouble with Bob Heinlein" Pohl, *The Way the Future Was,* 87.

he would reschedule his vacation JWC to RAH, March 5, 1940.

116   *Doña's mother had been sick* JWC to Robert Swisher, June 12, 1940.

"Heinlein puts on a bit of Annapolis manners" Ibid.

"The gag was that our mad scientist" RAH to JWC, November 2, 1940.

Irving Langmuir Strand, *The Brothers Vonnegut,* 160.

117   *"you and John are of the small group"* RAH to Doña Campbell, "Sunday morning," 1940.

"If you write to L. Ron Hubbard" RAH to JWC, May 4, 1940.

"a red-headed boy . . . He is our kind of people" RAH to John Arwine, January 1, 1945.

"No, I know you" Widder, *Master Storyteller,* 33.

118   *the departure of a college crush* Asimov, *In Memory Yet Green,* 267.

"Our personal contact" Doña Campbell to RAH, December 13, 1941.

Doña's water broke Doña Campbell to RAH, September 11, 1940.

Maple Hill Farms . . . in Scotch Plains, New Jersey Their mailing address was 2065 Hill Top Road, Westfield, New Jersey. As JWC explained to RAH in a letter dated July 25, 1940: "Legally, we live in the township of Scotch Plains, and must legally so state our address. However . . . all mail has to be addressed to Westfield."

"My personality is too cold" JWC to RAH and Leslyn Heinlein, January 8, 1942.

119   *"scaring the living daylights out of her"* Doña Campbell to RAH, September 11, 1940.

an operation for a uterine cyst JWC to Robert and Frances Swisher, September 9, 1939.

"That ought to make her a patroness" RAH to JWC, September 14, 1940.

Leslyn could be a fairy godmother JWC to RAH, September 16, 1940.

"D'ja mean it?" JWC to RAH, October 29, 1940.

"Among friends of our own generation" JWC to RAH, November 6, 1940.

120   *"You and Leslyn were the type of people"* JWC to RAH, November 23, 1940.

a list of potential plots RAH to JWC, August 11, 1940.

a generation starship JWC to RAH, September 20, 1940.

"bad clear through" Patterson, *Learning Curve,* 581n.

121   *"The Elder Gods"* Arthur J. Burks based the novel on a detailed synopsis

from JWC, but the submission was unusable. After Burks threatened to sue for payment, JWC rewrote it, allowing the author to keep most of the money. JWC to Robert Swisher, March 18, 1939 and April 18, 1939. JWC's outline can be found in the John W. Campbell compositions, Houghton Library, Harvard University, folder "The Elder Gods."

121 *all sides of his personality* "For *Astounding,* I want stories which are good and logical and possible. For *Unknown,* I want stories which are good and logical." JWC, quoted in Panshin, *The World Beyond the Hill,* 294.

"It represented, in a way" JWC to Robert Swisher, February 28, 1938.

if they found themselves in ancient Rome JWC to Robert Swisher, July 28, 1938.

as an editorial John W. Campbell compositions, Houghton Library, Harvard University, folder "Untitled."

122 *"You're not at all what I pictured"* Del Rey, *Early Del Rey,* 147.

on a dare from his girlfriend Ibid., 6.

the Neanderthals had died of heartbreak Ibid., 27.

paid him to print enlargements JWC to Robert Swisher, March 3, 1941.

"not merely as an idea" Lester del Rey, in *Locus,* July 12, 1971, 2.

"A human being should be able to change a diaper" RAH, "Intermission: Excerpts from the Notebooks of Lazarus Long," in *Time Enough for Love.*

123 *"to get some superman stories"* JWC to Clifford Simak, June 18, 1953.

standing up at a newsstand Panshin, *The World Beyond the Hill,* 455.

a superman was only believable JWC to Clifford Simak, June 18, 1953.

"Fans are slans" Warner, *All Our Yesterdays,* 42.

"No matter what may come after" Leigh Brackett, in *Locus,* July 22, 1971.

"They weren't very good stories" Leigh Brackett, interview with Dave Truesdale and Paul McGuire III, April 1976, https://www.tangenton line.com/interviews-columnsmenu-166/1270-classic-leigh-brackett-a -edmond-hamilton-interview (accessed December 2017).

"The 'Leigh' in 'Leigh Brackett'" JWC, Brass Tacks, *ASF,* July 1940, 155.

124 *"rather viciously"* Leigh Brackett, interview with Dave Truesdale and Paul McGuire III, April 1976, https://www.tangentonline.com /interviews-columnsmenu-166/1270-classic-leigh-brackett-a-edmond -hamilton-interview (accessed December 2017).

"Write me a story about a creature" Sturgeon, introduction to *Roadside Picnic.* In some versions, the statement includes "or *better* than a man," which the editor—who disliked superior aliens—was unlikely to have said.

"my best friend and my worst enemy" Theodore Sturgeon, interviewed in Platt, *Dream Makers Volume II,* 175.

124 *"I owe him more"* Theodore Sturgeon, at the panel "The Man John W. Campbell," Conclave III, Romulus, MI, November 4, 1978. Recording courtesy of the SFOHA Archives.

125 *in Paris when it fell* JWC to Robert Swisher, September 30, 1940.

remainders in England Moskowitz, *Seekers of Tomorrow*, 125.

the circulation of Astounding *declined* JWC to Robert Swisher, March 6, 1940.

"science fiction addicts" JWC, "Wanted: A Chronoscope," *ASF,* August 1940, 6.

"The battle of robots is on" Ibid.

"May we hope that attempts" JWC, In Times to Come, *ASF,* November 1939, 78.

CHAPTER 6: IN TIMES TO COME (1939–1941)

127 *"In 1939 and 1940"* RAH to JWC, December 21, 1941.

the largest check JWC to LRH, March 21, 1939.

128 *"If you have the interest"* JWC to LRH, June 26, 1939.

poker . . . voodoo drumming LRH, in a letter dated March 10, 1940, reprinted in LRH, *Literary Correspondence*, 136–37.

Sir Richard Francis Burton In *Slaves of Sleep* (*Unknown*, July 1939) LRH advises the reader to seek out Burton's translation of *The Arabian Nights* in the New York Public Library, while *The Ghoul* (*Unknown*, August 1939) takes place at the fictional Hotel Burton.

"I'm convinced that you do like fantasy" JWC to LRH, January 23, 1939.

129 *"When he starts to outline a story"* LRH, "How to Drive a Writer Crazy," reprinted in LRH, *Writer: The Shaping of Popular Fiction*, 101–3.

invited Hubbard to Thanksgiving JWC to Robert Swisher, November 11, 1939.

"kept things smooth" LRH, "An Introduction to Science Fiction," reprinted in LRH, *Writer: The Shaping of Popular Fiction*, 151.

make him bray with laughter Doña Campbell to Frances Swisher, December 14, 1939.

"a man who officiates" LRH, in a letter dated September 14, 1939, reprinted in LRH, *Literary Correspondence*, 123.

Final Blackout The story inspired a debate in Brass Tacks over its allegedly militaristic or fascistic themes, particularly from readers who were sympathetic toward communism. Carter, *The Creation of Tomorrow*, 237–40.

conceived over grilled steaks LRH, *Writer: The Shaping of Popular Fiction*, 114.

"landmark novel in my life" Widder, *Master Storyteller*, 84.

129 *privately recorded it as a play* Forrest J Ackerman, review of *Fear* and *Typewriter in the Sky, ASF,* August 1951, 143.

130 *"I wish to offer my services"* Miller, *Bare-Faced Messiah,* 87.
awakened one night by screaming Corydon, *Messiah or Madman?,* 291, and Wright, *Going Clear,* 84.
"five abortions" LRH, "Affirmations."

131 *"a deckhand"* LRH, *Master Mariner,* 27.
"I anchored and lashed up" Ibid., 48.
a swimming brown bear LRH, "It Bears Telling," reprinted in LRH, *Adventurer/Explorer,* 105–9.
"a slight case of shipwreck" JWC, Of Things Beyond, *Unknown,* December 1940, 5.
"Ron, I think, is in for some kidding" JWC to Robert Swisher, January 7, 1941.
"Cap'n, do you like to wrassle with bears?" LRH, "It Bears Telling," reprinted in LRH, *Adventurer/Explorer,* 105.
a satirical song in his honor JWC to RAH, February 19, 1941.
a flamboyant character Pohl, *The Way the Future Was,* 119.

132 *"I waited on the stairway with a gun"* Miller, *Bare-Faced Messiah,* 173.
"This will introduce" Ibid., 97.
"In personal relationships" Atack, *A Piece of Blue Sky,* 72.
"He was very beautiful" Doña Campbell to RAH, November 9, 1941.

133 *"There are about five consistent"* JWC to RAH, February 13, 1941.
"Asimov is one of those authors" JWC, Brass Tacks, *ASF,* November 1940, 115.
"work their way up" JWC, "Invitation," *ASF,* February 1941, 6.

134 *his mother grew fond of Pohl* "Her affection for you has lately passed all bounds (and it was big enough as it was)." Asimov to Frederik Pohl, November 29, 1939.
"You don't look at all like your stories" Asimov, *In Memory Yet Green,* 262.
"I can detect that fiendish look" Asimov, letter to *ASF,* April 1940, 159.
"Do you think, Asimov" Asimov, *Asimov on Science Fiction,* 196.
Campbell had inserted a new speech Patrouch, *The Science Fiction of Isaac Asimov,* 16.

135 *"Robert Heinlein . . . presents a civilization"* JWC, "It Isn't a Science—Yet!", *ASF,* February 1940, 164.
recurrent panic attacks "I understand psychologists and psychiatrists are supposed to report any consultations if the patient shows up at the Army and Navy lists. Mine probably wouldn't, but if he did, I'd be out rather quickly probably. I suspect the Navy Medical doesn't like 'Fear Syndrome' on the records." JWC to RAH, July 21, 1942.

135 *"The* Astounding Science Fiction *of the past year"* Lynn Bridges, letter to *ASF,* November 1940, 115–16.

"Psychology could improve a lot" JWC, Brass Tacks, *ASF,* November 1940, 115.

136 *"Remember, I want to see that story"* Asimov, *In Memory Yet Green,* 281.

"Asimov, when you have trouble" Ibid.

Campbell had ruthlessly cut John W. Campbell compositions, Houghton Library, Harvard University, folders "Dark," "Dead Language," and "Pandora."

inspired by Campbell's Penton and Blake Asimov, *Before the Golden Age,* 795.

"Look, Asimov, in working this out" Asimov, *In Memory Yet Green,* 286.

137 *"No, Asimov, I picked them out of your stories"* Ibid., 286–87.

"the basic desires of a small child" JWC to Isa D. Reed, July 2, 1951.

"a good many of the world's ethical systems" Asimov, "Evidence," *ASF,* September 1946, 121–40.

fewer Hitlers and more Einsteins Asimov, letter to *ASF,* January 1941, 158–59.

"Psychology isn't an exact science" JWC, Brass Tacks, *ASF,* January 1941, 158.

"What do you think would happen" Asimov, *In Memory Yet Green,* 295.

138 *who never read the essay himself* Asimov, *The Early Asimov,* 337.

"I never had anything write itself so easily" Asimov, *In Memory Yet Green,* 297.

"a lean and hungry" JWC to Jay Kay Klein, May 6, 1971.

"From what you told me" Asimov, *In Memory Yet Green,* 297n.

the greatest science fiction story It was ranked first by the Science Fiction Writers of America in Silverberg, *The Science Fiction Hall of Fame Volume One, 1929–1964.* In a poll by *Locus* in 2012, it fell to second, behind Daniel Keyes's "Flowers for Algernon." http://www.locusmag.com/2012/AllCenturyPollsResults.html (accessed December 2017).

139 *the comic opera* Iolanthe Asimov's description matches an illustration—by W. S. Gilbert himself—on page 272 of *Plays and Poems of W. S. Gilbert* (New York: Random House, 1934), which may have been the book that he was carrying that day.

"He felt in our discussion" Freedman, *Conversations with Isaac Asimov,* 40.

theories of history L. Sprague de Camp, "The Science of Whithering," *ASF,* July and August 1940.

139 *"I'm interested in theories"* Jack Williamson to JWC, April 16, 1941. Jack Williamson papers, Eastern New Mexico University.

"a scientific Shangri-La" Jack Williamson, "Backlash," *ASF,* August 1941, 150.

"politicotechnic theories" Jack Williamson, "Breakdown," *ASF,* January 1942, 21.

140 *"That's too large a theme"* Asimov, *In Memory Yet Green,* 311.

"You may need the second one later on" Panshin, *The World Beyond the Hill,* 535.

"I want that Foundation story" Asimov, *In Memory Yet Green,* 318.

141 *"Why? Do you think you would be any safer"* Ibid., 300.

"But Professor Urey" Ibid., 300–301.

Campbell argued about it Lester del Rey, in *Locus,* July 12, 1971, 3.

142 *Hitler's defeat was inevitable* Freedman, *Conversations With Isaac Asimov,* 46.

"Because I'm a Jew" L. Sprague de Camp, "Isaac and I," *Isaac Asimov's Science Fiction,* November 1992, 5.

"It might be of very real interest" JWC, "History to Come," *ASF,* May 1941, 6.

"Van Vogt probably could do a better job" RAH to JWC, September 27, 1940.

143 *a new, superior species* JWC to RAH, "Monday," circa December 15, 1940.

"Too reminiscent of Slan" RAH to JWC, December 17, 1940.

"The story is weak" JWC to RAH, December 27, 1940.

"Can any solution" JWC, note on "Solution Unsatisfactory," *ASF,* May 1941, 86.

Heinlein sent in the first section for notes RAH to JWC, March 5, 1941.

"cotton candy" RAH to JWC, October 4, 1941.

144 *"If you someday find it necessary"* RAH to JWC, November 2, 1940.

"To be classed" RAH to JWC, February 19, 1941.

145 *"Mrs. Heinlein and I"* James, "Regarding Leslyn," 22.

"The basic trouble" JWC to RAH, August 21, 1941.

"unofficial scout" RAH to JWC, August 27, 1941.

"We were delighted to see Asimov" RAH to JWC, August 27, 1941.

"Asimov is one of my personal finds" JWC to RAH, September 3, 1941.

"You are apparently under the impression" RAH to JWC, September 6, 1941.

146 *"pressure and uncertainty"* JWC to RAH, September 13, 1941.

"If you retire abruptly" JWC to RAH, September 17, 1941.

147 *"What you contributed to science fiction"* JWC to RAH, October 27, 1941.

147 *stories that felt like they could appear* Pohl, *The Way the Future Was*, 87–88.

Campbell proposed that he come out Patterson, *Learning Curve*, 292.

"If the Japanese start a war" RAH to T. B. Buell, October 4, 1973, quoted in Patterson, *Learning Curve*, 292.

"I would like to have been a synthesist" RAH to JWC and Doña Campbell, December 21, 1941.

148 *as if they had written it together* "As you may recall from *Beyond the Horizon* [*sic*], we don't share your own gloomy view." Leslyn Heinlein to Forrest J Ackerman, 1944, quoted in James, "Regarding Leslyn," 25.

"tall stories . . . Like that yarn about the grandfather clock" JWC, In Times to Come, *ASF*, March 1942, 76.

he asked Heinlein to spread the word JWC to RAH, November 24, 1941.

PART III: THE INVADERS (1941–1945)

149 *"In a short war"* JWC, "Invention," *ASF*, January 1941, 6.

CHAPTER 7: A COLD FURY (1941–1944)

151 *"You've told me that I was your best writer"* RAH to JWC, January 4, 1942.

When the telephone rang JWC to RAH and Leslyn Heinlein, December 8, 1941.

"I'm not kidding" Ibid.

"gloomy as hell" Ibid.

152 *"But do, both of you"* Doña Campbell to RAH and Leslyn Heinlein, December 7, 1941.

"Pearl Harbor isn't a point on a floor game" RAH to JWC, January 4, 1942.

"a cold fury" RAH to JWC, December 9, 1941.

"somewhere in the Pacific" JWC, In Times to Come, *ASF*, March 1942, 76.

153 *Ray Bradbury joked* Virginia Heinlein to William H. Patterson, Jr., August 15, 1999. A rather different account appears in Weller, *The Bradbury Chronicles*, 114–15.

a "bum" at a cigar store LRH, "Miracles in Dianetics," delivered on December 12, 1951.

the commander of the USS **Astoria** JWC to Robert Swisher, November 1939, and Doña Campbell to RAH, December 13, 1941.

"He'll probably turn up in Greenland" Doña Campbell to RAH, December 13, 1941.

153 *"none too enthusiastically"* Asimov, *In Memory Yet Green*, 323.
he was so furious with the Japanese JWC to RAH, December 17, 1941.
Campbell prepared a bomb shelter Ibid.
outside plant engineer JWC to Robert Swisher, December 12, 1941. John W. Campbell, Sr., and Linus E. Kittredge authored the article "War Emergency Stocks in the Bell System," *Bell Telephone Magazine*, September 1943, 178–87.
His sister Laura JWC to Robert Swisher, December 12, 1941.

154 *a Red Cross class for women* Doña Campbell to RAH, January 8, 1942.
"My own status is somewhat confusing" JWC to RAH, December 17, 1941.
"cannon fodder . . . I suppose it has already occurred" RAH to JWC, December 21, 1941.
"Of course, it would be kinda rough" Ibid.

155 *"I doubt [Doña would] get the job"* JWC to RAH, December 24, 1941.
"Ha! Such is the power of love" Doña Campbell, marginal note on letter from JWC to RAH, December 24, 1941.
the resident expert at the office JWC to RAH, January 8, 1942.
"the British once shot an admiral" JWC to RAH, December 17, 1941.
"perilously close to giving aid" RAH to JWC, December 21, 1941.
The editor missed the hint JWC to RAH, December 24, 1941.
"to stir you up off your fat fanny" RAH to JWC, January 4, 1942.

156 *"Don't you realize"* Leslyn Heinlein to JWC, January 4, 1942.
"a clumsy oaf" JWC to RAH, January 8, 1942.

157 *the emotional catharsis* RAH to JWC, January 17, 1942.
"Incidentally, how would you like" Buddy Scoles to RAH, January 14, 1942, quoted in Patterson, *Learning Curve*, 299.
"You are likely to have quite a lot" RAH to JWC, January 17, 1942.
"most ardently . . . The greatest disturbance" JWC to RAH, January 22, 1942.
"My concern lay solely" Doña Campbell to RAH, January 23, 1942.

158 *the National Defense Research Committee* JWC to RAH, May 13, 1942.
Heinlein was in town Ibid.
"Very far" Asimov, *In Memory Yet Green*, 337.
"Why didn't you call?" Ibid., 338.

159 *"It's a Coke"* Ibid., 338.
"one ounce of blended rye" Catherine de Camp, "An Unwritten Letter to Our Dear Friend Isaac Asimov," *Asimov's Science Fiction*, November 1992, 8.
"No wonder Isaac doesn't drink" Asimov, *In Memory Yet Green*, 338.
some nude photos Asimov later came to believe that these images were of

L. Sprague de Camp's wife, Catherine. *In Memory Yet Green*, 503. However, de Camp stated elsewhere that she only met the Heinleins after their move to Philadelphia. Catherine de Camp, foreword to Gifford, *Robert A. Heinlein: A Reader's Companion*, vi.

159 *"[Philinda] started making eyes at Bob"* JWC to Robert Swisher, April 14, 1942.

"They took us to shows" JWC to Robert Swisher, May 8, 1942.

160 *"L. Ron Hubbard's in town"* JWC to RAH, May 13, 1942.

"He collected a piece of Jap bomb" Ibid.

the **Don Isidro** A detailed account of this incident appears in the revised edition of Chris Owen's *Ron the War Hero*, which the author has reviewed in manuscript.

"By assuming unauthorized authority" Memorandum from US Naval Attaché to Australia to Commandant, Twelfth Naval District, February 14, 1942.

161 *"Frankly, I'm scared stiff"* Asimov to Frederik Pohl, May 13, 1942.

"My job is really a reasonable facsimile" Asimov to Frederik Pohl, May 29, 1942.

"Let's get together" Asimov, *In Memory Yet Green*, 329.

"Naturally with the dance" Asimov to Frederik Pohl, July 24, 1941.

162 *"a Russian chemist with a mustache"* Asimov, *In Memory Yet Green*, 330.

"I don't want to spoil things" Ibid., 331.

"Oh my, you are *smart"* Ibid., 336.

163 *he accidentally forced an evacuation* Wysocki, *An Astounding War*, 175.

164 *"Remember, Gittel"* Asimov, *I. Asimov*, 111.

"I am greatly relieved" Asimov, *Yours, Isaac Asimov*, 204.

165 *"What's this I hear about"* Asimov, *In Memory Yet Green*, 372.

"It was no great hardship" Ibid., 372.

166 *"I don't think they hit it off"* Ibid., 375.

He liked to snap their bras Ibid., 430.

"attractive and pleasingly quiet" Frederik Pohl to Asimov, July 13, 1942.

"For Christ's sake, Isaac" Frederik Pohl to Asimov, January 2, 1942.

"I don't know with what authority" Asimov to Frederik Pohl, January 5, 1942.

167 *"Try as I may"* Gertrude Asimov to Frederik Pohl, circa January 1942.

"You're lucky they weren't real" Joel Charles to RAH, April 5, 1988, quoted in Patterson, *Learning Curve*, 306.

168 *"I hate my job"* RAH to JWC, July 18, 1942.

"the perfect private secretary" Ibid.

"clip those beetling brows" Patterson, *Learning Curve*, 312.

168 *"It must have irked Heinlein"* De Camp, *Time and Chance,* 189.

"*A war requires subordination*" RAH to JWC, July 18, 1942.

"as the type of men wanted for real research" JWC to Robert Swisher, March 30, 1942.

169 *He even reached out to del Rey* Del Rey, *Early Del Rey,* 340.

"fear syndrome" JWC to RAH, July 21, 1942.

"Truthfully, we aren't shorthanded" RAH to JWC, July 18, 1942.

170 *"working my heart out"* RAH to G. Harry Stine, July 27, 1954. Virginia Heinlein later wrote in the essay "Science Fiction and John W. Campbell, Jr.": "It is my private opinion that John's lack of wartime service to his country did as much to destroy the friendship as anything which happened between the two men." RAH Archives, UC Santa Cruz.

"with poor grace" Asimov, *In Memory Yet Green,* 392.

171 *"Don't do that"* Ibid., 393.

"Well, then, suppose I figure out" Ibid.

172 *"Just doing everything she could"* Forrest J Ackerman, interview with Robert James, June 9, 2000, quoted in Patterson, *Learning Curve,* 313.

the same uniforms as the female workers Leslyn Heinlein, "Each Employee His Own Personnel Manager," reprinted in James, "Regarding Leslyn," 32.

"shapfu" JWC to RAH, January 1, 1943.

"in a location where I could not see" RAH to E. J. "Ted" Carnell, December 31, 1943, quoted in Patterson, *Learning Curve,* 319.

"having your asshole cut out" RAH to John Arwine, January 8, 1944, quoted in Patterson, *Learning Curve,* 319.

"no rectum to speak of" RAH to Horace Gold, October 27, 1952, quoted in Patterson, *Learning Curve,* 321.

to live with the Campbells RAH to JWC, October 23, 1944.

173 *"I'm simply going to be bored"* RAH to John Arwine, January 8, 1944, quoted in Patterson, *Learning Curve,* 324.

"Hubbard has been an adventurer" JWC, In Times to Come, *ASF,* November 1942, 42.

"I imagine that the thing" JWC to RAH, August 11, 1942.

CHAPTER 8: THE WAR OF INVENTION (1942–1944)

175 *"The position of America"* JWC, In Times to Come, *ASF,* February 1942, 35.

"Since reporting to this activity" Quoted in Owen, "Ron the 'War Hero.'"

"[Hubbard's] own feeling" JWC to RAH, May 19, 1942.

176 *"They've kidnapped him into a desk job"* JWC to Robert Swisher, "Friday," circa 1942.

176 *"the peoples, language, and customs"* Miller, *Bare-Faced Messiah*, 101.
trips to Los Angeles C. L. Moore to RAH, July 2, 1942, quoted in Patterson, *Learning Curve*, 308.
"He's back on sea duty" JWC to RAH, June 25, 1942.
"Hubbard has gone to collect" Doña Campbell to RAH, July 2, 1942.
"their braid dirty" Wright, *Going Clear*, 43.
a science fiction club in Cambridge Warner, *All Our Yesterdays*, 213. In a letter about this visit, JWC offered a rare contemporary description of Polly, whom he and Doña met for the first time in Boston: "She is fully as powerful and arresting a major personality as Ron himself. . . . She can talk as steadily and as fascinatingly, as intelligently as Ron. . . . She's the only caliber of person that could offer Ron companionship, but she's also so powerful a personality that the pair couldn't stay close to each other for long stretches." JWC to Anthony Boucher, October 14, 1942. William Anthony Parker White papers, Indiana University Bloomington.
177 *"not temperamentally suited"* Quoted in Owen, "Ron the 'War Hero.'"
"I have a feeling" JWC to Robert Swisher, October 21, 1942.
urinating blood Atack, *A Piece of Blue Sky*, 80.
"While training in Miami" LRH, "Affirmations."
"Boy was I able to catch up" Atack, *A Piece of Blue Sky*, 79.
he had graduated at the top of his class JWC to RAH, January 6, 1943.
"I took to dosing myself" LRH, "Affirmations."
178 *"The ship, sleepy and skeptical"* LRH, "An Account of the Action Off Cape Lookout," https://www.cs.cmu.edu/~dst/Cowen/warhero/battle.htm (accessed December 2017).
"every man on the bridge" Ibid.
179 *"two Jap subs without credit"* LRH, "Affirmations."
"a very arduous day" Quoted in Owen, "Ron the 'War Hero.'"
"At no time was I aware" Ibid.
His men lied to protect him "My crew lied for me at the Court of Inquiry." LRH, "Affirmations."
"lacking in the essential qualities" Quoted in Owen, "Ron the 'War Hero.'"
he had invented them to avoid punishment LRH, "Affirmations."
180 *"My salvation is to let this roll over me"* Miller, *Bare-Faced Messiah*, 110.
"I do not know whether" JWC, In Times to Come, *ASF*, February 1942, 35.
"That leaves de Camp" JWC to Jack Williamson, December 9, 1941, quoted in Williamson, *Wonder's Child*, 136.
a metalworker at McDonnell Aircraft Moskowitz, *Seekers of Tomorrow*, 183.
a hotel in Jamaica Davis, "The Work of Theodore Sturgeon," 24.

180 *"A. E. van Vogt is a Canadian"* JWC, In Times to Come, *ASF,* February 1942, 35.

"I would like to contract you" Van Vogt, *Reflections of A. E. van Vogt,* 65.

181 *"I'm genuinely trying to divert the stream"* JWC to A. E. van Vogt, June 12, 1942.

"For the past several months" JWC, In Times to Come, *ASF,* August 1942, 98.

Ace Magazines Knight, *The Futurians,* 132.

"Well, I think I'd better go, Fred" Ibid., 134.

Rocket to the Morgue The book included thinly veiled portraits of RAH, LRH, and Jack Williamson. Boucher had never met LRH, but based the portrayal on descriptions by others. JWC to Robert Swisher, October 21, 1942.

182 *their mutual friend H. P. Lovecraft* Moskowitz, *Seekers of Tomorrow,* 311.

"He's a homely little squirt" JWC to Robert Swisher, "Friday," circa 1942.

on the advice of the editor Panshin, *The World Beyond the Hill,* 589.

jokingly threatened to kill him Eller, *Becoming Ray Bradbury,* 70.

"mastered the mechanics of writing" Ibid., 72.

Campbell passed anyway "Chrysalis" was later published in *Amazing Stories,* July 1946.

183 *first look at such future landmarks* Moskowitz, *Seekers of Tomorrow,* 365.

wartime rationing JWC to RAH, January 6, 1943.

it would exceed the sales of **Astounding** JWC to Robert Swisher, April 4, 1939.

the same number of display issues JWC to A. E. van Vogt, April 4, 1943.

its print run would be reduced JWC, "—In Small Boxes," *Unknown Worlds,* October 1943, 6.

"for the duration" Asimov, *In Memory Yet Green,* 390.

"I interpret that as forever" Ibid., 390. As a result of the magazine's end, Asimov's "Author! Author!" wouldn't appear for years, and a sale by Bradbury, "The Emissary," ended up in limbo as well. JWC to Ray Bradbury, August 2, 1951.

184 *"The more we write about ingenious ruses"* Anthony Boucher, letter to *ASF,* June 1943, 162.

"I'm doing research work" JWC, "Too Good at Guessing," *ASF,* April 1942, 6.

"The consequence is that" Ibid.

184 *a terrible enemy in a conflict* JWC, "Invention," *ASF,* January 1941, 5–6.
"We have the highest potential" JWC, "Science-Fiction and War," *ASF,*
March 1942, 6.

185 *"The whole setup down there"* JWC to Robert Swisher, March 30,
1942.
"crash the gate" JWC to A. E. van Vogt, August 24, 1942.
"Among the writers and readers" Buddy Scoles to RAH, January 14,
1942, quoted in Wysocki, *An Astounding War,* 188.

186 *"I'll have to try helping"* JWC to RAH, July 21, 1942.
"problems of the Navy" JWC to RAH, October 9, 1942.
"gotten Navy authorization" JWC to Leslyn Heinlein, November 20,
1942.
The issue was censorship JWC to RAH, October 12, 1943.
"I'm a nuclear physicist, you know" Knight, *In Search of Wonder,* 18.
"stymied . . . But I'm running" JWC, In Times to Come, *ASF,* November
1942, 42.

187 *A pressure suit project* Wysocki, *An Astounding War,* 170–71.
"a very careful, long, and elaborate letter" Ibid., 191.
to weaken wing struts and disable boilers JWC to RAH, "Friday," circa
June 1942.
the "diabolic" notion JWC to RAH, February 2, 1943.
his own proposals JWC submitted these proposals, as well as others, to
RAH in letters dated "Friday," circa June 1942; July 9, 1942; August 11,
1942; February 2, 1943; and February 10, 1944. RAH later told him that
his best idea—to use AC motors as a power source for planes—was "already on the fire," adding encouragingly: "You were cooking with gas on
that one, John." RAH to JWC, August 2, 1945.
None were deemed practical JWC briefly became excited by another avenue of investigation. Felix Ehrenhaft, an Austrian physicist, announced
that he had discovered particles called "magnetic monopoles," which
could be used to develop generators, motors, and other machines analo-
gous to those based on electricity. JWC called it a greater discovery than
uranium fission—but the results were never duplicated. JWC, "Super-
Conservative," *ASF,* April 1944, 5–6, and "Beachhead for Science," *ASF,*
May 1944, 103–17.

188 *"There might be a story in this thought"* Berger, "The Astounding Investigation," 132, and Silverberg, "Reflections: The Cleve Cartmill Affair: One,"
4. JWC's assertion that uranium had been separated in "quantities measured
in pounds" was premature—Oak Ridge wouldn't possess such amounts until around the autumn of 1944. Berger, *The Magic That Works,* 69.

189 *"prophecy so close to home"* Berger, "The Astounding Investigation,"
132.

189 *"Censorship won't give any trouble"* Ibid.
"mediocre fantasy" M. Eneman, letter to *ASF,* July 1944, 151.
he might conceivably have been part of the effort "Practically all the nuclear physicists graduated in the United States since [1941] have graduated directly into the Manhattan Project." JWC, "Spanish Atoms," *ASF,* September 1946, 5.
190 *the reaction at Los Alamos was "astonishment"* Benford, "A Scientist's Notebook: The Science Fiction Century," 133.
He was a security officer "[Edward] Teller recalled a security officer who took a decided interest, making notes, saying little." Ibid., 134.

CHAPTER 9: FROM "DEADLINE" TO HIROSHIMA (1944–1945)

191 *"Atomic physics . . . could end the war in a day"* JWC, "Noncommunication Radio," *ASF,* August 1943, 7.
192 *the most detailed description* JWC to Jane Rice, April 23, 1956.
sixteen pounds of uranium For a detailed critique of the design of the bomb in "Deadline," see Wysocki, *An Astounding War,* 124–26.
193 *numerous stories* Examples include "Artnan Process" by Theodore Sturgeon, "Collision Orbit" by Jack Williamson, "Lunar Landing" and "Fifth Freedom" by Lester del Rey, and "Recoil" by George O. Smith.
alarms in the Counterintelligence Corps Most of the details in the following account are drawn from Berger, "The Astounding Investigation," and Silverberg, "Reflections: The Cleve Cartmill Affair."
"no technical knowledge" Silverberg, "Reflections: The Cleve Cartmill Affair: One," 7.
"The subject of atomic disintegration" Ibid.
"technically minded intimates and associates" Berger, "The Astounding Investigation," 128.
a copy of a journal Reynolds, *The Fiction Factory,* 264.
the story line of "Solution Unsatisfactory" Ibid.
"somewhat of an egotist" Silverberg, "Reflections: The Cleve Cartmill Affair: Two," 8.
"I am Astounding Science Fiction" Berger, "The Astounding Investigation," 127.
Wernher von Braun "In wartime days, Wernher von Braun had been able to get his treasured subscription copies only by means of a false name and a neutral mail drop in Sweden." Frederik Pohl, *"Astounding:* The Campbell Years, Part 2," December 7, 2009, http://www.thewaythefutureblogs .com/2009/12/astounding-campbell-years-part-2 (accessed December 2017). JWC wrote to John L. Nanovic on November 30, 1951: "Count von Braun, who developed the V-2 in Germany, and is now at White Sands, was reading *ASF* all during the war—at considerable expense and trouble."

194 *"Four Little Ships"* Wysocki, *An Astounding War,* 88–89.

"Tell me, have you ever read" Stallings and Evans, *Murray Leinster,* 93–94.

"conducted experiments" Berger, "The Astounding Investigation," 128.

Campbell had joked that he should try it on uranium JWC to Robert Swisher, "Friday," circa 1942.

He gave the sample to Asimov Berger, "The Astounding Investigation," 128.

195 *"In the opinion of informed persons"* Silverberg, "Reflections: The Cleve Cartmill Affair: One," 7–8.

"It stinks" Berger, "The Astounding Investigation," 130.

"He took the major portion of it" Ibid., 131.

"provoke public speculation . . . such highly particularized stories" Ibid., 134.

196 *"I tremble over venturing"* Silverberg, "Reflections: The Cleve Cartmill Affair: Two," 9, and Berger, "The Astounding Investigation," 135.

"such articles coming to the attention" Berger, "The Astounding Investigation," 135.

"publish additional material" Ibid., 134.

"atom smashing" Ibid., 132.

"We got the notice of censorship" "1945 Cassandra," The Talk of the Town, *The New Yorker,* August 25, 1945, 15.

197 *"One of the boys guessed too good"* JWC to Robert Swisher, "Summer" 1944.

"The really good ideas" JWC, Brass Tacks, *ASF,* January 1945, 149–50.

A legend later developed Brake and Hook, *Different Engines,* 101.

"Every major trade journal publishing company" JWC, "Denatured Atoms," *ASF,* July 1946, 5.

the drugstore near Oak Ridge De Camp, *Science Fiction Handbook,* 70.

198 *Manuals for sonar equipment* Information about this project is drawn primarily from the Completion Report of the UCDWR, UC San Diego Special Collections, University of California Division of War Research Reports, Box 1, 144–45.

Keith Henney Smith, *Worlds of George O.,* 26.

"[We] are, as usual" JWC to RAH, June 18, 1944.

199 *Heinlein came to think that Sturgeon* RAH, introduction to Sturgeon, *Godbody,* 11.

L. Jerome Stanton JWC to RAH, June 18, 1944. Stanton was there a year later on July 28, 1945, when a small plane crashed into the Empire State Building. Harriet Teal (Stanton), e-mail to author, August 27, 2017.

a weekend every month in New Jersey Smith, *Worlds of George O.,* 4–5.

199 **Popular Science** JWC's byline appeared on twenty articles between November 1942 and May 1946.

projects in the basement These included a remote baby monitor that JWC described in an article, complete with pictures of Doña listening at the speaker while Peedee slept in her crib. JWC, "Completing Your Carrier-Current Receiver," *Popular Science*, March 1945, 192–194.

"like a delicate flower" Doña Campbell to RAH, "Tuesday," circa 1943.

Smith moved into the house Doña Campbell to RAH and Leslyn Heinlein, August 19, 1944.

as Smith was coming upstairs Smith, *Worlds of George O.*, 27.

"The trouble with John Campbell" Quoted by A. Bertram Chandler in Bangsund, *JWC: An Australian Tribute*, 7.

an entire floor RAH, introduction to Sturgeon, *Godbody*, 11.

four editors, ten physicists Completion Report of the UCDWR, UC San Diego Special Collections, University of California Division of War Research Reports, Box 1, 145.

"two big and several dozen small rooms" JWC to RAH, June 18, 1944.

"like a ping-pong ball" JWC, "Meet the Authors," *Air Trails Pictorial*, December 1946, 106.

thirteen manuals Completion Report of the UCDWR, UC San Diego Special Collections, University of California Division of War Research Reports, Box 1, 145.

200 *"Inventions Wanted"* JWC, "Inventions Wanted," *ASF*, October 1944, 5–6.

"I couldn't keep up" JWC to Robert Swisher, November 30, 1944.

"Lieutenant, your slip is showing" Patterson, *Learning Curve*, 330.

"But he's your commander in chief!" RAH to Ted Carnell, May 13, 1945, quoted in Patterson, *Learning Curve*, 333.

201 *Asimov joined the crowd as well* Asimov, *In Memory Yet Green*, 407.

"very temperamental" Miller, *Bare-Faced Messiah*, 111.

202 *Heinlein's younger brother Clare* RAH to JWC, November 22, 1944.

"He'll go in with the first wave" JWC to Robert Swisher, November 30, 1944.

to make himself attractive to women In the "Affirmations," LRH attempted to dissuade himself from this approach: "Women are not impressed by your injuries. Clear exuberant good health is your passport to their hearts."

"He was in command" JWC to Robert Swisher, November 30, 1944.

"Ron had had a busy war" RAH, introduction to Sturgeon, *Godbody*, 13.

Hubbard also slept with Leslyn Virginia Heinlein to William H. Patterson, Jr., October 1, 1999. Patterson believed that this affair took place after the war, but the reference in the "Affirmations" clearly dates it to the Philadelphia period: "During my Princeton sojourn I was very tired and harassed . . . and spent weekends with a writer friend in Philadelphia. He almost forced me to sleep with his wife."

202 *"He almost forced me to sleep with his wife"* LRH, "Affirmations."

203 *her husband and Hubbard* Patterson, *Learning Curve*, 538n.

afraid of a recurrence of his gonorrhea LRH, "Affirmations."

he was sleeping at the same time "Meanwhile I had a affair with a woman named Ferne." LRH, "Affirmations." Asimov mentions a "friend of the Heinleins named Firn [*sic*]" in *In Memory Yet Green,* 412.

None of the team's ideas were ever put into practice De Camp suggested using a keyboard to designate targets, which was too slow to work, while E. E. Smith wrote to pitch a gigantic shotgun shell or a greater presence in the air. The most creative notions came from Jenkins, who proposed detecting planes with sound or with magnesium granules that would light up the sky. Wysocki, *An Astounding War,* 218–20.

"I can see him now" RAH, introduction to Sturgeon, *Godbody,* 13. On another occasion, after his attention was drawn to a dust devil in the room, LRH said casually: "Oh, that's just Kitten." The remark gave RAH the idea for the story "Our Fair City," which he wrote up a few years later. Patterson, *Learning Curve,* 336.

the music undulating on a cathode ray screen A. Bertram Chandler, in Bangsund, *JWC: An Australian Tribute,* 6.

"He has a low, magnificently mellow baritone voice" JWC to Robert Swisher, November 30, 1944.

204 *"swarmed all over her"* Asimov, *In Memory Yet Green,* 412.

the fact that de Camp outranked him De Camp, "El-Ron of the City of Brass."

"quietly as pussycats. . . . In after years" Asimov, *In Memory Yet Green,* 413.

"I recall [Hubbard's] eyes" Williamson, *Wonder's Child,* 185.

a box of candy bars Patterson, *Learning Curve,* 339.

"a supposedly hopeless cripple" LRH, "My Philosophy," 1965, http://www.lronhubbard.org/articles-and-essays/my-philosophy.html (accessed December 2017).

205 *Mark Hubbard* RAH provided information on Mark Hubbard's actions during the war in a letter to Poul Anderson, September 6, 1961. Hubbard's service number was 2032296. Details of his death were verified through a number of sources, including the database "Pacific POW Roster," http://www.mansell.com/pow_resources/pacific_pow_roster.html (accessed December 2017).

205 *"This is how a man gets to Valhalla"* RAH to Poul Anderson, September 6, 1961.

a restaurant with service so bad Asimov, *In Memory Yet Green*, 416.

"Both of you seem to be strung on taut wires" Henry Kuttner to RAH, February 8, 1945, quoted in Patterson, *Learning Curve*, 340.

"You see, I've never lost a member of my family before" RAH to Ted and Irene Carnell, April 2, 1952, quoted in Patterson, *Learning Curve*, 346.

206 *Heinlein took it down* RAH to Ted Carnell, May 13, 1945, quoted in Patterson, *Learning Curve*, 347.

"just enough of him left to sit down" RAH to JWC, June 3, 1945.

one day after he had predicted it James, "Regarding Leslyn," 25.

"That's the end" Patterson, *Learning Curve*, 354.

snide remarks about his Russian ancestry Asimov, *In Memory Yet Green*, 414.

207 *"I sent word to him"* RAH to JWC, June 3, 1945.

"No, no, no" Asimov, *In Memory Yet Green*, 415.

"What chart?" Ibid., 401.

"mild physical defects" Ibid., 421.

squashing radios in a compression machine De Camp, *Time and Chance*, 191.

208 *"Oh my God!"* Smith, *Worlds of George O.*, 66.

"During the weeks" JWC, "Atomic Age," *ASF*, November 1945, 5.

209 *"The fact that your life is in danger"* Quoted in Berger, *The Magic That Works*, 74.

"the kind of man who could talk a blue streak" Wollheim, *The Universe Makers*, 1.

"the economics of atomic power" JWC to RAH, August 8, 1945.

a contract with the publisher Henry Holt Ibid.

"Every major city" "1945 Cassandra," The Talk of the Town, *The New Yorker*, August 25, 1945, 16.

Laura had left her first husband "We find that John's sister presented us with an almost ex-brother-in-law. However she has another lined up, now a vice-consul in Lagos, Nigeria." Doña Campbell to RAH, January 1, 1942.

braved the Atlantic at the height of the war Obituary for William Laurence Krieg, *Sarasota Herald-Tribune*, December 5, 2010.

"she was invalided home" JWC to Asimov, December 8, 1955.

electroshock therapy Leslyn Randazzo, e-mail to author, July 31, 2016.

Campbell wrote favorably about the treatment JWC, "Science to Come," *ASF*, August 1945, 6.

210 *she got tipsy in the afternoons* Doña Campbell to RAH and Leslyn Heinlein, "Sunday," circa July 1945.

210 *she sometimes went out with George O. Smith* Doña Campbell to RAH and Leslyn Heinlein, November 8, 1944.

"It must be the life I lead" Doña Campbell to RAH, September 10, 1944.

"in very real danger" Theodore Sturgeon, at the panel "The Man John W. Campbell," Conclave III, Romulus, MI, November 4, 1978. Recording courtesy of the SFOHA Archives.

"a renovation, regeneration, or something" Doña Campbell to RAH, July 12, 1945.

"I also have been the victim" Doña Campbell to RAH, April 9, 1945.

211 *"She's in violent revolt"* JWC to RAH, October 10, 1945.

Doña met up with George O. Smith Ibid.

"rather impersonal" Ibid.

the science editor for all of Street & Smith JWC to RAH, November 10, 1945.

He finally cranked out "The Chromium Helmet" Davis, "The Work of Theodore Sturgeon," 26.

"Doña's mood is not improved greatly" JWC to RAH, January 3, 1946.

"May we call to your attention" JWC, introduction to "Atomic Power Plant: The Making of the Bomb," *ASF,* December 1945, 100.

212 *"What do you expect to do"* Doña Campbell to RAH, circa September 21, 1945.

"some of these superweapons" Alfred M. Klein, "Stranger than Fiction," *Philadelphia Record,* January 20, 1946. Reprinted in de Camp, *Time and Chance,* 186–88.

"drunk, hostile, or very, very careless" L. Sprague de Camp to RAH, February 4, 1946, quoted in Wysocki, *An Astounding War,* 178.

the article caused an "explosion" RAH to L. Sprague de Camp, February 13, 1946, quoted in Patterson, *Learning Curve,* 380.

Klein, the credited writer De Camp, *Time and Chance,* 188.

213 *the operations rooms on warships* Wysocki, *An Astounding War,* 138f.

"helped the Navy" JWC to Robert Swisher, September 12, 1945.

"Our present culture is finished" JWC, "Science to Come," *ASF,* August 1945, 6.

214 *"Science fiction better get stepping"* JWC to LRH, November 21, 1945.

PART IV: THE DOUBLE MINDS (1945–1951)

215 *"The art [of science fiction]"* S. I. Hayakawa, "From Science-Fiction to Fiction-Science," *Etc.,* Summer 1951.

CHAPTER 10: BLACK MAGIC AND THE BOMB (1945–1949)

218 *"Yes, Sarge"* Asimov, *In Memory Yet Green,* 432.

"What was yours?" Ibid., 446.

219   *"very pretty girl"* Ibid., 452.

"Isaac doesn't like the atomic bomb worth a damn" JWC to RAH, March 12, 1946.

220   *he did his best to break the habit* Asimov, *Treasury of Humor*, 415.

the rights to his story "Evidence" Asimov, *In Memory Yet Green*, 482.

"extraneous intrusion" Ibid., 491.

"lost in a maze of successful agencies" Asimov to Frederik Pohl, July 8, 1947.

221   *"Go to hell!"* Asimov, *In Memory Yet Green*, 508.

"Not interested in any work" Ibid., 505.

"What if it dissolved"... *"Go try it"* Ibid., 497–98.

"Hey, that was a funny satire"... *"I forgot"* Ibid., 517–18.

222   *"What can you tell us, Mr. Asimov"*... **"Doctor *Asimov*"** Ibid., 526.

223   *"Certainly"* Ibid., 552.

"the kind of girl" Ibid., 510.

Merril had actually grabbed at his crotch Judith Merril, signed footnote in Asimov, *In Memory Yet Green*, 653n.

"There was a question in my mind" Asimov, *In Memory Yet Green*, 556.

leaving some furniture Patterson, *Learning Curve*, 357.

"He left me on a street corner" Ibid., 358.

224   *"The men who built the atom bomb"* RAH to Henry Sang, September 15, 1945, quoted in Patterson, *Learning Curve*, 360.

Heinlein, Williamson, and Cartmill Patterson, *Learning Curve*, 374, and Pendle, *Strange Angel*, 171.

"a conspiracy to seize control" De Camp, "El-Ron of the City of Brass."

the Eleanor Hotel Owen, "Ron the 'War Hero.'"

impotent and depressed "The hormone further reduces my libido and I am nearly impotent." LRH, "Affirmations."

225   *"He always was that way"* Pendle, *Strange Angel*, 271.

"I . . . spent weeks in '45" RAH to JWC, March 28, 1953.

"the man who learned better" RAH, "On the Writing of Speculative Fiction," in Eshbach, *Of Worlds Beyond*, 15.

There was talk of Hubbard revising Patterson, *Learning Curve*, 374.

"wasted on pulp" Lurton Blassingame to LRH, November 5, 1945, quoted in Patterson, *Learning Curve*, 370.

Heinlein wanted to obtain the releases RAH to JWC, February 6, 1946.

"What do you mean by saying" RAH to JWC, February 16, 1946.

226   *Campbell handled it poorly* JWC to RAH, February 4, 1946.

"a supreme scissorbill" RAH to Lloyd Biggle, Jr., September 30, 1976, quoted in Patterson, *The Man Who Learned Better*, 518n.

"I hardly expect to sell to him again" RAH to L. Sprague de Camp, February 13, 1946, quoted in Patterson, *Learning Curve*, 380.

226 *"Never write down to them"* RAH Accession Notes for *Rocket Ship Galileo,* April 2, 1967, RAH Archives, UC Santa Cruz.

Will Jenkins had told him Ashley, *The Time Machines,* 195.

"speculative fiction" RAH, "On the Writing of Speculative Fiction," in Eshbach, *Of Worlds Beyond.*

"The market is there" RAH to John Arwine, May 10, 1946, quoted in Patterson, *Learning Curve,* 389–90.

"swan song" Patterson, *Learning Curve,* 402.

had even mentioned it in the magazine "Heinlein wants to tell the story of the Blind Singer of the Spaceways; you may remember mention of some of his poems in Heinlein stories." JWC, In Times to Come, *ASF,* April 1943, 65.

"miserable envy" Asimov, *In Memory Yet Green,* 489.

227 *"I deeply regret"* RAH to Henry and Catherine Kuttner, October 26, 1946, quoted in Patterson, *Learning Curve,* 404.

"I think about you all the time" RAH and Leslyn Heinlein to Virginia Gerstenfeld, March 9, 1947, quoted in Patterson, *Learning Curve,* 411.

Leslyn couldn't drive Virginia Heinlein to William H. Patterson, Jr., January 8, 2000.

"Leslyn slept in the studio" Grace Dugan Sang, quoted in Patterson, *The Man Who Learned Better,* 484.

"Oh, my darling" Virginia Gerstenfeld to RAH, circa April 1947.

"During the past eighteen months" RAH to John Arwine, March 15, 1947, quoted in Patterson, *Learning Curve,* 415.

228 *"I was simply a man"* RAH to Anthony Boucher, March 27, 1957.

"Bob feels that I am entirely to blame" Leslyn Heinlein to Jack Williamson, August 18, 1947, quoted in James, "Regarding Leslyn," 27.

"I took it to mean that his marital problems" Asimov, *In Memory Yet Green,* 499.

229 **Space Cadet** The novel would lend its title, though little else, to the television show *Tom Corbett, Space Cadet.* Patterson, *The Man Who Learned Better,* 55.

The rights dispute with **Astounding** JWC to RAH, August 10, 1948.

articles on the subject for hobbyist journals JWC wrote pieces for the June and July 1955 issues of *The Radio Amateurs' Journal,* as well as the article "How to Be an Amateur" in *Amateur Radio 73,* October 1960, 34–37. His call sign was W2ZGU.

they used it to discuss a new idea RAH to JWC, December 3, 1948.

a letter from a fan Richard A. Hoen, letter to *ASF,* November 1948, 111–12.

230 *"Another solution is for him to become a messiah"* RAH to JWC, January 27, 1949.

230 *"What makes a superman?"* Virginia Heinlein, note in RAH, *Grumbles from the Grave,* 52.

a publisher wanted to put out the Future History Erle Korshak of Shasta Press published landmark editions of JWC's *Who Goes There?* and *Cloak of Aesir,* LRH's *Slaves of Sleep,* and RAH's *The Man Who Sold the Moon, The Green Hills of Earth,* and *Revolt in 2100,* although all three men—as well as Asimov—expressed occasional irritation with his business practices. LRH to RAH, March 8 and March 31, 1949; RAH to JWC, April 11, 1949; Asimov to Pohl, October 18, 1949; JWC to Allen S. Porter, May 19, 1954; and JWC to Raymond F. Jones, October 28, 1954.

"If you don't say yes" LRH to RAH, February 17, 1949.

"She won't turn down a shipmate" RAH to LRH, February 19, 1949.

"No son of a bitch" RAH to LRH, March 4, 1949.

"If it drives you nuts" LRH to RAH, March 8, 1949.

231 **Lou Goldstone** Pendle, *Strange Angel,* 252.

"Must not believe in God" Wright, *Going Clear,* 51.

the best way to make money Miller, *Bare-Faced Messiah,* 119.

Heinlein bet him that he couldn't Patterson, *Learning Curve,* 563n.

Sara Northrup Sara, whose middle name was Elizabeth, was known as "Betty" while living with Parsons. Miller, *Bare-Faced Messiah,* 117.

he awoke after a drunken party Ibid., 172.

"Although he has no formal training in Magick" Ibid., 120.

232 *"like a starfish on a clam"* Pendle, *Strange Angel,* 255–56.

Hubbard and Parsons were fencing Ibid., 256.

"my very good friend" LRH, Philadelphia Doctorate Lectures, December 5, 1952.

"the perfect pioneer" Crowley, *The Confessions of Aleister Crowley,* dedication.

"He called" Parsons, *The Book of Babalon,* http://www.sacred-texts.com/oto/lib49.htm (accessed December 2017).

"It is done" Pendle, *Strange Angel,* 263.

233 **Marjorie Cameron** Cameron later married Parsons and became a prominent figure in occult circles, working with such artists as the director Kenneth Anger. Pendle, *Strange Angel,* 263, 303.

"varied and elastic nature" Miller, *Bare-Faced Messiah,* 122.

"The lust" Parsons, *The Book of Babalon,* http://www.sacred-texts.com/oto/lib49.htm (accessed December 2017).

"I thought I had a most morbid imagination" Miller, *Bare-Faced Messiah,* 126.

"Apparently Parsons or Hubbard" Ibid.

234 *"Any distaste I may have"* LRH, "Affirmations."

"China, knives, guns" Patterson, *Learning Curve,* 409.

234 *"I don't understand Ron's current activities"* RAH to John Arwine, May 10, 1946, quoted in Patterson, *Learning Curve*, 387.

"Suspect Ron playing confidence trick" Miller, *Bare-Faced Messiah*, 128.

235 *"[breaking] up black magic in America"* Ibid., 114. The Church of Scientology has asserted that RAH asked LRH to investigate Parsons on behalf of naval intelligence, but no evidence has emerged to support this claim. Wright, *Going Clear*, 431.

he began beating her in Miami Wright, *Going Clear*, 60.

stayed overnight in New Jersey LRH, in a letter dated November 26, 1946, reprinted in LRH, *Dianetics: Letters & Journals*, 8.

"He was a quivering psychoneurotic wreck" JWC to RAH, March 24, 1953.

"reeked of tension" JWC to Art Coulter, August 28, 1953.

"heartily and affectionately . . . the Heinlein doghouse" LRH to RAH, December 4, 1946.

"I no longer trust you" Patterson, *Learning Curve*, 409. A few months later, RAH told JWC that LRH had accused him of plagiarizing "The Green Hills of Earth." After warning him to watch out for libelous material in anything that LRH submitted, he concluded: "I have been at a loss to understand much of Ron's behavior for the past year. I just check it off to the actions of a battle-fatigued wounded veteran and skip it." RAH to JWC, February 14, 1947.

236 *"Here and there throughout the world"* LRH, as "Capt. B.A. Northrop," "Fortress in the Sky," *Air Trails and Science Frontiers*, May 1947, 70.

the "gravity gauge" "The first [strategic advantage] might be termed the 'gravity gauge' comparable to the weather gauge so desirable in the days of sailing ships of the line. . . . The gravity gauge is important in the ratio of six to one, in that a missile would have to travel with an initial velocity of six miles per second to leave Earth, but would only have to travel with a velocity of one mile per second to leave the moon." LRH, as "Capt. B.A. Northrop," "Fortress in the Sky," *Air Trails and Science Frontiers*, May 1947, 25. RAH briefly mentioned the gravity gauge in *Space Cadet*, and he would draw on the concept at length in *The Moon Is a Harsh Mistress*.

"I bought it quite largely because" JWC to RAH, March 24, 1953.

237 *"I broke it out"* LRH to Russell Hays, July 15, 1948, reprinted in LRH, *Dianetics: Letters & Journals*, 17.

"long periods of moroseness" Miller, *Bare-Faced Messiah*, 138.

many of the plots proposed by Sara Corydon, *Messiah or Madman?*, 310.

"strolling in astral form" Miller, *Bare-Faced Messiah*, 142.

"I went right down in the middle of Hollywood" Wright, *Going Clear*, 68.

238 *he had his subjects "writhing"* Ibid.
eight out of ten patients LRH to Russell Hays, July 15, 1948, reprinted in LRH, *Dianetics: Letters & Journals,* 17.
meetings of the Queens Science Fiction League LRH to RAH, September 25, 1948.
"I no longer start for the bridge" Ibid.
"a book risen from the ashes" LRH to RAH, November 24, 1948.
Thanksgiving with the Campbells Ibid.
a pulpwood plant LRH to RAH and Virginia Heinlein, March 3, 1949.
"rape women without their knowing it" LRH to Forrest J Ackerman, January 13, 1949.
Sara went to see her mother LRH to RAH, March 31, 1949.
the American Psychiatric Association Wright, *Going Clear,* 84. LRH mentioned speaking to a man named Davies at the A.P.A. in the cover letter to his unpublished manuscript "A Criticism of Dianetics," which is preserved in the microfilm reels of JWC, *The Complete Collection of the JWC Letters.* In the same letter, he also claimed to have spoken to an individual who can be identified as James B. Craig, a neurologist "largely responsible for the establishment of the psychiatric ward at St. Joseph's Hospital" in Savannah. *Southern Cross* (Savannah, Georgia), April 26, 1952.
the Gerontological Society in Baltimore LRH to the Gerontological Society, April 13, 1949, reprinted in LRH, *Dianetics: Letters & Journals,* 19–21.
239 *"the local psychiatrists"* LRH to RAH, April 21, 1949.
he was moving to Washington, D.C. LRH to RAH, April 30, 1949.
a woman named Ann Jensen Wright, *Going Clear,* 72.
"awful pretty" LRH to RAH, March 31, 1949.
he sent a letter to Parsons Pendle, *Strange Angel,* 287.
inviting him and Sara to New Jersey Miller, *Bare-Faced Messiah,* 148.

CHAPTER 11: THE MODERN SCIENCE OF MENTAL HEALTH (1945–1950)
241 *"Cybernetics is the big new idea"* Yvette Gittleson, "Sacred Cows in Collision," *American Scientist,* October 1950, 603–9.
the Marshall Islands JWC later wrote that he had received an offer to observe the tests in person, but had declined. JWC to William R. Burkett, Jr., September 14, 1965.
"The big cities" JWC, "Bikini Balance Sheet," *Air Trails Pictorial,* December 1946, 35.
242 *"If you want to know what a hell of a fix"* Dickson Hartwell, "Mister Atomic," *Pic,* February 1946, 20.
"At thirty-five" Ibid., 21.
"Despite [his] varied activities" JWC, "Meet the Authors," *Air Trails Pictorial,* December 1946, 106–7.

242 *"Questions about his personal life"* Dickson Hartwell, "Mister Atomic," *Pic,* February 1946, 21.

243 *"Mrs. Campbell has long since"* JWC, "Meet the Authors," *Air Trails Pictorial,* December 1946, 107.

"I learned more" Doña Campbell to RAH, circa September 21, 1945.

"I should work fifteen years" JWC to RAH, January 3, 1946.

the physicist Hans Bethe JWC to Joseph P. Martino, September 22, 1965.

"The uranium reaction" JWC, "—But Are We?," *ASF,* January 1946, 6.

244 *"Psychology must advance"* JWC, "Progress To Be Made," *ASF,* April 1946, 6.

"I hate to see a man" RAH to JWC, November 5, 1946.

"Java, Australia" JWC, In Times to Come, *ASF,* February 1946, 116.

"Against the Fall of Night" Clarke, *Astounding Days,* 109.

issues with foreign rights Arthur C. Clarke to JWC, January 1, 1952.

245 *an idea from Campbell* Harrison and Aldiss, *The Astounding-Analog Reader,* x.

at the urging of a fan Resnick, *Always a Fan,* 132. "When I saw Campbell at NyCon III, the 1967 Worldcon, I asked him about it—in a very general way, so as not to insult him. He muttered that maybe [the fan Ed Wood] had a little something to do with it, and then wandered off." Mike Resnick, e-mail to author, August 18, 2017.

"John, I wrote a story" Knight, *The Futurians,* 185.

trying to pull back from atomic doom JWC, Brass Tacks, *ASF,* September 1948, 155.

other ways of approaching the same material Some of the best stories on atomic themes were written by women, including "In Hiding" by Wilmar R. Shiras, about a mutant child prodigy reminiscent of the young JWC—he reads his textbooks from cover to cover and sells fiction to the pulps.

a teenage Neil Armstrong Wagener, *One Giant Leap,* 35.

John Michel Knight, *The Futurians,* 156.

246 *"It is up to each of us"* JWC, "Air Trails and New Frontiers," *Air Trails Pictorial,* September 1946, 22.

"We can already control atomic weapons" JWC, "The Greatest Power," *Air Trails Pictorial,* December 1946, 26.

L. Jerome Stanton Smith, *Worlds of George O.,* 67–68. Stanton first appears on the *Air Trails* masthead in the February 1947 issue.

"the original ball-bearing mousetrap" Ibid., 137–38. The story was "Rat Race," *ASF,* August 1947.

"Between you and me" LRH to RAH, September 25, 1948.

246 *tens of thousands more copies* JWC, In Times to Come, *ASF,* December 1947, 82.

advertising to be sold specifically JWC, *ASF,* April 1948, 35, and In Times to Come, *ASF,* May 1948, 148.

247 *Henry Holt had "rooked" him* JWC to Robert Swisher, October 1, 1947.

"These two incomplete sciences" JWC, *The Atomic Story,* 280, 292.

"a total reorganization" Ibid., 296.

"We must learn more about atomic forces" Ibid., 297.

248 *When Asimov was told the news* Asimov, *In Memory Yet Green,* 556.

most had college degrees JWC, The Analytical Laboratory, *ASF,* July 1949, 161.

"George, build me a good, stiff drink!" Smith, *Worlds of George O.,* 213.

249 *obsessed with Hubbard's new mental therapy* Smith—who said that he and Doña played bridge with the Hubbards—also claimed that LRH had spoken to him about dianetics before discussing it with JWC, saying that he didn't "want John to dive into this as his next hobby" until he was prepared to leak it. The timing of LRH's move to New Jersey and JWC's first known mention of his work makes this claim highly unlikely. Smith, *Worlds of George O.,* 138.

"She took a dim view . . . John was satisfied" Ibid., 213.

"having no interest in the future" JWC to RAH, July 27, 1950.

"underwife" JWC to Eric Frank Russell, April 6, 1958.

"only the last straw" Doña Campbell to RAH and Virginia Heinlein, May 8, 1950.

the magazine's offices had relocated JWC to LRH, April 21, 1948.

His father was in Germany JWC to Robert Swisher, April 5, 1948.

Laura was stationed with her husband Ibid.

a house that the editor found for them Miller, *Bare-Faced Messiah,* 148.

"more fiction than anything else" JWC to Cyril Vosper, April 30, 1970.

"The sparkle was back" JWC to RAH, March 24, 1953.

250 *"He's better off dead"* JWC to Joseph Winter, July 1949, quoted in Winter, *A Doctor's Report on Dianetics,* 4.

"I had known [Hubbard]" JWC to Raymond F. Jones, October 10, 1953.

"It'll be a great world" Joseph A. Winter, "Endocrinology is Tough," *ASF,* October 1948, 125.

251 *"L. Ron Hubbard, who happens to be an author"* JWC to Joseph Winter, July 1949, quoted in Winter, *A Doctor's Report on Dianetics,* 3.

"My vanity hopes" Winter, *A Doctor's Report on Dianetics,* 8.

"The recording of her sequence" LRH, *Dianetics,* 126.

"You'll forget all about this" JWC to RAH, September 15, 1949.

251 *"automatic restimulator . . . [I] was barely able to hold myself under control"* Ibid.

252 *suffered from itchiness* Ibid.
"I used the technique on one knee" Ibid.
"I firmly believe this technique" Ibid.
"You will appreciate" RAH to JWC, October 1, 1949.

253 *"a purple-plated doozy"* JWC to RAH, November 4, 1949.
Hubbard took Campbell back to a period before his birth Don Rogers to Jon Atack, July 20, 1984. Letter provided by Jon Atack.
Joseph Winter, Sr. JWC to Laura Krieg, May 20, 1953.
"I had nightmares of being choked" Winter, *A Doctor's Report on Dianetics*, 11.
a spiral painted on a record turntable Smith, *Worlds of George O.*, 213.
one of his Ole Doc Methuselah stories LRH, "Her Majesty's Aberration," *ASF*, March 1948, 126–40.
scopolamine JWC described his use of drugs with Winter and LRH in letters to Raymond F. Jones, October 10, 1953, and Bill Powers, November 4, 1953.
"nam" and "env" JWC, "Interpreters May Still Be Needed," *ASF*, June 1941, 6.
the fates of Norse mythology JWC discussed Norse mythology in a letter to John W. Campbell, Sr., May 15, 1953, and its influence can be seen in such early stories as "Out of Night" and "Cloak of Aesir."

254 *"rules of thumb"* JWC to RAH, September 15, 1949.
figuring out a story idea JWC to RAH, November 4, 1949.
"Although he did a lot of talking" Corydon, *Messiah or Madman?*, 190.
"So I just simply processed" LRH, Saint Hill Special Briefing Course, April 27, 1965.
"I guess I didn't like being ignored" Leslyn Randazzo, e-mail to author, July 31, 2016.

255 **Rocketship X-M** Patterson, *The Man Who Learned Better*, 43. LRH wrote on November 14, 1949: "I am working on a movie shooting script." Reprinted in LRH, *Dianetics: Letters & Journals*, 22. His contributions to the screenplay went uncredited, although one line bears his stamp: "Today, there is even the possibility that an unassailable base could be established on the moon to control world peace."
the publicity for **Destination Moon** LRH to RAH, December 30, 1949.
"Nothing of real interest" LRH to RAH, July 18, 1949.
"It is an article on the science of the mind" JWC, In Times to Come, *ASF*, December 1949, 80.

256 *"That's where the ghosts are"* Winter, *A Doctor's Report on Dianetics*, 14–16.

256 *Winter submitted a paper* Ibid., 18.

he cautioned a correspondent JWC to George F. Forbes, May 11, 1971.

"A Criticism of Dianetics" The unpublished manuscript was discovered by the author in the microfilm files of JWC, *The Complete Collection of the John W. Campbell Letters*, Reel 2.

"played . . . back very carefully" LRH to JWC, December 9, 1949.

257 *"it is in no sense an effort to be funny"* Ibid.

a contract was signed around Christmas JWC to RAH, January 25, 1950.

fifty thousand words of new material JWC, In Times to Come, *ASF*, August 1950, 60.

"There is something new coming up" Walter Winchell, "In New York," *New York Daily Mirror*, January 31, 1950.

Hubbard had kicked her in the stomach Wright, *Going Clear*, 84.

the world's first dianetic baby was unusually alert LRH to RAH, March 28, 1950.

"There was a greatly accelerated rate" Winter, *A Doctor's Report on Dianetics*, 218.

258 *"Anyone attempting to stop"* JWC, "Advice to the Pre-Clear," in LRH, *Dianetics*, 431.

259 *"While dianetics does not consider the brain"* LRH, "Terra Incognita: The Mind," *The Explorers Journal*, Winter/Spring 1950.

"Bob Heinlein sat down one time" Wright, *Going Clear*, 74.

"[Van Vogt] with his null-A" LRH to RAH, March 31, 1949.

"He became a big follower of Korzybski" Corydon, *Messiah or Madman?*, 286.

unable to finish any of Korzybski's books Wright, *Going Clear*, 74.

painful memories could be restimulated Corydon, *Messiah or Madman?*, 286–88.

"The analytical mind computes in differences" LRH, *Dianetics*, 336.

260 *"purpose tremor"* Wiener, *Cybernetics*, 127.

a piece on cybernetics E. L. Locke, "Cybernetics," *ASF*, September 1949, 78–87.

"There was one error in that book" LRH, "Affirmations."

"I'm up to eight comes" LRH to RAH, March 31, 1949.

261 *"Basically, the brain"* JWC to RAH, July 26, 1949.

"The human mind is a calculating machine" JWC to RAH, September 15, 1949.

psychoanalysis, hypnosis, and Christian Science Winter, *A Doctor's Report on Dianetics*, 9.

"Christian Science, Catholic miracle shrines" JWC to RAH, September 15, 1949.

261 *"clearing" an adding machine* "The brain, in the course of nature, never even approximately clears out its past records." Wiener, *Cybernetics,* 143.
"anxiety neuroses" Ibid., 176.
"demon circuit" LRH, *Dianetics,* 86.

262 *"He was a marvelous editor"* Corydon, *Messiah or Madman?,* 307.
"a new, logical theory" JWC to Helen Swick Tepper, March 30, 1950.
"be greatly interested" Kline, *The Cybernetics Movement,* 92.
"If you read science fiction" Soni and Goodman, *A Mind at Play,* 201.

263 *"They are parasitic"* LRH to RAH, March 28, 1950.
"the electronic computer idea" LRH, "Dianetics: The Evolution of a Science," *ASF,* May 1950, 53.
"The concept of the electronic brain" LRH, *Dianetics,* 70.
a long footnote JWC in LRH, *Dianetics,* 44n.
"You can tear that out" LRH, Saint Hill Special Briefing Course, August 10, 1961.
"Now with this engram" LRH, *Dianetics,* 107–8.

264 *"Shouldn't you be on your clandestine way"* Smith, *Worlds of George O.,* 214.
"Doña sort of blew her top" JWC to RAH, March 9, 1950. JWC attributed the separation to an engram planted by a prenatal memory of Doña's father, George, of whom her mother supposedly said while pregnant, "If I lose George, I'll die."
"If I don't get out of here" Doña Smith to RAH and Virginia Heinlein, January 20, 1952.
"This shows the word rate influence" Ibid.

265 *he audited her to remove the emotional charge* JWC to RAH, March 9, 1950.
When Leslyn figured it out JWC to Robert Swisher, September 7, 1950.
"I'd like to know just what the living hell" JWC to RAH, March 9, 1950.
"you'll also get a long discussion" Ibid.
"If the situation had seriously disturbed me" JWC to Robert Swisher, September 7, 1950.

266 *"the obvious move"* Doña Smith to RAH and Virginia Heinlein, January 20, 1952.

CHAPTER 12: THE DIANETICS EPIDEMIC (1950–1951)

267 *"If anyone wants a monopoly"* LRH, *Dianetics,* 168.
"Special Features" JWC, The Analytical Laboratory, *ASF,* October 1949, 57.
"This is not a hoax article" JWC, In Times to Come, *ASF,* December 1949, 80.
"I want to assure every reader" JWC, "Concerning Dianetics," *ASF,* May 1950, 4.

268 *"[Campbell] wanted to make certain"* Joseph A. Winter, introduction to "Dianetics: The Evolution of a Science," *ASF,* May 1950, 43.

many fans still thought that it was a gag "A lot of the fans think I have gone Palmer one better, with a new Shaverism." JWC to Jack Williamson, quoted in Williamson, *Wonder's Child,* 184. He was referring to the Shaver Mystery, a series of articles in *Amazing,* ghostwritten by the editor Raymond A. Palmer, that purported to describe a subterranean civilization reminiscent of the work of H. P. Lovecraft.

"The optimum computing machine" LRH, "Dianetics: The Evolution of a Science," *ASF,* May 1950, 44. This section is likely to have been written by JWC.

"the medicine man of the Goldi people" Ibid., 48.

"a well-greased Univac" Ibid., 60.

"Up there are the stars" Ibid., 87.

"straining a gut" JWC to RAH, January 25, 1950.

269 *a favorite of Heinlein and Asimov* Patterson, *Learning Curve,* 39, and Asimov, *In Memory Yet Green,* 425n. LRH also mentions Durant in "My Philosophy," 1965, http://www.lronhubbard.org/articles-and-essays/my -philosophy.html (accessed December 2017).

"Mother is saying" LRH, *Dianetics,* 265.

"Dianetics addresses war" Ibid., 406.

"Sometimes soldiers in the recent war" Ibid., 348–49.

"In twenty or a hundred years" Ibid., 408.

"For God's sake" Ibid., 410.

270 *the American Institute of Advanced Therapy* LRH to Attorney General, U.S. Department of Justice, May 14, 1951.

the Hubbard Dianetic Research Foundation Miller, *Bare-Faced Messiah,* 153.

C. Parker Morgan JWC discusses his treatment of "Parker" in a letter to RAH, March 9, 1950.

the treasurer would be Campbell himself Williamson, *Wonder's Child,* 184.

"The professional people" Winter, *A Doctor's Report on Dianetics,* 29–30.

two thousand letters LRH, letter in Brass Tacks, *ASF,* August 1950, 152.

"Happily for me" LRH, telegram to Otto Gabler, reprinted in LRH, *Dianetics: Letters & Journals,* 61.

"surplus army cots" JWC to Jack Williamson, quoted in Williamson, *Wonder's Child,* 184.

271 *more hours of free auditing* JWC to Don Purcell, August 13, 1951.

Leaving his daughters with the housekeeper JWC to RAH, July 27, 1950.

"Why, for God's sake" JWC to Eric Frank Russell, May 9, 1958.

271 *"homosexuals, alcoholics"* JWC to Jack Williamson, quoted in Williamson, *Wonder's Child*, 184.

"We have case histories on homos" JWC to RAH, December 29, 1950.

participating in debates at colleges Ibid.

"It is not the first" Advertisement on inside front cover, *ASF*, August 1950.

272 *"The professional journals"* JWC, Brass Tacks, *ASF*, August 1950, 158.

its circulation stood at 75,000 JWC to Eric Frank Russell, January 7, 1952.

over a thousand copies a day LRH to RAH, July 14, 1950.

"Well, I've got to go" Van Vogt, *Reflections of A. E. van Vogt*, 83.

his wife's sister . . . a cathartic sense of grief Miller, *Bare-Faced Messiah*, 159.

273 *"If you can get a reasoned explanation"* JWC to RAH, March 9, 1950.

"sorry as hell" RAH to JWC, March 18, 1950.

"If she is cleared" JWC to RAH, March 24, 1950.

"I fully expected to come down here" Doña Campbell to RAH, June 3, 1950.

"in the hands of a couple of crackpot world-savers" Doña Campbell to RAH and Virginia Heinlein, May 8, 1950.

Destination Moon Robert Silverberg, e-mail to author, September 20, 2016.

an orange space suit JWC to RAH, July 27, 1950.

274 *she was nicknamed "Irish"* JWC to Ted Carnell, August 5, 1957.

the University of Wisconsin JWC provides information on Peg's educational background in letters to E. N. Columbus, April 25, 1952; Dr. Albert P. Kline, May 5, 1952; and Gib Hocking, February 15, 1954.

a flour and feed company "Everett Kearney is Heart Victim: Prominent Business Man Dies Wednesday," *Ironwood Daily Globe* (Michigan), October 4, 1951.

embroidering crewel ski sweaters JWC to RAH, March 6, 1951.

investing five thousand dollars JWC to Don Purcell, March 14, 1955.

"You don't know anything" JWC to Don Purcell, January 23, 1954.

Peg's abilities as an auditor JWC to Raymond F. Palmer, March 17, 1954.

Asimov had heard about it from de Camp Asimov, *In Memory Yet Green*, 586.

the Hydracon convention Robert Silverberg, e-mail to author, September 21, 2016.

Doña married George O. Smith Doña and George O. Smith wedding announcement, August 19, 1950, in the RAH Archives, UC Santa Cruz.

275 *"with a stable, wise, honest, and intelligent personality"* JWC to Paul M. Springfield, April 4, 1968.

275 *"If you start cross-auditing"* JWC to "Mr. Allen," February 15, 1953.
"The next president" Smith, *Worlds of George O.,* 232.
"a good bull session" JWC, The Analytical Laboratory, *ASF,* September 1951, 102.

276 *"You don't know it"* Alfred Bester, "My Affair with Science Fiction," in Harrison and Aldiss, *Hell's Cartographers,* 58f.

278 *"Actually, that may be so"* Frederik Pohl, in a talk at The Tyneside Cinema, Newcastle upon Tyne, UK, June 26, 1978, http://www.thewaythefu tureblogs.com/2011/04/me-and-alfie-part-6-john-w-campbell-dianetics (accessed December 2017).
"Incidentally, my dianetics-induced headache" Frederik Pohl to JWC, April 3, 1950.

279 *"I know dianetics"* JWC to Jack Williamson, quoted in Williamson, *Wonder's Child,* 185.
"lunatic revision of Freudian psychology" Williamson, *Wonder's Child,* 183.
"If I concentrate hard enough" Eric Frank Russell to JWC, December 11, 1949.
he was just envious of Hubbard De Camp, *Time and Chance,* 221.
Willy Ley broke away entirely Lester del Rey, in *Locus,* July 12, 1971, 4.
"I guess we're not going to talk" Lester del Rey, interview with Alan Elms, LACon II, Anaheim, California, September 3, 1984. Recording courtesy of the SFOHA Archives.
"I have no connection" Kline, *The Cybernetics Movement,* 92.
"detrimental to my standing" Ibid.
Will Jenkins Stallings and Evans, *Murray Leinster,* 92.
Ross Rocklynne Menville, *The Work of Ross Rocklynne,* 10, 16–17.
Katherine MacLean In 1974, MacLean still listed "dianetics" as one of her interests in Reginald, *Science Fiction and Fantasy Literature, Volume 2,* 985.

280 *Nelson S. Bond* "I am glad you have been having good results from your dianetics and getting real psychosomatic relief." JWC to Nelson S. Bond, May 25, 1951.
James Schmitz "Most of my top authors have plunged into reverie, and haven't come up for story-writing since. . . . Ray Jones, James Schmitz, Nels Bond, and Bob Williams are all going full blast." JWC to RAH, July 27, 1950.
Robert Moore Williams "Bob Williams got a local psychiatrist interested in dianetics—chief psychiatrist at the St. Louis spin-bin." Ibid.
James Blish "My own personal tests of the therapy—on myself, my wife, and a friend (namely, Jerome Bixby)—haven't proceeded very far as yet. But as far as they've gone, they check with the claims. . . . It may well be the most important discovery of this or any other century." James Blish,

"Dianetics: A Door to the Future," *Planet Stories*, November 1950, 102. Blish describes JWC in the same article as "a government consultant in nuclear physics."

280 *"Brother, you're not kidding"* Raymond F. Jones to JWC, May 26, 1950.

Sturgeon, who was audited by Campbell himself Theodore Sturgeon, at the panel "The Man John W. Campbell," Conclave III, Romulus, MI, November 4, 1978. Recording courtesy of the SFOHA Archives.

"synthesis rather unlike anything done before" Davis, "The Work of Theodore Sturgeon," 31.

"If it does you that much good" RAH to LRH, March 26, 1949.

"I have heard from [Hubbard]" RAH to JWC, August 1, 1949.

"I most solemnly assure you" JWC to RAH, September 15, 1949.

"I am most anxious" RAH to JWC, September 19, 1950.

281 *"unallocated fear"* RAH to JWC, April 5, 1951.

to get the military to look into it RAH to JWC, February 26, 1951.

"You, for instance" JWC to RAH, December 29, 1950.

who annoyed Asimov Asimov, *In Memory Yet Green*, 601.

"Captain Dianetic" Patterson, *The Man Who Learned Better*, 506n.

"I would love to experiment a bit" RAH to JWC, September 19, 1950.

"I tried lying down" RAH to Robert Bloch, November 30, 1950, quoted in Patterson, *The Man Who Learned Better*, 50.

282 *"Hubbard's dabblings in amateur psychiatry"* Asimov, *In Memory Yet Green*, 570.

"Neither Sprague nor I" Ibid., 587.

"Damn it, Asimov" Ibid.

"lambasted dianetics" Ibid., 595.

"I want to maintain my loving relationship" Asimov to Frederik Pohl, November 21, 1949.

"All stories that go to magazines" Asimov to Frederik Pohl, January 6, 1950.

283 *"Fuck Eando Binder"* Asimov, *In Memory Yet Green*, 591.

"It was like having a stomachache in the mind" Asimov, *Gold*, 248.

"Have I done something?" Asimov, *In Memory Yet Green*, 592.

284 *"I kept my mouth shut"* Ibid., 602.

"fusser and tinkerer" RAH to Lurton Blassingame, October 13, 1951, quoted in Patterson, *The Man Who Learned Better*, 70.

Gold's personal issues JWC later fought with Gold over reprints of stories that had originally appeared in *Astounding*, and he wrote without apparent irony of the "psychological slant" of the fiction in *Galaxy:* "Horace Gold . . . is an acute agoraphobe and xenophobe. . . . A number of years of psychotherapy were signally unsuccessful; he is now engaged in developing his own therapeutic theory and attempting to work out his own problems." JWC to Steven G. Vandenberg, September 19, 1956.

284 *an accident of timing* By way of comparison, when F. Orlin Tremaine founded the rival magazine *Comet* in 1940, he failed to win over most of JWC's writers: "No, it won't ever be Tremaine. Sprague gave me an earful of how Tremaine had treated him. I resented it very nearly as much as if it had been addressed to me personally." RAH to JWC, February 17, 1941. Asimov recounts a similarly distressing encounter with Tremaine in *In Memory Yet Green*, 283–84.

285 *He had considered presenting Sara* Corydon, *Messiah or Madman?*, 308.

286 *"full and perfect recall"* Miller, *Bare-Faced Messiah*, 166.
"Well, Forry" Ibid., 167.
"When Ron wants to" JWC to RAH, December 29, 1950.
a Lincoln dealership Corydon, *Messiah or Madman?*, 307.
"Funds received by the foundation" LRH to foundation staff, November 22, 1950, reprinted in LRH, *Dianetics: Letters & Journals*, 89.

287 *"cold and uncordial"* Letter from "Andy" to "Charlie," July 8, 1950, reprinted in LRH, *Dianetics: Letters & Journals*, 85.
they were departing from orthodox techniques JWC to RAH, November 20, 1951.
"a dismal, expensive failure" Winter, *A Doctor's Report on Dianetics*, 190.
the American Medical Association Atack, *A Piece of Blue Sky*, 125.
"You don't know what it's like" Miller, *Bare-Faced Messiah*, 167–68.
"stiff and polite . . . I have proved to be" Bedford, *Aldous Huxley*, 498–99.

288 *"when the group decided"* JWC to RAH, March 6, 1951.
"a simple process of getting all the gripes I could" Ibid.
"desk-prying [and] wastebasket studying" Ibid.
"The thing blew sky-high" Ibid.
"Many clubs have been formed" "Hubbard Dianetic Research Foundation, Incorporated, Internal Security," FBI office memorandum, SAC (Newark) to Director (FBI), March 21, 1951.

289 *"What's magic about the instant of birth?"* JWC to RAH, July 26, 1949.
the board voted to discourage such research LRH, *Science of Survival*, 85.
a volunteer to run past lives LRH, memo to foundation, December 30, 1950, reprinted in LRH, *Dianetics: Letters & Journals*, 97.
Hubbard had forced her to take the medication Miller, *Bare-Faced Messiah*, 185.
the New Jersey Board of Medical Examiners JWC called the move "legal, but not just." JWC to RAH, December 29, 1950.
Countess Motorboat Telegram to foundation, February 5, 1951, reprinted in LRH, *Dianetics: Letters & Journals*, 94.

290 *"Don't sleep"* Corydon, *Messiah or Madman?*, 306.

"If you really loved me, you would kill yourself" "Author Sued for Divorce," *Wichita Beacon,* May 4, 1951.

"He said that he had cut [Alexis] into little pieces" Wright, *Going Clear,* 89.

291 *Campbell later claimed* JWC to James F. Pinkham, July 2, 1951.

no indication that he was planning to leave JWC may have tempered his enthusiasm toward LRH, but he still believed in dianetics. A few months earlier, Peedee had broken her leg while playing with her sister on the ice. After an auditing session that lasted for two hours, JWC allegedly discharged the pain. JWC to RAH, December 29, 1950.

watching the girls two days a week JWC to RAH, May 27, 1951.

seeing patients in New York JWC to R. Kelman, February 15, 1951.

"Joe [Winter] had been spreading rumors" JWC to Marge Winter, October 18, 1955.

"Privately, for your close-held information" JWC to RAH, March 6, 1951.

"I wish to thank you" J. Edgar Hoover to LRH, March 9, 1951.

292 *"a mental case"* FBI airgram to legal attaché, Havana, Cuba, April 27, 1951.

a crib covered in chicken wire Wright, *Going Clear,* 90.

"The story about Ron and another man" RAH to JWC, August 15, 1951.

the result of hypnosis Miller, *Bare-Faced Messiah,* 184.

"systematic torture" "Dianetics Author Crazy, Wife Charges," *Los Angeles Mirror,* April 23, 1951.

293 *"a scientist in the field"* LRH to Attorney General, U.S. Department of Justice, May 14, 1951.

"The original group" JWC to Harry B. Moore, May 25, 1951.

"I can tell you, Bob" JWC to RAH, May 27, 1951.

294 *"I wasn't yet competent for the job"* JWC to Art Coulter, August 28, 1953.

"extreme mismanagement" JWC to T. Scott, February 15, 1965.

"I departed from Hubbard's ideas" JWC to David Palter, May 12, 1971.

his sinusitis was back Gardner, *Fads and Fallacies,* 280.

"Peg and I have advanced" JWC to RAH, March 6, 1951.

295 *"I knew Campbell and I knew Hubbard"* Asimov, *In Memory Yet Green,* 625.

"I wish to lead a quiet and orderly existence" Miller, *Bare-Faced Messiah,* 193.

"You're going to get on that plane" Wright, *Going Clear,* 94.

PART V: THE LAST EVOLUTION (1951–1971)

297 *"The average [science fiction] author"* Jack Williamson, interview with Larry McCaffery, *Science Fiction Studies,* July 1991.

CHAPTER 13: A FUNDAMENTAL ATTACK ON THE PROBLEM (1951–1960)

299 *"Man molded the machine"* JWC, as "Arthur McCann," letter to *ASF,* April 1938, 151.
three teenage hitchhikers JWC to RAH, May 27, 1951.
the rights to "Who Goes There?" JWC to RAH, March 9, 1950.
Van Vogt had hoped to write the script A. E. van Vogt to JWC, March 29, 1950.

300 *one of the worst movies ever made* Asimov, "The Father of Science Fiction," in Harrison, *Astounding,* xi.
"I think they may be right" JWC to Nelson S. Bond, May 25, 1951.
"I have an impression" JWC to P. Schuyler Miller, June 28, 1951.
"It helps spread science fiction" Asimov, *Before the Golden Age,* 912n.
"utmost desire to drive Peg away from me" JWC to Laura Krieg, October 8, 1953.

301 *1457 Orchard Road* JWC to RAH, October 5, 1951.
embroidery supplies by mail JWC to George O. Smith, May 10, 1965.
Peg's first husband "Everett Kearney is Heart Victim: Prominent Business Man Dies Wednesday," *Ironwood Daily Globe* (Michigan), October 4, 1951.
"accepted me completely" JWC to RAH, October 5, 1951.
Joe suffered from asthma JWC to Joseph Winter, June 21, 1953.

302 *political science* Entry for Joseph Kearney in Williams College yearbook, 1955, 41.
an act of revolt JWC to Gib Hocking, April 10, 1955.
an independent dianetics newsletter in Florida The newsletter was *The ARC Light,* published by William and Dorothy Swygard. JWC to James F. Pinkham and R. M. Stevens, July 2, 1951.
"much less than Hubbard believed it to be" JWC, "Evaluation of Dianetics," *ASF,* October 1951, 6, 169.
"He's now operating" JWC to RAH, November 20, 1951.
"Peg's cordially hated Ron" JWC to Joseph Winter, October 12, 1953.
Hubbard had used hypnosis Ibid. Van Vogt described this visit in "My Life Was My Best Science Fiction Story," in Greenberg, *Fantastic Lives,* 195–96.
"But the deep self-understanding" JWC, "Evaluation of Dianetics," *ASF,* October 1951, 168.
"a kind of suicide pact" JWC to James H. Schmitz, February 20, 1970.

302 *ten pages of typewritten notes* The author has reviewed summaries of their session notes, which ultimately amounted to 1,800 stapled pages in sixty-four folders, dating primarily from October 1951 to November 1953, with a smaller amount of material from 1954 to 1956. Jim Gilbert, e-mail to author, January 30, 2018.

303 *Peg stitched at her embroidery* Author interview with Leslyn Randazzo, July 29, 2016.

twenty milligrams of Benzedrine JWC to Raymond F. Jones, October 28, 1954.

"mentally twanging" JWC to Asimov, September 21, 1957.

"the velvet glove" Asimov, *Asimov on Science Fiction*, 199–200.

"How do you think?" JWC to "Mrs. Curtis," December 13, 1952.

"with bright and gladdened face" JWC to RAH, March 6, 1951.

The term "psionics" Jack Williamson, "The Greatest Invention," *ASF*, July 1951, 56–96. The word was retroactively described as a portman-teau of "psychic electronics," but Williamson originally derived it from "psion," a unit of mental energy. Williamson, *Wonder's Child*, 189.

the editor's interest in telepathy JWC had written in the second issue of *Unknown*: "Is it so strange a thing that this unknown mass should have some unguessed power by which to feel and see beyond, directly, meeting mind to mind in telepathy, sensing direct the truth of things by clair-voyance?" JWC, as "Don A. Stuart," "Strange Worlds," *Unknown*, April 1939, 162.

304 *The dianetics group had taken them seriously* "Exhaustive tests were made on telepathy and ESP and in every case an explanation was found which did not need to go into mind reading or radar sight." LRH, *Dianet-ics*, 320.

"I know the general concept" JWC to Eric Frank Russell, October 1, 1952.

"He could not move his arms" JWC to Gotthard Gunther, June 5, 1954.

"various authors and key fans" JWC to John W. Campbell, Sr., May 18, 1953.

he mentioned the term for the first time JWC, "Unwise Knowledge," *ASF*, October 1953, 6–7, 160–62.

"Until I can demonstrate the phenomena myself" JWC to Eric Frank Russell, October 1, 1952.

partially paralyzing him JWC to Laura Krieg, May 5, 1953.

305 *"I'm in this for blood"* JWC to John W. Campbell, Sr., May 18, 1953.

Serendipity Inc. JWC to Gib Hocking, July 21, 1954.

he told him about a man named Welsford Parker JWC to Arthur Z. Gray, May 25, 1954.

the treasure hunter Mel Chappell Finnan, *Oak Island Secrets*, 71.

"condensers, vacuum tubes" JWC to Arthur Z. Gray, May 25, 1954.

305 *"Parker is not a fool"* Ibid.

306 *$150,000 into various avenues* JWC to John W. Campbell, Sr., June 24, 1954.
Campbell invested as well Arthur Z. Gray to JWC, July 7, 1954.
sixteen thousand dollars a year JWC to John W. Campbell, Sr., May 18, 1953.
"[A] larger-scale crackpot" JWC to Laura Krieg, November 11, 1954.
"for the express purpose" RAH to G. Harry Stine, July 18, 1954.
"I don't know your methods" RAH to JWC, December 4, 1952.

307 *"He said I had no right to say"* JWC to Gotthard Gunther, June 5, 1954.
"in about five minutes" JWC to Raymond F. Jones, June 15, 1954.
"I didn't say that" Ibid.
Campbell tapped Heinlein on the chest RAH to JWC, January 6, 1955.

308 *"I got preached at"* RAH to G. Harry Stine, July 18, 1954.
"After four hours of bullyragging" RAH to G. Harry Stine, July 27, 1954, quoted in Patterson, *The Man Who Learned Better*, 118.
"In the course of the evening" JWC to Gotthard Gunther, June 5, 1954.
"mashing Bob's face in" JWC to G. Harry Stine, September 7, 1954.
"I wish John would just let it be" RAH to G. Harry Stine, July 18, 1954.
"As for space flight" RAH to G. Harry Stine, July 27, 1954, quoted in Patterson, *The Man Who Learned Better*, 118.
The Living Brain JWC to Dr. W. Grey Walter, unsent, May 1, 1953. Several years later, the same book inspired William S. Burroughs, Ian Somerville, and Brion Gysin to construct a similar device known as the Dream Machine. Burroughs, *Rub Out the Words*, 46–48.

309 *"I will judge Mother"* JWC to Dorothy Middleton, October 9, 1954.
drove her to the hospital JWC to John W. Campbell, Sr., November 2, 1954.
"The trigger that caused her death" JWC to Theodore Sturgeon, September 7, 1956.

310 *Laura had converted to Christianity* Walter Hooper, in Lewis, *Collected Letters*, 602n.
"a deist" JWC to "Pease," February 10, 1953.
"You have found The Light" JWC to Laura Krieg, August 10, 1954.
"Christianity has failed" Ibid.
"He must be a corker of a boy" C. S. Lewis to Philinda (Laura) Krieg, June 6, 1955, quoted in Lewis, *Collected Letters*, 602–3.
Joseph Winter The details of Winter's death are taken from letters from JWC to Gib Hocking, June 8, 1955; Asimov, April 6, 1958; and Joseph Goodavage, January 23, 1965.
"There are men dead" LRH, *Manual of Justice*, 8.
Frank Kelly Freas JWC to Frank Kelly and Polly Freas, June 10, 1955.

311 *Joe Kearney* Information about Joe Kearney's accident is taken from

JWC, "Design Flaw," *ASF,* October 1955, 85–94, and letters from JWC to Gib Hocking, June 17, 1955; John W. Campbell, Sr., June 18, 1955; G. Harry Stine, June 19, 1955; Dwight Wayne Batteau, June 20, 1955; and Gotthard Gunter, June 20, 1955.

311 *"a very charming and intelligent young man"* Asimov to JWC, January 10, 1953.

312 *"It was a very good thing"* JWC to Gib Hocking, June 8, 1955.

313 *"You've really had it, kid"* JWC to Gotthard Gunther, June 21, 1955.
"It lets you consider the problem" JWC to G. Harry Stine, June 19, 1955.
"It didn't make Peg sleepy" JWC to Gotthard Gunther, June 21, 1955.
"It threw Peg" JWC to Gotthard Gunther, June 28, 1955.
"The experience ran through" Ibid.

314 *While packing the night before* JWC, "Design Flaw," *ASF,* October 1955, 88.
Joe had been killed by highway hypnosis JWC's first reference to highway hypnosis appeared the day after Joe's death, in a letter to John W. Campbell, Sr., June 18, 1955. The term's earliest appearance in print was in Griffith W. Williams, "Highway Hypnosis: Our Newest Hazard," *Parade,* August 21, 1949.
"I could have warned Joe" JWC to Gotthard Gunther, June 28, 1955.
"I am, as you see, seeking vengeance" JWC to John W. Campbell, Sr., August 1, 1955.
"Joe Kearney was sacrificed" JWC to Asimov, January 20, 1956.

315 *"I'm trying to rally the tribe"* JWC to Gotthard Gunther, June 21, 1955.
He reached out for help JWC to Gotthard Gunther, June 21, 1955; Gib Hocking and Bernard I. Kahn, June 22, 1955; Capt. Singleton Shearer, June 27, 1955; and John W. Campbell, Sr., July 26, 1955.
"Design Flaw" The article shared its title with a story by G. Harry Stine, writing as Lee Correy, in the February 1955 issue of *ASF.* JWC came up with the plot—in which the flicker of a guidance panel causes a series of airplane accidents—after reading *The Living Brain,* and he gave it to Stine in a letter dated April 10, 1954. After the accident, JWC wrote to Stine on June 19, 1955: "Joe Kearney, my stepson, was killed on the Pennsylvania Turnpike; he lived out the essential mechanism of 'Design Flaw.'"
the most powerful piece Asimov, *Asimov on Science Fiction,* 200.
"the Good Joes" JWC, "Design Flaw," *ASF,* October 1955, 94.
"No real solution to the problem" Ibid.
"The pragmatic, trial-and-error approach" JWC, Brass Tacks, *ASF,* February 1956, 152.

316 *"I've sort of slowed down"* JWC to Dwight Wayne Batteau, July 27, 1955.
"Define 'reality'" Ibid.
a source of objective data on the brain "We *must* study psi, *because it is*

the only objectively observable set of phenomena stemming from subjective forces. . . . The psi phenomena represent subjective phenomena that can be observed objectively." JWC, "We Must Study Psi," *ASF,* January 1959, 162.

316 *a second trip to Belleville* JWC to Welsford Parker, November 1, 1954.
Colonel Henry Gross JWC to Galen Hieronymus, June 19, 1956.

317 *"You stroke this plastic gimmick here"* JWC, "Psionic Machine—Type One," *ASF,* June 1956, 106–7.
the two men cooked up another test JWC to Poul Anderson, March 18, 1968.
"I got shown" Ibid.

318 *ceased to work during nuclear tests* JWC to Claude Shannon, May 22, 1957.
"I have a Campbell Machine" JWC to "Dr. Frey," May 26, 1956.
"I no longer trusted" Asimov, *In Joy Still Felt,* 53.
"Mr. Campbell, the plate feels slippery" Ibid.
"The articles we run" JWC, "The Problem of Psionics," *ASF,* June 1956, 5.
the Campbell Machine JWC, "Unprovable Speculation," *ASF,* February 1957, 54–70.

319 *"I am not compelled to defend my hunches"* Ibid., 70.
whether the Hieronymus Machine was a hoax Robin Johnson, in Bangsund, *JWC: An Australian Tribute,* 10.
Bell Aircraft and the RAND Corporation JWC to Galen Hieronymus, February 4, 1957.
Claude Shannon offered to test it JWC to G. Harry Stine, July 31, 1957.
"a tinker's damn" Hieronymus, *The Story of Eloptic Energy,* 123–24.
Bell Labs, the Harvard Computer Lab, and MIT "I'm welcome at Bell Labs, the G.E. labs, DuPont, Upjohn, Lederle, Brookhaven, MIT, etc." JWC to Helen Campbell, unsent, May 11, 1953. He frequently visited Cambridge, and his regular correspondents included John Arnold of MIT, who taught an undergraduate course on creativity; Mike Mihalakis, an inventor and former wrestler; and Dwight Wayne Batteau of Harvard and Tufts, a brilliant experimenter who died tragically in 1967.
he continued to give ideas to writers Works from this period based on JWC's ideas included "Noise Level" by Raymond F. Jones and *They'd Rather Be Right* by Mark Clifton and Frank Riley. The novel *Empire* by Clifford Simak was a reworking of one of the editor's early unsold stories: *"Empire* was essentially a rewrite of John's plot. I may have taken a few of the ideas and action, but I didn't use any of his words. And I certainly tried to humanize his characters." Simak, quoted in Currey, *Science Fiction and Fantasy Authors,* 446–47.

320 *"You gypped me"* JWC to Tom Godwin, October 29, 1953. At the time that the story was submitted, JWC had become interested in "the De-meaned Viewpoint technique," which involved coming up with a justifi-cation for a point of view that seemed indefensible. "The Cold Equations" was designed to undermine the premise that human sacrifice was unac-ceptable: "So we deliberately, knowingly and painfully sacrifice a young, pretty girl . . . and make the reader accept that it is valid!" JWC to Dwight Wayne Batteau, August 13, 1954.

The Moon Is Hell The novel was published, with minimal revision, by Lloyd Eshbach's Fantasy Press in 1951.

"The Idealists" The anthology was Raymond J. Healy's *9 Tales of Space and Time*, New York: Henry Holt, 1954. JWC's story had no discernible impact on readers, although he viewed it as a reinvention of the genre comparable to his work as Don A. Stuart: "I was learning new basic fac-tors of philosophy up to the last day before I wrote the yarn." JWC to Raymond J. Healy, October 10, 1953.

an unlikely pair Silverberg, *Other Spaces, Other Times*, 41–43.

"This is Robert Silverberg" Robert Silverberg, e-mail exchange with au-thor, September 20, 2016.

321 *"Bob Silverberg is a kid"* JWC to E. E. Smith, May 26, 1959.

"I was so excited at the thought" Robert Silverberg, in Solstein and Moos-nick, *JWC's Golden Age of Science Fiction*, 29.

writing up the editor's ideas "What difference does it make whether you do the actual typing yourself, or see to it that Silverberg and Garrett write exactly what you would have written if you had written it?" E. E. Smith to JWC, April 20, 1959.

a drunk and a sexual predator "You could follow [Garrett's] move-ments . . . by the squeals of the women whose bottoms he had just pinched." Frank Herbert, "Randall Garrett," in Garrett, *The Best of Ran-dall Garrett*, 135.

322 *Garrett was shockingly frank* Robert Silverberg, e-mail to author, Sep-tember 21, 2016.

"lack of breast development" JWC to Joseph Winter, May 7, 1953.

"What's the matter, Isaac?" Asimov, *In Joy Still Felt*, 78.

treated Garrett at the house JWC to Bernard I. Kahn, February 20, 1957.

the editor insisted on playing a tape Asimov, *In Joy Still Felt*, 78–79.

Garrett had "guessed" Ibid., 79.

323 *"It's been so long"* JWC to Randall Garrett, November 11, 1957.

"slob . . . complete bum" JWC to Leslyn Campbell, October 17, 1965.

"Well, by damn" JWC to Rick Cook, September 24, 1970.

"the brightest and kindliest" JWC to Asimov, January 1, 1962.

323 *bareback on a friend's horse* Author interview with Leslyn Randazzo, July 29, 2016.

"an Italian sunset color display" JWC to Carl A. Larson, December 9, 1969.

324 *"What happened?"* Author interview with Leslyn Randazzo, July 29, 2016.

"Leslyn got started right" JWC to Raymond F. Jones, April 29, 1953.

Heinlein had sent all of her letters Frederik Pohl, "The Wives (and Drives) of Robert Heinlein, Part 1," May 17, 2010, http://www.thewaythefuture blogs.com/2010/05/the-wives-and-drives-of-robert-heinlein-part-1 (accessed December 2017).

Martin Gardner "John Campbell, Jr., who had been introduced to dianetics many years earlier when Hubbard began treating him for sinusitis, and who in turn introduced dianetics to the world, has likewise been divorced. He married Dr. Winter's sister. And he still has his sinusitis." Gardner, *Fads and Fallacies*, 280.

"He hasn't creative ability enough" JWC to Theodore Sturgeon, June 19, 1958.

to push beyond the limits of the magazine JWC also tinkered in his workshop for several years with a "waveform generator" that he hoped would make him a fortune. Technological limitations forced him to scale it back, and a patent that he filed in 1956 lacked any practical application. United States Patent, "Electron Discharge Apparatus," J.W. Campbell, Jr., July 9, 1956. Patent number 2,954,466.

faith healing JWC underwent treatment with Doc Brinker, a faith healer in Pennsylvania, and the psionics researcher Curtis Upton, who also treated JWC's sister, Laura. JWC to Dr. L. H. Wallendorf, October 29, 1956; Leslyn Campbell, February 8, 1967; Asimov, June 10, 1958; and Curtis Upton, January 21, 1960.

other forms of pseudoscience These included the herbal cancer cure developed by Harry Hoxsey, whose work was denounced by the Food and Drug Administration. JWC to John W. Campbell, Sr., August 26, 1957.

"Bullshit!" De Camp, *Time and Chance*, 222.

a radio anthology series In the past, JWC had recommended stories—including RAH's "Requiem"—for the show *Beyond Tomorrow*, consulted for *Dimension X* and *X Minus One*, and served as a freelance editor for *The Planet Man*. He also corresponded with the producer Clement Fuller about a television series called *The Unknown*, but nothing ever came of it. JWC to Clement Fuller, March 5, 1952.

Exploring Tomorrow The series ran from December 4, 1957 to June 13, 1958, on the Mutual Broadcasting System. "Campbell often ended up just restating the theme or moral of the episode, regardless of how obviously those points had been made by the story itself. . . . John Campbell's talent and his enormous contributions to science fiction are beyond question, but acting as a radio host was apparently outside his expertise." DeForest, *Radio by the Book,* 190–91.

324 *Sputnik* "We agreed in our first conversation after the satellite went up that people were going to react by deciding science had caught up with science fiction." Del Rey, *The World of Science Fiction,* 371. The launch coincided with the demise of the American News Company, a distributor on which many pulps depended, which led to the failure of a dozen titles over two years. *Astounding* survived, but its circulation fell by almost half.

Interplanetary Exploration Society JWC, "Society for Amateurs," *ASF,* July 1958, 5–7.

325 *its inaugural meeting* Asimov, *In Joy Still Felt,* 140–41.

F. Darius Benham JWC to F. Darius Benham, July 24, 1957 and August 12, 1957.

"What's all this?" Asimov, *In Joy Still Felt,* 141.

Boston . . . an event at an arboretum Ibid., 234.

Street & Smith was bought by Condé Nast "Inherited Deal," *Time,* August 31, 1959, and Maier, *Newhouse,* 43–45.

"You—and many another" JWC to RAH, March 31, 1953.

he announced without warning JWC, In Times to Come, *ASF,* January 1960, 82.

326 *"I've already received a number of comments"* JWC, In Times to Come, *ASF,* February 1960, 37, 53.

"a name of memories and tradition" Asimov, *In Joy Still Felt,* 197.

"I have never quite managed to forgive Campbell" Ibid.

CHAPTER 14: STRANGERS IN A STRANGE LAND (1951–1969)

327 *"Under extreme environmental pressure"* JWC, "The Value of Panic," *ASF,* August 1956, 4.

328 *some of which belonged to Peg Campbell* JWC to Don Purcell, March 14, 1955.

"one of the most central points" "Dianetics Group to Quit City Because 'We're Not Wanted,'" *Elizabeth Daily Journal,* April 3, 1951.

Perry Chapdelaine Chapdelaine, who later preserved and published much of JWC's correspondence, described his experiences with LRH in his book *During the Dawn of Dianetics and Scientology.*

Ron Howes Atack, *A Piece of Blue Sky,* 136.

Purcell reached out to Campbell Purcell's first letter to JWC is dated

July 28, 1951, and the two men corresponded sporadically over the next few years.

328 **"Two of the early associates"** Miller, *Bare-Faced Messiah,* 187.

329 **"a heavy foe of dianetics"** LRH, letter to FBI, July 11, 1953.

Hubbard was happy to be the sole authority in Wichita LRH's visitors during this period included a teenager named Del Close, who later became renowned as one of the founders of modern improvisational comedy. Johnson, *The Funniest One in the Room,* 28–29. Close wrote up the encounter in "Del and Elron," an autobiographical story in the comic book *Wasteland,* August 1988, 1–8.

Volney Mathison Mathison, *Electropsychometry,* 101–3.

a lie detector that van Vogt had described "He emerged almost immediately carrying a small lie detector. He grasped the two hand grips firmly." Van Vogt, *The World of Null-A, ASF,* September 1945, 26.

electroencephalograph readings Winter, *A Doctor's Report on Dianetics,* 185.

"It works magnificently" JWC to A. S. Budgely, September 10, 1963.

forced on him by his publisher Hubbard Association of Scientologists to Better Business Bureau of Phoenix, Arizona, June 12, 1954.

330 **a session that Hubbard conducted in April** A recording of the tape was leaked in 2014 to *The Underground Bunker,* https://tonyortega .org/2014/06/17/rare-tape-reveals-how-l-ron-hubbard-really-came-up -with-scientologys-space-cooties (accessed December 2017).

"fantasies built upon reading and imagination" LRH, *Science of Survival,* 85.

implant stations on Mars "The report area for most has been Mars. Some women report to stations elsewhere in the Solar System. There are occasional incidents about Earth report stations. The report stations are protected by screens. The last Martian report station on Earth was established in the Pyrenees." LRH, *A History of Man* (previously titled *What to Audit*), 110.

a dozen case studies of past lives LRH, *Have You Lived Before This Life?*

He even claimed to have audited E. E. Smith Raine, "Astounding History," 15.

331 **"small-town booster"** In a lecture delivered on December 9, 1952, for the Philadelphia Doctorate Course, LRH said: "Mohammed decided to be a good small-town booster in Kansas, Middle East, or something of the sort." Compare to Bolitho: "Mahomet was a 'home-town booster,' and this conception will unlock the many obscurities of his life and his doctrine." Bolitho, *Twelve Against the Gods,* 125.

"The lever of his position" Bolitho, *Twelve Against the Gods,* 137.

331 *a machine that induced hypnosis using sound* Miller, *Bare-Faced Messiah*, 214.

one of his Ole Doc Methuselah stories LRH, "A Sound Investment," *ASF*, June 1949, 36–57.

"I await your reaction" Urban, *The Church of Scientology*, 65.

"If you want to get rich, you start a religion" Miller, *Bare-Faced Messiah*, 119 and 134. Harlan Ellison—who was a teenager in Ohio at the time— implausibly claimed to have been present on the night that LRH came up with the idea. Segaloff, *A Lit Fuse*, 119.

"It was, as a matter of fact" JWC to G. Harry Stine, May 16, 1956.

332 *"better controls . . . change of status of man"* LRH, *All About Radiation*, 120, 149.

"Of course Scientology" William S. Burroughs to Allen Ginsberg, October 30, 1959, quoted in Burroughs, *Rub Out the Words*, 3.

"If President Kennedy did grant me an audience" LRH, "A Second Statement by L. Ron Hubbard," January 6, 1963. FBI file on LRH.

333 *"Things go well"* LRH to JWC, August 29, 1964.

"intellectual garbage" JWC to Cyril Vosper, April 30, 1970.

"Some of [Hubbard's] claims" Wright, *Going Clear*, 111–12.

"It is carefully arranged" Atack, *A Piece of Blue Sky*, 193.

334 *"Very space opera"* A copy of the original handwritten Xenu story can be viewed at https://www.cs.cmu.edu/~dst/OTIII (accessed December 2017).

including William S. Burroughs In his correspondence, Burroughs clearly refers to the OT III material: "So leaving aside galactic federations and Zmus [sic] there may be some validity in Hubbard's procedure. . . . Exactly how are these body thetans contacted and run? Are they addressed directly and if so in what terms? Do they have names? Do they have dates? Are they run through the alleged shooting freezing and bombing incidents as if you are an auditor running an internal parasite through these incidents?" William S. Burroughs to John Cooke, October 25, 1971, quoted in Burroughs, *Rub Out the Words*, 374.

335 *white uniforms with silver boots* Atack, *A Piece of Blue Sky*, 211.

"They have lived on this little earth" Bolitho, *Twelve Against the Gods*, 117.

Jack Parsons The fullest account of Parsons's death appears in Pendle, *Strange Angel*, 1f.

a party hosted by Ron Howes Patterson, *The Man Who Learned Better*, 94.

the inventor of the Easy-Bake Oven Barry M. Horstman, "Ronald Howes, inventor of Easy-Bake Oven, dies at 83." *Cincinnati Enquirer*, February 19, 2010.

335 *"Ron is a jerk"* RAH to George O. Smith, circa May 10, 1953, quoted in Patterson, *The Man Who Learned Better*, 94.

336 *including George O. and Doña Smith* The Smiths visited the Heinleins in 1952 and again around 1957. RAH to Lurton Blassingame, July 16, 1952, quoted in Patterson, *The Man Who Learned Better*, 81; and Doug Smith, e-mail to author, October 11, 2017.
"a fake utopia" RAH to Robert A. W. Lowndes, March 13, 1956.
"a revolting son of a bitch . . . I thank heaven that I live" Ibid.
"traitors" and "custard heads" RAH, *Tramp Royale*, 63.
Irving Pichel Hoberman, *An Army of Phantoms*, 52–54.
Dalton Trumbo Ibid., 126.
Chan Davis Davis, a prolific contributor to *ASF*, was sentenced to six months in prison after refusing to answer questions before the House Un-American Activities Committee. De Baets, *Censorship of Historical Thought*, 569.
Bernhard J. Stern Price, *Threatening Anthropology*, 137–38.
a record by Tom Lehrer RAH to JWC, August 30, 1954.

337 *"Isaac, your books are so proper"* Asimov, *In Joy Still Felt*, 117.
tired of Campbell's provocations RAH's reluctance to work with JWC was clearly a matter of choice, not ability. When Theodore Sturgeon wrote to ask for financial help, RAH sent him a check and a letter filled with story ideas that he knew would sell to *ASF*. Patterson, *The Man Who Learned Better*, 125.
"Half the time at least" RAH to JWC, July 17, 1956.
including several to Doña Doña Smith to RAH, January 20, 1952.
"The only thing that really worries me" RAH to Lurton Blassingame, February 12, 1952, quoted in Patterson, *The Man Who Learned Better*, 77.
The Door into Summer On May 11, 1957, JWC wrote of the novel to Asimov: "Bob can write a better story, with one hand tied behind him, than most people in the field can do with both hands. But Jesus, I wish that son of a gun would take that other hand out of his pocket!" In the end, Boucher bought it for *Fantasy & Science Fiction,* and Asimov raved: "This is the best thing you've ever done, which means, for my money, it's the best thing anyone has ever done. . . . I love *The Door Into Summer* and I love you." Asimov to RAH, August 25, 1956.
Campbell rejected the former, but bought the latter JWC to RAH, April 5, 1957.

338 *"Two changes, admittedly easy"* RAH to Lurton Blassingame, May 17, 1957, quoted in Patterson, *The Man Who Learned Better*, 142.
"very shook up" RAH to Buddy Scoles, October 9, 1957, quoted in Patterson, *The Man Who Learned Better*, 145.
Campbell was tantalized by it JWC to RAH, December 23, 1957.

338 *"I do not think"* RAH to Alice Dalgliesh, December 24, 1957, quoted in Patterson, *The Man Who Learned Better*, 147.

"Consciously or unconsciously" RAH, "Who Are the Heirs of Patrick Henry?," *Expanded Universe*, 392.

"You do realize" Patterson, *The Man Who Learned Better*, 153.

Campbell was skeptical of the whole approach JWC to RAH, June 10, 1958.

"I therefore played a very small part" Asimov, *In Joy Still Felt*, 10.

339 *"I fear Bob's going to induce"* JWC to Lurton Blassingame, March 4, 1959.

"the pious critic" RAH to Theodore Sturgeon, March 5, 1962, quoted in Patterson, *The Man Who Learned Better*, 185.

"the best setup for a novel" RAH to Theodore Sturgeon, February 11, 1955, quoted in Patterson, *The Man Who Learned Better*, 125.

340 *"ignoring length [and] taboos"* RAH to Lurton Blassingame, October 21, 1960, quoted in Patterson, *The Man Who Learned Better*, 203.

"I thought I was getting a saga" JWC to RAH, August 12, 1962.

"There ain't no such thing as a free lunch" The phrase was introduced to Heinlein by Jerry Pournelle in December 1964. Patterson, *The Man Who Learned Better*, 264.

he reluctantly rejected it JWC to RAH, July 6, 1965.

341 *"The central problem of today"* RAH to Rex Heinlein, December 4, 1960, quoted in Patterson, *The Man Who Learned Better*, 206.

in the absence of other strong personalities Asimov, *I. Asimov*, 76. Asimov incorrectly dated the shift in his political views to 1946, when RAH floated the idea that President Truman should appoint a Republican successor, laying the groundwork for a later return to power. Asimov misinterpreted the proposal: "This was the first indication to me that he had grown conservative." Asimov, *In Memory Yet Green*, 488.

a talk by Linus Pauling Asimov, *In Joy Still Felt*, 238.

"I think Bob Welch's methods" RAH to Dorothea Faulkner, July 27, 1961.

"psychogenic" JWC to RAH, May 3, 1957.

"a parasitic excrescence" RAH to Elizabeth Price, November 11, 1967, quoted in Patterson, *The Man Who Learned Better*, 277.

he had sampled marijuana "I'm afraid that I'm too square to have tried marijuana, but Robert did try it in his youth." Virginia Heinlein to Leon Stover, February 1982.

"as much of a failure as other drugs" RAH to Elizabeth Price, November 11, 1967, quoted in Patterson, *The Man Who Learned Better*, 277.

342 *"If a male and a female"* RAH to Marie Browne, December 18, 1968, quoted in Patterson, *The Man Who Learned Better*, 294.

342 *"innuendo for innuendo"* Asimov, *In Memory Yet Green*, 681.

"looked around" Frederik Pohl, "Our continued reminiscences of Isaac Asimov," November 10, 2010, http://www.thewaythefutureblogs.com /2010/11/isaac-asimov-part-6 (accessed December 2017).

"Well, what the hell do you do?" Asimov, *In Joy Still Felt*, 279.

343 *"I was having a stronger and stronger impulse"* *In Memory Yet Green*, 669.

Campbell turned it down JWC to Asimov, February 20, 1955.

they often quarreled over money White, *Isaac Asimov*, 156.

he hated that she smoked Asimov, *I. Asimov*, 106–8.

"In all those years I had not made her happy" Asimov, *In Joy Still Felt*, 32.

344 *"Genius at Work" and "Great Lover"* Freedman, *Conversations with Isaac Asimov*, 14.

"Gertrude complains" Asimov to RAH, January 27, 1955.

"miserably unhappy" Asimov to RAH, February 5, 1955.

Asimov was still selling stories to Campbell One of these stories, "Pâté de Foie Gras," was based on a premise from Peg. JWC to John Pomeroy, September 19, 1956.

"I would write one for him" Asimov, *In Joy Still Felt*, 52.

losing it would disappoint both his father and Campbell Poul Anderson, "In Memoriam," *Isaac Asimov's Science Fiction*, November 1992, 9–10.

"I berated myself" Asimov, *In Joy Still Felt*, 106.

345 *"What's your name?"* Ibid., 66.

"There's no need to end the evening, I hope" Ibid., 154.

He had grown closer to his other editors "I suppose it must have been Campbell's imprinting in the first place, but I have the tendency to look upon editors as security figures." Ibid., 250.

"I am glad to see" Ibid., 173.

"telling jokes" Asimov, *Asimov on Science Fiction*, 200.

346 *"Suppose you meet a man"* Asimov, *In Joy Still Felt*, 235.

"You'll regret all the years" This exchange is compiled from Asimov, *Opus 100*, xiv, and Asimov, *In Joy Still Felt*, 221.

a toy typewriter Asimov to RAH, August 25, 1956.

"They just sound too much like you" Asimov, *In Joy Still Felt*, 362.

psychiatrists and neurologists Asimov, *I. Asimov*, 175.

"Suppose you had to choose" Asimov, *In Joy Still Felt*, 221.

347 *a celebrity in the mainstream* Asimov was even mentioned briefly in Saul Bellow's 1964 novel *Herzog*, which treated him as a representative of the entire genre: "Was it mystery novels (Josephine Tey), or science fiction (Isaac Asimov)?"

"Say, Asimov" Asimov, *In Joy Still Felt*, 413.

347 *"God, Asimov"* White, *Isaac Asimov*, 151.

"We would, naturally, furnish some suitable posteriors" Earl Kemp to Asimov, December 11, 1961, reprinted in Stephanie Zvan, "We Don't Do That Anymore," *The Orbit*, September 9, 2012, https://the-orbit.net/almost diamonds/2012/09/09/we-dont-do-that-anymore (accessed December 2017).

"Of course, I could be persuaded" Ibid.; Asimov to Earl Kemp, December 14, 1961.

"the man with a hundred hands" Judith Merril, signed footnote in Asimov, *In Memory Yet Green*, 653n.

"The question then is not whether or not a girl should be touched" Asimov, *The Sensuous Dirty Old Man*, 108.

"Whenever we walked up the stairs" Segaloff, *A Lit Fuse*, 181.

348 *"hugging all the young ladies"* Asimov, *In Memory Yet Green*, 678.

"All you want to do is kiss" Asimov, *In Joy Still Felt*, 253.

the women found excuses to leave the building Gordon Van Gelder, e-mail to author, December 6, 2017. The source for this anecdote was the late Ruth Cavin, a former editor for Walker & Company.

Cele Goldsmith Davin, *Partners in Wonder*, 4.

"harmless" Asimov, *In Memory Yet Green*, 678.

"I kiss each young woman" Asimov, *In Joy Still Felt*, 175.

"Asimov . . . instead of shaking my date's hand" Edward L. Ferman, interviewed in Platt, *Dream Makers Volume II*, 246.

"It's like the old saying" Frederik Pohl, "Our continued reminiscences of Isaac Asimov," November 10, 2010, http://www.thewaythefutureblogs.com/2010/11/isaac-asimov-part-6 (accessed December 2017).

"unbearable convention manners" Asimov to Mildred Clingerman, September 5, 1956.

"Isaac says John made them up" Asimov, *In Joy Still Felt*, 304.

349 *"I would like to thank Mr. John W. Campbell, Jr."* Asimov to JWC, September 10, 1966.

investigated by the FBI Asimov's FBI file, which was released through the Freedom of Information Act, can be viewed at https://www.muck rock.com/foi/united-states-of-america-10/fbi-file-on-isaac-asimov-8300 (accessed December 2017).

a flying saucer Asimov, *In Joy Still Felt*, 397.

"He nearly had a heart attack" Dave Itzkoff, "Trying to Meet the Neighbors," *New York Times*, March 11, 2007.

350 *Roman Polanski* "At one of the embassy parties, Roman Polanski found Heinlein and introduced him to his wife, the stunningly beautiful Sharon Tate. She had been filming in Europe but had taken a break to join her husband at the festival. Ginny was off, circulating, as she usually did." Patterson, *The Man Who Learned Better*, 301. Patterson's source was evi-

dently Virginia Heinlein, but other sources indicate that Tate had flown to Europe on March 24, 1969, and no record exists of any such visit to Rio. Bugliosi, *Helter Skelter*, 281–82.

350 *"the greatest spiritual experience I've undergone in my life"* Patterson, *The Man Who Learned Better*, 307.

"This is the greatest event" Ibid., 309.

a television panel moderated by Rod Serling Video of the panel can be found online at https://www.youtube.com/watch?v=tFkqGDEAi_4 (accessed December 2017).

Analog *sent a press representative* The reporter was Russell Seitz, a graduate student at MIT. JWC, In Times to Come, *Analog,* December 1969, 155.

Campbell attended his funeral Lester del Rey, in *Locus,* July 12, 1971, 4.

"the greatest show ever staged" JWC, "7/20/69," *Analog,* November 1969, 4.

"Annette or Nanette or something" Patterson, *The Man Who Learned Better,* 313. Patterson identifies the writer as Lynette "Squeaky" Fromme, but a source within the Manson Family states: "Gypsy [Catherine Share], who also used another alias, Manon Minette, spent her time writing letters to Robert Heinlein to see if he would help bail us out. . . . He wrote her back a nice letter admitting he had done some pranks in his youth, but unlike the character in his book *Stranger in a Strange Land,* he was unable to offer any other type of legal or financial support. He was, however, very sympathetic." Lake and Herman, *Member of the Family,* 336.

"Honey, this is worse" Patterson, *The Man Who Learned Better,* 313.

351 *"In the psychotic mind"* "A Martian Model," *Time,* January 19, 1970, 44–45.

Manson subsequently denied J. Neil Schulman, "Manson and Heinlein," letter to the *Los Angeles Times,* January 20, 1991. A copy of *Stranger in a Strange Land* was found at Barker Ranch in Death Valley National Park, where Manson was arrested in October 1969. Gifford, *Robert A. Heinlein: A Reader's Companion,* 247n.

letters from members of the Manson Family "Some weeks ago, a fan letter came in from the jail in Independence, California. In a burst of generosity, Robert tried to do something about this girl who'd written him. It turned out that she was one of the Manson family. So if we're knifed in our beds like Sharon Tate, it's because of three letters from members of the family." Virginia Heinlein to Lurton Blassingame, January 7, 1970, quoted in RAH, *Grumbles from the Grave,* 240–41.

"the new mental health cult" Bugliosi, *Helter Skelter,* 200.

"A cell partner turned me on to Scientology" Manson, *Manson in His Own Words,* 70.

"What do you do after 'clear?'" Bugliosi, *Helter Skelter,* 318.

352 *"That girl is insane"* Ibid., 291.

the Aum Shinrikyo cult "In an interview, [Hideo] Murai would state matter-of-factly that Aum was using the Foundation series as the blueprint for the cult's long-term plans." David E. Kaplan and Andrew Marshall, "The Cult at the End of the World," *Wired*, July 1, 1996.

"There's somebody on the moon today" Guinn, *Manson*, 229–30.

CHAPTER 15: TWILIGHT (1960–1971)

353 *"For each human soul"* JWC, "On the Nature of Angels," *Analog*, September 1971, 160.

"I've seen some pictures of a gadget" JWC, "The Ultrafeeble Interactions," *ASF*, December 1959, 160.

354 *"a contraption of rotating eccentric weights"* Ibid.

"I believe the true space drive" JWC, "The Space-Drive Problem, *ASF*, June 1960, 100.

who met Dean at the editor's house Asimov, *In Joy Still Felt*, 196.

John R. Pierce of Bell Labs Harrison, *Harry Harrison! Harry Harrison!*, 264.

the roboticist Marvin Minsky Knight, *In Search of Wonder*, 50.

the government had conducted a lynching JWC, "Scientific Lynch Law," *Analog*, October 1961, 4–5, 176–78.

"Now, Sprague!" De Camp, *Time and Chance*, 222.

355 *the new principles of physics* Dr. William O. Davis, "The Fourth Law of Motion," *Analog*, May 1962, 83–104.

dowsing JWC came to believe that dowsing was a better introduction to psionics than the Hieronymus Machine, since it was easier to demonstrate. The author Poul Anderson was impressed by how reliably a homemade dowsing rod could find an underground water pipe—although his daughter noted that there was a visible depression in the grass. Author interview with Astrid Bear, August 19, 2016.

astrology JWC ran weather forecasts by the astrologer Joseph F. Goodavage, who had correctly predicted that Kennedy would die in office: "It is coincidental that each American president in office at the time of these conjunctions [of Jupiter and Saturn in an earth sign] either died or was assassinated before leaving the presidency. . . . John F. Kennedy was elected in 1960 at the time of a Jupiter and Saturn conjunction in Capricorn." Joseph F. Goodavage, "The First Science," *Analog*, September 1962, 109–10. The first of his astrological weather forecasts appeared in *Analog* in October 1962.

his discoveries tended to stay within **Analog** Damon Knight thought that this was a conscious strategy: "He deliberately cultivated technically oriented writers with marginal writing skills. . . . Campbell was building a new stable he knew he could keep." Quoted in Westfahl, *The Mechanics of Wonder*, 285–86.

355 *"Fred, you did real good"* Pohl, *The Way the Future Was*, 91.

356 *"[Campbell] considered my writing"* Dick, *The Minority Report*, 379.
Dick sold just one story to Campbell "Impostor," *ASF*, June 1953, 58–70. Dick said that JWC asked him to revise it repeatedly, adding that he would "rather write several first-draft stories for one cent a word than spend time revising a single story for Campbell, despite the higher pay." Davin, *Partners in Wonder*, 147.
"He liked his ideas better than mine" Author interview with Larry Niven, August 20, 2016.
"Sprague de Camp can't make the magazine" JWC to Gotthard Gunther, July 29, 1957.
"a book-learning follower" JWC to William R. Burkett, Jr., July 1, 1968. JWC refers to Asimov only as "a professor of chemistry," but his identity is clear from context.
"The Great Old Authors" JWC, in Rogers, *A Requiem for Astounding*, xxi.
"rejected discussion of his ideas" JWC to "Spring," May 30, 1957.
"He's scared blue-with-chartreuse-spots" JWC to E. E. Smith, April 11, 1959.
"[Heinlein is] much more concerned" JWC to Col. F. W. Ott, February 23, 1967.

357 *"as an effort to confine his artistic creativity"* Ibid.
"ten pages of his arrogant insults" RAH, *Grumbles from the Grave*, 152.
"really bitter" arguments Theodore Sturgeon, at the panel "The Man John W. Campbell," Conclave III, Romulus, MI, November 4, 1978. Recording courtesy of the SFOHA Archives.
"invalidated" himself as an editor Robert Silverberg, in Solstein and Moosnick, *JWC's Golden Age of Science Fiction*, 26.
"I can't speak for Isaac or Ted" Robert Silverberg, e-mail exchange with author, September 20–21, 2016.
"adolescent demigod" JWC to Tom Godwin, September 19, 1953.
"Congratulations!" JWC to Frank Herbert, June 3, 1963.

358 *"Sorry to see her go"* JWC to Frank Herbert, January 22, 1964.
ideas for sequels JWC to Frank Herbert, March 25, 1964.
"Paul was a damn fool" JWC to Frank Herbert, summer 1968, quoted in Herbert, *The Road to Dune*, 293.
"In this one, it's Paul" JWC to Lurton Blassingame, October 15, 1968.

359 *"slightly open-mouthed adoration"* RAH to JWC, January 4, 1942.
"somewhat of a lesbian" JWC to Eric Frank Russell, May 9, 1958.

359 *he was unaffected by the change in ownership* Apart from the new title, the most visible effect on the magazine was a brief experiment with a larger format, which was published from March 1963 to March 1965.

he employed the company to get his ideas out JWC to Ronald E. Graham, September 8, 1969, reprinted in Bangsund, *JWC: An Australian Tribute*, 86.

"carefully expurgated to suit the most prudish" JWC to John W. Campbell, Sr., May 15, 1953.

"And since when does the Condé Nast Publications, Incorporated" Bova, "John Campbell and the Modern SF Idiom."

Alan Dean Foster Author interview with Alan Dean Foster, August 29, 2016.

Vietnam wasn't ready for democracy JWC, "Keeperism," *Analog*, July 1965, 5–6, 159–62.

a statement in support of American intervention In an advertisement that appeared in the June 1968 issue of *Galaxy*, the signatories in favor of the United States remaining in Vietnam included Heinlein, de Camp, Williamson, and dozens of others. A statement opposing the war was signed by an even greater number, including Asimov, Bradbury, del Rey, and Gene Roddenberry.

Gregory Benford Speech at Campbell Conference Awards banquet, MidAmeriCon II, Kansas City, Missouri, August 18, 2016.

360 *Campbell had written dismissively of tachyons* "Most scientists aren't up on [tachyons] either, and a large number seem to feel there's nothing to be up on!" JWC, Brass Tacks, *Analog*, June 1968, 167.

"a bit too esoteric" JWC to Gregory Benford, March 5, 1970.

"something for nothing" JWC, "Impossible Problem," *Analog*, November 1967, 178.

"The problem with this country" Gregory Benford, at the panel "The World of Tomorrow is Today," MidAmeriCon II, Kansas City, Missouri, August 20, 2016.

"There is such a thing as a nigger" JWC to Reese Danley Kilgo, August 31, 1966.

361 *"All human beings are not equal"* JWC to Poul Anderson, February 14, 1956.

"If you deny the existence of racial differences" JWC to Asimov, December 2, 1955.

"The result is that the old question" JWC to Asimov, December 21, 1955.

362 *"Essentially, I am forced to answer"* JWC to Asimov, January 20, 1956.

"I think [Campbell] saw himself" Asimov to Tom Cole, June 13, 1989, reprinted in Tom Cole, "Postcard That Isaac Asimov Sent to Me," http://

www.tomhascallcole.com/asimovpostcardtome.html (accessed December 2017).

362 *"Any more and the friendship will be destroyed"* Asimov, *Asimov on Science Fiction*, 199.

And their differences The argument erupted again in a series of letters that began in late 1961. In a note in his archives, Asimov stated that they corresponded less frequently toward the end of JWC's life because of their disagreement over social issues. Isaac Asimov Collection, Howard Gotlieb Archival Research Center, Boston University, Box 139.

"a high-order civilization" JWC to Asimov, October 12, 1957.

"a new heresy" Anderson, *All One Universe*, 70.

"Slavery is a useful educational system" JWC to RAH, April 5, 1957.

363 *"interesting letter"* RAH to JWC, April 18, 1957.

"Slavery is a system" JWC, "Unimaginable Reasons," *ASF*, July 1960, 176.

"Gentlemen, you can't reduce everything" Harrison, *Harry Harrison! Harry Harrison!*, 265.

unsympathetic to calls for social justice "Sure, it's mighty easy for a brilliant Negro to feel that all his troubles are race prejudice. Never having been a brilliant Caucasian, he can't possibly have the experience that the brilliant white is just as roundly rejected, and just as thoroughly frustrated." JWC, "Evolution Without Mutations," *ASF*, June 1957, 162. On May 22, 1957, JWC wrote to RAH: "Ike Asimov had suffered for a good many years under the pressure of antisemitism . . . until he discovered it was anti-intellectualism he was suffering from!"

an unfair traffic ticket JWC, "It Ain't My Job," *Analog*, January 1962, 4–5, 173–78.

"The police have as their function" JWC, "Breakthrough in Psychology," *Analog*, December 1965, 159–60.

"Think about it a bit" JWC to Ron Stoloff, May 1, 1969.

"If Negro authors are extremely few" Ibid.

"minimizing race problems" JWC to Elinore Wackernagel, July 29, 1952.

364 *"The guy can write"* JWC to Henry Morrison, September 29, 1965 and October 17, 1966.

who had briefly met Campbell Samuel R. Delany, e-mail to author, January 12, 2018.

"Campbell . . . didn't feel his readership" Delany, "Racism and Science Fiction." At the following year's Nebulas, another win by Delany prompted Asimov to venture an awkward joke: "You know, Chip, we only voted you those awards because you're Negro."

"a black main character" Two apparent exceptions were the serials "Black Man's Burden" and "Border, Breed Nor Birth" by Mack Reynolds, which ran their first installments in the December 1961 and July 1962 issues of

Analog. Reynolds recalled that the stories, about a group of black activists in North Africa, "were written at a suggestion of John Campbell's and whole chunks of them were based on his ideas." Most of the characters, regardless of race, sounded just like JWC. Mack Reynolds, introduction to "Black Sheep Astray," in Harrison, *Astounding,* 202.

365 *Joe Haldeman* Author interview with Joe Haldeman, August 20, 2016.
"The aboriginal race of Australia" JWC, "No Other Race," *ASF,* May 1939, 50.
"And Ike, my friend" JWC to Asimov, November 13, 1958.
homosexuality was a sign of cultural decline JWC, "Situation Normal: Explosive," *ASF,* November 1957, 158.
"My God!" JWC to RAH, March 9, 1950.
When it came to women The author Leslie F. Stone claimed that JWC said to her in 1938, "I do not believe that women are capable of writing science fiction—nor do I approve of it!" Even if he held this opinion at the time, it was soon contradicted by experience. Davin, *Partners in Wonder,* 144–45.
"girlish special privileges" JWC to Jack Wodham, June 28, 1971.
"Are you sure, dear?" JWC to Poul Anderson, March 28, 1953.

366 *"No woman has ever attained"* JWC to Asimov, January 20, 1954.
Pauline Ashwell JWC loved Ashwell's first story, "Unwillingly to School," but was discouraged by its lukewarm reception: "It didn't go over so hot—our readers appear to be less than enthusiastic about the peculiarities of teenage girl's thinking." JWC to RAH, March 25, 1962.
Campbell admired Islam JWC to Raymond F. Jones, March 17, 1954.
"He never, not once" Asimov, *The Early Asimov,* 203.
"a fairly decent little Jew-boy" JWC to Robert Swisher, March 7, 1937.
"You ever hear of Isaac Asimov?" Robert Silverberg, e-mail exchange with author, September 20, 2016.
"Phil, I want you to know something" Philip Klass, in Solstein and Moosnick, *JWC's Golden Age of Science Fiction,* 29–30.

367 *to complain about the excess of psionics* Harlan Ellison to JWC, April 15, 1958.
he had a "shocker" JWC to Harlan Ellison, December 6, 1965.
their differences were more temperamental Author interview with Ben Bova, September 15, 2016.
the editor's submissive circle of writers Harlan Ellison, *Dangerous Visions,* 512.
"John W. Campbell, Jr., who used to edit a magazine" Ibid., xxi.
"destructive, rather than constructive" JWC to Perry Chapdelaine, June 30, 1969.
"He needs a muzzle" JWC to Anthony Lewis, June 28, 1971.
"He's buying it?" Bova, *Future Crime,* 152.

367 *"Harlan's always wanted to win your approval"* Ben Bova to JWC, January 9, 1970.

"I don't know whether it's the hyper-defensive attitude" JWC to Joe Poyer, October 23, 1967.

368 *"In fact, John"* Asimov to JWC, September 30, 1963, quoted in Asimov, *Yours, Isaac Asimov*, 99–101.

Krebiozen JWC, "Fully Identified," *Analog*, January 1964, 7, 95.

"I want a chance to vote for a different approach!" JWC, "Political Entropy," *Analog*, November 1968, 178.

"a terrible choice" JWC to Leigh Atkinson, October 31, 1968.

the protesters at Kent State JWC, "The New Stone Age," *Analog*, September 1970, 4–7, 175–78.

the ecologist Rachel Carson JWC, "Deadly Poison," *Analog*, February 1971, 162.

"a crypto-fascist deeply philistine magazine" Moorcock, "Starship Stormtroopers," reprinted in *The Opium General and Other Stories*.

369 **Mother Night** Howard W. Campbell, Jr., also appears briefly in *Slaughterhouse-Five*.

she had suffered a heart attack JWC to Will Jenkins, April 9, 1962.

"These are the issues that are going to matter" Malzberg, *The Engines of the Night*, 73f.

370 *turned on to science fiction in his teens* Alexander, *Star Trek Creator*, 31.

371 *counted Asimov and Heinlein* Ibid., 188n.

The names on his list of potential writers Ibid., 238.

unable to work within the confines of television Ibid., 239.

"Hey, fellow, stop talking" Ibid., 266.

"No breath of prescience" Asimov, *In Joy Still Felt*, 404.

how to make better use of William Shatner Alexander, *Star Trek Creator*, 280–81.

"It might be well to unify" Ibid., 282.

372 *"I will follow your advice"* Ibid., 283.

"overly generous, to put it mildly" RAH to Harlan Ellison, December 29, 1967, quoted in Patterson, *The Man Who Learned Better*, 289.

he had lifted the basic notion Patterson, *The Man Who Learned Better*, 289.

a telegram to go out over Asimov's name Alexander, *Star Trek Creator*, 301.

the rights to **I, Robot** Ibid., 331, 357.

"My major sadness" Ibid., 313.

"I'm joining in the campaign" JWC to Gene Roddenberry, January 23, 1968.

373 *"Too often they've taken old space toys"* Alexander, *Star Trek Creator*, 342.

the problems of trade between aliens Ibid.

373 *a visit to Desilu Studios* JWC to Poul Anderson, November 19, 1968.

offered to send him a kalliroscope JWC to J. Russell Seitz, September 19, 1968.

"Well, for that week" Alexander, *Star Trek Creator*, 343.

his opinion that slavery Ibid., 347–48.

"I can see no signs" Ibid., 348.

"Time, I think, to wash **Star Trek***"* Robb, *A Brief Guide to Star Trek*, 62.

374 *"lousing up the one good science fiction show"* JWC to Poul Anderson, January 13, 1969.

"I'm afraid I can't use **Analog***"* JWC to Gene Roddenberry, February 20, 1969.

Walking down Madison Avenue Theodore Sturgeon, at the panel "The Man John W. Campbell," Conclave III, Romulus, MI, November 4, 1978. Recording courtesy of the SFOHA Archives.

severe hypertension Leslyn Randazzo, e-mail to author, July 31, 2016.

suffered from gout JWC first mentioned the possibility of gout in a letter to Asimov on February 17, 1958, but it only appears on a regular basis in his letters starting toward the end of 1965.

painful tophi Peg Campbell to A. E. van Vogt, August 3, 1971.

he scooted around on a stool Leslyn Randazzo, e-mail to author, July 31, 2016.

pain in one arm JWC, memo to Toni Thompson, September 26, 1966. Brown University, *Analog Science Fiction & Fact* editorial records, Box 3.

unable to manage the walk Moskowitz, "Inside John W. Campbell," 3.

Benford saw him fall down Gregory Benford, at the panel "The World of Tomorrow is Today," MidAmeriCon II, Kansas City, Missouri, August 20, 2016.

Poul Anderson found him so crippled Anderson, *Going for Infinity*, 185.

375 *tobacco might even suppress cancer* JWC, note on "Possible Relationships Between Smoking and Lung Cancer," *Analog*, May 1964, 83.

"Tobacco is not habit-forming" JWC, "The Lynch-Mob Philosophy," *Analog*, July 1969, 176.

to quit or die Green, "Our Five Days With John W. Campbell."

he experimented with marijuana JWC to H. R. Ralston, April 16, 1962. He also said that he had sampled "an African witch doctor drug" that a friend was researching.

his poor health left a mark on his personality The writer John Brunner believed that JWC had blacklisted him from the magazine in retaliation for an exchange at a panel in 1965, concluding: "John was a man who knew how to hold a grudge." John Brunner, in a letter to George Hay, quoted in *The John W. Campbell Letters, Vol. 1*, 5.

375 *"Patience, tolerance, and forgiveness"* JWC to Frank Herbert, February 8, 1971.
376 *"the distant, dark horizon"* Green, "Our Five Days With John W. Campbell."
Roger Ebert Roger Ebert to JWC, April 17, 1962. In a letter dated April 23, JWC asked to see the article, but it never appeared in the magazine.
"my hero" Roger Ebert, "Sunshine," *Chicago Sun-Times,* July 19, 2007.
serving up beer and pretzels Ben Bova, interview with Alan Elms, LACon II, Anaheim, California, September 1, 1984. Recording courtesy of the SFOHA Archives.
the fanzine editor Arnie Katz John Foyster, in Bangsund, *JWC: An Australian Tribute,* 79.
"My God, you talk together" Peg Campbell, in JWC, *The Best of JWC,* 306.
remedial reading in Ohio JWC to Poul Anderson, December 5, 1967.
Tarrant as a role model JWC to Leslyn Campbell, November 6, 1964.
When Leslyn left to see Doña Leslyn Randazzo, e-mail to author, July 31, 2016.
377 *Campbell felt unwell* The most complete account of JWC's death appears in Moskowitz, "Inside John W. Campbell," 2.
professional wrestling JWC may have enjoyed wrestling because it reminded him of his old friend Mike Mihalakis, who had been a professional wrestler before becoming an inventor. JWC to Mike Mihalakis, May 11, 1971.
378 *"a walking time bomb"* Leslyn Randazzo, e-mail to author, July 31, 2016.
Sam Moskowitz had driven by the house Author interview with Stanley Schmidt, May 13, 2016.
He usually turned in his editorials Ibid.
"It never occurred to me" Asimov, introduction to Harrison, *Astounding,* xiv.
Asimov picked up the del Reys Asimov, *In Joy Still Felt,* 573.
Dickson's room at the Algonquin Harrison, *Harry Harrison! Harry Harrison!,* 268.
"I know he's not here" Ibid.
"one of the nasty ones" Ibid.
379 *a recording of Campbell's voice* Philip Klass, in Solstein and Moosnick, *JWC's Golden Age of Science Fiction,* 65.
Leslyn's husband said Leslyn Randazzo, e-mail to author, July 31, 2016.
a dirty joke about a parrot Sam Moskowitz, handwritten notes for *Seekers of Tomorrow,* Sam Moskowitz Collection, Texas A&M University, Series VIII: Subject Files, Box 3-150, "Campbell, John W." It is tempting

to identify this joke with the one with the punch line "Brother Ignatius, put down your beads. Our prayers have been answered!" Asimov, *Treasury of Humor*, 401.

379 *"I'm sorry, Peg"* Asimov, *Asimov on Science Fiction*, 201.

"The field has lost its conscience" Malzberg, *The Engines of the Night*, 66.

The Society for Creative Anachronism Elliot Shorter, interview with Alan Elms and Paul Pearson, LACon II, Anaheim, California, September 2, 1984. Recording courtesy of the SFOHA Archives.

The Forever War Joe Haldeman, at the panel "The Legacy of John W. Campbell," Nebula Conference, May 13, 2016.

"One never can tell" JWC to Harold Schwartzberg, July 13, 1971.

380 *"to keep our soul's b value"* JWC, "On the Nature of Angels," *Analog*, September 1971, 160.

"This is science fiction" Harrison, *The Astounding-Analog Reader*, ix–x.

"You know—things can go into a black hole" JWC, "Those Impossible Quasars," *Analog*, December 1971, 178.

"Who, in your opinion" Asimov, *In Joy Still Felt*, 575.

EPILOGUE: BEYOND THIS HORIZON

381 *"The very act of trying to look ahead"* Octavia E. Butler, "A Few Rules for Predicting the Future," *Essence*, May 2000, 166.

the ocean liner SS Statendam Details of the cruise are drawn primarily from Weiner, "A Stowaway to the Thanatosphere"; Asimov, *In Joy Still Felt*, 621–24; and Patterson, *The Man Who Learned Better*, 336–38.

"a ship of fools" Asimov, *In Joy Still Felt*, 622.

382 *wondered what they were supposed to be doing* Author interview with Rex Weiner, August 19, 2017.

"Did anyone ever tell you" Asimov, *In Joy Still Felt*, 587.

"monumentally boring" Weiner, "A Stowaway to the Thanatosphere."

383 *Pohl saw Asimov, Heinlein, and Sturgeon* Frederik Pohl, "The Ship of Foolishness, Part 3: Apollo 17," November 24, 2010, http://www.theway thefutureblogs.com/2010/11/the-ship-of-foolishness-part-3-apollo-17 (accessed December 2017).

Heinlein compared it to an atomic explosion Heinlein makes the comparison in the 1972 short documentary film "Voyage Beyond Apollo," which can be viewed at https://www.youtube.com/watch?v=JTrzxIh8jX8 (accessed December 2017).

"Oh, shit" Asimov, *In Joy Still Felt*, 623. Rex Weiner confirmed the story in an interview with the author on August 19, 2017.

he could speak for only fifteen minutes Patterson, *The Man Who Learned Better*, 338.

383 *"rather wandering"* Asimov, *In Joy Still Felt,* 624.
the journalist Tom Wolfe Wolfe, *The Right Stuff,* ix.

384 *had to be cut by thirty thousand words* RAH to Gregory Benford, October 31, 1973.
he had never ceased to see as a war hero "Thank fortune that Robert never saw [Miller's *Bare-Faced Messiah*], because he had a lot of faith in Hubbard and did not realize what a four-flusher he was." Virginia Heinlein to William H. Patterson, Jr., July 17, 1999.
"I am trembling as I write this" Philip K. Dick to RAH, February 11, 1974, quoted in Patterson, *The Man Who Learned Better,* 358.

385 *"If Isaac doesn't know the answer"* Tom Collins, "Tonight I Met Robert Heinlein," *Transient* #31, 1974. Quoted in Patterson, *The Man Who Learned Better,* 607n.
never written a memorable character Virginia Heinlein to William H. Patterson, Jr., November 7, 1999.
"Fuck the other writers!" McAleer, *Visionary,* 223.

386 *"Now they're accusing us old-timers"* LRH to RAH, December 24, 1980, reprinted in LRH, *Literary Correspondence,* 168.
a commercial ticket to the moon RAH, "Spinoff," *Expanded Universe,* 511.
Dalgliesh had "disliked" him RAH, *Expanded Universe,* 207, 354.
"the only story of mine" Ibid., 93.
George R. R. Martin Author interview with George R. R. Martin, August 19, 2016.
"It sometimes seems to me" Asimov, *I. Asimov,* 529.

387 *he had sliced up his novels for serialization* RAH, *Expanded Universe,* 276.
Harry Harrison, Poul Anderson, and Fred Pohl *Locus,* July 30, 1971, 1.
"in ability and character" Asimov, *In Joy Still Felt,* 581.
Bob Lapham Ben Bova, interview with Alan Elms, LACon II, Anaheim, California, September 1, 1984. Recording courtesy of the SFOHA Archives.
"Here we've had a good lunch" Stallings and Evans, *Murray Leinster,* 93.
a negative review of **Expanded Universe** Alexei Panshin, "Expanded Universe," *Omni,* April 1981, 32–34. Bova published a more positive review by Jack Williamson in the July 1981 issue.

388 *"I don't think Star Wars is feasible"* William J. Broad, "Sci-Fi Authors Use Their Vision In Defense Debate," *New York Times News Service,* May 2, 1985.
"technological obscenities" McAleer, *Visionary,* 253. Clarke delivered his remarks by videotape.

389 *"a bucket of nails"* Arthur C. Clarke, "War and Peace in the Space Age," *Analog,* July 1983, 163.

389 *"But Max, I learned everything"* Patterson, *The Man Who Learned Better*, 445.

"He accused me of typically British arrogance" McAleer, *Visionary*, 255.

"I can't help the British" Ibid., 256.

"Does this remind you of anything?" Ibid.

"Though I felt sad about this incident" Arthur C. Clarke, "Robert Heinlein," in Kondo, *Requiem*, 264.

390 *"[Heinlein] had a definite feeling"* Asimov, *I. Asimov*, 76.

he banished all of Heinlein's books Author interview with Greg Bear, August 19, 2016.

"If [his enemies] caught up with him" Miller, *Bare-Faced Messiah*, 296.

391 *a typewriter that was discarded after a single use* Atack, *A Piece of Blue Sky*, 253.

"Your good friend, J. Edgar Hoover" Wright, *Going Clear*, 146.

"He was a mess" Author interview with James Randi, August 9, 2017.

the names of the Seven Dwarfs Wright, *Going Clear*, 151.

the Snow White Program Accounts of this program often refer to it as "Operation Snow White," but this usage was unknown within the church itself. Tony Ortega, e-mail to author, October 20, 2017.

392 *a third of the crew* Atack, *A Piece of Blue Sky*, 233.

"a wonderful trip" Miller, *Bare-Faced Messiah*, 329.

"He was talking about people" Ibid., 347.

393 *"That stupid fucking kid!"* Ibid., 342.

"And that poses the interesting probability" Atack, *A Piece of Blue Sky*, 293.

one of his favorite movies LRH's favorite films included *Star Wars, Diva, Citizen Kane, Slaughterhouse-Five,* and *Patton.* Ibid., 393.

394 *a teenager named David Miscavige* Ibid., 300.

"an insatiable lust for power and money" Miller, *Bare-Faced Messiah*, 356.

some of which were drawn from his old stories "Another time [LRH] was on a disabled spaceship that landed here before life began and realized the potential and brought seeds back from another planet to fertilize planet earth." Kima Douglas, quoted in Miller, *Bare-Faced Messiah*, 360. This recalls LRH, "The Emperor of the Universe," *Startling Stories,* November 1949, 132–41.

395 *fifty thousand members* Atack, *A Piece of Blue Sky*, 389.

"deeply involved" Declaration of Lawrence H. Brennan, Merrimack County, New Hampshire, May 6, 2008.

seven hundred pages of handwritten notes LRH, *Writer: The Shaper of Popular Fiction*, 143.

Man: The Endangered Species "About the Author," note to LRH, "The Were-Human," *Fantasy Book,* October 1981, 43.

395 *Mitt Romney* Jim Rutenberg, "Romney Favors Hubbard Novel," The Caucus, *New York Times,* April 30, 2007, https://thecaucus.blogs.ny times.com/2007/04/30/romney-favors-hubbard-novel (accessed December 2017).

396 *Van Vogt couldn't finish it* Miller, *Bare-Faced Messiah,* 366.
"It's a great story, Ron" RAH to LRH, December 16, 1982, reprinted in LRH, *Literary Correspondence,* 169.
John Travolta Wright, *Going Clear,* 209.
Miscavige personally delivered Robert Vaughn Young, "L. Ron Hubbard's *Mission Earth,*" February 19, 2000, http://www.lermanet.com/cos /MissionEarth.htm (accessed December 2017).
their price tags still attached Robert W. Welkos and Joel Sappell, "Costly Strategy Continues to Turn Out Bestsellers," *Los Angeles Times,* June 28, 1990.
The Dick Cavett Show Asimov, *In Joy Still Felt,* 521. Asimov doesn't identify the actress by name, and the only other guest mentioned in listings for the episode is the humorist Sam Levenson.

397 *"Yes, I am"* Ibid.
she was suffering from arthritis Asimov, *I. Asimov,* 335.
"You know, my apartment" Asimov, *In Joy Still Felt,* 533.

398 *"exasperating—but fascinating"* Ibid., 565.
Woody Allen Allen met with Asimov to discuss the script for his film *Sleeper* and offered him the position of technical director, which ultimately went to Ben Bova. Ibid., 625–26.
Paul McCartney McCartney wanted to collaborate on a movie about "two sets of musical groups: a real one, and a group of extraterrestrial impostors." Asimov wrote a treatment, but after he was asked to start over from scratch, he "bowed out politely." Ibid., 693.
Steven Spielberg Spielberg asked him to work on the film *Close Encounters of the Third Kind,* but Asimov was reluctant to participate in a movie that "glorified flying saucers." *In Joy Still Felt,* 716, and Clarke Taylor, "Isaac Asimov and Science Fiction," *Los Angeles Times,* February 7, 1988. Asimov called the result "a rotten picture." Asimov, *Asimov on Science Fiction,* 292.

399 *"I keep telling you to be careful"* Asimov, *I. Asimov,* 340.
"If it hadn't been a mild one" Asimov, *In Joy Still Felt,* 775.
"I expected cheerful volubility" Amis, *Visiting Mrs. Nabokov,* 220.
"There's Asimov, applauding his own name" Asimov, *I. Asimov,* 367.
to put its horrors on-screen "Bill [Lancaster] wrote the screenplay with the monster in shadows, the old Hollywood cliché stuff, which everybody still talks about even to this day. Rob Bottin was the guy who said, 'No, you've got to put him in the light, then the audience really goes nuts.

They really go nuts because there it is in front of them.' I wasn't sure, but that's what we did." John Carpenter, interviewed by Erik Bauer, *Creative Screenwriting*, July 22, 2014, https://creativescreenwriting.com/the-thing (accessed December 2017).

399 *"pointless, dehumanized freeway smashup"* Ellison, *An Edge in My Voice*, 293.

400 *"Type faster"* Asimov, *I. Asimov*, 205.
"Listen, I must have plenty of oxygen" Ibid., 484.
"There was an old doctor named Paul" Ibid., 486.
Asimov came down with a fever Janet Asimov, in Asimov, *It's Been a Good Life*, 251.

401 *"a debt to science fiction"* Carl Sagan, "Growing Up with Science Fiction," *New York Times*, May 28, 1978. On October 10, 1968, JWC wrote to Sagan to propose a meeting in Cambridge, but it isn't clear if they ever met.
she underwent a sudden decline George O. Smith, in Reginald, *Science Fiction and Fantasy Literature, Volume 2*, 1080.
Peg sold her crewel business George O. Smith, "In Memoriam: Margaret Winter Campbell," *Isaac Asimov's Science Fiction Magazine*, February 1980, 10–11.
"Personally, I don't give a fuck" Michael Kurland, e-mail to author, November 8, 2017.
"no matter that we may leave the surface" LRH, "Flag Order 3879: The Sea Org & The Future," January 19, 1986.

402 *"Let's get this over with!"* Wright, *Going Clear*, 226.
"L. Ron Hubbard discarded the body" Miller, *Bare-Faced Messiah*, 372–73.
they later settled with the estate Atack, *A Piece of Blue Sky*, 397.
At three remote compounds The plans to preserve LRH's work are described in detail in "Preservation for Eternity," *International Scientology News 64*, 26–39.
including his fiction Author interview with Chuck Beatty, August 28, 2017.

403 *"Now all there is to worry about"* Virginia Heinlein, circular letter, August 18, 1986, quoted in Patterson, *The Man Who Learned Better*, 454.
"I'm just going to do it" Patterson, *The Man Who Learned Better*, 461.

404 *"Now you know the answer"* Virginia Heinlein to RAH, June 29, 1988, quoted in Patterson, *The Man Who Learned Better*, 470.
"spouted off in his usual fashion" Ibid., 473.
"When Robert died" Virginia Heinlein, "Relationships," biographical essay in the RAH Archives, UC Santa Cruz.

405 *in an unresponsive state* Mark Cole, "The Clown Prince of Science Fic-

tion: Inside the Wild and Undisciplined Mind Of Randall Garrett," *The Internet Review of Science Fiction*, September 2009, http://www.irosf .com/q/zine/article/10578 (accessed December 2017).

405 *He suffered "wipeouts"* Asimov, *I. Asimov*, 533–34.

"You clearly don't know my husband's work" Grazer, *A Curious Mind*, 99.

Marilyn vos Savant Julie Baumgold, "In the Kingdom of the Brain," *New York Magazine*, February 6, 1989, 41.

"Well, you might have been ready to die" Asimov, *I. Asimov*, 538.

it came back positive Janet Asimov, in Asimov, *It's Been a Good Life*, 252.

406 *"I'm seventy-one and a half"* Ben Bova, "Isaac," *Isaac Asimov's Science Fiction*, November 1992, 15.

Gertrude had died of breast cancer White, *Isaac Asimov*, 222.

"David's great hobby" Asimov, *I. Asimov*, 176.

"the biggest child pornography collection" Eric Brazil, "Charges shatter Asimov son's reclusion," *San Francisco Examiner*, March 15, 1998.

three years' probation PACER case locator search, accessed on November 14, 2017.

"It has always been my ambition" Asimov, "Farewell Farewell," *The Magazine of Fantasy and Science Fiction*, August 1992, quoted in Asimov, *I. Asimov*, 551.

"Do you have a typewriter I can use?" Asimov, *Asimov Laughs Again*, 145.

407 *"Isaac, you're the best there is"* Janet Asimov, epilogue to Asimov, *I. Asimov*, 551–52.

"I love you, too" Ibid., 551.

"We are now living in a science fictional world" Asimov, in Solstein and Moosnick, *JWC's Golden Age of Science Fiction*, 21.

408 *"I want—"* Janet Asimov, epilogue to Asimov, *I. Asimov*, 551.

BIBLIOGRAPHY

Aldiss, Brian. *Billion Year Spree*. Garden City, NY: Doubleday, 1973.

Alexander, David. *Star Trek Creator: The Authorized Biography of Gene Roddenberry*. New York: Roc, 1994.

Amis, Kingsley. *New Maps of Hell*. New York: Arno, 1975.

Amis, Martin. *Visiting Mrs. Nabokov*. London: Jonathan Cape, 1993.

Anderson, Poul. *All One Universe*. New York: Tor, 1997.

———. *Going for Infinity*. New York: Tor, 2002.

Ashley, Mike. *Gateways to Forever: The Story of the Science-Fiction Magazines from 1970 to 1980*. Liverpool: Liverpool University Press, 2007.

———. *The Time Machines: The Story of the Science-Fiction Pulp Magazines from the Beginning to 1950*. Liverpool: Liverpool University Press, 2000.

———. *Transformations: The Story of the Science Fiction Magazines from 1950 to 1970*. Liverpool: Liverpool University Press, 2005.

Asimov, Isaac. *Asimov Laughs Again*. New York: HarperCollins, 1992.

———. *Asimov on Science Fiction*. Garden City, NY: Doubleday, 1981.

———. *Before the Golden Age*. Garden City, NY: Doubleday, 1974.

———. *The Early Asimov*. Garden City, NY: Doubleday, 1972.

———. *Gold: The Final Science Fiction Collection*. New York: Harper Voyager, 2003.

———. *I. Asimov: A Memoir*. New York: Doubleday, 1994.

———. *In Joy Still Felt*. New York: Avon, 1980.

———. *In Memory Yet Green*. New York: Avon, 1979.

———. *Isaac Asimov's Treasury of Humor*. Boston: Houghton Mifflin, 1971.

———. *It's Been a Good Life*. Amherst, NY: Prometheus, 2002.

———. *Opus 100*. Boston: Houghton Mifflin, 1969.

———. *Opus 200*. Boston: Houghton Mifflin, 1979.

———. *Opus 300*. Boston: Houghton Mifflin, 1984.

———. *The Sensuous Dirty Old Man*. New York: Signet, 1971.

———. "The Sword of Achilles." *Bulletin of the Atomic Scientists*, November 1963, 17–18.

———. *Yours, Isaac Asimov: A Lifetime of Letters*. Edited by Stanley Asimov. New York: Doubleday, 1995.

Asimov, Isaac, ed. *The Hugo Winners, Volumes One and Two*. Garden City, NY: Doubleday, 1962.

Atack, Jon. *Let's Sell These People a Piece of Blue Sky*. North Charleston, SC: CreateSpace, 2013.

Bangsund, John. *John W. Campbell: An Australian Tribute*. Canberra, Australia: Parergon, 1972.

Bedford, Sybille. *Aldous Huxley*. New York: Knopf, 1974.

Benford, Gregory. "A Scientist's Notebook: The Science Fiction Century." *Fantasy & Science Fiction*, September 1999, 126–137.

Berger, Albert I. "The Astounding Investigation." *Analog Science Fiction/Science Fact*, September 1984, 125–136.

———. *The Magic That Works: John W. Campbell and the American Response to Technology*. San Bernardino, CA: Borgo, 1993.

Bleiler, Everett F. *Science-Fiction: The Gernsback Years*. Kent, OH: Kent State University Press, 1998.

Bolitho, William. *Twelve Against the Gods*. New York: Simon & Schuster, 1929.

Bova, Ben. *Future Crime*. New York: Tom Doherty, 1990.

———. "John Campbell and the Modern SF Idiom." *Fantasy Review*, July/August 1986, 13–16.

Brake, Mark, and Neil Hook. *Different Engines: How Science Drives Fiction and Fiction Drives Science*. Basingstoke, Hampshire, England: Macmillan, 2008.

Bretnor, Reginald, ed. *Modern Science Fiction: Its Meaning and Its Future*. New York: Coward-McCann, 1953.

Budrys, Algis. *Benchmarks Continued*. Reading, England: Ansible Editions, 2014.

———. *Benchmarks Revisited*. Reading, England: Ansible Editions, 2013.

Bugliosi, Vincent, with Curt Gentry. *Helter Skelter*. New York: Norton, 2001.

Burks, Arthur J. *Monitors*. Lakemont, GA: CSA Press, 1967.

Burroughs, William S. *Rub Out the Words: The Letters of William S. Burroughs 1959–1974*. Edited by Bill Morgan. New York: Ecco, 2012.

Campbell, John W. *The Atomic Story*. New York: Henry Holt, 1947.

———. *The Best of John W. Campbell*. Edited by Lester del Rey. Garden City, NY: Doubleday, 1976.

———. *Collected Editorials from* Analog. Edited by Harry Harrison. Garden City, NY: Doubleday, 1966.

———. *The Complete Collection of the John W. Campbell Letters.* Edited by Perry A. Chapdelaine, Sr. Franklin, TN: AC Projects, 1987. Microfilm.

———. Introduction to *The Black Star Passes.* Reading, PA: Fantasy Press, 1953.

———. Introduction to *Cloak of Aesir.* Chicago: Shasta, 1952.

———. Introduction to *The Man Who Sold the Moon* by Robert A. Heinlein. New York: Signet, 1979.

———. *The John W. Campbell Letters, Volume 1.* Edited by Perry A. Chapdelaine, Sr., Tony Chapdelaine, and George Hay. Franklin, TN: AC Projects, 1985.

———. *The John W. Campbell Letters with Isaac Asimov and A. E. van Vogt, Volume 2.* Edited by Perry A. Chapdelaine, Sr. Fairview, TN: AC Projects, 1993.

Carr, John F. *H. Beam Piper: A Biography.* Jefferson, NC: McFarland, 2014.

Carter, John. *Sex and Rockets: The Occult World of Jack Parsons,* Venice, CA: Feral House, 1999.

Carter, Paul A. *The Creation of Tomorrow: Fifty Years of Magazine Science Fiction.* New York: Columbia University Press, 1977.

Chapdelaine, Perry A. *During the Dawn of Dianetics and Scientology.* North Charleston, SC: CreateSpace, 2015.

Clarke, Arthur C. *Astounding Days: A Science Fictional Autobiography.* New York: Bantam, 1989.

Corydon, Bent. *L. Ron Hubbard: Messiah or Madman?* Fort Lee, NJ: Barricade, 1992.

Crowley, Aleister. *The Confessions of Aleister Crowley.* New York: Penguin, 1989.

Currey, L. W. *Science Fiction and Fantasy Authors.* Boston: G. K. Hall, 1979.

Davin, Eric Leif. *Partners in Wonder: Women and the Birth of Science Fiction, 1926–1965.* Lantham, MD: Lexington, 2006.

Davis, Matthew. "The Work of Theodore Sturgeon." *Steam Engine Time,* March 2012, 15–66.

De Baets, Antoon. *Censorship of Historical Thought: A World Guide, 1945–2000.* Westport, CT: Greenwood, 2002.

De Camp, L. Sprague. "El-Ron of the City of Brass." *Fantastic,* August 1975.

———. *Time and Chance: An Autobiography.* Hampton Falls, NH: Donald M. Grant, 1996.

De Camp, L. Sprague, and Catherine C. de Camp. *Science Fiction Handbook, Revised.* Philadelphia: Owlswick Press, 1975.

DeForest, Tim. *Radio by the Book: Adaptations of Literature and Fiction on the Airwaves.* Jefferson, NC: McFarland, 2008.

Del Rey, Lester. *Early Del Rey.* Garden City, NY: Doubleday, 1975.

——. *The World of Science Fiction.* New York: Ballantine, 1979.

Delany, Samuel R. "Racism and Science Fiction." *New York Review of Science Fiction,* August 1998.

Dick, Philip K. *The Minority Report.* New York: Citadel Press, 2002.

Doctorow, Cory. *Information Doesn't Want to Be Free.* San Francisco: McSweeney's, 2014.

Eller, Jonathan R. *Becoming Ray Bradbury.* Champaign: University of Illinois Press, 2011.

Ellison, Harlan. *Again, Dangerous Visions.* New York: Signet, 1973.

——. *Dangerous Visions.* New York: Berkley, 1967.

——. *An Edge in My Voice.* New York: Open Road Media, 2014.

Eshbach, Lloyd. *Of Worlds Beyond.* Chicago: Advent, 1964.

Finnan, Mark. *Oak Island Secrets.* Halifax, Novia Scotia: Formac, 2002.

Franklin, H. Bruce. *Robert A. Heinlein: America as Science Fiction.* Oxford: Oxford University Press, 1980.

Freas, Frank Kelly. *The Art of Science Fiction.* Norfolk, VA: Donning, 1977.

Freedman, Carl, ed. *Conversations with Isaac Asimov.* Jackson: University Press of Mississippi, 2005.

Gardner, Martin. *Fads and Fallacies in the Name of Science.* Mineola, NY: Dover, 1957.

Garrett, Randall. *The Best of Randall Garrett.* Edited by Robert Silverberg. New York: Timescape, 1982.

Gifford, James. *Robert A. Heinlein: A Reader's Companion.* Aurora, CO: Nitrosyncretic, 2000.

Gingrich, Newt. *To Renew America.* New York: HarperCollins, 1995.

Grazer, Brian. *A Curious Mind.* New York: Simon & Schuster, 2015.

Green, Joseph. "Our Five Days With John W. Campbell." *Challenger,* Winter 2005–2006.

Greenberg, Martin H., ed. *Fantastic Lives: Autobiographical Essays by Notable Science Fiction Writers.* Carbondale: Southern Illinois University Press, 1981.

Guinn, Jeff. *Manson: The Life and Times of Charles Manson.* New York: Simon & Schuster, 2014.

Gunn, James. *Isaac Asimov: The Foundations of Science Fiction.* Oxford: Oxford University Press, 1982.

Hagedorn, Ann. *Savage Peace.* New York: Simon & Schuster, 2007.

Harrison, Harry. *Harry Harrison! Harry Harrison!* New York: Tor, 2014.

Harrison, Harry, ed. *Astounding: John W. Campbell Memorial Anthology.* New York: Random House, 1973.

Harrison, Harry, and Brian Aldiss, eds. *The Astounding-Analog Reader*. Garden City, NY: Doubleday, 1972.

———. *Hell's Cartographers*. New York: Harper & Row, 1975.

Hartwell, David G. *Age of Wonders: Exploring the World of Science Fiction*. Rev. ed. New York: Tor, 1996.

Hartwell, David G., and Milton T. Wolff, eds. *Visions of Wonder*. New York: Tor, 1996.

Heinlein, Robert A. *Expanded Universe*. New York: Ace, 1980.

———. *Grumbles from the Grave*. Edited by Virginia Heinlein. New York: Del Rey, 1989.

———. Introduction to *Godbody*, by Theodore Sturgeon. New York: D. I. Fine, 1986.

———. *Tramp Royale*. New York: Ace, 1992.

Herbert, Frank. *The Road to Dune*. Edited by Brian Herbert. New York: Tor, 2005.

Hieronymus, T. Galen. *The Story of Eloptic Energy*. Lakemont, GA: Institute of Advanced Sciences, 1988.

Hoberman, J. *An Army of Phantoms: American Movies and the Making of the Cold War*. New York: New Press, 2011.

Hubbard, L. Ron. *All About Radiation*. Los Angeles: Bridge, 1989.

———. *Dianetics: Letters & Journals*. Los Angeles: Bridge, 2012.

———. *Dianetics: The Modern Science of Mental Health*. New York: Hermitage House, 1950.

———. *Early Years of Adventure: Letters & Journals*. Los Angeles: Bridge, 2012.

———. *Have You Lived Before This Life?* Los Angeles: Bridge, 1990.

———. *A History of Man*. Los Angeles: Bridge, 2007. Previously titled *What to Audit*.

———. *Literary Correspondence: Letters & Journals*. Los Angeles: Bridge, 2012.

———. *Master Mariner: At the Helm Across Seven Seas*. Los Angeles: Bridge, 2012.

———. "Science Fiction and Satire." Introduction to *The Invaders Plan*. Los Angeles: Bridge, 1985.

———. *Science of Survival*. Los Angeles: Bridge, 2001.

———. *Writer: The Shaping of Popular Fiction*. Los Angeles: Bridge, 2012.

Hutchisson, James M. *The Rise of Sinclair Lewis, 1920–1930*. University Park: Pennsylvania State University Press, 1996.

James, Robert. "More Regarding Leslyn." *The Heinlein Journal*, July 2002, 11–13.

———. "Regarding Leslyn." *The Heinlein Journal*, July 2001, 17–36.

Johnson, Kim. *The Funniest One in the Room*. Chicago: Chicago Review Press, 2008.

Kline, Ronald R. *The Cybernetics Movement.* Baltimore: Johns Hopkins University Press, 2015.

Knight, Damon. *The Futurians.* New York: John Day, 1977.

———. *In Search of Wonder.* Chicago: Advent, 1996.

Kondo, Yoji, ed. *Requiem: New Collected Works by Robert A. Heinlein and Tributes to the Grand Master.* New York: Tom Doherty, 1992.

Lake, Dianne, and Deborah Herman. *Member of the Family: My Story of Charles Manson, Life Inside His Cult, and the Darkness That Ended the Sixties.* New York: William Morrow, 2017.

Lewis, C. S. *The Collected Letters of C. S. Lewis, Volume III: Narnia, Cambridge, and Joy 1950–1963.* Edited by Walter Hooper. New York: HarperOne, 2007.

McAleer, Neil. *Visionary: The Odyssey of Sir Arthur C. Clarke.* Baltimore: Clarke Project, 2012.

Maier, Thomas. *Newhouse: All the Glitter, Power, and Glory of America's Richest Media Empire and the Secretive Man Behind it.* Boulder, CO: Johnson, 1997.

Malzberg, Barry N. *The Engines of the Night.* Garden City, NY: Doubleday, 1982.

Manson, Charles. *Manson in His Own Words.* New York: Grove, 1988.

Mathison, Volney G. *Electropsychometry.* Los Angeles: Mathison Psychometers, 1954.

Menville, Douglas Alver. *The Work of Ross Rocklynne.* San Bernardino, CA: Borgo, 1989.

Miller, Russell. *Bare-Faced Messiah.* London: Silvertail, 2014.

Moorcock, Michael. *The Opium General and Other Stories.* New York: HarperCollins, 1986.

Moskowitz, Sam. *The Immortal Storm.* Westport, CT: Hyperion, 1974.

———. "Inside John W. Campbell." *Fantasy Commentator,* Spring 2011, 1–157.

———. *Seekers of Tomorrow.* New York: Ballantine, 1967.

Nevala-Lee, Alec. "The Campbell Machine." *Analog Science Fiction and Fact,* July/August 2018, 125–33.

———. "Xenu's Paradox: The Fiction of L. Ron Hubbard and the Making of Scientology." *Longreads.* https://longreads.com/2017/02/01/xenus-paradox-the-fiction-of-l-ron-hubbard. Accessed December 2017.

Olander, Joseph D., and Martin Harry Greenberg, eds. *Isaac Asimov.* New York: Taplinger, 1977.

———. *Robert A. Heinlein.* New York: Taplinger, 1978.

Owen, Chris. "Ron the 'War Hero': L. Ron Hubbard and the U.S. Navy, 1941–50." Carnegie Mellon University. https://www.cs.cmu.edu/~dst/Cowen/warhero. Accessed December 2017.

Page, Michael R. *Frederik Pohl*. Champaign: University of Illinois Press, 2015.

Panshin, Alexei. *Heinlein in Dimension*. Chicago: Advent, 1968.

Panshin, Alexei, and Cory Panshin. *SF in Dimension*. Chicago: Advent, 1980.

———. *The World Beyond the Hill: Science Fiction and the Quest for Transcendence*. Los Angeles: Tarcher, 1989.

Patrouch, Joseph F., Jr. *The Science Fiction of Isaac Asimov*. Garden City, NY: Doubleday, 1974.

Patterson, William H., Jr. "The Hermetic Heinlein." *The Heinlein Journal*, July 1997, 15–23.

———. *Robert A. Heinlein: In Dialogue With His Century: Volume 1, 1907–1948: Learning Curve*. New York: Tor, 2010.

———. *Robert A. Heinlein: In Dialogue With His Century: Volume 2, 1948–1988: The Man Who Learned Better*. New York: Tor, 2014.

Pendle, George. *Strange Angel: The Otherworldly Life of Rocket Scientist John Whiteside Parsons*. London: Weidenfeld & Nicholson, 2005.

Platt, Charles. *Dream Makers Volume II: The Uncommon Men and Women Who Write Science Fiction*. New York: Berkley, 1983.

Pohl, Frederik. *The Early Pohl*. Garden City, NY: Doubleday, 1976.

———. *The Way the Future Was*. New York: Del Rey, 1978.

Price, David H. *Threatening Anthropology: McCarthyism and the FBI's Surveillance of Activist Anthropologists*. Durham, NC: Duke University Press, 2004.

Raine, Susan. "Astounding History: L. Ron Hubbard's Scientology Space Opera." *Religion*, 2015, Issue 1, 66–88.

Reginald, Robert, Douglas Menville, and Mary A. Burgess. *Science Fiction and Fantasy Literature*. Detroit: Wildside Press, 2010.

Resnick, Mike. *Always a Fan: True Stories From a Life in Science Fiction*. Detroit: Wildside Press, 2009.

Reynolds, Quentin. *The Fiction Factory*. New York: Random House, 1955.

Rhodes, Richard. *The Making of the Atomic Bomb*. New York: Touchstone, 1986.

Rich, Mark. *C. M. Kornbluth: The Life and Works of a Science Fiction Visionary*. Jefferson, NC: McFarland, 2009.

Robb, Brian J. *A Brief Guide to Star Trek*. Philadelphia: Running Press, 2012.

Rogers, Alva. *A Requiem for Astounding*. Chicago: Advent, 1964.

Sagan, Carl. *Broca's Brain*. New York: Presidio Press, 1980.

Scithers, George H., Darrell Schweitzer, and John M. Ford, eds. *On Writing Science Fiction*. Philadelphia: Owlswick Press, 1981.

Segaloff, Nat. *A Lit Fuse: The Provocative Life of Harlan Ellison*. Framingham, MA: NESFA Press, 2017.

Silverberg, Robert. *Other Spaces, Other Times*. Greenwood, DE: NonStop, 2009.

——. "Reflections: The Cleve Cartmill Affair: One." *Asimov's Science Fiction,* September 2003, 4–8.

——. "Reflections: The Cleve Cartmill Affair: Two." *Asimov's Science Fiction,* October/November 2003, 4–9.

Silverberg, Robert, ed. *The Science Fiction Hall of Fame Volume One, 1929–1964.* Garden City, NY: Doubleday, 1970.

Smith, George O. *Worlds of George O.* New York: Bantam, 1982.

Solstein, Eric, and Gregory Moosnick. *John W. Campbell's Golden Age of Science Fiction: Text Supplement to the DVD.* New York: Digital Media Zone, 2002.

Soni, Jimmy, and Rob Goldman. *A Mind at Play: How Claude Shannon Invented the Information Age.* New York: Simon & Schuster, 2017.

Stallings, Billee J., and Jo-an J. Evans. *Murray Leinster: The Life and Works.* Jefferson, NC: McFarland, 2011.

Stover, Leon. *Robert Heinlein.* Boston: Twayne, 1987.

Strand, Ginger. *The Brothers Vonnegut.* New York: Farrar, Straus & Giroux, 2015.

Sturgeon, Theodore. Introduction to *Roadside Picnic,* by Arkady and Boris Strugatsky. New York: Macmillan, 1977.

Urban, Hugh. *The Church of Scientology.* Princeton, NJ: Princeton University Press, 2011.

Van Vogt, A. E. *Reflections of A. E. van Vogt.* Lakemont, GA: Fictioneer, 1975.

Wagener, Leon. *One Giant Leap.* New York: Tom Doherty, 2005.

Warner, Harry, Jr. *All Our Yesterdays.* Chicago: Advent, 1969.

Weiner, Rex. "A Stowaway to the Thanatosphere." *The Paris Review,* December 31, 2012. https://www.theparisreview.org/blog/2012/12/31/a-stowaway-to-the-thanatosphere-my-voyage-beyond-apollo-with-norman-mailer. Accessed December 2017.

Weller, Sam. *The Bradbury Chronicles.* New York: Harper Perennial, 2006.

Westfahl, Gary. *The Mechanics of Wonder.* Liverpool: Liverpool University Press, 1998.

White, Michael. *Isaac Asimov: A Life of the Grand Master of Science Fiction.* New York: Carroll & Graf, 2005.

Widder, William J. *The Fiction of L. Ron Hubbard: A Comprehensive Bibliography & Reference Guide to Published and Selected Unpublished Works.* Los Angeles: Bridge, 1994.

——. *Master Storyteller: An Illustrated Tour of the Fiction of L. Ron Hubbard.* Los Angeles: Galaxy, 2003.

Wiener, Norbert. *Cybernetics, or Control and Communication in the Animal and the Machine.* New York: Technology Press, 1948.

——. *The Human Use of Human Beings.* New York: Avon, 1967.

Williamson, Jack. *Wonder's Child: My Life in Science Fiction.* New York: Bluejay, 1984.

Winter, J. A. *A Doctor's Report on Dianetics.* New York: Julian Press, 1951.

Winter, Nevin O. *A History of Northwest Ohio, Volume II.* Chicago and New York: Lewis, 1917.

Wolfe, Tom. *The Right Stuff.* New York: Bantam, 1980.

Wollheim, Donald A. *The Universe Makers: Science Fiction Today.* New York: Harper & Row, 1971.

Wright, Lawrence. *Going Clear: Scientology, Hollywood, and the Prison of Belief.* New York: Vintage, 2013.

Wysocki, Edward M., Jr. *An Astounding War.* North Charleston, SC: CreateSpace, 2015.

———. *The Great Heinlein Mystery.* North Charleston, SC: CreateSpace, 2012.

INDEX

ABOUT THE AUTHOR

Alec Nevala-Lee was born in Castro Valley, California, and graduated from Harvard College with a bachelor's degree in classics. He is the author of three novels, including *The Icon Thief*, and his stories have been published in *Analog Science Fiction and Fact*, *Lightspeed Magazine*, and *The Year's Best Science Fiction*. His nonfiction has appeared in the *Los Angeles Times*, the Daily Beast, Salon, Longreads, the Rumpus, and the *San Francisco Bay Guardian*. He lives with his wife and daughter in Oak Park, Illinois.